Lesbianism and the Criminal Law

Caroline Derry

Lesbianism and the Criminal Law

Three Centuries of Legal Regulation in England and Wales

palgrave
macmillan

Caroline Derry
Law School
The Open University
Milton Keynes, UK

ISBN 978-3-030-35299-8 ISBN 978-3-030-35300-1 (eBook)
https://doi.org/10.1007/978-3-030-35300-1

This Palgrave Macmillan imprint is published by the registered company Springer Nature Switzerland AG.
The registered company address is: Gewerbestrasse 11, 6330 Cham, Switzerland

To Angela

Acknowledgements

I owe particular thanks to Rosemary Auchmuty who has helped and supported me from the very beginning, when she supervised both my LLM dissertation and PhD thesis, and continues to be a valued friend and advisor. My sister Angela has also provided invaluable support from the start: not only reading, commenting, assisting, and encouraging me but also offering good sense and perspective when needed! Thanks are also due to everyone who has read or discussed various parts of this work at various stages, suggested sources, or offered information, including Erika Rackley, Judith Bourne, Carina Bartleet, Rictor Norton, Jeffrey Weeks, Julia Laite, the anonymous reviewers for my articles in the *Journal of Legal History* and *History Workshop Journal*, my PhD examiners Didi Herman and Oliver Phillips, and a number of colleagues from London Metropolitan University and the Open University, including but not limited to Janet Loveless, Maggie Conway, Mischa Allen, Lisa Claydon, Carol Howells, Matt Howard, and Stephanie Pywell. Janet mentored me as an academic, was a greatly valued colleague, but is most missed as a treasured friend.

A project of this type would be impossible without the assistance of a number of librarians and archivists. In particular, thank you to the staff of the Open University library, the London Metropolitan Archives, the National Archives, Somerset County Records Office, York Archives and Local History Service, the British Library, University of Reading Special

Collections, the Wellcome Library, and the Women's Library (now the Women's Library at LSE). Thank you also to Gladstone's Library, which offered a wonderful environment to stay and write, and to Liam Inscoe-Jones and Josie Taylor at Palgrave Macmillan.

Finally, thank you to Mum, Dad, and Shaun.

Contents

Abbreviations

AMSH	Association of Moral and Social Hygiene
CHOP	Committee on Homosexual Offences and Prostitution
HC	House of Commons Hansard
HL	House of Lords Hansard
LMA	London Metropolitan Archives
MWF	Medical Women's Federation
NUSEC	National Union of Societies for Equal Citizenship
NVA	National Vigilance Association
SA	Somerset Archives
TNA	The National Archives
UR	University of Reading Special Collections
WC	Wellcome Library at Wellcome Collection
WL	The Women's Library at LSE

Table of Statutes

Table of Reported Cases

1

Introduction

There is a surprisingly persistent myth that lesbians have never been punished by the criminal law of England and Wales because of Queen Victoria. She supposedly refused to believe that women would do such things (or, in an alternative version, ministers were unwilling to raise the subject with her). As a result, there could be no prohibition in the Criminal Law Amendment Act 1885 equivalent to that criminalising 'gross indecency' between men. Sex between women, the myth assures us, has been the subject of nothing worse than benign legal neglect.[1]

The story is false: no amendment addressing gross indecency between women had been suggested. Even if it had been proposed and passed, the Queen could not have refused her assent to an individual section, only to the Act as a whole—and she would have caused a constitutional crisis in the process. That is even assuming that Victoria was as innocent of the possibilities as the story assumes, which is questionable (Weintraub 1987; Hall 2000; Loch 2015). And the tale does nothing to explain the lack of explicit criminalisation before 1885: the secular law had proscribed many

[1] A complete account of the myth's appearances could probably fill the rest of this book. For a few recent examples, see Hodgson (2017), Venning (2017), and Professor Kate Williams in Dowd (2019).

C. Derry, *Lesbianism and the Criminal Law*,
https://doi.org/10.1007/978-3-030-35300-1_1

other forms of 'deviant' sexual activity beginning with the Buggery Act of 1533, over three centuries before Victoria became monarch.

So much for Queen Victoria; what of the criminal law? This book seeks to challenge the mythology on several grounds. First, the absence of a specific crime should not be confused with benign neglect. Rather, it was central to a policy of silencing which aimed to keep lesbianism outside the knowledge of, or at least unspeakable by, 'respectable' white, British women of higher social class. That silencing was required precisely because of acute anxieties about female sexual autonomy: relationships between women were seen as a potent threat to the patriarchal family. Second, the lack of a discrete crime did not entirely prevent the prosecution of sex between women using other offences. Such relatively rare moments of legal visibility form many of the case studies around which each chapter is centred. These case studies allow us to identify both the consistent factors and the significant developments in the law's approach over three centuries. Third, there has not been a smooth progression from invisibility to social acceptance, and this book will examine the ways in which the criminal justice system has responded to recent social and political changes. Now that straightforward silencing of lesbianism is no longer a realistic policy, there is a more troubled relationship between lesbianism, the criminal law, and their wider social contexts. In other words, demythologising this subject is important not only as a matter of historical accuracy but also because of its continuing—and damaging—effects today.

This book traces the emergence and evolution of silencing through case studies ranging from 1746 to 2013. These case studies encompass the distinct but interlinked approaches of courts and legislators, and relate these to the social and medical regulation of women's sexuality. The earliest case study explores the prosecution of Mary/Charles Hamilton, severely punished by the courts for marrying a woman and thereby usurping patriarchal sexual and social privileges. It is followed by the very different prosecution of Victorian midwife Louise Mourey, who was convicted of indecent assault for examining a girl without her father's consent. Her case, in which the legal status of sex between women was confirmed without reference to women's sexual conduct, represents the high-water mark of silencing. Yet while silenced in the criminal courts, lesbianism faced medical regulation which could meet autonomous female sexuality with highly coercive responses including surgery or incarceration. Meanwhile, first-wave feminism challenged the sexual double standard and questioned the assumptions of female sexual passivity upon which silencing rested, prompting the first explicit parliamentary debate on lesbianism, our third case study. Not only feminists but also sexual scientists and doctors were complicating assumptions around women's sexuality, particularly through newer models of 'congenital inversion'. These treated male and female homosexuality as parallel phenomena and influenced the next case study: the prosecution of Victor/Valerie Barker in 1929. Yet social and medical challenges were slow to affect the criminal law, and silencing endured with surprising effectiveness until after the Second World War. The 1957 Wolfenden Report marked a turning point: rather than treating male and female sexuality as opposites, it took lesbians as the obvious comparators for gay men. By then immediately dismissing female homosexuals as less prevalent, troublesome, or libidinous than their male counterparts, it marked the start of a new form of silencing. Our final case studies, sexual assault prosecutions from the 1990s onwards, demonstrate that the criminal justice system continues to represent lesbians as lesser versions of gay men while nonetheless punishing them harshly when they do come to the courts' attention.

This book, in exploring the development of silencing and its changing forms, argues that some themes have remained relatively consistent. One is that lesbian subjectivities have been ignored and obscured, whether through outright denial that lesbians exist or through assuming that they can be equated with gay men. Another is that the treatment of lesbianism is closely connected to the wider treatment of women's sexuality and that both have been fundamental to the maintenance of patriarchy. Lesbianism has become a matter for the criminal courts when heteropatriarchal privileges have apparently been threatened. In setting the scene for a substantive discussion of lesbianism and the criminal law, this introduction will explore several questions. First, what is lesbianism? Second, what is silencing, and why has it been used for women in particular? Finally, methodological approaches to writing the lesbian legal past and present will be discussed.

What Is Lesbianism?

So far, both 'sex between women' and 'lesbianism' have been used to discuss the subject-matter of this book, but they are clearly not interchangeable terms. Before defining the latter, it is worth repeating that this book is concerned with the regulation of lesbianism, which is not quite the same as the regulation of lesbians: not every defendant in these pages was a lesbian, but in most cases the courts believed or acted as if they were. (Midwife Louise Mourey, discussed in Chap. 3, is an obvious exception.) Further, the legal system did not use this terminology for most of its history and often took great care to avoid recognising that relationships were what we could term lesbian, so there are no formal legal definitions.

This book is focused upon what parliament and the legal system talked about and what they thought they were regulating. We will see that historically, there was little recognition of any deviance from heterosexuality other than lesbianism, and limited recognition even of that. In the eighteenth-century courtroom, the emphasis was not upon women's own subjectivities but rather their lack of, and potential for, heteropatriarchal conformity and propriety. By the twentieth century, women who were not attracted uniquely to other women were 'really' pseudo-lesbians, potential heterosexuals deceived or corrupted into a same-sex entanglement. The courts, in other words, did not pay attention to bisexual or pansexual possibilities. Similarly, some of the defendants discussed in this book look to contemporary readers like trans men rather than lesbians, but the courts have generally treated them as women in male disguise (and, as we will see in Chap. 8, sometimes still do). As the legal system believed it was regulating lesbianism, its approach is relevant here whether or not the subjects thus regulated were in fact lesbians.

Anachronism?

Since this book covers a period of about 300 years, using 'lesbianism' is open to criticism as anachronistic. For that reason as well as the others discussed here, I have avoided describing individual women as 'lesbian' without some evidence that they were likely to have identified in that way (if not with that precise term), but I do use 'lesbian' and 'lesbianism' to describe types of activity or identities. I have not followed the practice of historians who modify 'lesbian' to constantly highlight its contingent or tactical use: Valerie Traub italicises it throughout her book to remind readers of its historical contingency, while Judith M. Bennett prefers the term 'lesbian-like' (Traub 2002, p. 16; Bennett 2006). I considered but ultimately rejected both strategies. Italicisation is distracting for the reader; while that effect is not without purpose, it can also disrupt reading in ways which are unhelpful (and physically uncomfortable for my own autistic brain). As for 'lesbian-like', the suffix '-like' indicates 'not lesbian'. Someone can be 'child-like' because they are not a child; 'lawyer-like' because they are not a lawyer. Bennett (2006, p. 118) argues that the term's decentring of 'lesbian' brings 'productive uncertainty', which encompasses a wider range of women with affinities to the contemporary lesbian identity. However, decentring lesbianism would run counter to the very centring which this book attempts. It also means the shift from 'lesbian-like' to 'lesbian' would really matter, but when should we make that shift? The date at which something akin to contemporary sexual identities may have emerged has been moved further and further back by historians since Foucault suggested 1870: Vicinus is surely right to suggest that the question is 'impossible to answer' (1996a, p. 237). I have decided to trust the reader to bear this caveat in mind. After all, we routinely expect ourselves and others to do the same with any number of other terms such as 'family' or 'marriage' (Brooten 1998, p. 18).

The risk of anachronism is closely related to another important caveat, which is that the very definition of 'lesbian' is inherently political and thus complex and controversial. Uses of the term by lesbians and feminists are neither identical with the concepts used by courts or the legislature, nor uniform. By understanding 'lesbian' as a historical descriptor and a descriptor with history, we can see that far from inevitably representing an essentialised identity, 'lesbian' has always been questioned and debated; rooted in a past, but not static; both recognisable and indefinable (see, e.g. L. Garber 2001). Its specificity should not be dismissed as necessarily collapsing into essentialism. Rather, it is vital if we are to ensure that lesbians are not subsumed within masculinised categories of 'homosexual' or 'queer' (Lanser 2014, p. 5). There is a particular political force to using it here, in exploring contexts where lesbianism has been denied a name or had that name silenced for centuries.

Definitions

What, then, is this thing that we might term 'lesbian'? There is no agreement about the answers; but crucially, the questions the law poses are very different to those asked by women themselves. We will see that courts and legislators have resisted defining (or even mentioning) lesbianism, but in identifying what should be regulated they have broadly taken two approaches. The first is to consider the relationship as a facsimile of heterosexual marriage, with the question of sexual conduct secondary and often silenced. The second is to focus upon it as a purely sexual offence, which revolves around whether there was genital contact, whether it involved penetration, and how closely it resembled penis-in-vagina sexual intercourse. For both approaches, the question of identity has been less important to the courts than that of rehabilitative potential: might either woman return to heterosexuality and resume her place in the patriarchal family? Or better still, and as Parliament has asked, could women be prevented from deviating from heterosexuality in the first place?[2]

Departures from, rather than dalliances outside, heterosexuality were the real concern: the women whose prosecutions are discussed here were engaged in more than a specific kind of sexual behaviour. They were involved in relationships (sometimes long term and often alleged to be one of a series of such relationships). It was precisely that wider context which concerned courts and legislators, who demonstrated distaste for sexual acts between women but showed deeper anxiety about the affective element whose threat to the patriarchal family required silencing or punishment. In other words, they were seeking to regulate something akin to lesbianism rather than discrete, purely sexual acts.

The need for a term which points beyond sexual activity alone is therefore apparent and has always been fundamental to the 'lesbian' of lesbian

[2] For example, the 1921 debates on criminalising sex between women (Chap. 4) and section 28's prohibition of its 'promotion' (Chap. 7).

history. It is also central to this book: its approach is lesbian-centred, so who is the lesbian around whom it centres? She has proved remarkably persistent: despite postmodern challenges, there is wide acceptance that 'lesbian' continues to serve a purpose. For Judith Butler, the 'sign of lesbian' should not be abandoned but left 'permanently unclear what precisely that sign signifies' (Salih 2004, p. 121). Paula Blank (2011, p. 134) chooses to use it both to avoid further limiting an already sparse vocabulary describing same-sex desire among women, and for the possibilities and pleasures in its very complexities. Kevin Henderson (2018), drawing upon Monique Wittig, argues for the continued value of the lesbian to queer, feminist, and trans theorists. As Beresford contends, the term is vital in providing 'a site of resistance to dominant normative heteropatriarchal identity' (2016, p. 67). Laura Doan and Jane Garrity point out that women who loved and desired other women have 'existed all along', even if under different names or no name at all (2016, p. 4). And Heather Love argues that we should not seek to 'overcome' identity but rather treat our 'recognitions not as consoling but as shattering' (2007, p. 45). In other words, we do not need to discard lesbian identity but must accept its complexities, and our ambivalences and grief towards it, in a move away from attempting only affirmative history.

What does lesbian identity involve, though? In particular, does it require sexual activity, and if so, of what kind? For Parliament and the criminal courts, superficially it has not, although the sexual elements of lesbian relationships have formed a vital undertone. Parliament has continued to carefully avoid defining what 'lesbian sex' is, most recently in the 2013 Marriage (Same-Sex Couples) Act which excluded consummation as an element of same-sex marriages. In the courts, sexual offences have only been the primary means of regulation for a few decades. Historians have also eschewed a focus on proven sexual activity, although for different reasons. The meanings of different actions change over time, so that it is not always easy to interpret whether a particular act was understood as sexual by its participants (Traub 2016, p. 14).[3] More fundamentally, the heteropatriarchal focus upon penile penetration means that for Marilyn Frye, talking of 'sex' between women is 'like speaking of

[3] Indeed, the question remains difficult to answer in the present (Richardson 1992).

ducks who engage in arm-wrestling' (1983, pp. 157–58). Further, proof of the sexual activities a person engaged in is rarely expected when establishing the presumed heterosexuality of historical subjects. Only when considering other identities is the demand to prove genital contact routinely raised; this higher, rarely achievable standard of proof obscures, denies, and silences non-heterosexual lives and relationships. Thus it has been broadly rejected by lesbian and other historians (M. Vicinus 1994; Cook 1979; Jeffreys 1989; Faderman 1996). For example, Bennett (2006, p. 118) suggests that we can find the 'lesbian-like' in a range of practices including genital sex, direction of primary emotions towards other women, non-marriage, cross-dressing, and flouting norms of sexual propriety. Vicinus has also urged an open definition rather than an insistence upon 'knowing-for-sure' (1996b, p. 2).

Is there a more concrete meaning to be discerned? For Terry Castle, there is, and it 'is instantly (even dangerously) clear': 'primary emotional and erotic allegiance … to my own sex' (1993, p. 15). We thus return to the point that any definition of 'lesbian' is inherently political. To allow a meaningful discussion of our history, our present, and our future, we need to allow for specificity as well as productive uncertainties. It is this coexistence of openness and particularity which is captured in Ruthann Robson's formulation: 'Lesbian identity is something I have known, have felt, have recognized across a room and across years' (1998, p. 13).

(Not) Defining Individuals

Such recognition may be tentative or absent for a number of the cases in this book. If a person is genitally female but lived and married as a man, are they better understood as a trans man or a lesbian woman? The short answer to this question is neither and both. For historical cases, we cannot know how these people would identify today and cannot do more than speculate as to how they saw themselves, an issue explored in more detail in Chap. 2. Perhaps more surprisingly, uncertainties persist in contemporary cases, as discussed in Chap. 8. What we do know is that, on the whole, local communities and the courts—though not necessarily partners—viewed such defendants straightforwardly as women in male disguise. Since the law was certain that it was regulating sex between women when it dealt with these cases, they fit within the story of the criminal regulation of lesbianism whether or not their subjects were themselves lesbian.

This book will not attempt to identify whether individuals were 'really' lesbians or trans men. Not only does this do violence to the realities under which these people lived, but it does political harm: historians of trans men and lesbian women, as well as contemporary lawyers, have much to offer to each other. We share many common concerns including the exclusion of lives outside heteropatriarchal norms from mainstream history, and need to keep our attention on the real loci of power and erasure. The attempt to define and enforce clear boundaries is thus politically, as well as historically, problematic. It also denies the complexities of lived experiences (Gross 2009, p. 216). Alison Oram (2006) has discussed in some depth the difficulty of distinguishing historically between cross-dressing, transsexuality or transgender, and lesbianism, and notes that the interrelationship between these has diverged only relatively recently. Marjorie Garber (1992, p. 10) argues that the ambiguities of historical cross-dressing are such that it cannot be reduced to any innate identity or gender but is always ambiguous. We should not, then, impose contemporary divisions upon subjects who had more complex understandings of their own identity. Nor should we imagine that those divisions are clear today. Expansive definitions of trans can overlap with lesbianism, as when Susan Stryker includes those who 'want to strike out toward some new location' or who 'simply feel the need to get away from the conventional expectations bound up with the gender that was initially put upon them' (2017, chap. 1; see also Halberstam 2018). The relationship between gender non-conformity, female masculinities, and trans identities is undefined and complex: not all butch lesbians, for example, would adopt or refuse the label 'trans'. It should be unsurprising, then, that single lives may have a place in multiple histories: their inclusion in lesbian history does not preclude their having a place in others, too (Laurie 2009, p. 350).

This book, therefore, discusses those who have been treated by the criminal justice system as women who felt desire for other women: in other words, those for whom the model imposed on them by the judicial process was a broadly lesbian one. Their inclusion here is not an attempt to claim 'ownership' of them as lesbians: we cannot 'own' our subjects. Rather, we have an ethical responsibility to do our best not to misrepresent them. Where the evidence is constrained by the requirements of legal proceedings, heavily mediated by the tropes and attitudes of the popular press, and restricted by our own limited understandings of the context in which they live or lived, we must be cautious about claiming a single, specific identity as theirs. What we can do is identify the ways in which their lives (or some part of them) are relevant to lesbian history, without foreclosing the possibility of their also being part of other histories.

A Note on Pronouns

A number of the people whose prosecutions are discussed in this book were living as men when they came to the attention of the criminal justice system. However, their identities and motivations are often opaque or shifting even in the contemporary cases, while the application of current understandings of lesbian and trans identities to historical defendants is necessarily anachronistic. It is thus frequently not obvious which pronoun is the most appropriate to use in referring to these defendants. In the absence of any wholly satisfactory solution, the approach I have taken is to use the pronoun appropriate to the person's presentation at the time under discussion. For example, many of the defendants are referred to as 'he' if living as men before discovery; 'she' during the court proceedings; and by the pronoun relevant to their presentation after conviction. While the use of shifting pronouns is not ideal, it does seem preferable to the imposition of a single pronoun which would falsely suggest a known and fixed identity.

Silencing

The distinction between silence and silencing is central to this book. Silence—the absence of discussion of lesbianism—can have many causes. It may be accidental or deliberate, ignorant or knowing, an attempt at toleration or an act of passive-aggression. That does not mean it is unimportant, or even unsystematic: silence has long been recognised as an element of discourse which works with and alongside speech. It does, though, encompass chosen, accidental, shamed, embarrassed, or imposed silences, communicative and uncommunicative, emanating from an immense variety of causes.

Silencing, by contrast, is used here specifically to describe a deliberate suppression of communication. It thus implies intention and the exercise of power. While it can describe the silencing of particular agents (e.g. lesbians), or words (e.g. sexual terms), in this book it is used to describe the silencing of a concept (lesbianism) before those potential agents could access it. This form of silencing, used to regulate the possibility of sexual relationships between women, is not an accidental, benign, or careless absence. It is a method of policing women's sexualities. The myth that Queen Victoria or anyone else thought women didn't do those things is a story of denial and consequent *silence*. The reality that lawmakers believed women did do those things, but designated them as unspeakable and enforced that unspeakability, is *silencing*. One can only silence something if one admits that it exists and that, in the absence of constraints, it might be spoken about.

A more detailed sense of what silencing means here can perhaps be gained through comparison with other, related uses. For example, while this book considers material practices and empirical data alongside texts and textual practices, consideration of silencing in critical discourse theory is helpful in clarifying my usage of the term here. Discourse analysis embraces language usage and conceptual evaluation of its relations with social norms and political ideologies (Thiesmeyer 2003, p. 1). Schröter and Taylor (2018) suggest silencing occurs through censorship (attempts by powerful actors to control others' speech) or through marginalisation of certain points of view or groups. These conceptualisations of silencing are closely related to, but not quite the same as, that discussed here. For much of the period under consideration, the powerful legal actors who silenced lesbianism did not do so with the aim of censoring or marginalising its discussion. Rather, they aimed to make it legally incomprehensible so that there was no discussion to control. In other words, silencing did not make such ideas 'unacceptable' or 'forbidden' so much as inconceivable.

Or at least, inconceivable for certain women: silencing was never total. Specifically, the silencing of lesbianism was centred upon 'respectable' women. Respectable men, the lawyers and legislators themselves, were not silenced. They granted themselves the freedom to allude to lesbian possibility existing among those whom legal and parliamentary discourse constructed as 'other'. Thus they engaged in what Schröter describes as 'talking *about* them rather than talking *with* them' (2013, p. 4), although it differs from her account in its intentionality. In that sense, it is closer to her definition of censorship, but with a few exceptions (e.g. the 1928 *Well of Loneliness* obscenity trial considered in Chap. 5), 'censorship' feels too legally loaded a term to use in relation to the criminal justice system. Nor does the notion of a conspiracy of silence, a 'collective effort of avoidance' of something offensive to a community's beliefs (Schröter 2013, p. 5), quite work here. Lesbianism was not so much offensive to those responsible for criminal justice, as threatening: it would be dangerous knowledge in the hands of their wives and daughters. Outside that particular context, though, it could be entertaining or even titillating. Perhaps the crucial difference between the silencing Schröter and others describe, and the way the term is used here, is that their conception centres upon *people* being silenced where they might otherwise speak; this book looks at how the *topic* is silenced with the aim that potential actors do not even have an awareness of the concept. It is the difference between silencing the experiences and subjectivities of an oppressed group, on the one hand, and preventing that group from forming through lack of awareness, let alone vocabulary, on the other.

Legal Silencing

When Lamble recognises the contemporary use of silencing, particularly in the Canadian context, she talks of lesbianism being silenced in the courts through 'wilful acts of ignorance' (2009, p. 112). In this book, I argue that these are primarily acts not of ignorance but of suppression. One might use an analogy from the criminal courts. When a judge refuses to admit a confession, they do not claim ignorance of it (they will have seen the confession and, usually, heard evidence about the way it was obtained). Rather, they are deliberately concealing its very existence from the jury. The expectations are that the jury will therefore not discover that there was a confession; and that had they known, it would have had a significant effect upon their behaviour. Not only judges but also other institutional agents including legislators took on this role in silencing lesbianism. The process was generally less overt (although not always, as considered in Chap. 4). Nonetheless, it was similarly rooted in concealment from others of what one knew, as well as what one chose not to know, oneself.

Jen Jack Gieseking uses not an oral but a visual metaphor: she refers to the 'invisibilization' of lesbian history (2015, p. 29). It is a close synonym but, in the legal context, silencing has a particular resonance. It explicitly suggests a refusal of verbal representation: words or language have been denied to women who were not even granted the oppressive vocabulary of criminality. It invokes the English criminal trial's peculiar emphasis upon the principle of orality: the speaking of evidence inside the courtroom gives it a weight it would not have if presented in other forms. It also has some scope to encompass the situation of those (working-class women, non-British women, and women of colour in particular) who have occasionally been made *visible* in the courtroom, represented as sufficiently far outside norms of feminine respectability to engage in such sexual activity, but who were not allowed a voice. Their alleged experiences, appearances, and proclivities have been discussed by the men of law while the women themselves were absent and unheard, or present but constrained in their permitted speech. Beyond the courtroom, the legislative process is also heavily dependent upon oral debate. In a system of representative democracy, of which women have only been members for a little over a century, it was inevitable that lesbians would not be literally visible for most of history. What is significant is that their experiences and existence were rarely articulated either. Finally, the notion of visibility carries a lot of weight in the field of sexuality where its political equation with empowerment has been both celebrated and complicated (Sullivan 2002; Lamble 2009; G. Mason 1995). Silencing does not escape those complexities (and nor should it), but it is less weighed down by them.

Paradoxically, the principle of orality makes silencing as central to criminal justice as speech. A trial is as much (and sometimes more) about determining what can be spoken, and by whom, as what can be inferred from speech (e.g. Fridland 2003). Thus there is little silence, but much that is silenced.[4] The rules of evidence achieve this through the application of legal precedents and statutes. No such published authorities were produced to guide the regulation of sex between women in the courtroom: the act of silencing was itself silenced. Sexual conduct has been converted by the criminal justice system into financial crime, vagrancy, or perjury. Evidence of sexual behaviour has thus been rendered legally irrelevant; or has been elicited in ways which prevent the public from hearing it; or has been given a heteronormative gloss. This tactic has also extended far beyond the trial, working with wider social and cultural understandings and ideologies. The decision not to enact a specific offence criminalising sex between females is only its most obvious form. We will see throughout this book that there have been many other, often more subtle ways of silencing lesbian possibility. Lamble (2009) distinguishes silencing through careless thinking, limited thinking, and refusal to know; this book will also emphasise that silencing can involve an even more deliberate process. Parliament and the courts have asserted the facts of female sexuality as *privileged* knowledge for them to control and withhold as they felt appropriate. That had effects far beyond the criminal justice system, given the extent to which the law frames and creates vocabulary for the discussion of certain subjects including 'deviant' sexual behaviour.[5] As Phyllis Chessler put it, lesbianism was 'completely legislated out of the realm of possibility' (quoted in Crane 1982, p. 8; see also Mason 1995). At the same time, legal discourses have always carefully maintained their distinctiveness and that is evident throughout this book as we see the legal system operating on understandings which have fallen behind or are at odds with popular and cultural understandings.

Those legal discourses were profoundly raced and classed, drawing upon and reinforcing notions of virtuous white British womanhood. It is

[4] For lawyers' discomfort with silence see Bassett (2015, pp. 519–26).

[5] For example, Walker (1998) discusses the extent to which in early modern England rape was culturally defined by the law, so that even rape stories told outside legal contexts drew upon the common law definition.

no coincidence that silencing's emergence became apparent in the same period that Britain was anxiously redefining its relationship with both its empire and its own bourgeoisie. Britain used the supposed moral superiority of its women as a justification for 'civilising' its colonies, while the middle class was using its own claims to virtue as an argument for greater political rights. Unspoken anxieties about lesbianism were displaced onto women outside the white, British, 'respectable' classes.

Given the work that it was doing, it is apparent that the silence around lesbianism was not, as many authors have assumed, generally beneficial.[6] On the contrary, it was an attempt at fundamental suppression and erasure of lesbian possibility; Anna Marie Smith even argued in the 1990s that its cost to lesbians had been so great that it was 'well worth taking' the risk of criminalisation to breach it (1992, p. 210). One way of understanding this is by drawing upon Judith Butler's discussion of how the interpellation of the policeman ('hey you!') socially constitutes the subject, transferring them from the 'outer region' of impossibility into the social domain (Butler 1993, p. 121).[7] Conversely, as Leslie Moran has recognised, the criminal law's silence is a denial of legal subjectivity to 'the embodied genital female'. While he suggests that it occurred through 'indifference' (1996, p. 12), Eve Kosofsky Sedgwick has concentrated upon precisely these silences as 'strangely specific' speech acts in their own right, 'as pointed and performative as speech' (1990, pp. 3–4), which should not be subjected to 'sentimental privileging … as an originary, passive innocence' (p. 7). Indeed, ignorance (actual or wilful) can be a function of power—the 'privilege of unknowing'—just as knowledge.

As a coercive approach which actively prevents and penalises speech about the silenced subject, silencing equates unauthorised knowledge with guilt.[8] Lesbianism is not just unspoken, but unspeakable. This is not

[6] For example, Atkins and Hoggett suggested it was viewed as 'an unthreatening curiosity' (1984, p. 67); Lynn Friedli claimed a lack of both legal attention and public disapproval (1987, p. 235).

[7] This example was taken from Althusser; later she would point out two problems with Althusser's example. First, it is 'constrained by a notion of a centralized state apparatus'; second (and crucially), there is no explanation of *why* the person so hailed turns round, a shortcoming Foucault's notion of discourse aimed to address (Butler 1997, pp. 5–6).

[8] See for example the Maud Allan libel case discussed in Chap. 5. Inappropriate sexual knowledge has been used against women and girls in other ways: Pamela Cox (2013, p. 41) describes how in the early twentieth century, children with the vocabulary to describe their sexual abuse were not

a benign form of regulation: it is to have one's identity denied so comprehensively that one is not told 'you cannot be a lesbian' but rather 'lesbians do not exist'—or told nothing of lesbianism so that one cannot articulate one's own desires. By implication, it renders the unspeakable as unspeakably awful, but allows no opportunity to respond. As the pursuers in the early nineteenth-century Scottish case of *Woods and Pirie* put it (1975, pp. 20–21, emphasis in original):

> the half-sentences,—hints,—insinuations,—allusions to something too horrible to be spoken of,—seals of secrecy, &c., far from mitigating, aggravated the injury tenfold ... It was stabbing ... in the dark,—wounding them where they had no defence,—producing all the mischief, whether they were guilty or innocent,—while, to their rights as parties uncondemned, to the possibility of their innocence, *not one chance* of innocence or vindication was left.

Nearly two centuries later, Marilyn Frye contrasted the large vocabulary for gay male sex and the lack of language for lesbian sex: the latter meant that as a lesbian, she had 'in one important sense, no knowledge' (1990, p. 311).

To discuss silencing as a policy or form of legal regulation is not to suggest that a committee of ruling-class men sat down together and drew up a formal agreement. Rather, it has been what Lamble describes as 'a culmination of social, institutional and political forces' (2009, p. 114) in which defence arguments as well as state actions and wider forces played a part. In particular, we will see that different legal institutions (courts, Parliament, and prosecutors) often had differing attitudes and approaches. Silencing evolved not through explicit discussion (though that did occasionally happen) but through the intersections of elite male interests, anxieties, and attitudes with particular cultural understandings and ideals of sexuality and femininity.[9] In particular, the construction of knowledge about women's bodies and sexuality as a matter of secrets knowable only

'innocent', so were assumed both to have encouraged it and to be a contamination risk to other children.

[9] For explicit discussions, see the *Woods and Pirie* case in Chap. 3 and the parliamentary debates in Chap. 5.

by male 'experts' had a pedigree reaching back into and beyond the early modern period (Traub 2016, p. 22).

While silencing is a consistent theme throughout this book, it has not been static in nature. The policy arguably emerged in the eighteenth century, when sexual misconduct was becoming a matter for the secular rather than ecclesiastical courts and when criminal prosecutions began their move from being a matter for individuals to being understood as of wider public concern. However, it has older roots in the legal language of buggery and would reach its zenith in the nineteenth century when ideologies of separate spheres and female sexual purity were at their height. Silencing became a more complex policy to maintain during the twentieth century, and has transformed significantly in the twenty-first. We will see that it may have lost its earlier clarity and force, but its effects are lingering with surprising persistence.

Why Silencing for Women but Not Men?

Legal silence has at least nominally extended to sex between men, most famously in the standard wording of the indictment for buggery, a crime 'not to be named amongst Christians' (Coke 1681, p. 58).[10] However, the very existence of a statute, a standard indictment, prosecutions, and overt articulations of the desirability of silence make it clear that silencing was not the primary legal strategy for policing male homosexual acts. Indeed, as Leslie Moran has pointed out, the 'silence' produced a great deal of text about as well as 'substitute names' for buggery (L. Moran 1996, chap. 3). Edward Deacon (1831, p. 125) was not untypical of legal commentators when he wrote at great length on the desirability of silence around

> that horrible sin against, nature, and the ordinance of the Almighty, which the English law (in the language of the indictment for the offence) most fitly describes as one not even to be named among Christians. The least notice, that could be taken of this detestable crime, would certainly be the best; but those who profess to expound the criminal law, as well as those whose duty is to administer it, must not shrink from the task, disgusting

[10] Moran notes that this wording was not a statutory requirement (1996, p. 33).

> though it be, of explaining with clearness and precision that dreadful crime, of which the inevitable consequence is death to those convicted of it, besides indelible and lasting infamy to their names,—which the slightest suspicion of the least propensity to drives them as pestilential outcasts from society,—and which, even to mention by its odious appellation, is pollution to the lips that utter it, or the pen transcribing it.

Silence was thus not literal, nor a *silencing*, but it was explicitly connected with shame: an association we will see made for women too, particularly in the twentieth century.

The ways in which women's behaviour is policed have made silencing a more successful strategy than was the case for men. As considered in the following chapters, female sexuality has been constructed as passive, receptive, but also potentially dangerous and therefore in need of close control. That control has not been primarily entrusted to the courts. Rather, there are a number of social, economic, and medical mechanisms which have policed women's behaviour alongside wider legal structures which significantly constrained women's lives. One of the most significant historically is perhaps less obvious to many modern readers: religion. Early modern people did not rely on earthly courts alone for justice and punishment; as Kenneth Borris points out, an assumption that they would attract divine retribution 'cannot be considered tolerant' (2004, p. 80).

As society became more secular, the social policing of women centred upon their division into respectable and not-respectable. To contravene the norms of femininity was to become a 'loose' woman in the eighteenth century, a 'fallen' woman in the nineteenth, and a 'slut' in the twentieth and twenty-first. All these epithets indicated a lack of sexual morality *and* a failure to perform respectable domesticity: 'slut', for example, can describe a slovenly housekeeper as well as a woman seen to transgress sexual norms. Kittredge argues that the breadth of behaviours constructed as transgressive by this binary is part of its power: women are made to fear 'crossing a line that cannot be seen'. Drawing upon Lynda Hart, she indicates the role this plays in obscuring lesbianism and bisexuality, which become subsumed in a wider othering of everything outside the white, middle-class, feminine norm as transgressive (Kittredge 2003; Hart 1994).

Susan S Lanser has demonstrated that the eighteenth century saw a proliferation of discourses around the sapphic, arguing that there was an attempt to construct the sapphic body as an other against which hetero-femininity was defined (2003, pp. 22–23). That century's changing models of sexual difference are explored in Chap. 2, but for the moment it is worth noting that they marked the emergence of sexuality as a medical question, an approach which would grow in importance in the following centuries. It worked within a web of financial, legal, educational, and cultural constraints on women's agency which limited the possibility of lesbian relationships. Even educated women did not typically receive education in Latin or Greek considered essential for most higher-class men,[11] and which gave access to texts describing lesbianism and male homosexuality.[12] Women earned less than men, and the cultural model of the male provider was used to justify lower wages for women before (and after) the Equal Pay Act 1970 came into force. Until late in the nineteenth century, a married woman's property and income became her husband's while the law also allowed him to dictate most aspects of her life including where she lived. Medical theories of sex difference and of women's irrationality have provided further support for patriarchal authority. All of these factors have made relationships between women considerably more difficult to pursue, and the establishment of lesbian families incredibly so. Patriarchal oppression thus made the criminalisation of lesbianism almost redundant, with silencing enough to fill most of the gaps in this extra-criminal regulation.

Finally, legal silencing has coexisted with non-legal visibility in a range of material from popular satires to Classical texts to pornography. Their existence does not contradict the legal ideology, in part because it has been specific to the criminal justice system and in part because the presumed readership for such literature, as well as medical and scientific texts, was historically male and higher-class. We are brought back to the crucial point that silencing was targeted at a very specific section of

[11] Anthony Fletcher notes that even those girls' schools which taught classics nonetheless aimed to educate their students 'for the marriage market' (1995, p. 374).

[12] Anne Lister, who recorded sexual relationships with women in her diaries, privately studied the Classics herself but publicly declared them unsuitable for women for the material they revealed (Clark 1996, p. 32).

women: those who shared their social status, race, and nationality with the elite men who gave this policy effect. It was based upon ideals and ideologies of women's sexual innocence, not empirical realities. A striking (non-lesbian) illustration of the gulf between them is offered by *R v. Penguin Books Limited* [1961] Crim LR 176, the *Lady Chatterley's Lover* case of 1960. Mr Justice Byrne discreetly shielded his copy of D H Lawrence's controversial novel from view in a bag sewn by his wife Lady Byrne, who had read and annotated the key passages for him. That she also sat alongside him in court did not deter prosecution counsel from asking the jury whether they would wish their own wives to read the book (Rich 2019).

Making Lesbian Legal History

While the attention in later chapters to current and recent law fits clearly within legal literature, the historical focus of earlier chapters may seem more surprising given the apparent absence of a lesbian legal past. The lack of a specific offence criminalising lesbianism has long served as a reason for wider histories to effectively ignore it, equating its absence with lack of a readily recoverable history.[13] This book contributes a specifically legal perspective to the growing and now considerable body of research which proves otherwise. It draws upon existing historical and legal literatures but shifts the perspective by centring lesbianism in the criminal law. Eschewing a narrative of progress, it moves into the present to ask what is happening now, how it is informed by history, and how we might move into the future.

It does so specifically in relation to the law of England and Wales. The Laws in Wales Acts 1535 and 1542, like the Buggery Act, were enacted during the reign of Henry VIII. They extended the English legal system to Wales, so that the laws discussed in this book were applicable in both countries. Scotland and Ireland, by contrast, retained separate legal

[13] Its consequences are apparent in popular as well as academic culture: 'Lesbianism wasn't illegal. There was *absolutely no British law* … for the entire nineteenth century' (Naomi Wolf in Smith 21 May 2019, 14 minutes; emphasis added).

systems. It is noticeable, though, that there is very little material from Wales in this book. The question of whether that reflects a lack of prosecutions or simply a lack of known evidence deserves further research.

As a legal account, this book's view of and approaches to the material are different to those of social and literary histories. As an account which puts lesbianism at its centre, it offers a different perspective to most legal histories and texts. As an interdisciplinary account, it takes law, the criminal justice system, and the wider social context seriously as profoundly interconnected frameworks for the regulation of lesbian relationships. The position of women in relationships with each other is not treated as a footnote, side comment, or symptom of a larger issue, but is at the heart of the analysis. Inevitably, the legal terrain looks rather different from this viewpoint. Assumptions about tolerance are not taken at face value; nor are the prosecutions and punishments undergone by defendants minimised through comparison to other penalties or groups. At the same time, it is an account of the *regulation* of lesbianism, rather than of lesbianism or lesbians themselves: that means it explores where and how the law saw relationships between women, and makes no claim that this ever accurately reflected what women were actually doing.

Sources

Historical and Legal Literature

Being a silenced history, the story of regulation is not easily recovered. Anyone researching in this field is, then, particularly indebted to her predecessors. Popular interest has probably existed 'as far back as there were lesbians in history' (Laurie 2009, p. 351); certainly Britain's first lesbian magazine *Arena Three* published historical articles in the mid-1960s. The emergence of lesbian history in the academy is often traced back to in the 1975 publication of Carroll Smith-Rosenberg's essay 'The Female World of Love and Ritual', which established women's intimate friendships as a subject of scholarly attention. Almost immediately, explicitly lesbian histories began to appear. By 1979, Judith Schwarz could cite various local archives and oral histories in the United States as well as national conference sessions and publications by Blanche Wiesen Cook and Nancy Sahli (Schwarz 1979). Lesbian history became widely recognised as a viable area of study upon the publication of Lillian Faderman's *Surpassing the Love of Men* in 1981. That influential volume provided evidence extending across Europe and the United States from the sixteenth century to the present day. Its emphasis on women's romantic friendships in the eighteenth and nineteenth centuries as essentially asexual and socially acceptable received considerable criticism, stimulating critical engagement with questions of what lesbian history should do, who might fall within it, and what its scope should be.[14] Those questions and others were engaged with by members of the Lesbian History Group established in Britain in 1984, whose 1989 essay collection was another important milestone (Laurie 2009, p. 353; Lesbian History Group 1989).

The field has blossomed, but much recent work has come from literary scholars.[15] For example, Fielding's fictional account of the Hamilton case considered in Chap. 2 has received more attention than the surviving court records (Lanser 2014, pp. 166–67; Blackwell 2002; Clayton 2010; Nicolazzo 2014; O'Driscoll 2003). Specifically legal history remains sparse although it began in 1980 with Louis Compton's article 'The Myth of Lesbian Impunity'. Using sources from across Europe and America, he demonstrated that the assumption lesbians had been unaffected by the criminal law was false, although his emphasis upon executions effectively excluded England and Wales from significant consideration. The distinctive English approach to regulation has received only limited attention. A notable exception is the *Lesbian History Sourcebook* (Oram and Turnbull 2001) which has a chapter dedicated to lesbians and the law. Its authors highlight the lack of research in this area, and their collection of materials including case reports, parliamentary debates, and state papers offers a starting point. Their challenge has not yet been fully met by legal historians, but it is hoped that this book will play a part in doing so.

[14] For example, Moore (1997) is a direct engagement with and rejection of the notion that 'romantic friendship' received universal social approbation. For a review of the evolving questions addressed by lesbian history see Binhammer (2010, pp. 1–7).

[15] This can bring limitations as well as different emphases: Doan (2007, pp. 29–30) criticised some of the lesbian history produced within cultural studies for its reliance upon secondary sources rather than archival research, as well as lack of national specificity or attention to changing cultural meanings of 'lesbian'.

The seeds of a legal history can also be found within more general works. Faderman briefly addressed the criminalisation of 'female husbands' who married other women in *Surpassing the Love of Men*; they were also considered by Emma Donoghue (1993), Julie Wheelwright (1989), and Fraser Easton (2003) among others and are discussed here in Chap. 2. Faderman returned to the law in *Scotch Verdict* (1983), but this book-length account concerned a Scottish case, a civil suit rather than a criminal prosecution, and centred upon its social history rather than its legal specificities. There has been important work on the earlier part of the twentieth century, particularly from Alison Oram and Laura Doan, which has shed significant light on the operation of the criminal law, although again with a primary focus on social rather than legal history. *Her Husband Was A Woman!* (Oram 2007) is based upon a comprehensive examination of two Sunday newspapers, and in consequence offers invaluable sources and analysis of prosecutions related to gender-crossing during the twentieth century. Given the difficulties of locating primary sources, discussed below, the value of this aspect of her work alone is enormous and informs several chapters of this book. Both Oram and Doan have considered the prosecution of Victor Barker, the central case study of Chap. 5, although primarily for its cultural significance. While Doan paid more attention to the legal context in *Fashioning Sapphism* (2001), her emphasis was upon the law's role in the emergence of a lesbian subculture in the interwar years rather than upon criminal regulation *per se*.

The English legal literature has had even less to say about lesbians: Sarah Beresford's 2016 survey of seven leading criminal law textbooks found 52 references to 'homosexuality' but only one to 'lesbian', which simply noted the absence of a specific prohibition (Beresford 2016). Discussion in more specialist texts is similarly sparse. The first comprehensive contemporary surveys of sex between women and the criminal law were those of Tony Honoré (1978), Susan S M Edwards (1981), and Paul Crane (1982). Honoré began his chapter on homosexuality by warning that most of what followed would be about men; his discussion of lesbianism under the law was directed towards supporting the different legal treatment of male and female homosexuality. Edwards was therefore the first British legal writer to treat lesbianism and the criminal law as a matter of interest purely in its own right. Her work, though brief and not entirely accurate, gave the topic visibility and provided a basis from which to develop further accounts. For example, Matthew Waites's analysis of the history of the lesbian age of consent (2002, 2005) explicitly references Edwards in its consideration of age of consent laws and prosecutions from the nineteenth century to the end of the twentieth. Although focused upon just one aspect of the history of the legal regulation of lesbian sexuality, it is important for its sustained consideration of a surprisingly complex aspect of the criminal law. Waites places the age of consent in the wider cultural context of lesbianism's continuing social invisibility, although this book will dispute his assumption that such invisibility arose out of lesbianism being 'unthreatening' prior to the 1920s. Meanwhile, Crane's brief discussion (1982, pp. 8–11) was focused on the contemporary criminal law but recognised that the absence of a specific offence reflected the use of extra-legal sanctions rather than toleration.

Primary Sources

Turning to primary sources, researchers of sexual histories have been pushed towards court records and crime reports by their relative availability and discoverability. While those offer some kind of continuous historical record of sex between men, albeit very imperfect, silencing ensures that cases involving women are both sparser and harder to find. Often, no prosecution was brought at all; where it was brought, this was until recently for non-sexual crimes such as vagrancy, fraud, or breach of the peace. Many cases are likely to have been prosecuted in the petty sessions whose records have rarely survived and are generally incomplete, and where broad and unrevealing offence descriptions such as 'nuisance' or 'disturbing the peace' were common even in the early twentieth century (Turner 2012, p. 59). How can those gaps be filled? Newspaper reports, as our main source for many prosecutions particularly where case papers do not survive, are used extensively.[16] The impact of digitisation of historical records has thus been significant—and complex. In recent years, the

[16] I primarily consider them as historical sources rather than literary texts; for a contrasting approach see Oram (2007). Similarly, fiction including pornography is little used: those literatures employed very different discourses to the law and require detailed and careful treatment in their own right which can be found in, for example, Moore (1997) and Traub (2002).

creation of huge new databases has made vast amounts of material more accessible. In turn, that has brought new approaches to historical research as well as fresh challenges and dangers (Upchurch 2013; Hitchcock 2018). These include the distortions brought about by selections of sources for digitisation; the limitations of optical character recognition (OCR) software; and the loss of surrounding context when individual records are returned. Source selection is driven by many factors including availability, commercial considerations, and often, the particular requirements of family historians. There is also the tantalising promise of new material to be discovered as digitisation projects advance and OCR improves. Whether or not that promise is kept, it is a reminder that our histories are necessarily incomplete and our conclusions always open to revision.

One of the key issues in using online databases is the formulation of appropriate search terms, which poses particular problems when researching the history of sexuality (Upchurch 2013, pp. 17–20). Modern terms do not always have direct equivalents, while familiar words can have very different meanings: Erasmus's *Adages*, widely circulated in sixteenth-century England, drew on ancient Greek sources to define *lesbiari* as to behave like a Lesbian and, specifically, to perform fellatio (Blank 2011, pp. 108–09). To add to the complexity, several seventeenth-century sources list 'fellatrice' alongside 'tribade'—a woman who achieved sexual pleasure by rubbing her genitals against those of another woman—suggesting a categorisation based on something rather different to the current understandings of sexuality (Fellatrix 2017). Without a relatively consistent legal language to draw upon, terms for relations between women have been diverse, transient, and period-specific; have varied by region, context, and class as well as era—when they were used at all; were also applied in other contexts such as child abuse (Bingham et al. 2016, p. 416) or male homosexuality or non-sexual offences (Upchurch 2013, p. 96); and were often deliberately euphemistic to the point of obfuscation. Silencing encouraged and enforced such an approach. Some archives and databases are doing excellent work to address these issues, but there are no quick solutions.[17]

[17] For example, both the National Archives and London Metropolitan Archives have guides to finding LGBT materials (The National Archives n.d.-b; London Metropolitan Archives 2016). The National Archives also adds, and allows users to add, tags including 'lesbian' and 'lgbt' to records (The National Archives n.d.-a).

Methodology

These difficulties encourage qualitative rather than quantitative approaches. Methodologically, this book is centred around case studies analysed using a lesbian-centred and feminist approach. In other words, it assumes that the legal regulation of lesbianism is important in its own right rather than as a comparator for or side-note to the regulation of other gendered or sexual categories: as Ruthann Robson and Sarah Valentine (1990) have explained, it is 'a way to examine the laws affecting lesbians from both individualistic and communitarian lesbian perspectives'. It challenges the disappearance of lesbians within the categories 'woman' and 'LGBT': lesbianism is not a less-important subset of either but, positioned at the intersection of misogyny and homophobia, has much to say about both. Within those parameters, the interdisciplinary nature of the project has required me to become something of a methodological magpie. For example, I have borrowed insights from queer theory and historiography, although my own approach is not queer.[18] Rather than focusing upon disruption of the category 'lesbian', this book takes the law's conceptualisation and regulation of that category as its starting point—although in the process, disruption necessarily occurs. Its primary attention is upon lesbianism and its regulation as lived experiences and material practices rather than upon 'female homoeroticism as idea and image' within the wider 'social imaginary' (Lanser 2014, p. 2), although again, the two are not separate.[19] Nor can—or should—sexuality be separated from its intersections with class, race, and nationality.

As Samuel Clowes Huneke notes, lesbian history has a 'long-established convention' of reliance upon case studies (2017, p. 7). This book is no exception, using a particular historical moment to open each chapter and lead into a wider examination of the criminal justice system's approach to regulating lesbianism at that period. Case studies also allow attention to

[18] There is a significant literature exploring, from a range of perspectives, queer theory's debt to and areas of common ground with feminism (e.g. L. Garber 2001; Jagose 2009; Doan 2007; Richardson et al. 2006; Marinucci 2016; Barker 2012, pp. 7–12).

[19] Queer theory has been subjected to extensive criticism for its focus upon discourse at the expense of lived experience and the need to talk of a lesbian subject: for a summary, see Beresford (2014, pp. 766–67).

be given to the classed and racialised elements of the regulation of sexuality. By discussing these 'cases' in depth and placing them within a wider historical and theoretical context, the breadth of existing evidence can be considered without obscuring either its limitations or its possibilities. Since legal history is not found only in the courtroom, the use of case studies allows proper attention to be paid to the legislature, which in passing statutes both makes the law thereafter applied in courtrooms and develops and expresses its own discourses, approaches, and priorities. In Doan's term, these case studies are 'hubs' whose spokes can reach out into related areas (2007, p. 32), including social and medical developments and press representations.

It is not only lack of data which commends this qualitative approach to many feminist legal historians. Walker and Kermode comment upon the particular value of qualitative material in the context of studying women, who 'get lost in the broad overview' (1994, p. 5). That point is particularly true for women's relationships with other women. It also fits within a wider awareness among historians of the deficiencies of metanarratives and quasi-metanarratives (Fraser and Nicholson 1990, p. 27). A focus upon particular historical moments, using them to identify changes in legal discourse and social context, offers an important corrective and encourages the 'constant conversation between the general and the specific' urged by Katherine Binhammer (2010, p. 8). It pays sustained attention to the specific experiences of women who fell outside dominant norms of class, race and sex. It also recognises geographic specificities: the policy of silencing described here is one which was either not followed, or applied in very different ways, outside England and Wales.

Conversely, one should be cautious of allowing concerns about false universalising to prevent the making of valid and important connections. As Andrew Scull warns in a slightly different context (the history of psychiatry), too narrow a view becomes 'neo-solipsism', distorting and obscuring through its lack of a wider contextual frame (Scull 1999, p. 298). In this book, links and connections are drawn out alongside important patterns of change over three centuries; the wider themes and commonalities are often striking. Valerie Traub has challenged the assumption that we must choose between alterity (which emphasises historical difference and denies any continuous lesbian identity at all) and continuism (which assumes a fundamentally unchanging lesbian identity through history) in her influential essay 'The Present Future of Lesbian Historiography' (2015). She argues that the history of lesbianism has 'recurrent explanatory metalogics', which might be understood as 'cycles of salience', typically linked to moments of social crisis (pp. 84–85, 93). The task of the historian is to be both attentive to their recurrence and alert to the differences between recurrences: to stage a dialogue not only between past and present but also between 'one queer past and another' (p. 99). For Traub, the appearance of continuity comes not from a consistent lesbian identity across time, but rather from external preoccupations about the meanings of women's behaviours (p. 85). Insofar as it focuses on the criminal justice system, this book shares her concern with such external preoccupations, their correspondences, and their changes. Indeed, the legal system claims to derive its authority in large part through the doctrine of precedent and the continuance of tradition: it actively looks to the past as a way of maintaining its dominion in the present. For this reason, the links between past and present are notably strong—though rarely straightforward—in legal history.

This book perhaps tilts less towards alterity than Traub, given its identification of significant continuities in the legal treatment of women's relationships that, in the criminal law context at least, do not so much cycle as persist and evolve. It nonetheless documents considerable ideological shifts and, crucially, the uneven nature of those shifts. Ideas on different aspects of women's lives changed at different rates so that dominant views within one field were often inconsistent with those in another. Not everybody was subject to the same ideologies in the same ways: some people fell outside their ambit, others resisted them. They were, after all, ideologies rather than laws of nature. Nonetheless, they are discussed because enough people of influence shared enough of them sufficiently simultaneously for them to have had influence upon the criminal justice system's approach to lesbianism. They are overwhelmingly the ideologies of white, ruling-class men because for much of history, these were the only people who had the power to make and administer criminal law, and they retain a great deal of that power today. Their views found concrete form in the processes of the criminal justice system (albeit in inconsistent and sometimes contradictory ways). Naturally there are differences within the group—we will see them openly debated in Chap. 4, for example—but one can at least identify broad themes which enjoyed precedence at particular times.

Finally, the chapters dealing with the recent past and present raise further methodological and ethical issues and demands (see Robson 1995). While there are more data to draw upon, both primary sources and secondary legal literature remain relatively sparse. As Beresford (2016) has noted, much recent material referencing 'lesbian' tends to conflate women within 'lesbian and gay' and to be written from a gay male or heterosexual feminist perspective, while specifically lesbian material is predominantly focused upon family law. Exceptions include Beresford's own article which, although focusing on lesbian BDSM, raises wider questions around the legal invisibility of lesbians as sexual subjects, and Lamble's analysis of lesbian and trans invisibility in the 2002 Canadian case of *Hornick* (Lamble 2009).

Analyses of the current law have often been constrained by the lack of a sustained and accessible history. For example, Anna Marie Smith's first (1992) article on the 1991 trial and conviction of Jennifer Saunders (discussed in Chaps. 7 and 8) suggested that if the complainants had been working-class there would have been no prosecution, an assertion contradicted by the history of such cases as well as later developments. Diane Hamer did refer to historical prosecutions but claimed a 'discursive shift' in *Saunders* where the dildo was a 'tabloid invention' rather than the material presence of earlier cases (Hamer 1992). Yet in both *Saunders* and its historical counterparts, the dildo was physically absent from (and often unarticulated within) the courtroom.[20]

While the Sexual Offences Act 2003 may have been presented as a rupture with earlier legal approaches to the regulation of sexual activity, Chap. 8 will demonstrate that, in fact, history remains important to understanding the current law. Rather than essentialising identities and interpretations, it encourages us to understand their complexities and nuances. Such understandings are particularly important if we are to critically address current trends in prosecution rather than retreat into constructing oppositions between trans, lesbian, and feminist interests,

[20] See Chaps. 2, 7 and 8.

which are neither useful nor inevitable. Thus historical approaches are not discarded in the later chapters but combined with feminist legal methodologies. Our historical past both assists and complicates our analysis of the current law and its reform, even as contemporary developments in our understandings of gender, sexuality, and the limits of the criminal law raise new questions and challenge us to find fresh solutions.

Arrangement of Chapters

The overarching argument of this book is that lesbianism was regulated primarily by silencing, but the focus upon maintaining the sexual ignorance of white, British, middle-class women did leave space for the strategic prosecution of women thereby constructed as 'other'. That approach still affects the law's operation today. The argument is developed through chapters whose division into periods and themes is a matter of organisation rather than an assertion that this history can be divided so neatly. Each chapter is centred around a moment of visibility whose significance is explored. Common themes, idiosyncrasies, specificities, and context are all considered, making each case study a qualitative exploration of silencing and its exceptions.

A broadly chronological approach is taken, beginning in Chap. 2 with a case study from the start of our period. Charles/Mary Hamilton, a travelling quack doctor, was prosecuted by the Corporation of Glastonbury for a vagrancy offence. However, it was not the peripatetic sale of quack medicine which attracted the Corporation's attention but Hamilton's marriage to one Mary Price. Several months after the wedding, Price announced that she had discovered her husband to be a woman. Hamilton's prosecution was one of at least half a dozen 'female husband' cases during the eighteenth century, although such prosecutions were more usually brought by the victims and, in London at least, charged as financial fraud. These cases have a great deal to tell us about when and why silencing would give way to criminal sanction during this period and who fell outside its terms.

Chapter 3 moves forward to the nineteenth century and explores the growing professionalisation and state control of the criminal justice system, increasing statutory regulation of sexual offences, and changing attitudes to sex and gender, which came together in the events of 1885. These coalesce around the prosecution of Louise Mourey for indecent assault on a female. Mourey was not the complainant's lover but a midwife who examined her to establish her virginity. The absence of erotic motivation on the defendant's part perhaps makes this case more rather than less revealing about the justice system's approach at a time when silencing was arguably at its height.

As the following chapters progress through the twentieth century, they also take us into a period when there was overt if limited acknowledgement of lesbianism in Parliament. They therefore alternate between the political and judicial treatment of lesbianism. Chapter 4 takes up the story after 1885 and examines a unique instance of visibility: the 1921 parliamentary debates on a proposed offence of gross indecency between females. That offence was never passed into law—indeed, its proposers almost certainly did not intend that it should—but the debates were a rare instance of open discussion about lesbianism and its regulation. While they marked both silencing's existence and its breach, subsequent decline of the policy would be surprisingly slow and uneven. Chapter 5 returns to the courtroom with the prosecution of Colonel Victor Barker, identified in court as Valerie Arkell-Smith, for making a false entry in a marriage register. The case centred around an apparently heterosexual marriage in which the husband was later found to be biologically female, closely echoing the female husband prosecutions of the eighteenth century. Tellingly, the defendant's life also had strong parallels with that of the protagonist in Radclyffe Hall's lesbian novel *The Well of Loneliness* which had achieved notoriety the previous year. While the Barker case may have been framed by that controversy, its impact would prove short-lived. The reasons for this are explored with reference to legal, social, cultural, and scientific developments which promoted or prevented meaningful rupture in the policy of silencing.

Official discussion would re-emerge in public only after the Second World War when the Wolfenden Committee heard evidence on homosexuality and the law. The exclusion of evidence on lesbianism from the final report is the subject of Chap. 6. It explores not only how and why lesbianism was silenced but also the relationship of this official report from a Home Office departmental committee to Parliamentary, prosecutorial, and courtroom decisions. In doing so, it identifies the response to the Wolfenden Report as a key moment in the development of silencing. There was a distinct shift away from attempting the complete silencing of lesbian possibility among 'respectable' women. Instead, lesbianism was incorporated into the category of 'homosexual', within which patriarchal gender relations could be reproduced: lesbians were constructed as less sexual, less public, and less worthy of (negative or positive) attention than gay men.

The consequences of that shift are evident in Chap. 7, which brings us to the latter half of the twentieth century. It takes *Allen*, an age of consent case, as the starting point for consideration of the law's response to wider cultural and social changes around sexuality and gender. The limits of liberalism and formal equality are considered, and the equation of visibility with acceptance is problematised. It was during this period that lesbianism was explicitly addressed in legislation for the first time when section 28 of the Local Government Act 1988 forbade local authorities from 'promoting homosexuality'. By using this apparently gender-neutral blanket term, the Act drew upon a new form of silencing which became prominent at this period and continues today: the elision of non-heterosexual women with gay men in a way which takes men as the norm. The chapter ends with the Sexual Offences Act 2003, whose effects in the present are the subject of Chap. 8. It looks at the current legal position, and in particular the complex issue of 'gender fraud' in prosecutions such as that which forms its central case study, *McNally*. Finally, the conclusion considers where the law is now, and how we might move forward in future.

References

Atkins, Susan, and Brenda Hoggett. 1984. *Women and the Law*. Oxford: Basil Blackwell.

Barker, Nicola. 2012. *Not the Marrying Kind: A Feminist Critique of Same-Sex Marriage*. Basingstoke: Palgrave Macmillan.

Bassett, Debra Lyn. 2015. Silencing Our Elders. *Nevada Law Journal* 15: 519–536.

Bennett, Judith M. 2006. *History Matters: Patriarchy and the Challenge of Feminism*. University of Pennsylvania Press.

Beresford, Sarah. 2014. The Age of Consent and the Ending of Queer Theory. *Laws* 3 (4): 759–779. https://doi.org/10.3390/laws3040759.

———. 2016. Lesbian Spanners: A Re-Appraisal of UK Consensual Sadomasochism Laws. *Liverpool Law Review* 37 (1–2): 63–80. https://doi.org/10.1007/s10991-016-9182-2.

Bingham, Adrian, Lucy Delap, Louise Jackson, and Louise Settle. 2016. Historical Child Sexual Abuse in England and Wales: The Role of Historians. *History of Education* 45 (4): 411–429. https://doi.org/10.1080/0046760X.2016.1177122.

Binhammer, Katherine. 2010. Accounting for the Unaccountable: Lesbianism and the History of Sexuality in Eighteenth-Century Britain. *Literature Compass* 6 (6): 1–15.

Blackwell, Bonnie. 2002. An Infallible Nostrum': Female Husbands and Greensick Girls in Eighteenth-Century England. *Literature and Medicine* 21 (1): 56–77.

Blank, Paula. 2011. The Proverbial 'Lesbian': Queering Etymology in Contemporary Critical Practice. *Modern Philology* 109 (1): 108–134. https://doi.org/10.1086/661977.

Borris, Kenneth. 2004. *Same-Sex Desire in the English Renaissance: A Sourcebook of Texts, 1470–1650*. London: Routledge.

Brooten, Bernadette J. 1998. *Love Between Women: Early Christian Responses to Female Homoeroticism*. Chicago: University of Chicago Press.

Butler, Judith. 1993. *Bodies That Matter: On the Discursive Limits of "Sex"*. New York: Routledge.

———. 1997. *The Psychic Life of Power*. Stanford, CA: Stanford University Press.

Castle, Terry. 1993. *The Apparitional Lesbian: Female Homosexuality and Modern Culture*. New York: Columbia University Press.

Clark, Anna. 1996. Anne Lister's Construction of Lesbian Identity. *Journal of the History of Sexuality* 7 (1): 23–50.

Clayton, Susan. 2010. Can Two and a Half Centuries of Female Husbands Inform (Trans)Gender History? *Journal of Lesbian Studies* 14 (4): 288–302. https://doi.org/10.1080/10894160903048106.

Coke, Edward. 1681. *The Third Part of the Institutes of the Laws of England*. London: Thomas Basset.

Cook, Blanche Wiesen. 1979. The Historical Denial of Lesbianism. *Radical History Review* 20: 60–65. https://doi.org/10.1215/01636545-1979-20-60.

Cox, Pamela. 2013. *Bad Girls in Britain: Gender, Justice and Welfare, 1900–1950*. Basingstoke: Palgrave Macmillan.

Crane, Paul. 1982. *Gays and the Law*. London: Pluto Press.

Deacon, Edward E. 1831. *A Digest of the Criminal Law of England; as Altered by the Recent Statutes and the Consolidation and Improvement of It*. London: Saunders and Benning.

Doan, Laura. 2001. *Fashioning Sapphism: The Origins of a Modern English Lesbian Culture*. New York: Columbia University Press.

———. 2007. Lesbian Studies After The Lesbian Postmodern. *Journal of Lesbian Studies* 11 (1–2): 20–35.

Doan, Laura, and Jane Garrity. 2016. Introduction. In *Sapphic Modernities: Sexuality, Women, and National Culture*, ed. Laura Doan and Jane Garrity, 1–13. Basingstoke: Palgrave Macmillan.

Donoghue, Emma. 1993. *Passions Between Women: British Lesbian Culture 1668–1801*. London: Scarlet Press.

Dowd, Geraldine. 2019. Insert Name Here, Series 4.4: Emma. UK: BBC.

Easton, Fraser. 2003. Gender's Two Bodies: Women Warriors, Female Husbands and Plebeian Life. *Past and Present* 180: 131–174.

Edwards, Susan S.M. 1981. *Female Sexuality and the Law: A Study of Constructs of Female Sexuality as They Inform Statute and Legal Procedure*. Oxford: Martin Robertson.

Faderman, Lillian. 1981. *Surpassing the Love of Men: Romantic Friendship and Love Between Women from the Renaissance to the Present*. London: The Women's Press.

———. 1983. *Scotch Verdict: Miss Pirie and Miss Woods V Dame Cumming Gordon*. New York: William Morrow.

———. 1996. Who Hid Lesbian History? In *The New Lesbian Studies: Into the Twenty-First Century*, ed. Bonnie Zimmerman and Toni A.H. McNaron, 41–47. New York: The Feminist Press at the City University of New York.

Fellatrix, N. 2017. Oxford English Dictionary. http://www.oed.com/view/Entry/45625778#eid1209624430.

Fletcher, Anthony. 1995. *Gender, Sex and Subordination in England 1500–1800*. Yale University Press.

Fraser, Nancy, and Linda J. Nicholson. 1990. Social Criticism without Philosophy: An Encounter between Feminism and Postmodernism. In *Feminism/Postmodernism*, ed. Linda Nicholson, 19–38. London: Routledge.

Fridland, Valérie. 2003. Quiet in the Court: Attorneys' Silencing Strategies during Courtroom Cross-Examination. In *Discourse and Silencing: Representation and the Language of Displacement2*, ed. Lynn Thiesmeyer, 119–138. Philadelphia: John Benjamins Publishing Company.

Friedli, Lynne. 1987. Passing Women'—A Study of Gender Boundaries in the Eighteenth Century. In *Sexual Underworlds of the Enlightenment*, ed. G.S. Rousseau and Roy Porter, 234–260. Manchester: Manchester University Press.

Frye, Marilyn. 1983. *The Politics of Reality: Essays in Feminist Theory*. New York: The Crossing Press.

———. 1990. Lesbian 'Sex'. In *Lesbian Philosophies and Cultures*, ed. J. Allen. New York: State University of New York Press.

Garber, Linda. 2001. *Identity Poetics: Race, Class and the Lesbian-Feminist Roots of Queer Theory*. New York: Columbia University Press.

Garber, Marjorie. 1992. *Vested Interests: Cross—Dressing and Cultural Anxiety*. London: Routledge.

Gieseking, Jen Jack. 2015. Useful In/Stability. *Radical History Review* 2015 (122): 25–37. https://doi.org/10.1215/01636545-2849504.

Gross, Aeyal. 2009. Gender Outlaws before the Law: The Courts of the Borderland. *Harvard Journal of Law & Gender* 32 (1): 165–231.

Halberstam, Jack. 2018. Trans*: *A Quick and Quirky Account of Gender Variability*. Oakland, CA: University of California Press.

Hall, Lesley A. 2000. *Sex, Gender and Social Change in Britain Since 1880*. Basingstoke: Macmillan Press.

Hamer, Diane. 1992. The Invention of the Dildo. *Australian Gay and Lesbian Law Journal* 2: 41.

Hart, Lynda. 1994. *Fatal Women: Lesbian Sexuality and the Mark of Aggression*. London: Routledge.

Henderson, Kevin. 2018. Becoming Lesbian: Monique Wittig's Queer-Trans-Feminism. *Journal of Lesbian Studies* 22 (2): 185–203. https://doi.org/10.1080/10894160.2017.1340009.

Hitchcock, Tim. 2018. Digital Affordances for Criminal Justice History. *Crime, History & Society* 21 (2): 335–342.

Hodgson, Nichi. 2017. Lesbian Sex Was Never Illegal in the UK. But Women Fought for Visibility. *The Pool*. https://www.the-pool.com/life/love-sex/2017/7/nichi-hodgson-on-how-lesbians-became-visible.

Honoré, Tony. 1978. *Sex Law*. London: Duckworth.

Huneke, Samuel Clowes. 2017. The Duplicity of Tolerance: Lesbian Experiences in Nazi Berlin. *Journal of Contemporary History* (Apr.): 1–30. https://doi.org/10.1177/0022009417690596.
Jagose, Annamarie. 2009. Feminism's Queer Theory. *Feminism & Psychology* 19 (2): 157–174. https://doi.org/10.1177/0959353509102152.
Jeffreys, Sheila. 1989. Does It Matter If They Did It? In *Not a Passing Phase: Reclaiming Lesbians in History 1840–1985*, ed. Lesbian History Group, 19–28. London: The Women's Press.
Kittredge, Katharine. 2003. Introduction: Contexts for the Consideration of the Transgressive Antitype. In *Lewd and Notorious: Female Transgression in the 18th Century*, ed. Katharine Kittredge, 1–17. Ann Arbor: University of Michigan Press.
Lamble, Sarah. 2009. Unknowable Bodies, Unthinkable Sexualities: Lesbian and Transgender Legal Invisibility in the Toronto Women's Bathhouse Raid. *Social & Legal Studies* 18 (1): 111–130. https://doi.org/10.1177/0964663908100336.
Lanser, Susan S. 2003. Queer to Queer': The Sapphic Body as Transgressive Text. In *Lewd and Notorious: Female Transgression in the 18th Century*, ed. Katharine Kittredge, 21–46. Ann Arbor: University of Michigan Press.
———. 2014. *The Sexuality of History: Modernity and the Sapphic, 1565–1830*. Chicago: University of Chicago Press.
Laurie, Alison J. 2009. Introduction: A History of 'Lesbian History'. *Journal of Lesbian Studies* 13 (4): 349–361. https://doi.org/10.1080/10894160903048015.
Lesbian History Group. 1989. *Not a Passing Phase: Reclaiming Lesbians in History 1840–1985*. London: The Women's Press.
Loch, Jason. 2015. The Curious Case of Queen Victoria and the Lesbians. *A Venerable Puzzle*. https://venerablepuzzle.wordpress.com/2015/09/18/the-curious-case-of-the-queen-victoria-and-the-lesbians/.
London Metropolitan Archives. 2016. *Lesbian, Gay, Bisexual, Transgender (LGBT) Community Archives at London Metropolitan Archives*. London: London Metropolitan Archives.
Love, Heather. 2007. *Feeling Backward: Loss and the Politics of Queer History*. Cambridge, MA: Harvard University Press.
Marinucci, Mimi. 2016. *Feminism Is Queer: The Intimate Connection between Queer and Feminist Theory*. 2nd ed. London: Zed Books.
Mason, Gail. 1995. (Out)Laws: Acts of Proscription in the Social Order. In *Public and Private: Feminist Legal Debates*, ed. Margaret Thornton, 66–88. Oxford: Oxford University Press.

Moore, Lisa L. 1997. *Dangerous Intimacies; Toward a Sapphic History of the British Novel.* London: Duke University Press.
Moran, Leslie. 1996. *The Homosexual(Ity) of Law*. London: Routledge.
Nicolazzo, Sarah. 2014. Henry Fielding's The Female Husband and the Sexuality of Vagrancy. *The Eighteenth Century* 55 (4): 335–353. https://doi.org/10.1353/ecy.2014.0038.
O'Driscoll, Sally. 2003. The Lesbian and the Passionless Woman: Femininity and Sexuality in Eighteenth-Century England. *The Eighteenth Century* 44 (2–3): 103–131.
Oram, Alison. 2006. Cross-Dressing and Transgender. In *The Modern History of Sexuality*, ed. H.G. Cocks and Matt Houlbrook, 256–285. London: Palgrave Macmillan.
———. 2007. *Her Husband Was a Woman! Women's Gender-Crossing in Modern British Popular Culture*. London: Routledge.
Oram, Alison, and Annmarie Turnbull. 2001. *The Lesbian History Sourcebook: Love and Sex between Women in Britain from 1780 to 1970*. London: Routledge.
Rich, Barbara. 2019. Lady Chatterley's Embroidery. *Medium*. https://medium.com/@abarbararich/lady-chatterleys-embroidery-896b8b978ae2.
Richardson, Diane. 1992. Constructing Lesbian Sexualities. In *Modern Homosexualities: Fragments of Lesbian and Gay Experience*, ed. Ken Plummer, 187–199. London: Routledge.
Richardson, Diane, Janice McLaughlin, and Mark E. Casey. 2006. *Intersections Between Feminist and Queer Theory*. Basingstoke: Palgrave Macmillan.
Robson, Ruthann. 1995. Convictions: Theorizing Lesbians and Criminal Justice. In *Legal Inversions: Lesbians, Gay Men and the Politics of Law*, ed. Didi Herman and Carl F. Stychin, 180–194. Philadelphia: Temple University Press.
———. 1998. *Sappho Goes to Law School.* New York: Columbia University Press.
Robson, Ruthann, and Sarah Elizabeth Valentine. 1990. Lov(h)Ers: Lesbians as Intimate Partners and Lesbian Legal Theory. *Temple Law Review* 63 (3): 511–542.
Salih, Sara, ed. 2004. *The Judith Butler Reader*. Oxford: Blackwell Publishing.
Schröter, Melani. 2013. *Silence and Concealment in Political Discourse*. Philadelphia: John Benjamins Publishing Company.
Schröter, Melani, and Charlotte Taylor. 2018. Introduction. In *Exploring Silence and Absence in Discourse: Empirical Approaches*, ed. Melani Schröter and Charlotte Taylor. Basingstoke: Palgrave Macmillan.

Schwarz, Judith. 1979. Questionnaire on Issues in Lesbian History. *Frontiers: A Journal of Women Studies* 4 (3): 1–12.

Scull, Andrew. 1999. Rethinking the History of Asylumdom. In *Insanity, Institutions and Society, 1800–1914: A Social History of Madness in Comparative Perspective*, ed. Joseph Melling and Bill Forsythe, 295–315. London: Routledge.

Sedgwick, Eve Kosofsky. 1990. *Epistemology of the Closet*. Berkeley, CA: University of California Press.

Smith, Anna Marie. 1992. Resisting the Erasure of Lesbian Sexuality: A Challenge for Queer Activism. In *Modern Homosexualities: Fragments of Lesbian and Gay Experience*, ed. Ken Plummer, 200–213. London: Routledge.

Smith-Rosenberg, Carroll. 1975. The Female World of Love and Ritual: Relations between Women in Nineteenth-Century America. *Signs: Journal of Women in Culture and Society*. https://doi.org/10.1086/493203.

Stryker, Susan. 2017. *Transgender History: The Roots of Today's Revolution*. 2nd ed. New York: Seal Press.

Sullivan, Sheila. 2002. What Is the Matter with Mary Jane?' Madeleine Smith, Legal Ambiguity, and the Gendered Aesthetic of Victorian Criminality. *Genders* 35: 32.

"The Additional Petition of Miss Mary-Ann Woods and Miss Jane Pirie." 1975. In *Miss Marianne Woods and Miss Jane Pirie against Dame Helen Cumming Gordon*. New York: Arno Press.

The National Archives. n.d.-a Help Us Tag Records in Our Collection. *Discovery*. Accessed July 25, 2019a. https://discovery.nationalarchives.gov.uk/tags/index.

———. n.d.-b Sexuality and Gender Identity History. *Research Guides*. Accessed July 25, 2019b. http://www.nationalarchives.gov.uk/help-with-your-research/research-guides/gay-lesbian-history/.

Thiesmeyer, Lynn. 2003. Introduction: Silencing in Discourse. In *Discourse and Silencing: Representation and the Language of Displacement*, ed. Lynn Thiesmeyer, 1–36. Philadelphia: John Benjamins Publishing Company.

Traub, Valerie. 2002. *The Renaissance of Lesbianism in Early Modern England*. Cambridge: Cambridge University Press.

———. 2015. The Present Future of Lesbian Historiography. In *Thinking Sex with the Early Moderns*, 82–100. Philadelphia: University of Pennsylvania Press.

———. 2016. *Thinking Sex with the Early Moderns*. Philadelphia: University of Pennsylvania Press.

Turner, Joanne. 2012. Summary Justice for Women: Stafford Borough, 1880–1905. *Crime, Histoire & Sociétés* 16 (2): 55–77. https://doi.org/10.4000/chs.1359.

Upchurch, Charles. 2013. Politics and the Reporting of Sex between Men in the 1820s. In *British Queer History: New Approaches and Perspectives*, ed. Brian Lewis, 17–38. Manchester: Manchester University Press.

Venning, Annabel. 2017. The Secret Passion between Queen Anne and Sarah Churchill | Daily Mail Online. *Daily Mail*. https://www.dailymail.co.uk/news/article-4636386/The-secret-passion-Queen-Anne-Sarah-Churchill.html.

Vicinus, M. 1994. Lesbian History: All Theory and No Facts or All Facts and No Theory? *Radical History Review* 60 (60): 57–75. https://doi.org/10.1215/01636545-1994-60-57.

Vicinus, Martha. 1996a. Introduction. In *Lesbian Subjects: A Feminist Studies Reader*, ed. Martha Vicinus, 273. Indiana University Press.

———. 1996b. 'They Wonder to Which Sex I Belong': The Historical Roots of the Modern Lesbian Identity. In *Lesbian Subjects: A Feminist Studies Reader*, ed. Martha Vicinus, 233–260. Bloomington: Indiana University Press.

Waites, Matthew. 2002. Inventing a 'Lesbian Age of Consent'? The History of the Minimum Age for Sex between Women in the UK. *Social & Legal Studies* 11 (3): 323–342.

———. 2005. *The Age of Consent: Young People, Sexuality and Citizenship*. Basingstoke: Palgrave Macmillan.

Walker, Garthine. 1998. Rereading Rape and Sexual Violence in Early Modern England. *Gender & History* 10 (1): 1–25.

Walker, Garthine, and Jenny Kermode. 1994. Introduction. In *Women, Crime and the Courts in Early Modern England*, ed. Jenny Kermode and Garthine Walker, 1–25. London: UCL Press.

Weintraub, Stanley. 1987. *Victoria: An Intimate Biography*. New York: Dutton.

Wheelwright, Julie. 1989. *Amazons and Military Maids: Women Who Dressed as Men in the Pursuit of Life, Liberty, and Happiness*. London: Pandora.

2

Mary/Charles Hamilton: Eighteenth-Century Female Husband Prosecutions

Mary/Charles Hamilton, Female Husband

The eighteenth century saw changes in medical, social, and legal understandings which together formed the background to an emerging policy: the legal silencing of lesbianism. Part of the evidence for this developing approach comes, somewhat contrarily, from public criminal trials and newspaper reports. They concern a very particular set of prosecutions which became known as female husband cases, thanks to a popular pamphlet about the case study for this chapter, the trial of Charles/Mary Hamilton. In 1746, the itinerant quack doctor Charles Hamilton had come to Wells, a small city in Somerset. Within months, he would be the defendant in a case presented as extraordinary.[1] Although the newspapers of the day focused upon the apparently unique facts, Hamilton's actions were not as unprecedented as those reports suggested, but the legal responses were indeed unusual.[2]

[1] As explained in Chap. 1, this book will use male names and pronouns to refer to the accused while they lived as men and female names and pronouns while they lived as women.

[2] The case was widely reported, including in the *Bath Journal*; *Gentleman's Magazine*, *Annual Register*, and *Newgate Calendar*. The original case papers are in Somerset Archives (SA), Q/SR/314.

C. Derry, *Lesbianism and the Criminal Law*,
https://doi.org/10.1007/978-3-030-35300-1_2

In Wells, Hamilton had taken lodgings in the home of Mary Creed and her niece Mary Price. Hamilton courted Price, and they put up the banns in St Cuthbert's church where they married on 16 July.[3] Hamilton resumed travelling around Somerset, now with his wife, and by September they were in nearby Glastonbury. There, Price announced that she had discovered her husband was in fact a woman. Hamilton was arrested and appeared before the local magistrates as Mary Hamilton on 13 September 1746. At this hearing, a deposition (a sworn witness examination recorded in writing by the magistrates' clerk) was taken from Hamilton, although Price did not give hers until 7 October. They offer us an account of the spouses' lives and marriage, almost in their own words.

According to Hamilton, she had been born in Somerset before moving to Scotland as a child. Aged fourteen and for reasons which were not explained, she put on her brother's clothes and travelled to Northumberland, working for 'mountebank' Dr Edward Green for two or three years and Dr Hinly Green for nearly a year (Mary Hamilton, Deposition, 13 September 1746, SA Q/SR/314/172). A newspaper report recounts Dr Edward Green's 'incredible Performances' in which he 'perfectly cur'd several Gentlemen and others in this Place of all manner of Hesitation and Stammering in the Speech' (*Caledonian Mercury* 1728). He died before 1735 according to an advertisement for his son Dr William Green which also gave a flavour of what Hamilton's highly itinerant professional life would have been like. Green described a stay of '6 or 8 Weeks' in the Newcastle area, during which he would attend the market days at 'Durham, Auckland, Barnard-Castle, &c.' The self-described 'Oculist' also offered advice to the 'Deaf, Blind, and Diseased' and described treatments ranging from the fitting of spectacles to surgery on a 'Hair-lip' (*Newcastle Courant* 1735). Hamilton travelled through England working as a 'Quack Doctor' and had reached Somerset the previous May.

[3] Banns are oral notice of a forthcoming marriage, typically read out in church on the three Sundays preceding the wedding. The entry in the marriage register gave the groom's name as James Hamilton (SA D/P/W ST C 2/1/4 p. 63) although the marriage certificate gave it as Charles (SA Q/SR/314/159).

In court, Hamilton admitted courting and marrying Price and travelling around Somerset thereafter, but 'further this examinant saith not' (Hamilton, Deposition, SA Q/SR/314/172). We therefore do not know whether Hamilton agreed that Price had been deceived. Price's account was that Hamilton had 'entered her body several times', making her 'believe, at first, that the said Hamilton was a real man. But soon had reason to judge otherwise', a slightly disingenuous claim when 'soon' represented several months' marriage (Mary Price, Deposition, 7 October 746, SA Q/SR/314/173). The means by which Hamilton 'entered her body' are not discussed further in the court papers.

In the eighteenth century, prosecutions were usually brought by complainants but, unusually, the Corporation of Glastonbury—the town council—took on that role in Hamilton's case. In his letter of instruction to barrister Henry Gould, solicitor Thomas Hughes emphasised the Corporation's wish to see Hamilton punished 'in the severest manner the Quarter Sessions can'. He concluded that '[i]f she be well whipt, will be Satisfactory' (Thomas Hughes to Henry Gould, 9 October 1746, SA Q/SR/314/169). The Quarter Sessions were a higher court with greater sentencing powers than the Petty Sessions which initially heard the case. While the latter tended to be relatively informal, frequently presided over by local justices of the peace (magistrates) in their own homes, Quarter Sessions cases were heard by a panel of magistrates and a jury. They met, as the name suggests, only four times a year. Thus Hamilton was held in Shepton Mallet gaol until the next sessions on 7 October, in Taunton. Hamilton passed the time selling quack remedies to the 'great Numbers of People' who visited the prison, still in male attire according to the *Bath Journal*: 'very gay and impudent, with Perriwig, Ruffles and Breeches' (*Bath Journal* 1746a).

The first issue for the Quarter Sessions was what the charge should be. According to the *Bath Journal*, it required 'a great Debate for some time' before the decision was reached to charge Hamilton under the Vagrancy Act 1744 with 'imposing on his Majesty's subjects' (*Bath Journal* 1746c). The emphasis upon the charge as a vagrancy offence was unusual since we shall see that other cases of this kind were presented as fraud offences.[4]

[4] The actual charge may, in at least one of those cases, have been the same (fraud was an umbrella term for a variety of charges, not a single and distinct offence) but its presentation in court and the press were different.

Despite Hamilton's plea of not guilty and committal for trial, the Vagrancy Act allowed the court to detain her immediately and order her to be whipped, which they did. The gaol calendar for 7 October records that she was to be imprisoned with hard labour for six months and whipped publicly in four Somerset towns: Taunton on 11 October, Glastonbury on 1 November, Wells on 22 November, and Shepton Mallet on 19 December (General Kalendar of Prisoners, 7 October 1746, SA Q/SR/314/165). On 13 October, after already enduring one public whipping, Hamilton withdrew her not guilty plea. The remaining three whippings were carried out as ordered by the court, and she was discharged from gaol on 28 April 1747 (Quarter Sessions Minute Book, 1747, SA CD2.2/3(6), p. 339). At that point, Hamilton disappears from the historical record.

The case's move into the realms of fiction had begun with newspaper reports which added colourful details to the court hearings and gave Hamilton an improbable fourteen wives.[5] It was completed by the publication of an anonymous pamphlet, the work of Henry Fielding. *The Female Husband: or, the surprising history of Mrs. Mary, alias Mr. George Hamilton* is almost entirely fictional, a sensational version of Hamilton's life which has obscured the case's place in eighteenth-century law and culture (Baker 1959; Bowles 2010). Not only was Hamilton's decision to live as a man far from unique but the marriage was one of a small series which ended in the criminal courtroom. These tend to be referred to by today's historians as well as their peers by Fielding's term 'female husband', and I follow that usage since it highlights the contradictory position and interpretations within which they appeared. As Susan Clayton (2010, p. 291) suggests, it also seems to correspond to the identity these defendants constructed for themselves.

In 1694, an unnamed defendant had appeared in a case whose details survive only in a letter from antiquary Anthony à Wood to a friend (Powys 1932, pp. 306–07):

[5] According to the *Bath Journal* (1746c), this was alleged by Gould in his opening speech; no trace of the claim survives in the court records.

> appeared at the King's Bench in Westminster hall a young woman in man's apparel, or that personated a man, who was found guilty of marrying a young maid, whose portion he had obtained, and was very nigh of being contracted to a second wife. Divers of her love letters were read in court, which occasion'd much laughter. Upon the whole she was ordered to Bridewell to be well whipt and kept to hard labour till further order of the court.

The attribution of a financial motive to the marriage, the random use of pronouns, and the mocking of the relationship were devices which were frequently used to undermine and ridicule these relationships, neutralising any threat they might otherwise pose. Indeed, the account mirrored a popular ballad of the same period, *Comical News from Bloomsbury*, which described just such a fraudulent marriage as a 'jest' ("Comical News from Bloomsbury" 1690; quoted in Toulalan 2003, p. 60). While à Wood does not specify the offence with which the unnamed young woman was charged, the emphasis upon the marriage portion and alleged plan for a second marriage suggests that it was prosecuted as a financial crime. That was certainly true for Sarah Ketson, brought before the court by Ann Hutchinson and her mother Christian in 1720 'for being a loose person and pretending to be a man courting … Ann Hutchinson by the name of John Ketson with an intent to marry defraud and cheat her' (True Kalendar, March 1720, LMA MJ/SR/2344; Easton 2003, p. 152). Few details of the case survive, although it is apparent that Ketson was imprisoned for several months in New Prison, London.

Hardwicke's Marriage Act 1753 imposed stringent requirements upon legal marriages, as well as penalties for their breach. Although it is often seen as a point of rupture in marriage practices, Rebecca Probert (2009) has argued persuasively against such a radical shift. Certainly it seems to have neither dissuaded subsequent female husbands nor affected the courts' approach to their cases, one of which came just seven years later. In 1760, when he was about twenty years old, Samuel Bundy married Mary Parlour in South London. Parlour soon discovered her husband's secret but chose to keep it. However, their neighbours were suspicious of the couple's failure to have sexual relations and unconvinced by Bundy's explanation that he was being cured of 'a bad distemper'. They 'thought proper to make a strict Search; upon which they found the Bridegroom to be a perfect Female' (*London Evening Post* 1760). Parlour appears to have been swept along by them into bringing the matter before a justice of the peace. Bundy, now identified as Sarah Paul, was accused of 'defrauding a young woman of money and apparel, by marrying her' on the basis that Parlour had pawned some clothes when her husband was out of work.[6] Paul was committed to Southwark Bridewell where Parlour kept 'the prisoner company in her confinement' (*London Chronicle* 1760).

There was enormous local interest in the case, and one hearing was postponed because of the crowd gathered outside the court (*Whitehall Evening Post* 1760a). Despite the pressures upon Parlour from this public interest and the involvement of her neighbours, she ended the prosecution by not appearing at the next hearing. Without a prosecutor, the case had to fail and the prisoner was discharged. However, readers of the press reports were reassured that order had been restored and punishment rendered unnecessary since Paul claimed a heterosexual past and a return to feminine propriety. She had supposedly been dressed in men's clothes by her male seducer to avoid discovery; despite this one lapse, she 'never knew any other man than her seducer' (Norton 2005; *London Chronicle* 1760). The press were so eager to believe this story of feminine (near-) virtue that they failed to question why she not only remained in male clothes once apart from him but also married another woman. Instead the *London Chronicle* hurried to reassure readers that Paul 'has made herself known, sent for her mother, and appears to be a very sensible woman' (*London Chronicle* 1760). Nor did readers need to trust to Paul's good sense alone since the magistrate had ordered Paul's male clothes to be burned. We do not know what happened to the couple after these events, but six years later Paul died in the workhouse of St Sepulchre (*St James's Chronicle* 1766).

The last of the eighteenth-century cases was the prosecution of Charles/Ann Marlow, also named in the court papers as Marrow, Morhow, and Marrish.[7] Marlow had apparently married three women and obtained

[6] In light of this, it is surprising that Easton (2003, p. 131) argues that the case illustrates a shift in perceptions of female husband cases away from fraud and towards disorderly lesbian sexuality.

[7] The *Annual Register* chose to use 'Marrow'. However, as the accused's male name had been given as Marlow, this seems more likely to be correct.

'Money, Cloathes, and other Things' from them before being identified as Ann (*Public Advertiser* 1777); no details of those marriages or the circumstances of discovery survive. The prosecutor was a Hammersmith schoolmaster, George Field, whose interest in the case is unrecorded. It was certainly sufficient for him to bring proceedings some distance from his home and to enter into a recognisance (a sum which would become payable to the court if he did not pursue the prosecution) for £40 (True Kalendar, March 1720, LMA MJ/SR/2344; Easton 2003, p. 152). The recognisance gives the accused's name as Charles, later amended to Ann, suggesting that Marlow was still believed to be physically male when first brought before the court.

Marlow was convicted of fraud and sentenced to an unusually severe punishment: six months' imprisonment, during which she was to stand for an hour in the pillory at Charing Cross, the busiest site in London (Persons in Custody, Middlesex Sessions, June 1777, LMA MJ/SP/1777/07/026; Ann Marrish, Petition, 1777, LMA MJ/SP/1777/07/026). Exposure in the pillory was a fairly unusual punishment by this time, occurring on average five times a year, primarily for 'unnatural' sexual offences and perjury. It was also a highly dangerous prospect as the audience would throw various items ranging from dirt to rotten eggs, dead cats, bricks, and stones (Shoemaker 2004, pp. 235, 240; McLynn 1989, p. 283). One of the policy concerns of the period was precisely the control this method of punishment gave to the crowd (Shoemaker 2004, p. 245): some prisoners received approval and collections of money from spectators,[8] while others were killed.[9]

Marlow petitioned the court for mercy on the basis of her 'most alarming terror at that truly shameful and most dangerous punishment' rather than any mitigating features of the offence (Ann Marrish, Petition, 1777, LMA MJ/SP/1777/07/026). However, the petition was clearly rejected as she was pilloried and suffered terrible injuries from 'a severe pelting'

[8] For example, John Williams in 1765 and Daniel Eaton in 1812, both convicted of sedition (Shoemaker 2004, p. 245); and a Mr Parsons who invented a 'ghost' to haunt his creditor: when pilloried, the crowd gave him money to pay the debts (McLynn 1989, p. 282).

[9] Two people died in the pillory between 1775 and 1799, although for one of these, William Smith in 1780, the death may have been due to an improperly set-up pillory rather than the actions of the crowd (Shoemaker 2004, pp. 244–45).

(*Morning Chronicle* 1777). A week later, the *London Evening Post* reported that she had lost her sight and her death was imminent (*London Evening Post* 1777). There was no report of her death, so the *Annual Register* was probably correct in saying that Marlow was blinded (*Annual Register* 1778, pp. 191–92). Perhaps the most extraordinary feature of this case is the lack of reported detail about a crime which attracted such popular opprobrium.

Female Husbands and Silencing

Public trials and punishments might seem a strange starting-point for a history centred on silencing. However, these very moments of visibility give us important insights into how the policy developed and functioned, why it generally worked, and when it did not. Few policies are absolute or meet with universal success in practice; nor are they static across centuries. Silencing was no exception, and the eighteenth-century female husband cases offer much potential insight into its development and operation.

The policing of 'deviant' sexual conduct had been a matter for the ecclesiastical courts until after the Reformation, when the enactment of the Buggery Act 1533 made penile penetration of the anus punishable by death. A gradual shift in the policing of sexuality from the ecclesiastical courts to the secular courts followed, generally using public order and assault offences: a discrete framework of sexual offences had not yet developed. Nor was the state responsible for most criminal prosecutions, involving itself only with a few major offences. Generally the decision to investigate a crime and bring a case was left to those directly affected. Criminal trials were usually conducted without lawyers, whose role was heavily restricted even when they were instructed. Despite some moves towards a greater role for police and the legal profession, this was the 'golden age of discretionary justice' (King 2000, p. 1). Nonetheless, the judiciary exercised oversight of trials and had a great deal of influence upon their conduct and outcome. Hamilton's case makes this exercise of power most obvious because, unusually, the prosecutor was an official body, the Corporation of Glastonbury, who instructed prosecuting counsel.

The Corporation's current and former mayors were also the magistrates who dealt with the hearings and took the depositions; the barrister it had instructed would become the town's Recorder within two years (Battestin 1980, p. 207).

They worked together to identify an offence under the Vagrancy Act 1744: both a necessary task, since there was no specific law addressing female husbands, and a means of obscuring the true nature of the crime as far as possible. Vagrancy laws served a primarily economic function, sparing parishes from supporting paupers who did not have strong connections to them. The particular provision under which Hamilton was charged was fraud committed by 'using any subtil Craft to deceive and impose on any of His Majesty's Subjects'. Hamilton was thus cast as both vagrant and impostor: the word 'impose' still shared its close connections with 'imposture' at this period (Oxford English Dictionary 2004). The Corporation of Glastonbury's charter had been granted as recently as 1705 following a petition arguing that 'the morall of the inhabitants are corrupt' due to a lack of local judicial oversight, so the maintenance of public order was central to its purpose. A vagrancy charge both emphasised that Hamilton was a disruptive outsider to the otherwise-orderly town (Derry 2008) and ensured the case could be dealt with promptly and publicly.[10] While Jones and Stallybrass were right to suggest that the charge established Hamilton as 'out of place', there was too much else at stake for her to be 'simply and literally' so (Jones and Stallybrass 1991, p. 90). Silencing, then, did not necessarily require that cases were not brought at all, but did strongly influence how they were conducted and the offences used.

Identities and Perceptions

Before more fully exploring the legal and social context for these cases, it is important to consider the experiences and subjectivities of the parties themselves. Such consideration needs to take careful account of the

[10] Beattie (1986, p. 18) suggests the Vagrancy Act was used similarly to briefly imprison those suspected of theft.

limitations of the primary sources. The female husbands prosecuted for 'frauds' were plebeian, some of them living marginal or disreputable lives even before they came to the courts' attention. They did not write their own stories: the information we have has been heavily mediated by the court process, the desire of the press to present these cases as strange and sensational, and outright fictionalisation in popular accounts. The surviving archival records give us only one relatively direct narrative, Hamilton's deposition. Even there, the story was told in response to the court's questions, so its structure and scope were dictated by the magistrates. It was written down by someone else and confirmed by a mark rather than a signature, suggesting Hamilton was illiterate and could not read its contents. The defendant would also have good reason to shape her account in certain ways: for example, the claim that she had been born in an unknown Somerset parish seems unlikely but could have been an attempt to improve her position under the Vagrancy Act by suggesting a local connection.[11] Nonetheless, the deposition does appear to be a verbatim transcript: in several places, the words 'I' and 'my' have been crossed through and replaced with 'she' and 'her'. Hamilton was also not wholly compliant with the court, refusing to say anything about the marriage.

The evidence does not tell us much about how the defendants understood their own behaviour. Their motivations have been the subject of debate in recent years: were they women who dressed as men for purely economic reasons, with the marriage simply part of their charade? Did they assume male dress for a combination of economic motives, personal safety, and the possibility it offered of pursuing relationships with women partners? Were they trans men? It is unlikely that the marriages were motivated by economic considerations alone. However, information needed to answer the other questions is simply not available. What data we do have are often contradictory and their reliability uncertain. For example, Paul/Bundy is described as sometimes receiving prison visitors in female dress, sometimes male (*Whitehall Evening Post* 1760b). Is that an accurate piece of reporting? If so, were these changes of dress made

[11] The *Bath Journal* (1746b) stated 'we hear that she was born at Yeovil' but did not specify their source, and there is no corresponding information in the court record.

according to mood, to entertain (paying) visitors, or for practical reasons of limited washing facilities? Which clothes did Paul prefer and why?

There are more fundamental reasons not to attempt definitive answers. Modern lesbian and trans identities are different to eighteenth-century understandings of sex, gender, and sexuality. And these were real people: we have an ethical duty to recognise that they had their own agency and subjectivity. They can be part of lesbian history *and* trans history; we may conclude that they do not belong in either or both; but we should be very wary of imposing definitive interpretations upon them. What is most relevant to this book is how these defendants were seen and treated by the courts and the wider culture within which they lived. That is an easier question to answer: they were treated as women in male disguise.

Motivations for Marriage

As far as we can tell, the defendants had been living as men without attracting suspicion before their marriages. Why, then, might they take the great risk of marrying and becoming vulnerable to exposure by their wives? Although they were charged with fraud offences, those charges could not conceal the lack of financial motive in most if not all of the cases. To court and marry an impoverished young woman just so she would pawn her clothes to pay for a few meals would require a level of effort wholly disproportionate to the scant material gain. The courts framed the charges in this way precisely to conceal the defendants' real motives; but what were they?

The obvious motive would be emotional and sexual desire between husband and wife. The courts had strong ideological reasons for denying that, but it has also been doubted by some more recent commentators including Randolph Trumbach, who posited that most female husbands 'did not seek to have sexual relations with women' (1991, p. 115). Yet the strong relationships in at least some of these cases suggest sexual love between the couple was likely in fact, even if unspeakable in court. Emma Donoghue has argued (1993, p. 61) that while women often married men through financial need, it is fair to assume that desire was a motive for their marrying a woman. Indeed, love and attraction are perhaps the likeliest motivators for taking such a great risk. Connected to that is the loneliness which many female husbands must have felt. Always having to be on their guard against discovery, rewrite their personal histories, and carefully measure their actions would have been exhausting enough in itself, but having no one in whom to confide would have made life even harder. If they did feel able to trust a wife with their secret, as Bundy did, then simply being less lonely would have improved their lives. The risk of disclosure was so high, however, that a great deal of mutual affection and trust would be required.

The other reasons any man married (with the exception of having children) might also apply here. A husband would gain someone to keep the home and offer support in daily life, and would fulfil the strong social expectation that people should marry. A female husband may have thought that the marriage would consolidate their masculine presentation and reduce external scrutiny of the relationship. There might also have been specific pressures upon some defendants to marry their wives. Hamilton and Parlour both lived in the home of Parlour's aunt, who would have been concerned about her niece's reputation and the intentions of her lodger. Ketson's relationship with Ann Hutchinson was clearly of concern to Hutchinson's mother. Third-party involvement in other prosecutions suggests that the wives' reputations were the subject of wider interest. For some husbands at least, the choice may have been either to marry or to end the relationship and leave the area. The evidence, then, strongly suggests that a financial motive was secondary or absent in most cases.

Wives

By definition, a marital relationship requires the involvement of more than one person. While the legal focus was firmly upon the husband, we also need to take seriously the position of the wife. The first question to ask is why the wives in these cases do not seem to have feared or faced any negative legal consequences when bringing their relationships before the court. A superficial answer is that the wives were prosecutors rather than defendants. In a largely victim-led criminal justice system, they had effectively protected themselves when they seized the legal initiative. That is not a complete answer, though, as not all the prosecutions were brought by wives. Since Glastonbury's Corporation brought the prosecution against Hamilton, charges against Price were legally possible, but she was not even criticised. Parlour actually chose to discontinue the proceedings against Paul, again without apparent legal repercussions.

A better answer is that the lack of a specific sexual offence meant these women's actions were not criminal even if they were aware that their partner was female. Nonetheless, this answer is not sufficient: we have seen the ingenuity of prosecutors and courts in framing charges against husbands for whose conduct 'fraud' was not a natural or obvious description. Similar ingenuity could have been attempted to frame charges against wives, had the will existed. Courts were not generally averse to finding slightly questionable offences when the need arose, as judge and professor of law Edward Christian would later explain:

> Complaints are made to magistrates, with respect to a thousand immoral and wicked actions, over which they have no jurisdiction whatever. In such cases, it will be prudence to conceal the infirmity of their authority: but they will frequently find that [the statute against swearing] has been violated by one or both parties. I should then recommend, that they should exert their full authority in the punishment of *this* offence; and to dismiss the parties, with an admonition or a reprimand, where the law has given them no power to act. (Christian 1819, p. 291)

Rather, wives were protected by cultural and ideological understandings of gender and sexuality which made prosecution undesirable. They were framed as gullible, naïve girls duped by a fraudster's charms; the active prosecutorial role taken by others denied them both agency and, to some extent, visibility in the court process. Popular attention could be further diverted from an individual wife by rumours of previous marriages, such as the fourteen claimed for Hamilton. Keeping the wife firmly in the role of legal and sexual innocent left the notion that two women could choose to share all aspects of their lives, including the sexual, unspoken. Instead of being about a relationship which might challenge patriarchal norms and structures, the case became that of one individual, both ridiculous and wicked, who could safely be dismissed as an aberration. To suggest the complicity of the wife would be to challenge such a comforting and unthreatening view. There was also strong cultural support for the idea that relationships between women would not last and that the parties involved (or at least those who retained some femininity) would return to the superior pleasures of heterosexuality (Lanser 2003, pp. 37–38; Faderman 1981, p. 47).

While bringing a case against her husband might have posed few legal risks, it did carry significant disadvantages for the wife. A criminal case was public: her vulnerability to deception would become common knowledge, possibly exaggerated through gossip. Her status would be ambiguous: a woman who had been married, and often sexually active, yet without having experienced either marriage or sexual activity in socially recognised forms. While Mary Price remarried within two years, her husband was a soldier not a local man.[12] Ann Steel of Bolton Piercy, Yorkshire had been married to John Brown for five years before his attempt to enlist in the army at York ended in his identification as Barbara Hill. Steel 'came to town in great affliction, begging that they might not be parted', and it is almost certain that no prosecution followed,[13] but effective extra-judicial action was taken. Despite Steel's pleas, there is a note on the Bolton Piercy marriage register that Hill was 'of course separated from the said Ann Steel' (Borthwick Institute for Archives n.d.). Although Steel would later marry someone from her own parish, the gap of five years before her second marriage is suggestive. And local gossip might prove less willing than the courts to assume innocence. In 1839 James Allen was found at post-mortem to be physically female. His wife Abigail was questioned informally but assumed to be innocent (1829; Clayton 1999). Nonetheless, within days she applied through a friend to Bow Street magistrates' court asking to swear a public affidavit asserting her ignorance of her husband's sex, because she had 'been dreadfully

[12] The marriage register for St John, Glastonbury records her marriage to George Newton, soldier, on 1 March 1748 (SA D/P/GLAJ 2/1/4 p 2).

[13] Borthwick Institute's account of the case notes the lack of entries in the ecclesiastical court records. There is no reference to court proceedings in local or national newspapers or the quarter sessions records held in York Archives and Local History Service.

annoyed by some of her neighbours who doubted the truth of her statement' (*London Evening Standard* 1829).

In line with gender norms of the period, wives were depicted as passive participants in their marriages. Mary Price portrayed herself in those terms: her deposition attributes the active role entirely to Charles Hamilton in courting her, marrying her, and entering her body. However, norms are often far from reality and there are clear indications of these women's agency. Price did in fact agree to marry Hamilton, wed him in church, move from her aunt's house and travel with him, and publicly denounce him as a woman. Parlour's passivity seems to have been confined to the point at which she allowed herself to be drawn into prosecuting her husband: she had earlier discovered that Bundy/Paul was female, chosen to stay in the marriage, taken active steps to keep the couple financially afloat, and subsequently continued the relationship during Bundy/Paul's imprisonment and possibly beyond. Given the degree of public scrutiny she had endured, first for failing to consummate her marriage and then for her husband's sex, the decision to remain with her partner demonstrates a great deal of commitment.

Wives who wanted to end the relationship could establish their own virtue by appearing as wholly innocent victims of deception. The cultural status of the penis as the sole source of 'real' sex posited it as potently unique, not interchangeable with an 'instrument': deception would only be credible when explained by sexual naivety. As a popular ballad at the start of this period ("Comical News from Bloomsbury" 1690) had put it:

> The innocent Bride no difference knew,
> And seem'd to be greatly delighted;
> But Lasses I'll warrant there's none among you
> That would be so cleverly cheated.

The reassertion of sexual virtue was not the only reason a wife might bring or support a prosecution. Another was purely practical: under the doctrine of coverture, a wife's legal personality was subsumed by her husband's, making all her possessions and earnings his and giving him rights over her body including sexual access and physical chastisement. A trial's costs in terms of prosecution expenses and social embarrassment may well have seemed lower than those of being legally tied to a now-unwanted spouse. If the marriage ended on bad terms, for example because the wife had been genuinely deceived, then criminal proceedings also offered a measure of retribution or revenge. It is apparent, however, that wives rarely acted alone in these cases: their communities took an active and sometimes crucial role (Derry 2017).

Wives, then, were actors with their own agency as well as members of wider social networks. They had faced reactions while the marriage subsisted ranging from pity to contempt for their apparent infertility. They bore the disadvantages of the relationship without the concomitant benefits of (albeit precarious) male privilege. While the nature of the sources and the fascination of many historians with the more colourful, more obviously non-conformist parties have meant that attention remains on the husband in these cases, it is as important to note the lack of legal censure for those who retained their expected female role as the punishment of those who did not.[14] Some women freely chose to live in and even acknowledge such relationships: they too deserve a place in our histories.

Sexual Offences and the Bloody Code

The criminal statutes of the eighteenth century are known collectively as the 'Bloody Code' because of the sheer number of capital offences they contained, estimated to have increased from fifty to over two hundred during the century (Hay 1975, pp. 17–63; McLynn 1989, p. xi). However, there was a gap between the harshness of statute law and the reality of its implementation. Not only were offenders frequently pardoned, so that conviction for a capital offence did not necessarily result in execution; the law itself also constrained the scope of these offences. Some were extremely specific: for example, there were separate offences for the destruction of separate bridges. Their scope was also narrowed by

[14] Liberty Smith's article (2002) is a rare but flawed exception. Unfortunately, it both depends heavily upon literary accounts and makes some questionable claims, notably that these couples were engaged in a joint project of challenging heteronormativity.

strict judicial interpretation. Thus the discussion about what Hamilton's offence might be was important not only in framing its interpretation but also because a mistake at this stage could result in acquittal. That stringent approach might seem at odds with the creativity endorsed by Edward Christian. In reality, both served the same end of reinforcing the power of the law. Christian's magistrates were hiding the law's inadequacies when dealing with the disputes of their neighbours, while stern application in the higher courts highlighted its strengths. Douglas Hay argues that attention to legal technicalities made law 'a power with its own claims' higher than those of the men within it, and instilled belief in its 'disembodied justice' (1975, p. 33). This was not a consciously cynical exercise: Emsley points out that the judiciary's conduct was influenced by their belief in impartiality, independence, and equality before the law as well as their class interests and prejudices (2018, p. 15).

The offences so carefully interpreted were mostly property crimes (McLynn 1989, p. xii). These were the early days of the Industrial Revolution with its emphasis upon industry and capital, and political theory reflected those priorities. John Locke asserted that 'Government has no other end but the preservation of property'; by legislating to that end, Parliament would secure the common good (Locke 1690, sects. 1–2; Linebaugh 1982, p. 50).[15] Even when one considers that the meaning of 'property' could include one's own life and personal liberty, this philosophy offered little impetus to extend criminal legislation into the purely moral realm (Locke 1690, sect. 27; Hay 1975, pp. 18–19). The law's concern with sexual offences was largely limited to those involving penile penetration: rape and buggery. The English secular law's definition of buggery was narrower than ecclesiastical definitions of sodomy, which had the potential to encompass any non-procreative sexual activity including masturbation and oral sex (Murray 1996), or the legal definitions used in other European countries.[16] Its emphasis upon penile

[15] Locke's views were by no means universally accepted; his *Second Treatise* was written in the context of a debate with Sir Robert Filmer over absolute monarchy and the divine right of kings.

[16] For example, there were several cases in sixteenth- and seventeenth-century France where the death penalty was imposed (Faderman 1981, p. 51; Laqueur 1990, pp. 136–37; Jones and Stallybrass 1991, pp. 88–89; Fletcher 1995, p. 84); in the Netherlands, Henrika Schuria's death sentence for tribadism was reduced to removal of the clitoris and exile (Laqueur 1990, p. 137);

penetration has been central to the treatment of sexual offences in the English criminal justice system from the eighteenth century to the present.

However, female husbands' behaviour impinged upon elements of concern to the courts: fraudulent assumption of men's sexual, financial, and social privileges. It touched a particular cultural nerve since gender disorder was seen as both symptom of and metaphor for societal breakdown, with prints on the theme of 'the world turned upside down' featuring women performing male roles throughout the eighteenth century (O'Connell 1999, pp. 122–24; Castle 1982, p. 615). While lesbianism remained legally invisible, relationships which came to the courts' attention could be punished through fraud offences which focused legal attention on the material aspects of the marriage. Their silencing of the sexual and emotional elements ensured that the possibility women might want and have sexual relationships together was disregarded. Shared lives were transformed into a one-sided deception, the wife reduced from participant to victim. Curiosity about what two women did together could be reframed as a question of method: how did a woman pass as a man in the marital bed? That question could be answered as briefly or obliquely as the court wished, but it transformed the couple's intimacies into a cynical performance. The possibility that such a relationship might not require the presence of a penis substitute was not considered. It was, after all, of no legal relevance.

Why Were Female Husbands Prosecuted?

Prosecutions were an uncommon response to the relatively many men discovered to be physically female. The lives of unmarried women were heavily constrained in the eighteenth century, legally, socially, and economically. While not all women were subject to the same regulation at all times, its possibility was present even when it was not being exercised. There were thus powerful external incentives for women to live as men even without same-sex attraction or what would now be understood

German Catherina Margaretha Linck was executed for marrying another woman and using a dildo (Faderman 1981, pp. 51–52; Hill 2001, p. 139; Peakman 2004, pp. 182–84).

as trans identities. As a result, there are numerous reports of men in both military and civilian life who were discovered to be biologically female (Duggaw 1989; Wheelwright 1989a). For some, their time living as men was intended to be transient, to achieve specific ends; others spent their whole lives as men and their female physiology was only discovered on death (*An Authentic Narrative of the Extraordinary Career of James Allen* 1829). These very diverse experiences drew similarly diverse responses, with female husband cases alone attracting prosecution. While wives often had good reason to bring a case before the courts, officials also felt able and even eager to respond punitively. What drew hostile attention to female husbands at this period? We will consider three broad factors—social, medical, and legal changes—before exploring precisely what kind of wrong these defendants were being punished for committing.

Social Change

British society was being transformed by the Industrial Revolution and the growth of empire, two deeply intertwined processes as many of the raw materials and much of the wealth upon which new industries were built came from colonialism and slavery. Within England, new wealth was upsetting old social orders with the emergence of East India Company nabobs and newly rich industrialists making their fortunes from cotton, sugar, and tobacco (Bowen 1998; Nechtman 2010). Migration from rural communities to larger industrial towns and major cities brought its own anxieties. By the latter part of the century, the French Revolution added new urgency to fears of working-class agitation. Britain's sense of its place in the world was also transforming as its empire expanded and it needed to attempt to justify its colonial endeavours to itself, a task the British found more challenging as the century progressed. From the publication of former slave Olaudah Equiano's autobiography and the formation of anti-slavery groups in the 1780s to concerns about the East India Company's activities in India culminating in the 1788 impeachment of Warren Hastings, difficult moral questions were increasingly being asked (Equiano 1789; Dirks 2006).

This general disquiet about society and nation fed into anxieties about the roles of men and women. Respectability grew in importance, with self-control in the area of sexual conduct a key way of distinguishing white Britons from the colonised Other (Peakman 2016, p. 37). Lynne Friedli has linked these anxieties to the legal preoccupation with fraud, suggesting that the proliferation of such offences indicated 'a general fear about deception and disorder' (1985, p. 25). London was a particular focus for concern: the capital, with its higher and growing rates of theft and violent crime, was unlike the rest of England (Beattie 1986, p. 14; McLynn 1989, p. 1). It held both abject poverty and a major share of the country's wealth, and its population included a large number of immigrants from outside the city and a high ratio of unmarried, disproportionately male, young people (Rogers 2007).

Such concerns were accompanied by a national trend for more women to marry, and to marry younger. The number of never-married women dropped in the mid-eighteenth century, only rising again in the 1780s (Hunt 1999, p. 278). This was partly facilitated by greater wage-earning possibilities (Cook 2005, p. 115) but also came alongside a new emphasis upon vaginal intercourse; at the start of the century, that had probably not been the main sexual activity in which most people engaged (Traub 2016, pp. 150–52). Tim Hitchcock (2012, pp. 826–29) argues persuasively that the growth in both marriage and birth rates from 1700 demonstrates that more penis-in-vagina sex was happening, and that this reflected a narrowing of the definition of sex to penile penetration of a vagina. The purpose of sexual activity was emphasised as procreative, with the most popular sex manual of the period, *Aristotle's Masterpiece* (1684), a guide to achieving conception rather than pleasure. Production of children was a matter of national interest, understood by political economists as central to the future wealth of the nation (Bannet 1997; Lanser 1999b).

Those factors contributed to an increasingly hostile environment for single women. Bridget Hill has identified a growing tendency to see unemployed single women as sexually suspect (Hill 2001, p. 101). Terry Castle and Susan S Lanser point to an increase in hostile depictions of lesbianism in literature, although Lanser also notes that the spinster was generally discredited not as a lesbian but as a woman who wanted a man and could not get one: a way of keeping them 'attached to the hetero-sexual order' (Lanser 1999b; Castle 1993). Lone women also faced risks to their personal safety which constrained their mobility and ability to live independently, not least the threat of seduction or sexual violence should they stray from the shelter of the patriarchal family (Kittredge 2003, p. 7).

Single women were also subject to rising economic constraints. Wages were falling in rural occupations, with a drastic drop in earnings for spinning, the paradigm occupation for single women. While most in London described themselves as financially self-supporting, albeit many presumably lived with other family members (Hunt 1999, p. 280), urban trades were generally closed to them. There was very little poor relief for single unemployed women, a deliberate strategy intended to force them into domestic service (Hill 2001, pp. 25–29, 96–97, 101). It was not a new policy: the Statute of Artificers 1563, which allowed magistrates to order unmarried women aged between twelve and forty into domestic service, was still in use during the first part of the eighteenth century (Mendelson and Crawford 1998, pp. 96–98, 246–47). One attraction for the authorities of placing women in service was exactly its disadvantage from many women's perspective: it put them firmly under the control of a patriarchal household.

At the same time, industrialisation brought fresh possibilities for leaving female life behind to seek new opportunities. The decision to live as a man, while not exactly common, was far from unknown and offered definite advantages. Jobs for men were available in cities, and moving to a new town made a change of identity possible. It was this mobility rather than the relative anonymity of London which facilitated reinvention. As Paul/Bundy's case demonstrates, urban communities were liable to be as diligent in policing their neighbours as their rural counterparts (see also Hill 2001, pp. 119–22). This is not to argue that female husbands were primarily motivated by economic or practical considerations. As already discussed, for someone biologically female to live as a man and enter into a marriage was fraught with risk. Unlike women who adopted male dress for relatively short periods or specific purposes, female husbands went beyond what was required by economic motivations and the need to pass.

In considering the social context for these cases, it is important to keep in mind that 'society' was not a singular mass. The evidence from communities, the print press, and popular culture paints a more complex picture. Community reaction might seem clearly hostile since neighbours supported or instigated the majority of prosecutions. However, both Paul and Hamilton drew sufficient benign curiosity to earn relatively large sums of money from their prison visitors. The *Bath Journal* reported that Hamilton was visited in prison by 'great numbers of people … to whom she sells a great Deal of her Quackery', a testament to popular curiosity rather than the reputation of her potions and nostrums (*Bath Journal* 1746a). Although prison visits could be motivated by horrified disgust or prurient curiosity as well as more sympathetic interest, the willingness to offer a financial contribution suggests a significant element of the latter. Paul similarly benefited financially from the public fascination with her case, effectively performing the role in which the court and media had cast her (*Whitehall Evening Post* 1760b):

> Since in Prison she has got, through the Folly of her Visitants, upwards of 30s. a Day; dresses herself occasionally in Women's Apparel, and some Times in a neat Sailor's Habit; and has since under Confinement been visited by above 12 young Women, to whom she paid her Respects as a Man for Marriage.

The presence of Parlour alongside her suggests that the flirtation at least was a performance. It was not appreciated by commentators of the middling sort who were scathing about popular approval: the *Public Ledger* referred sarcastically to 'so celebrated a heroine' (*Public Ledger* 1760). Such reactions may even have hardened rather than moderated court attitudes to the defendants.

Press reports often seemed to straddle a similar line between prurient, but not necessarily hostile, curiosity, and outrage or disgust. The effect was partly achieved by consistently emphasising the extraordinary nature of these cases. While newspapers were frequently inaccurate, Fielding's anonymous account of the Hamilton case was altogether unconstrained by facts; its value lies in showing what content appealed to a general readership rather than to learned or professional gentlemen—and, as Emily

Bowles (2010) argues, in exposing Fielding's construction of normative sexual categories. Having begun by explicitly asserting that heterosex is natural, necessary for procreation, virtuous, delightful, and rational, Fielding went on to describe Hamilton's conduct as 'monstrous and unnatural', 'in the highest manner criminal', a 'wicked crime', 'vile amours', 'most monstrous and unnatural desires', and 'foul and unnatural crimes' (1746, pp. 1, 3, 4, 23). By contrast, heterosexuality's 'delights infinitely surpass[ed] the faint endearments' between women (p. 4). The book ended with a nod to silencing: 'notwithstanding the subject of this narrative be of a nature so difficult to be handled inoffensively, not a single word occurs through the whole, which might shock the most delicate ear, or give offence to the purest chastity' (p. 23).

The last of the eighteenth-century cases, however, was reported differently. The *Newgate Calendar* began its account by contextualising Marlow's prosecution as one of a number, opening with a reference to the Hamilton trial three decades earlier. Its comment that the punishment in that case had not been adequate, 'the law not contemplating such an offence', contradicted the original report of Hamilton's case (Knapp 1810, pp. 125–26), which had expressed sadistic pleasure rather than dissatisfaction at the sentence. Now, Marlow's loss of sight was reported with evident glee (Knapp 1826, p. 395). While the unknown facts of the case may have accounted for courtroom reactions, they cannot explain the tone of this report whose vagueness suggests the author did not have access to them. Rather, the attitude of the *Newgate Calendar*'s authors had hardened alongside the sentencing of the court. Even the sparsity of detail may be symptomatic of wider changes in the latter part of the century: reporting of the 1797 sodomy prosecution of William Winklin was similarly vague because 'being extremely indecent, the Court ordered the publication of it to be suppressed' ("February 1797, Trial of William Winklin" 2012; and see Peakman 2016, p. 22).

These publications were ostensibly written by and for the middling sort. While plebeian neighbours could also be vocal in their disapproval, as in the Paul/Bundy case, social rank was a significant factor. Lanser makes a convincing case that sapphism was viewed as a lower-class behaviour which could 'infect the worthier classes from 'below'' (and as an aristocratic decadence which might infect them from above); by contrast, appropriate female friendships were a status symbol for the middling sort (Lanser 1999a, p. 186). Prosecution of plebeian female husbands was therefore a way both to constrain inappropriate female intimacies before they reached respectable women and to valorise appropriate behaviour by way of contrast. Societal determination to constrain women's behaviour within acceptable limits hardened during the century, as suggested by the hostility directed at Marlow. At the same time, the expressions of affection permitted *within* respectable friendships were crucial to silencing: the construction of affectionate and even romantic expression between women as appropriate for non-sexual friendship obscured alternative possibilities. This tension between romantic friendship as a space for women's homosocial (and possibly sexual) relationships to flourish, and its denial of lesbian sexuality, has to some extent been mirrored in subsequent disputes over their place in lesbian history (Faderman 1981; Love 2007, pp. 75–76; Castle 1993, p. 95; Donoghue 1993).

The eighteenth century thus offered a potent combination of geographic mobility, industrialisation, changing gender roles, and class anxieties. It is unsurprising that these issues sometimes found their focus in the female husband who embodied many of their threats. A growing public appetite for crime literature, satisfied by pamphlets, broadsides, and Old Bailey sessions papers, as well as increasing access to newspapers (King 2007, pp. 73–75), enabled such stories to be spread more quickly and widely (though not more accurately) than before (Ward 2014). However, social changes alone do not fully explain the relative visibility of these cases in the eighteenth century.

Changing Medical Theories

Crucially, there were also important changes in medical theory, now divided between competing models of sexual difference. The older approach was an essentially one-sex model, albeit with significant differences according to whether one followed Aristotelian or Galenic principles. Galen of Pergamum, a second-century writer, had believed that men and women shared one fundamental structure, which differed only in its arrangement. It was humans' greater 'vital heat' which made them superior to other animals, and the greater heat of men which caused their genitalia to be placed externally. Women, being inferior to men in heat (and thus further from perfection), kept their genitalia internally (Hitchcock 1997, p. 42). Thus the model was one of hierarchy rather than biological difference: the organs were the same, but crucially differed in location. The male was taken as the norm and model for understanding both sexes, so the woman was assumed to contribute 'semen' necessary to conception, with orgasm required for its release.

Aristotle also put forward a one-sex model; its key difference was that the female was understood as contributing no 'semen' to conception, so her orgasm was not required for it to occur (Connell 2000; Salisbury 1996).[17] Based in part upon Galen's later interpretations of this theory, the suggestion is often made that Aristotle viewed the female as an incomplete male, both intellectually and morally inferior (e.g. Bullough 1996, p. 225). Connell points out that this overstates Aristotle's position which in some aspects did more than Galen's to value women's reproductive role (Connell 2000). Aristotelian theory was less influential than Galenic in the eighteenth century, but important nonetheless (Hitchcock 1997, p. 47).[18] Thomas Laqueur (1990, p. 35) suggests that notions of sexual biology did not give rise to but rather acted as illustrations of wider truths: physical differences were interpreted according to the model of female inferiority which they in turn justified.

Under the Galenic model in particular, women were seen as sexually insatiable. Such a view may seem inconsistent with the belief that they were essentially passive, but this was a passive kind of insatiability: women did not act as sexual aggressors but rather were open to receiving men's semen as a source of dry heat. They posed a risk to men rather than themselves: there was less concern, at least among medical writers, with female masturbation than male since semen was a precious source of energy and masculinity, while female secretions were toxic and thus better purged than conserved (Salisbury 1996, p. 91).

---

[17] For a critical discussion of both theories, see Connell (2000).

[18] Harvey describes this dominance of Galenic over Aristotelian theory as 'a relatively short-lived blip' (2002, p. 211).

This conception of human sex differences was changing dramatically. The new two-sex model understood men's and women's physiology as fundamentally different. It was no coincidence that the scientific move to a two-sex model went in tandem with the rise of liberalism, since Laqueur (1990) argues that the liberal focus on individual rights required fixed, qualitative differences between men and women to justify inequalities. The transition did not occur overnight,[19] and there were often significant divergences between elite and popular understandings (Harvey 2002). It was at a time when both the Galenic or Aristotelian and the new two-sex models enjoyed currency that female husbands were increasingly visible. Emily Bowles (2010) argues that popular accounts of these cases played a role in codifying new understandings of sexual difference.

Adoption of a two-sex model had consequences detrimental to women, since by removing the analogy of the clitoris with the penis it also removed any emphasis upon women's sexual pleasure. Ornella Moscucci draws on Laqueur to argue that while the Galenic model had seen the clitoris as the seat of women's sexual pleasure, the possibilities it offered for sexual satisfaction independently of men now became perceived as a threat to the social order (Moscucci 1996). Sally O'Driscoll (2003) also maps the eighteenth-century emergence of the passionless woman in both medicine and literature. However, this argument should not obscure the disadvantages of a one-sex model for women. Female sexual pleasure was relevant only under the Galenic model, which nonetheless constructed women's 'lustfulness' as a danger to men except for those brief times when it was needed for conception. As Connell points out (2000, p. 414), tying it to conception meant that it was endorsed only when achieved through vaginal penetration for procreative purposes. One particularly cruel outcome was the conclusion of jurists that where there was conception there could not have been rape (Histed 2004). More generally, the assumption that sexual intercourse in moderation was vital to women's health may have allowed them to be recognised as sexual beings, but only in limited and heteropatriarchal terms. Sexual intercourse became something women passively submitted to or 'suffered' (Walker 1998), while its

[19] Indeed, several historians have argued persuasively that the shift began in the seventeenth century (Fissell 1995; Fletcher 1995; Gowing 1998).

absence was associated with female ill-health and specifically the condition of 'greensickness' (Blackwell 2002, pp. 61–65). Thus Ebenezer Sibly wrote that the 'animating effluvia' of coition rendered women 'robust, and beautiful, and active', while the 'ancient virgin' was 'generally consumed with infirmity, ill-temper, or disease' (1796, p. 43).

The increasing dominance of penis-in-vagina intercourse as the only acceptable form of sex was accompanied by a rise in anti-masturbation literature, which O'Driscoll (2003, p. 104) argues expressed an anxiety about women's sexuality amounting to cultural 'delusion'. It framed lesbianism as mutual masturbation, both a lower-class contagion and a source of physical danger. *Onania; or the Heinous Sin of Self-Pollution* (1710) described the case of a young woman whose sexual activity began when she 'was taught it by [her] Mother's Chamber Maid' and had led to 'a Swelling ... as big, and almost as hard, and as long or longer than [her] Thumb, which inclines [her] to excessive lustful Desires'. The preface to the eighth edition outlined a case in a girls' boarding school, in which they 'Practis'd it, *cum Digitis & aliis Instrumentis* [with fingers and other instruments]' (1723, p. vii). *Satan's Harvest Home* (1749) excoriated women's lack of virtue and men's effeminate preference for sodomy but, in concluding with 'the game of flatts', described lesbianism as 'a new and most abominable Vice' best illustrated with a story from Turkey (1749, pp. 60–61). *A Treatise on the Crime of Onan* (Tissot 1766) offered a comprehensive summary of the horrors of autonomous female sexuality, in which masturbation led to conditions ranging from 'elongations of the clitoris' to 'a desperate death' (pp. 46–48), but excessive chastity could also cause 'melancholy, disrelish of life, emaciation, and pollutions' (p. 200). Special disgust was reserved for 'clitoridian' or lesbian 'contamination' by 'monstrous beings' who 'usurped the functions of virility' thanks to a clitoris of 'supernatural size'. These women, distinguished from hermaphrodites, were dangerous seducers of 'innocent accomplices' (pp. 52–54).

If the differences between men and women altered the very content and construction of their bodies, then how to explain those who did not conform to their expected roles? Randolph Trumbach (1991, pp. 112–13) argued that there was a move from three biological sexes (male, female, and hermaphrodite) and two genders (male and female) to two biological sexes (male and female) but four genders (male, female, effeminate homosexual 'molly', and 'sapphic', with the sapphic woman a later and less fully incorporated 'gender'). Subsequent research, notably that of Emma Donoghue (1993), revealed the extent to which lesbian identities were constructed in this period. Susan S. Lanser identifies this process as involving a shift in the understandings of same-sex desire towards being socially rather than anatomically transgressive. By mid-century there was a move away from the hermaphrodite as a site of same-sex desire, which became located in external masculinity rather than atypical genitalia (Lanser 2003, pp. 23–29).[20]

Hermaphroditism had been a common explanation of sexual relationships between women in both medical and popular literature in the seventeenth and earlier eighteenth centuries, likely to be within the knowledge of parties and courts (see Jones and Stallybrass 1991; Donoghue 1993). It was implicitly considered and discounted in Paul/Bundy's case when neighbours described her as 'a perfect female'. Had any of these defendants been recognised as hermaphrodites rather than women, their legal position would have been different—although not necessarily better. Those classed as hermaphrodites seem sometimes to have had some limited agency to determine the sex to which they belonged: Sir Edward Coke (1628) had asserted that 'an Hermaphrodite may purchase according to that sexe which prevaileth', a decision made by lawyers, doctors, and/or the person themselves. Alice Domurat Dreger (1998, pp. 116–17) notes that although British doctors were relatively reticent about patients' sexual behaviour, they did treat it as a powerful indicator of their 'true' sex. However, it was to be a once-and-for-all choice with no legal scope for gender fluidity. Thus, just as the possibility of a third sex was legally or medically recognised, it was carefully corralled back into the binary system. As the century progressed, even the possibility fell out of favour, albeit slowly and unevenly (e.g. Clark 1996, p. 47).

[20] This view is supported by the near-absence of the hermaphrodite from the legal texts I have considered.

Changes in the Criminal Justice System

Throughout this chapter, we have seen the significance of court practice and procedure. The criminal justice system was undergoing a critical transition in both its practices and its underlying ideologies, informed by liberalism's focus upon rights and processes. The eighteenth-century norm of private rather than state prosecutions meant a criminal case would be brought only when somebody, usually but not always the victim, thought the time, expense, and inconvenience were merited.[21] It might not be brought where either community justice or direct compensation from offender to victim was available instead; where the victim did not want to bring a capital charge against the offender; or where the victim was either too embarrassed or too intimidated by the offender and their associates (Emsley 2018, pp. 187–90; Beattie 1986, pp. 39–40). If it was pursued, the private prosecutor had a great deal of discretion in choosing the charge and thus the potential severity of punishment (Emsley 2018, pp. 192, 196). By dropping the case, they could ensure that the alleged offender went unconvicted and unpunished—although prosecutors could be bound by recognisances for substantial sums to discourage this (Hay 1975, p. 41). The various ways in which these elements of discretion were exercised in the prosecution of female husbands has been a pervasive theme of this chapter.

However, the eighteenth century also saw the initial stages of a significant move from lawyer-less private prosecutions involving amateur magistrates and constables, to trials involving professional counsel. While police forces would only be established in the nineteenth century, prosecuting lawyers were already becoming more common. In response, defence counsel were permitted to cross-examine prosecution witnesses in many more types of criminal trial from the 1730s (Langbein 2003, pp. 3–4). Their presence subtly changed the role of the jury as courtroom

[21] Costs awards at the Surrey quarter sessions of 1767 ranged between seven shillings and a guinea, but probably did not represent the full cost of bringing the prosecution (Beattie 1986, pp. 46–47). A rough translation into current money values places those costs as between £30 and £91.62 at 2017 values, or between three and ten days' wages for a skilled tradesman (The National Archives 2018). Lost earnings while attending court were also a significant cost for poorer prosecutors (Emsley 2018).

evidence and proper procedure were increasingly emphasised over local knowledge. The final stage of the criminal process, the punishment of a convicted offender, would also gain greater formality: there was growing uneasiness at crowd involvement in the kinds of public punishment discussed in the following section (Shoemaker 2004, p. 245). Those concerns, combined with late eighteenth-century arguments for penal reform, saw a shift towards private punishments and particularly imprisonment. The eighteenth-century female husband cases thus coincided with the last days of amateur justice and crowd punishment. The consequences of the move to state investigation and prosecution and professionalised trials, not least their relationship with the increasing silencing of lesbianism, will be considered in Chap. 3.

Why Were Female Husbands Punished?

We therefore come back to the question of why, despite the difficulties and expense of prosecution, female husbands were brought before the courts by wives or neighbours. Clearly there was something about these accused which drew strong reactions from all levels of society. The *Newgate Calendar*'s account of Mary Hamilton's case suggests that this hostility was not confined to those directly affected but would be shared by a wider readership: it ends with the assurance that she 'was imprisoned and whipped accordingly, in the severity of the winter of the year 1746' (Crook 1926, p. 136). This reference to the harsh weather was designed to remind the reader that Hamilton would have been stripped to the waist when whipped publicly through the streets. Such an evocation of nakedness and public humiliation, in the same sentence as a reference to Hamilton as 'the monopoliser of her own sex', is sadistic and sexualised in tone. Given the pitch of the rest of the passage, it seems unlikely that such allusion was accidental. The punishment of women often had a sexual component for male viewers (Knelman 1998; Gatrell 1994, p. 264). The visceral physicality and sadism directed towards lesbians in particular may be related to the fact that their presence in seventeenth and eighteenth-century literature was largely in pornographic and semi-pornographic writing aimed at men (Castle 1982, pp. 612–13; Toulalan 2003).

Identification of the response to female husbands as both hostile and motivated by their perceived lesbianism calls into question the argument that lesbians were lightly treated in the context of the time.[22] On the contrary, the punishments endured by these defendants were severe even if they were not capital. The majority of crimes were dealt with by the Petty and Quarter Sessions, which did not have the power to impose capital punishment (Hay 1975, p. 59; Emsley 2018, p. 249). Whipping of female husbands was in line with other fraud sentences in these courts. Hamilton's sentence of multiple whippings and imprisonment was the maximum available for her vagrancy offence (Adolphus 1824, pp. 7–8), while Marlow's pillorying was unusually harsh. Implicit in the idea that lesbians were treated tolerantly is the measurement of their treatment against that of male sodomites. However, if we centre the treatment of lesbians rather than drawing on a male comparator, the level of physical violence inflicted upon these defendants is striking.

Such sentences could expect popular support as lesbianism was popularly considered criminal. Hester Thrale defined 'Sapphist' as a woman who liked 'her own sex in a criminal way' (quoted in Donoghue 1993, p. 4); an anonymous pamphlet talked of 'Tommies' as committing 'Unnat'ral Crimes' (quoted in Donoghue 1993, p. 5); James's *Medical Dictionary* (1742) defined 'Tribades' as women with enlarged clitorises who 'make Attempts to converse in a criminal manner with other Women'; while the anonymous author of *Plain Reasons for the Growth of Sodomy* referred to women 'criminally *amorous* of each other, in a *Method* too gross for expression' (1728, p. 12). Yet allegations which reached eighteenth-century courtrooms were specifically female husband cases: what about these in particular was seen to require official censure and retribution?

Historians have focused upon two elements: sexual behaviour and the adoption of male clothing. For Faderman, what was being punished was

[22] See Faderman (1981, p. 52), Fletcher (1995, p. 85), Heidensohn (1996, p. 39) which suggest lesbianism was immune from legal intervention; Hitchcock (1997, p. 77) which claims no lesbians were prosecuted *qua* lesbians. Peakman (2004, p. 193) argues sex between women was not criminalised because it posed less threat to the social order than sex between men.

transvestism with its explicit seizing of male prerogatives. Although she identified its combination with sexual acts, particularly use of a dildo, as the trigger for 'extreme societal anger', she maintained that the impersonation of men was key to the seriousness of these offences (1981, p. 52). Vicinus and Friedli similarly focused upon the deception with its usurpation of male privileges as more significant than the sexual conduct in itself (Vicinus 1996, pp. 242–44; Friedli 1987, p. 237). However, these interpretations do not fully account for the general lack of legal censure for other women who lived as men. Should we instead focus upon the sexual behaviour as central? Emma Donoghue favoured that approach, arguing that lawmakers felt threatened by lesbianism and cross-dressing in combination: this was a crime 'neither purely social nor purely sexual' (1993, p. 61). Castle offered an alternative suggestion: that clear distinctions between the sexes were essential for the maintenance of male dominance and sexual hierarchy (1982, p. 615).

All these elements—the assumption of male privilege in association with sexual deviance, the dangerous blurring of gender boundaries—were clearly significant. Also crucial, however, was another factor: the attempt to live together without male involvement. A recognised survival strategy crossed the line into criminality at the point where it went beyond limited assumption of male privileges into an outright rejection of male authority. It is significant that female husbands chose to establish their own homes with their wives: this meant not only a sexual component to their lives apparently absent in other cases but also a failure to remain under direct male authority in the form of an employer or superior military officer. As Fraser Easton mentions (2003, p. 133), women warriors were perceived as 'properly subordinate and industrious'. By contrast, Hamilton was self-employed and lived largely outside any settled community context; Bundy had abandoned an apprenticeship before joining and quickly running away from the Navy and then from a merchant ship (*London Chronicle* 1760). Such withdrawal from patriarchal control was seen to pose a real threat and thus to be deserving of criminal sanction. Lesbian relationships which did not prevent the women involved from marrying men and remaining firmly within patriarchal structures were less problematic, as were incidents of cross-dressing whose perpetrators demonstrated (or pretended) at least some willingness to submit to heteropatriarchal norms. What the courts needed to prosecute and punish was the adoption of a lifestyle based upon female self-sufficiency, mutual support, and overt independence from men. The particular method of achieving that independence, by emulating heterosexual marriage, left female husbands in a uniquely vulnerable position. Ironically, their imitation of conventional marital relationships neutralised much of the danger of prosecuting and thereby publicising lesbianism. They could be presented not as offering an alternative to the heteropatriarchal household but rather as having attempted a poor, often laughable facsimile of it. Further, the nature of their disguise precluded any building of a network or movement: as Wheelwright points out (1989b, p. 11), their status as 'staunch individualists' prevented them from posing any real threat.

Conclusion: Silencing and the Dildo

The female husband cases are paradoxical: they both breached and reinforced the silencing of lesbian possibility. On the one hand, they brought marriages between women into view not only through court hearings and media reports but also through the infliction of public punishment. On the other, the possibility of a meaningful relationship between two women was discounted at the very moment it was exposed. These marriages were presented as fraudulent, unsatisfactory counterfeits which no respectable woman would willingly choose and which could not survive the scrutiny of any but the most naïve young woman. At the centre of their presumed inferiority was a sexual absence: the lack of a penis with which to satisfy a wife.

Fielding's fictional account of the Hamilton case clearly illustrated that strange absence. Although it offered ever-more elaborate details of Hamilton's invented life, including multiple marriages, the sexual activity was characterised as unmentionable. The phallus was referred to through its absence: Hamilton lacked '*the werewithal*' on one occasion (Fielding 1746, p. 39), while the second wife discovered that 'you have not … what you ought to have' (p. 3). Even when the dildo finally made an appearance in court, it remained unnamed and undescribed, 'something of too vile, wicked and scandalous a nature'. It was also, as Sarah Nicolazzo (2014, p. 340) explores, constructed as a tool primarily for financial fraud rather than sexual pleasure. This was an elaboration of the press reports. The *Bath Journal* had made clear to readers that the two women had sexual relations 'owing to the Prisoner's using certain vile and deceitful Practices, not fit to be mentioned' (*Bath Journal* 1746c). In court, Price's deposition had revealed that Hamilton 'did enter [Price's] body' and at least some contemporary readers including Fielding had no difficulty in assuming this meant some kind of fake penis.[23] However, they had to do so on the basis of a narrative, which, as Terry Castle explains, 'at once describes and doesn't describe, tells and doesn't tell', making the female husband a paradoxical, 'notorious and unmentionable' figure (1982, pp. 602–03).

O'Driscoll (2010, pp. 45–46) describes how the dildo had moved by the mid-eighteenth century from a tool which sexually unsatisfied women might use to a symbol of 'unnatural' masculine desire. It paralleled, then, the shift from women as sexually desiring, even voracious, to the newer model of the passionless woman. What remained consistent was the underlying analogy of the dildo with the penis, so that overly public relationships between women could be punished, and publicised, without suggesting a lesbian alternative not modelled upon vaginal penetration by a dominant (pseudo-)male. By focusing upon the inferiority of the husbands' attempts to pass as male, popular accounts portrayed them as laughable deceivers of gullible women rather than feasible role models. Consequently, they elicited 'recoil and fascination', in Castle's phrase, but I would suggest that the 'subversiveness of the masquerade' she also claims for Hamilton (1982, p. 604) was largely absent. The potential for subversion was undermined by the inadequacy of the imitation of heterosexuality and by the ultimate vulnerability of the husband.

Ending as we began, with Hamilton's case, we can see that life as a man allowed a career as a travelling quack, independence, and geographical mobility. However, it became more dangerous following marriage to Price, culminating in conviction and punishment. Yet Price, despite

[23] Indeed, Fielding added a passage describing its discovery and use in evidence, an incident entirely absent from the actual records of the case.

being the chief witness and giving her own deposition, remains a shadowy figure: reports of the case evaded awkward questions about whether she might actually have known the truth, a notion too threatening to be seriously entertained. Hamilton and Price lived within a wider context where women who lived as men might go unpunished and even admired—until they seized sexual and social autonomy. Thereafter, they could suffer serious legal consequences, usually through fraud prosecutions which both hid the true motivations for their behaviour and reflected wider social anxieties. The eighteenth-century development of silencing, then, did not leave lesbianism unpunished and tolerated but required a *selective* approach to prosecution and punishment. The cases which appeared in courts and periodicals were those whose close but unsuccessful mimicry of patriarchal marriages could leave the overall policy, and with it patriarchal power relations, unchallenged. These early days of legal silencing, when sexual offences were a relatively recent concern for the secular criminal courts, effectively set a pattern for the following centuries. We will see in following chapters that many features persisted even as the criminal justice system and the wider social context changed. The next chapter will explore silencing's development in the nineteenth century when female husbands largely disappeared from legal view—but silencing's role in the criminal regulation of lesbianism was confirmed.

References

Adolphus, John. 1824. *Observations on the Vagrant Act*. London: John Major.

An Authentic Narrative of the Extraordinary Career of James Allen, the Female Husband, Who Was Married for the Space of Twenty-One Years, without Her Real Sex Being Discovered, Even by Her Wedded Associate. 1829. London: I.S. Thomas.

Annual Register for the Year 1777. 1778. 4th ed. London: J Dodsley.

Aristotle's Masterpiece; or, the Secrets of Generation Display'd in All the Parts Thereof. 1684. London.

Baker, Sheridan. 1959. Henry Fielding's The Female Husband: Fact and Fiction. *Proceedings of the Modern Language Association* 74 (3): 213.

Bannet, Eve Tavor. 1997. The Marriage Act of 1753: 'A Most Cruel Law for the Fair Sex'. *Eighteenth-Century Studies* 30 (3): 233–254.

Bath Journal. 1746a. No Title, September 22.

———. 1746b. No Title, September 29.

———. 1746c. No Title, November 3.

Battestin, Martin. 1980. Fielding and the Glastonbury Waters. *Yearbook of English Studies* 10: 205.

Beattie, J.M. 1986. *Crime and the Courts in England 1660–1800.* Princeton: Princeton University Press.

Blackwell, Bonnie. 2002. 'An Infallible Nostrum': Female Husbands and Greensick Girls in Eighteenth-Century England. *Literature and Medicine* 21 (1): 56–77.

Borthwick Institute for Archives. n.d. The Story of Barbara Hill. Lesbian, Gay, Bisexual & Transgendered History. Accessed September 6, 2019. https://www.york.ac.uk/borthwick/holdings/guides/research-guides/lgbt/barbara-hill/.

Bowen, H.V. 1998. British India, 1765–1813: The Metropolitan Context. In *The Oxford History of the British Empire: The Eighteenth Century*, ed. P.J. Marshall, 530–551. Oxford: Oxford University Press.

Bowles, Emily. 2010. You Have Not What You Ought: Gender and Corporeal Intelligibility in Henry Fielding's The Female Husband. *Genders* 52. https://www.colorado.edu/gendersarchive1998-2013/2010/10/01/you-have-not-what-you-ought-gender-and-corporeal-intelligibility-henry-fieldings-female.

Bullough, Vern L. 1996. Cross Dressing and Gender Role Change in the Middle Ages. In *Handbook of Medieval Sexuality*, ed. Vern L. Bullough and James A. Brundage, 223–242. New York: Garland Publishing.

Caledonian Mercury. 1728. Edinburgh, December 12.

Castle, Terry. 1982. Matters Not Fit to Be Mentioned: Fielding's The Female Husband. *ELH* 49 (3): 602–622.

———. 1993. *The Apparitional Lesbian: Female Homosexuality and Modern Culture*. New York: Columbia University Press.

Christian, Edward. 1819. *Charges Delivered to Grand Juries in the Isle of Ely, upon Libels, Criminal Law, Vagrants, Religion, Rebellions, Assemblies, &c. & c. for the Use of Magistrates and Students of the Law*. 2nd ed. London: W Clarke and Sons.

Clark, Anna. 1996. Anne Lister's Construction of Lesbian Identity. *Journal of the History of Sexuality* 7 (1): 23–50.

Clayton, Susan. 1999. Does the Dress Make the Husband? An Example of a Female Husband, James Allen (1787–1829). *Clio* 10: 90–116.

———. 2010. Can Two and a Half Centuries of Female Husbands Inform (Trans)Gender History? *Journal of Lesbian Studies* 14 (4): 288–302. https://doi.org/10.1080/10894160903048106.

Coke, Edward. 1628. *The First Part of the Institutes of the Laws of England*. London: Society of Stationers.

Comical News from Bloomsbury. 1690. The Female Captain: Or, The Counterfeit Bridegroom. London.

Connell, Sophia M. 2000. Aristotle and Galen on Sex Difference and Reproduction: A New Approach to an Ancient Rivalry. *Studies in the History and Philosophy of Science* 31 (3): 405–427.

Cook, Hera. 2005. The English Sexual Revolution: Technology and Social Change. *History Workshop Journal* 59: 109–128.

Crook, G.T., ed. 1926. *The Complete Newgate Calendar*. London: Navarre Society.

Derry, Caroline. 2008. Sexuality and Locality in the Trial of Mary Hamilton, 'Female Husband'. *King's Law Journal* 19 (3): 595–616. https://doi.org/10.1080/09615768.2008.11427709.

———. 2017. 'Female Husbands', Community and Courts in the Eighteenth Century. *Journal of Legal History* 38 (1): 54–79. https://doi.org/10.1080/01440365.2017.1289674.

Dirks, Nicholas B. 2006. *The Scandal of Empire: India and the Creation of Imperial Britain*. Cambridge, MA: Harvard University Press.

Donoghue, Emma. 1993. *Passions Between Women: British Lesbian Culture 1668–1801*. London: Scarlet Press.

Dreger, Alice Domurat. 1998. *Hermaphrodites and the Medical Invention of Sex*. London: Harvard University Press.

Duggaw, Dianne. 1989. *Warrior Women and Popular Balladry, 1650–1850*. Cambridge: Cambridge University Press.

Easton, Fraser. 2003. Gender's Two Bodies: Women Warriors, Female Husbands and Plebeian Life. *Past and Present* 180: 131–174.

Emsley, Clive. 2018. *Crime and Society in England 1750–1900*. 5th ed. London: Routledge.

Equiano, Olaudah. 1789. *The Interesting Narrative of the Life of Olaudah Equiano, or Gustavus Vassa, the African*. London: Olaudah Equiano.

Faderman, Lillian. 1981. *Surpassing the Love of Men: Romantic Friendship and Love Between Women from the Renaissance to the Present*. London: The Women's Press.

"February 1797, Trial of William Winklin (T17970215-46)." 2012. Old Bailey Proceedings Online. https://www.oldbaileyonline.org/browse.jsp?id=t17970215-46&div=t17970215-46&terms=winklin.

Fielding, Henry. 1746. *The Female Husband: Or, the Surprising History of Mrs. Mary, Alias Mr. George Hamilton*. London: M. Copper.
Fissell, Mary. 1995. Gender and Generation: Representing Reproduction in Early Modern England. *Gender and History* 7: 433–456.
Fletcher, Anthony. 1995. *Gender, Sex & Subordination in England 1500–1800*. New Haven, CT: Yale University Press.
Friedli, Lynne. 1985. Women Who Dressed as Men. *Trouble and Strife* 6: 25–28.
———. 1987. 'Passing Women'—A Study of Gender Boundaries in the Eighteenth Century. In *Sexual Underworlds of the Enlightenment*, ed. G.S. Rousseau and Roy Porter, 234–260. Manchester: Manchester University Press.
Gatrell, V.A.C. 1994. *The Hanging Tree: Execution and the English People 1770–1868*. Oxford: Oxford University Press.
Gowing, Laura. 1998. *Domestic Dangers: Women, Words and Sex in Early Modern London*. Oxford: Clarendon Press.
Harvey, Karen. 2002. The Substance of Sexual Difference: Change and Persistence in Representations of the Body in Eighteenth-Century England. *Gender & History* 14 (2): 202–223.
Hay, Douglas. 1975. Property, Authority and the Criminal Law. In *Albion's Fatal Tree: Crime and Society in Eighteenth-Century England*, ed. D. Hay, P. Linebaugh, J.G. Rule, E.P. Thompson, and C. Winslow, 17–63. Harmondsworth: Penguin.
Heidensohn, Frances. 1996. *Women and Crime*. 2nd ed. London: Macmillan.
Hill, Bridget. 2001. *Women Alone: Spinsters in England 1660–1850*. New Haven, CT: Yale University Press.
Histed, Elise Bennett. 2004. Mediaeval Rape: A Conceivable Defence? *Cambridge Law Journal* 63 (3): 743–769.
Hitchcock, Tim. 1997. *English Sexualities, 1700–1800*. Basingstoke: Macmillan.
———. 2012. The Reformulation of Sexual Knowledge in Eighteenth-Century England. *Signs* 37 (4): 823–832.
Hunt, Margaret. 1999. The Sapphic Strain: English Lesbians in the Long Eighteenth Century. In *Singlewomen in the European Past 1250–1800*, ed. Judith M. Bennett and Amy M. Froide, 270–296. Philadelphia: University of Pennsylvania Press.
James, Robert. 1742. *A Medicinal Dictionary*. London: T. Osborne.
Jones, Ann Rosalind, and Peter Stallybrass. 1991. Fetishizing Gender: Constructing the Hermaphrodite in Renaissance Europe. In *Body Guards:*

The Cultural Politics of Gender Ambiguity, ed. Julia Epstein and Kristina Straub, 80–111. London: Routledge.

King, Peter. 2000. *Crime, Justice, and Discretion in England 1740–1820*. Oxford: Oxford University Press.

———. 2007. Newspaper Reporting and Attitudes to Crime and Justice in Late-Eighteenth- and Early-Nineteenth-Century London. *Continuity and Change* 22 (1): 73–112.

Kittredge, Katharine. 2003. Introduction: Contexts for the Consideration of the Transgressive Antitype. In *Lewd and Notorious: Female Transgression in the 18th Century*, ed. Katharine Kittredge, 1–17. Ann Arbor: University of Michigan Press.

Knapp, Andrew. 1810. *The New Newgate Calendar, Volume 2*. London: J and J Cundee.

———. 1826. *The New Newgate Calendar, Volume 3*. London: J Robins and Company.

Knelman, Judith. 1998. *Twisting in the Wind: The Murderess and the English Press*. Toronto: University of Toronto Press.

Langbein, John H. 2003. *The Origins of the Adversary Criminal Trial*. Oxford: Oxford University Press.

Lanser, Susan S. 1999a. Befriending the Body: Female Intimacies as Class Acts. *Eighteenth-Century Studies* 32 (2): 179.

———. 1999b. Singular Politics: The Rise of the British Nation and the Production of the Old Maid. In *Singlewomen in the European Past 1250–1800*, ed. Judith M. Bennet and Amy M. Froide, 297–323. Philadelphia: University of Pennsylvania Press.

———. 2003. 'Queer to Queer': The Sapphic Body as Transgressive Text. In *Lewd and Notorious: Female Transgression in the 18th Century*, ed. Katharine Kittredge, 21–46. Ann Arbor: University of Michigan Press.

Laqueur, Thomas. 1990. *Making Sex: Body and Gender From the Greeks to Freud*. Cambridge, MA: Harvard University Press.

Linebaugh, Peter. 1982. *The London Hanged: Crime and Civil Society in the Eighteenth Century*. 2nd ed. London: Verso.

Locke, John. 1690. *The Second Treatise of Government*. London.

London Chronicle. 1760. A Female Husband Exposed, March 22.

London Evening Post. 1760. No Title, March 18.

———. 1777. No Title, July 31.

London Evening Standard. 1829. The Female Husband, January 22.

Love, Heather. 2007. *Feeling Backward: Loss and the Politics of Queer History*. Cambridge, MA: Harvard University Press.
McLynn, Frank. 1989. *Crime and Punishment in Eighteenth-Century England*. London: Routledge.
Mendelson, Sara, and Patricia Crawford. 1998. *Women in Early Modern England*. Oxford: Oxford University Press.
Morning Chronicle and London Advertiser. 1777. News, July 23.
Moscucci, Ornella. 1996. Clitoridectomy, Circumcision, and the Politics of Sexual Pleasure in Mid-Victorian Britain. In *Sexualities in Victorian Britain*, ed. Andrew H. Miller and James Eli Adams, 60–78. Bloomington: Indiana University Press.
Murray, Jacqueline. 1996. Twice Marginal and Twice Invisible: Lesbians in the Middle Ages. In *Handbook of Medieval Sexuality*, ed. Vern L. Bullough and James A. Brundage, 191–222. New York: Garland Publishing.
Nechtman, Tillman W. 2010. *Nabobs: Empire and Identity in Eighteenth-Century Britain*. Cambridge: Cambridge University Press.
Newcastle Courant. 1735. Dr. William Green, Oculist, January 11.
Nicolazzo, Sarah. 2014. Henry Fielding's The Female Husband and the Sexuality of Vagrancy. *The Eighteenth Century* 55 (4): 335–353. https://doi.org/10.1353/ecy.2014.0038.
Norton, Rictor. 2005. A Female Husband Exposed, 1760. Homosexuality in Eighteenth-Century England. http://rictornorton.co.uk/eighteen/1760fema.htm.
O'Connell, Sheila. 1999. *The Popular Print in England*. London: British Museum.
O'Driscoll, Sally. 2003. The Lesbian and the Passionless Woman: Femininity and Sexuality in Eighteenth-Century England. *The Eighteenth Century* 44 (2–3): 103–131.
———. 2010. A Crisis of Femininity: Re-Making Gender in Popular Discourse. In *Lesbian Dames*, ed. John C. Beynon and Caroline Gonda. New York: Ashgate.
Onania or the Heinous Sin of Self Pollution. 1710. London.
Onania; or, the Heinous Sin of Self-Pollution. 1723. London: Thomas Crouch.
Oxford English Dictionary, 2nd Edition. 2004. http://athens.oed.com.
Peakman, Julie. 2004. *Lascivious Bodies: A Sexual History of the Eighteenth Century*. London: Atlantic Books.
———. 2016. *Amatory Pleasures: Explorations in Eighteenth-Century Sexual Culture*. London: Bloomsbury.
Plain Reasons for the Growth of Sodomy in England. 1728. London: A Dodd and E Nutt.

Powys, Llewellyn, ed. 1932. *The Life & Times of Anthony à Wood*. London: Wishart & Company.

Probert, Rebecca. 2009. *Marriage Law and Practice in the Long Eighteenth Century: A Reassessment*. Cambridge: Cambridge University Press.

Public Advertiser. 1777. No Title, July 8.

Public Ledger or the Daily Register of Commerce and Intelligence. 1760. No Title, March 26.

Rogers, Pat. 2007. Fielding on Society, Crime, and the Law. *The Cambridge Companion to Henry Fielding* (May): 137–152. https://doi.org/10.1017/CCOL0521854512.011.

Salisbury, Joyce E. 1996. Gendered Sexuality. In *Handbook of Medieval Sexuality*, ed. Vern L. Bullough and James A. Brundage, 81–101. New York: Garland Publishing.

Satan's Harvest Home: Or the Present State of Whorecraft. 1749. London.

Shoemaker, Robert S. 2004. Streets of Shame? The Crowd and Public Punishments in London, 1700–1820. In *Penal Practice and Culture, 1500–1900: Punishing the English*, ed. Simon Devereaux and Paul Griffiths, 232–257. Basingstoke: Palgrave Macmillan.

Sibley, Ebenezer. 1796. *The Medical Mirror, or Treatise on the Impregnation of the Human Female*. 2nd ed. London.

Smith, Liberty. 2002. Listening to the 'Wives' of the 'Female Husbands': A Project of Femme Historiography in Eighteenth-Century Britain. *Journal of Lesbian Studies* 6 (2): 105–120.

St James's Chronicle or the British Evening Post. 1766. No Title, May 29.

The National Archives. 2018. Currency Converter: 1270–2017. *The National Archives*. http://www.nationalarchives.gov.uk/currency-converter/.

Tissot, Samuel. 1766. *A Treatise on The Crime of Onan*. 3rd ed. London: B Thomas.

Toulalan, Sarah. 2003. Extraordinary Satisfactions: Lesbian Visibility in Seventeenth-Century Pornography in England. *Gender & History* 15 (1): 50–68.

Traub, Valerie. 2016. *Thinking Sex with the Early Moderns*. Philadelphia: University of Pennsylvania Press.

Trumbach, Randolph. 1991. London's Sapphists: From Three Sexes to Four Genders in the Making of Modern Culture. In *Body Guards: The Cultural Politics of Gender Ambiguity*, ed. Julia Epstein and Kristina Straub, 112–141. London: Routledge.

Vicinus, Martha. 1996. They Wonder to Which Sex I Belong': The Historical Roots of the Modern Lesbian Identity. In *Lesbian Subjects: A Feminist Studies Reader*, ed. Martha Vicinus, 233–260. Bloomington: Indiana University Press.

Walker, Garthine. 1998. Rereading Rape and Sexual Violence in Early Modern England. *Gender & History* 10 (1): 1–25.
Ward, Richard M. 2014. *Print Culture, Crime and Justice in 18th Century London*. London: Bloomsbury.
Wheelwright, Julie. 1989a. *Amazons and Military Maids: Women Who Dressed as Men in the Pursuit of Life, Liberty, and Happiness*. London: Pandora.
———. 1989b. *Amazons and Military Maids*. London: Pandora.
Whitehall Evening Post or London Intelligencer. 1760a. No Title, March 25.
———. 1760b. No Title, April 1.

3

Louise Mourey and the 'Maiden Tribute of Modern Babylon'

Louise Mourey

In 1885, Louise Mourey was convicted of indecent assault on a female: the first known prosecution of a woman for that offence.[1] She had been caught up in one of the most high-profile criminal prosecutions of the century, but her part within it attracted relatively little attention. She had played a more fleeting role than her co-defendants, but received the heaviest sentence. And she was convicted of a sexual offence, for acts which had offered her no sexual gratification. Those paradoxes were a consequence not only of the unusual case itself but also of the policy of silencing lesbian possibility, which was then at its height.

That July, 'A Frank Warning' of 'an actual pilgrimage to a real hell' had whetted readers' appetites for a new series in the *Pall Mall Gazette*, 'The Maiden Tribute of Modern Babylon'. The articles cast London as the modern Babylon, and its teenage girls as the maiden tribute sacrificed to the sexual perversions of wealthy men. In the first instalment, campaigning

[1] Mourey's surname was also sometimes written as Mourez (e.g. "October 1885, Trial of Rebecca Jarrett et al." 2012a; Walkowitz 1992, pp. 106–08); the defendant herself used Mourey (e.g. *Post Office London Directory* 1880, p. 1108).

C. Derry, *Lesbianism and the Criminal Law*,
https://doi.org/10.1007/978-3-030-35300-1_3

journalist and *Gazette* editor W T Stead gave a lurid account of his 'purchase' of thirteen-year-old 'Lily' from her mother, apparently for the purpose of prostitution, for £5. The articles also described brothels, trafficking, bribery, and entrapment but it was this buying of a young girl, later identified as Eliza Armstrong, which really caught public attention. It also brought Stead and his confederates, including Mourey, before an Old Bailey judge and jury ("October 1885, Trial of Rebecca Jarrett et al." 2012a; Gorham 1978; Bland 1995; Walkowitz 1992). The trial would be a source of future pride to Stead, who saw himself as a martyr for a just cause; Mourey did not survive her sentence.

These events occurred in the context of wider campaigns against child prostitution and trafficking of girls to brothels on the Continent. Both were facilitated by a legal age of consent to sexual intercourse of just thirteen. Campaigners wanted it raised to at least sixteen, but their strenuous efforts had not yet met with success: several Bills had died in the House of Commons, and the latest looked liable to fail (Gorham 1978, p. 360). Public outrage at the 'Maiden Tribute' would provide the final impetus to get the Criminal Law Amendment Act passed the following month. Despite that success, the series was controversial and heavily criticised. One concern was the graphic and potentially corrupting material it placed before the public, including the young (Wendelin 2012, pp. 378–79). Another was Stead's methods. In court, Armstrong's mother strongly denied his version of events, claiming that she had agreed to her daughter becoming a servant and only received a small advance on wages. Further, Stead had not stopped at the 'purchase': having apparently proved his point that girls could be bought for prostitution, the court heard that he nonetheless chose to continue the charade by having Armstrong's virginity certified by Mourey and bringing her to a brothel where he visited but did not have sex with her. He then had her virginity confirmed again, this time by Harley Street practitioner Dr Heywood Smith, following which she was taken to France in the care of the Salvation Army until her parents and the police forced her return.

Criminal charges were brought against six people involved in the 'purchase'; four, including Mourey and Stead, were convicted. Unfortunately for Stead, although he had the mother's consent to the 'purchase', he did not have her husband's; the father of a legitimate child, not her mother, was the legal guardian.[2] Rebecca Jarrett, a former brothel procuress and recovering alcoholic, had been working with leading campaigner Josephine Butler when Stead requested her assistance in obtaining a girl. Sampson Jacques was an employee of Stead's *Pall Mall Gazette*. They were found guilty of offences including unlawfully taking Armstrong out of the possession of her father as well as indecent assault. Two Salvation Army members—worker Mrs Combe, who had helped Jarrett take Armstrong to Paris, and chief of staff Branwell Booth—were acquitted.

Mourey, a French midwife and 74-year-old widow, was the only defendant not involved in anti-prostitution campaigns. She had examined the girl to ensure she was a virgin, a service which she allegedly performed often for brothels ("October 1885, Trial of Rebecca Jarrett et al." 2012a; Plowden 1974, p. 20). Stead had portrayed her actions in lurid terms with fictitious, pornographic embellishments:

> [Lily] was taken in a cab to the house of a midwife, whose skill in pronouncing upon the physical evidence of virginity is generally recognized in the profession. The examination was very brief and completely satisfactory. But the youth, the complete innocence of the girl, extorted pity even from the hardened heart of the old abortionist. 'The poor little thing,' she exclaimed. 'She is so small, her pain will be extreme. I hope you will not be too cruel with her'—as if to lust when fully roused the very acme of agony on the part of the victim has not a fierce delight. To quiet the old lady the agent of the purchaser asked if she could supply anything to dull the pain. She produced a small phial of chloroform. 'This,' she said, 'is the best. My clients find this much the most effective.' […] £1 1s. was paid for the certificate of virginity—which was verbal and not written—while £1 10s. more was charged for the chloroform, the net value of which was probably less than a shilling. An arrangement was made that if the child was badly injured Madame would patch it up to the best of her ability, and then the party left the house (Stead 1885).

The conversation was Stead's invention: Armstrong expressly denied it had happened and confirmed that the midwife's English was poor

[2] Although Stead later claimed that Armstrong's parents were not legally married and so her father's consent should not have been required after all (Stead 2018), her legitimacy was not challenged at trial.

("October 1885, Trial of Rebecca Jarrett et al." 2012a). A physical examination, though, had taken place and resulted in the charge of indecent assault against Mourey. Defence counsel's submission that this offence could only be committed by a male perpetrator was given short shrift by the judge. The jury duly found Mourey guilty and she was sentenced to six months' imprisonment with hard labour. Her age and state of health meant that she was unable to do the work assigned to her, and within a fortnight she was admitted to the prison infirmary where she later died (*Devon and Exeter Daily Gazette* 1886).

The Development of Indecent Assault

During the nineteenth century, a specific body of sexual offences legislation emerged, partly as a result of the changing rationale for this area of law. It was moving (albeit imperfectly) from the protection of male property rights towards the safeguarding of female sexual innocence and, to a much lesser extent, female sexual autonomy. Historically, the main sexual offences had been buggery and rape, whose actus reus required penile penetration of the anus or vagina respectively. Rape was in practice the offence of primary relevance to women. It had been conceived of as an offence against a woman's father or husband since her value to him resided in her virginity or chastity, vital to ensuring the proper transmission of property to legitimate heirs (Peakman 2016, p. 34). That concern was also apparent in related offences concerned with the abduction of heiresses. However, sexual assaults which did not involve marriage or sexual intercourse, or upon women who had already engaged in extra-marital sexual activity, did not pose the same threats and were treated as a species of assault and battery:

> So, if a master take indecent liberties with a female scholar, though she does not resist, it is an assault; Rex v. Nichol, R. & R. 130. If a medical man unnecessarily strip a female patient naked, pretending that he cannot otherwise judge of her illness, it is an assault if he himself take off her clothes; Rex v. Rosinski, R. & M. 19. (Matthews 1833)

The Offences Against the Person Act 1861 consolidated and reformed this field of criminal law.[3] Indecent assault was enacted as a discrete sexual offence rather than aggravated common assault. This was done through two separate offences distinguished by the victim's sex: indecent assault on a female (section 52) and indecent assault on a male (section 62). They differed significantly in their penalties: the maximum sentence for indecent assault on a female was two years' imprisonment, compared to the much higher ten-year maximum for indecent assault on a male. Since a male accused was assumed, the disparity in penalty reflected the difference between supposedly natural (albeit non-consensual) sexual activity between a male and a female, and 'unnatural' sexual conduct between two males.

The offences were apparently gender-neutral as to perpetrator: 'whosoever shall be convicted of any indecent Assault upon any Female' and 'Whosoever [...] shall be guilty [...] of any indecent Assault upon any Male Person'. However, women were not necessarily included in such gender-neutral terms, as a line of cases denying women's right to vote (*Chorlton v Lings* (1868) L.R. 4 C.P), be admitted to universities (*Jex-Blake v Senatus of Edinburgh University* (1873) 11 M. 784), or practise a profession (*Bebb v Law Society* [1914] 1 Ch 286) would confirm,. An additional complication was that the offence against male victims appeared under the sub-heading 'Unnatural Offences', in a part of the Act which also addressed behaviour specific to male offenders such as attempted buggery. The issue of female culpability was addressed in *Mourey* (1885) 49 *Justice of the Peace* 745:

> There is one point which was decided by Lopes, J., in the recent Armstrong abduction case which deserves to be remembered. The counsel for one of the defendants contended that there could not be an indecent assault by one woman upon another. The contention was a bold one but was evi-

[3] Offences involving sexual intercourse with a woman or girl over twelve continued to focus upon the protection of heiresses from undesirable marriages: it was a crime if it was procured by false pretences (section 49) or involved abduction of a girl under sixteen, or abduction 'from motives of lucre' where the victim was an heiress or had interests in property (section 53), or abduction by force with intent to marry her (section 54).

> dently untenable.—Lopes, J., explained that the striking or touching of another without his or her consent was an assault, and if accompanied by indecent circumstances was an indecent assault.

Indecency

Although 'indecency' was the primary difference between indecent assault and other forms of assault, its meaning was not defined by statute. The courts were therefore left to formulate vague tests such as 'what all right-minded men, men of sound and wholesome feelings would say was indecent' (William Brett J, quoted in L. A. Jackson 2000, p. 25). Such vagueness ensured that the interpretation of what constituted indecent assault was carried out on masculine terms: those right-minded men were the twelve who composed the jury, from which women were excluded by law until 1919 and often in practice thereafter (Crosby 2017). There would be little change to the formula in the following century or so. The leading modern case of *Court* [1989] AC 28 HL repeated the definition of indecency as 'an assault which right-minded persons would think was indecent' (*per* Lord Ackner, p. 42); Lord Griffiths offered an alternative definition of indecency as 'conduct that right-thinking people will consider an affront to the sexual modesty of a woman' (p. 34). Such appeals to an assumed shared—and gendered—moralism encouraged considerations such as the complainant's conduct or the perceived immorality of same-sex relations. This disadvantaged women generally and lesbians in particular, but would remain central to the law throughout the twentieth century.

The vagueness of 'indecency' also meant that there was no need to define exactly what an indecent assault by one female upon another might involve. In other words, the nature and scope of lesbian sex could remain undefined. Mourey's conduct involved digital penetration rather than, as in the female husband cases, implied use of a dildo. However, no acknowledgement or discussion of this needed to be openly given. That theme of undefinability, shading into unimaginability, is an element of silencing which has persisted ever since.

Age of Consent

As the law moved from protecting male property towards protecting female innocence, so the age of consent for indecent assault gained significance. While the 1861 Act included an offence of unlawful sexual intercourse with a girl under the age of 12 (raised to 13 by the Criminal Law Amendment Act 1880), there was no equivalent for indecent assault. The factual consent of the complainant was thus a complete defence regardless of her age. The inadequacy of this provision became apparent when a defendant was acquitted of indecently assaulting a child of six on the basis that the child consented (see *K* [2001] UKHL 41, para. 6). An age of consent was subsequently created by the Criminal Law Amendment Act 1880, section 2, which read:

> It shall be no defence to a charge or indictment for an indecent assault on a young person under the age of thirteen to prove that he or she consented to the act of indecency.

The age would eventually be raised to 16 by section 1 of the Criminal Law Amendment Act 1922, in circumstances considered in Chap. 4.

The 1861 and 1880 Acts had therefore possibly created an age of consent for sex between women. While *Mourey* confirmed that it did apply to indecent assaults by females upon females, the question has tended to be viewed as remaining controversial until the mid-twentieth century. Annabel Faraday wrote the first contemporary analysis of the Mourey case, although as a non-lawyer, she did overestimate its potential significance in suggesting it was an attempt to criminalise lesbian acts (Faraday 1988, p. 12). In fact its consequences were less drastic: only non-consensual sexual activity between women was illegal, whether the lack of consent was factual or was due to the complainant's young age. Both Faraday and legal writers have emphasised the seeming isolation of the decision: Matthew Waites, who published the first sustained analysis of the lesbian age of consent, followed Susan Edwards in dismissing it as 'apparently isolated' (Waites 2002, p. 327; Edwards 1981, p. 43). As the *Justice of the Peace* commentary made clear, the judgment was legally unexceptional: it was isolated not as a matter of law but through the policy of silencing.

Social and Legal Context

Female Husbands in the Nineteenth Century

It is characteristic of this period that the most legally significant case on sex between women did not, in fact, involve sex between women. Before considering why that was so, it is worth exploring how that point had been reached by taking up the story where we left it in Chap. 2. Eighteenth-century female husbands had been punished severely by the courts but societal reactions were more ambiguous: responses ranged from condemnation, through ridicule, to curiosity. Towards the end of the century, however, there seems to have been a more consistently hostile reaction: in 1777, not only was Ann/Charles Marlow pilloried but the earlier 'satisfactory' whipping of Mary/Charles Hamilton was reinterpreted as inadequate. Attitudes would continue to evolve during the nineteenth century.

In the century's first decades, the Scottish case of *Marianne Woods and Jane Pirie v Dame Helen Cumming Gordon* made its slow way to the House of Lords, then the highest appellate court for Scotland as well as England and Wales (*Miss Marianne Woods and Miss Jane Pirie against Dame Helen Cumming Gordon* 1975; L. L. Moore 1997). This libel claim had been brought in 1811 by two women teachers whose school closed when Cumming Gordon withdrew her granddaughter and advised her acquaintances to do likewise for unspecified reasons. In court, the teachers discovered that a pupil had accused them of having sex together; the hearings explored the question of whether such behaviour could have occurred. A scant majority of judges had initially found that it could. On review, an equally bare majority concluded that it could not, but they were not making a general statement on the possibility of sex between women. Rather, through careful examination of the facts and authorities combined with a reliance on imperialist 'common sense' imbued with race and class prejudices, they found that these specific (white, British, middle-class) women could not have had sex in the specific factual circumstances alleged. Rather, the forbidden sexual knowledge was attributed to the two accusers, a half-Indian pupil and a domestic servant. The House of Lords, through a combination of distaste and discretion, upheld the claim without substantive discussion. The whole process was undertaken in secrecy, with closed hearings, elaborate restrictions upon access to the case papers, and assertions of the unspeakable nature of the alleged sexual conduct. In the Court of Session, Lord Meadowbank had even spelled out that this was a social necessity: 'the virtues, the comforts, and the freedom of domestic intercourse, mainly depend on the purity of female manners, and that, again, on their habits of intercourse remaining, as they have hitherto been,—free from suspicion' (Meadowbank 1975, p. 2). In other words, silencing and its rationale were spelled out within the confines of the courtroom. They were also elaborately performed there: as the pursuers pointed out, 'the senior counsel of the defender confessed his total inability to give any name' to the misconduct alleged despite having produced copious evidence and authorities to support the defence ("The Additional Petition of Miss Mary-Ann Woods and Miss Jane Pirie" 1975, p. 27).

Bill Chapman lived and worked in a very different milieu, residing in the notorious London slum of St Giles's and travelling the country as a ballad-seller with his common-law wife Isabella Watson. Only when the police became involved in a dispute between Watson and her sister in January 1835 was Chapman found to be physically female. Watson was brought before Hatton Garden magistrates' court for assault but discharged; Chapman, who gave the name Mary to the court, was accused of being a common cheat (*Morning Chronicle* 1835). While a police inspector gave evidence that he had known Chapman for ten years and until this incident had not doubted he was a man, the discovery that Chapman was physically female utterly transformed perceptions. The criminal justice system and the press treated the defendant as clearly a woman, albeit a deeply troubling one who raised the spectre of a sexual relationship between two women. The magistrate stated he 'never saw a figure more like a man', and expressed both his disapproval and his impotence: 'She may be a disorderly and disreputable character, which, in fact, her dressing as a man clearly shows; but I know of no law to punish her.' Nor did Chapman or Watson promise any change for the future: on leaving court, Watson was reported to tell her partner, 'Never mind, my lad, if we live a hundred years we will be in this manner.'

An account which appeared in numerous papers including the *Morning Chronicle* reported the prosecution with a mixture of hostility and confusion more pronounced than those of the previous century, terming Chapman 'the thing' or 'creature'. It both disavowed and obliquely invoked the lesbian undercurrents of the case, balancing Chapman's claim that the relationship was one of unmarried companionship against the magistrate's disquiet: 'She may have more than one reason for dressing in that manner, and passing as the husband of the woman Isabella Watson, and I wish it was in my power to imprison her' (*Morning Chronicle* 1835). That was reinforced by a comparison to male cross-dressing which would have recalled the recent case of Lavinia Edwards, discovered on death to be physically male and suspected of fathering his 'sister's' child (*Morning Post* 1833). The report also offered a heteronormative gloss, supposedly quoting Chapman: 'I own I am disguised, and it was owing to the cruelty of a father-in-law that I was first dressed in this manner.' *Bell's Weekly Messenger* published a longer and slightly different version of the story which was not taken up elsewhere (*Bell's Weekly Messenger* 1835). Its key variations were that Chapman claimed to have adopted a male persona to avoid marriage; Watson's sister had recently discovered Chapman's sex and threatened to expose it, which precipitated the fight; and those who watched Chapman leave the court were described as showing 'the most excessive disgust'. The discrepancies are suggestive: while the *Bell's* report had more in common with those of the previous century, the more popular *Morning Chronicle* version recast its account of marriage avoidance and hostile community reactions into one of essentially domestic disharmonies. In other words, the differences all tended in one direction, simultaneously privatising and discrediting the relationship.

Chapman's itinerant lifestyle, conduct, and the apparent charge of being a common cheat were similar to those of Mary/Charles Hamilton, whose 1746 case was considered in Chap. 2; but the prosecution and its outcome were different. The later case was brought by a professional police officer and heard by a (salaried and legally qualified) stipendiary magistrate who explicitly declared his powers to be constrained by the letter of the law. The possibility of sexual activity was simultaneously carefully unspoken, anxiously repudiated, and the subject of hostility. Similar judicial impotence was reported in 1838 after a Manchester woman Harriet Stoakes consulted a solicitor because her husband Henry, a master bricklayer with a successful business, ill-treated her and withheld housekeeping money. She mentioned having discovered several years earlier that her husband of over twenty years was a woman, so the solicitor brought the case to the attention of a magistrate who directed the police to conduct private examinations of the spouses. Admissions were made and the police surgeon certified that the husband was female; the police then mediated a financial arrangement between the spouses but 'no legal proceedings have been, *or indeed could be*, taken' in the criminal courts (*Royal Cornwall Gazette* 1838; *Kendal Mercury* 1838, emphasis added).

The financial theme was even more heavily stressed in reports of the posthumous discovery of female husband John Smith, a knife-grinder in Macclesfield who had cohabited with a woman for fourteen years. Smith's partner claimed that her motivation for being in the relationship was to receive maintenance for herself and her eleven children from a former marriage, and identified Smith as Sophia Locke. The report assigned similar practical and financial motives to earlier relationships: Smith's first marriage had been to a pregnant woman in return for £5 from the baby's father, and 'she could have had no object in living with women as she had done, unless it was to keep down suspicion. The promises she made of keeping them were, perhaps, an inducement for them to live with her' (*Leeds Times* 1848). Yet the tentative tone of this conclusion serves to undermine it, leaving the spectral possibility of another, unspeakable motive for cohabitation.

Following the 1830s' acquittals, there seem to have been no reported female husband prosecutions for the remainder of the century. That is consistent not only with the increasing effectiveness of the silencing of lesbianism but also with a wider silencing around illicit sexual knowledge. It became legally marked out as something which was to be reserved to higher-class men: the Obscene Publications Act 1857 was debated in Parliament as a way to keep sexual material from being widely and cheaply available. Its availability to educated men including MPs themselves was supposedly unproblematic since they were accustomed to similar content in classical literature (Shanley 1989, p. 41). Opponents of the Act focused on the risks it posed to the libraries of respectable gentlemen and booksellers, and the dangers of publicising obscene material through its prosecution (Roebuck, HC 12/08/1857, cols. 1476–1477; Monckton Miles, HC 12/08/1857, col. 1479).

When female husbands came to the criminal courts' attention, they did so for other offences. In March 1862 John Jones appeared before Manchester magistrates for creating a disturbance by threatening to beat his wife Sarah. In court, he was identified as Ann McGaul alias Ann Hughes, but discharged after promising not to repeat the behaviour (*Western Daily Press* 1862). Later that year, the couple moved to Bolton where Hughes was prosecuted for obtaining money by false pretences after collecting payments due to an ex-employer. Hughes's sex had been discovered around the time of the offence but far from being the subject of legal interest, the 'marriage' was ruled by the magistrate to be irrelevant (*Bolton Chronicle* 1862).

Sarah Geals had lived as William Smith for over a decade, working for bootmaker James Giles and living as husband and wife with Caroline Smith in Hackney, London. Caroline disclosed her husband's sex to Giles while nursing his wife in her final illness, and soon after he married Caroline while financially supporting Geals, who returned to female dress at his insistence. The reasons for these changing relationships are unclear from the court evidence, and Giles was apparently abusive to Caroline, but that did not stop *Bell's Weekly Messenger* from insisting that Caroline 'naturally enough, of her two husbands, preferred the man to the woman'. In June 1865 Geals shot Giles, but the pistol was not properly loaded and he was unharmed. Geals was tried at the Central Criminal Court for attempted murder, convicted of the lesser offence of attempted grievous bodily harm, and sentenced to five years' penal servitude ("September 1865, Trial of Sarah Geals" 2012). Once again, the press emphasised an imagined financial motivation: the *Illustrated Times* reported that Geals assumed male dress 'probably with the object of obtaining more remunerative employment' (*Illustrated Times* 1865). A little over a year after leaving prison on ticket of leave (parole), Geals died in Rotherhithe Workhouse and was buried in Hackney on 1 April 1870 (Non-Conformist Burials: Victoria Park Cemetery Vol. 7, TNA RG/8/48).

Barman Thomas Walker was identified as Mary Walker when arrested for embezzlement in 1867. Arthur Munby, present at Walker's first court appearance, wrote in his diary that she had 'confessed her sex to avoid the prison bath' (L. Jackson 2001). Walker pleaded guilty at the Central Criminal Court, which was told of her remorse and the victim's lack of 'desire to press the case harshly'—and, most importantly, heard a version of her life story in which she was forced into male dress to obtain employment after her father's death. Sentence was adjourned (*Ashton Weekly Reporter* 1867; "February 1867, Trial of Mary Walker" 2012). When a further embezzlement from the previous year came to light, the magistrate was informed at the committal hearing that a young woman had visited Walker in prison and 'told the governor that she was about to be married to her'. A solicitor in court confirmed that Walker had committed no further criminal offence in relation to her (*Essex Herald* 1867), but this second case and the stain of sexual impropriety were clearly enough to harden the court's attitude (*Bury Times* 1867). According to the *Penny Illustrated Paper* (1867), Walker was imprisoned and then sent to a reformatory but expelled for bad behaviour. Walker then worked as a railway porter under the name Charles Arnold before fleeing with a railway pass when discovered by her landlady. Walker's past was now rewritten as a disreputable one of absconding from school in male dress and refusing help from respectable relations.

Eight years later William Seymour/Margaret Honeywell, a cab-driver with a wife, was convicted of stealing meat. The magistrate asked questions about cross-dressing—but not the marriage—in court, but he was at pains to say he would not treat Seymour differently from any other prisoner (Oram and Turnbull 2001, pp. 31–33).

In summary, female husbands had not completely disappeared from the criminal courts, but the sexual possibilities they suggested had become too dangerous to air. Instead, the law on sex between women could more readily develop through *Mourey*, a case centred on the gratification of men's sexual desires. This change was the result of wider legal and cultural developments in the nineteenth century when the professionalisation of criminal justice complemented changing medical, social, and political norms. Those norms were themselves subject to increasing feminist challenge as the century progressed.[4]

Attitudes to Gender and Sexuality

The eighteenth century had been a period of transition between models of sexual difference, with new norms of domestic femininity emerging among the middling sort (Armstrong 1987, p. 66; O'Driscoll 2010, p. 49). In the nineteenth century, ideologies of separate spheres and female desirelessness solidified. That is not to say that everyone now accepted a two-sex model, believed that women lacked sexual desire, or saw society as divisible into rigidly separated public and private spheres. Those did, though, become dominant understandings which underpinned many judicial pronouncements and legislative reforms—partly as a way of resisting growing political and social challenges to patriarchal structures. Chapman's trial was separated from its predecessors by the revolutionary disquiet of the later eighteenth century when liberalism threatened to upset not only the established political order but also the gender order. It provided a language of individual rights from which to claim equality not only for men but also between women and men. Inspired by liberal politics and the French Revolution, Mary Wollstonecraft had published *A Vindication of the Rights of Woman* (1792), asserting that women were entitled to the same moral agency and education as men. Her arguments would be taken up by campaigners for women's legal rights, who gathered strength as the century progressed and had notable male supporters, including MP and philosopher John Stuart Mill.

As liberalism gained ground, new ideologies were required to counter the threat of class and gender upheaval. The oppression of women was given fresh justifications: sex differences and the patriarchal family structure were not simply god-given, but medically and scientifically ordained. The two-sex model under which women were fundamentally biologically

[4] While the term 'feminism' was not yet in common use, it is used here as a helpful way of identifying the concerns of the women's movement.

different to men became generally accepted.[5] Catherine Hall argues that the Evangelicals played a significant mediating role in changes to the image and function of the middle-class home and family (1992, p. 79; see also Bland 1995, pp. 49–50). These members of the Church of England, who sought to reform not only the Church but also national morality, placed particular emphasis on women's domestic roles as wives and mothers (Hall 1992, p. 75; Bland 1995, p. 50). Foremost among them was Hannah More who, horrified by Wollstonecraft's *Vindication of the Rights of Woman*, argued for very different roles for men and women within their separate spheres; however, while women ought to be dependent and domestic, their superior moral qualities gave them a vital purpose as improvers of male morality and, in Hall's phrase, 'moral regenerators of the nation' (Hall 1992, pp. 82–86). It may be no coincidence that Yorkshire landowner Anne Lister, the antithesis of this model as she pursued both roles in the public sphere and relationships with other women, was a Tory gentrywoman with little time for liberalism or Evangelism (Liddington 1998; Clark 1996).

By mid-century, the ideological transition from the household as economic unit to a middle-class family model of male economic activity and female domestic activity had largely been achieved. Marriage was a moral duty: since men and women were by nature so different, each was required to supply the defects of the other (Fletcher 1995, pp. 396–97). One should be careful of overstating this as a practical rather than ideological transformation. In 1851, nearly half of women in Britain were not currently married, while one in four wives were in employment; in 1862, Frances Power Cobbe claimed that 25 per cent of women would never marry—and that 25 per cent of men were bachelors, although they were not seen as 'redundant' or problematic; and by 1891, almost a third of women were in the workforce (Richardson 2003, pp. 35–37; C. Hall 1992, p. 176; M. Jackson 1994, p. 15). As David Rayside has pointed out (1992, pp. 128–29), norms of family, gender, and sexuality were not

[5] See discussion in Chap. 4. Michael Mason (1994, pp. 180–81) highlights the risks of assuming that there had been a universal change from the older one-sex model of female sexuality, particularly among GPs who might not want to offer uncomfortable new ideas to patients.

always adhered to; the point was that those who transgressed them could legitimately be criticised.

With increased emphasis upon the division between the public sphere of masculine political and economic activity and the feminised, private domestic sphere, sexual attitudes also changed. Scientific theories such as Darwinian evolution were used to further arguments for men and women's essential differences (Richardson 2003, p. 40). Women's whole bodies, skeletons, and nervous systems, as well as their reproductive organs, were now perceived as sexed: 'she exists only through her ovaries' (Jozé (1895) in Laqueur 1990, p. 149). Female virtue became synonymous with sexual virtue, while the feminine ideal located women's role wholly within the family and home (Shanley 1989; C. Hall 1992; Bland 1995; Zedner 1991, pp. 12–15).[6] These understandings of gender developed in tandem with scientific racism: as Lisa Moore has described, British middle-class superiority was asserted in the face of its national and colonial violence by defining British feminine virtue against the threats posed by those who were racially and sexually other (Moore 1997, p. 12). Rather than the passive but voraciously 'open' creature feared in previous centuries, who must struggle to preserve chastity despite 'fierce and unruly desire' (Steele 1714, p. 155; quoted in Fletcher 1995, p. 392), the ideal Victorian Englishwoman was more-or-less desireless.

The combination of female innocence with sexual passivity left little cultural space for lesbianism. The doctor William Acton had described the ideal 'English wife and mother' as 'utterly ignorant of and averse to any sensual indulgence'. His claim that 'the majority of women (happily for society) are not very much troubled with sexual feeling of any kind' (1865, p. 112) was a sentiment shared to varying extents by many but by no means all Victorian doctors and much of wider Victorian society (Bland 1995, p. 55).[7] The clitoris was now dismissed as irrelevant, leaving women with no site of active desire as they submitted to an act of

[6] Lynda Nead (2000) has discussed not only the ways in which women were discouraged from negotiating London's streets alone, but also the pleasures they nonetheless achieved in doing so. Note that of the 4.5 million women working in 1891, almost half were in domestic service and thus still firmly in the domestic sphere (Richardson 2003, p. 37).

[7] Acton's professional stature is disputed: Lesley Hall (2004) says his reputation was high while Janet Oppenheim (1991, p. 201) argues that he was not highly regarded.

penetration which they should not actively solicit.[8] It would hardly make sense for two sexually unknowing or undesiring beings to come together to engage in sexual activity unless there was some external impetus for doing so. That reinforced the logic of silencing: left to themselves, respectable women would not disturb each other's purity.[9] Thus the whole logic of this model depended upon lesbianism being silenced, leaving the penis uncontested as the essence of active sexuality.

Vicinus (1997, p. 72) argues that this period saw 'an eloquent silence': lesbianism existed, but acknowledgement of it was withheld. As in the eighteenth century, friendships between respectable women thus offered a space in which homoerotic relationships could hide, but whose acceptable limits were policed as vital markers of middle-class respectability. To exceed them by engaging in sexual activity was highly deviant. Vicinus focuses upon the 1864 Codrington divorce case, where the friendship between the respondent Helen Codrington and her 'mannish' younger friend Emily Faithfull was central although its strong hints of lesbianism were never made explicit. In particular, a sealed packet apparently contained the reason Admiral Codrington had expelled Faithfull from the marital home; Robert Browning wrote to a friend that 'one of the counsel in the case told an acquaintance of mine that the 'sealed letter' contained a charge I shall be excused from even hinting to you' (quoted in Vicinus 1997, p. 92). His knowing silence is a reminder that the myth of female sexual passivity, although dominant in legal discourse, was used strategically: in other words, it served particular ideological aims and purposes but was not universally believed, even by those putting it forward. However, by denying women knowledge about their own bodies, it made professional men the acknowledged experts on female sexuality, empowered to share or withhold knowledge as they saw fit.

Even those who accepted the existence of autonomous female desire tended to emphasise the importance of its control by women's natural modesty: it was 'an *unconscious* quality' all too easily lost through exposure

---

[8] The most famous legal example of this attitude came at the end of this period: the Punishment of Incest Act 1908, with its language of men *having* sexual intercourse and women *permitting* sexual intercourse.

[9] This did leave space for a rich range of familial and friendship bonds between women, as explored in Marcus (2007).

to bad habits, companions, or ideas (Bland 1995, p. 56, emphasis in original). Women's enforced and artificial ignorance regarding sexuality meant that while men were expected to gain experience and 'sow wild oats', women were kept in deliberate ignorance even of issues as fundamental as menstruation and pregnancy. Sexual knowledge was interpreted as a sign of female sexual impropriety—Josephine Butler, for example, had been vilified for speaking out publicly about prostitution (L. A. Hall 2001; Hunt 1999, p. 154). Conveniently, pointed out Dr Louisa Martindale, the denial of knowledge also made innocent and submissive young women easier to seduce (M. Jackson 1994, p. 45). That was evident in Mourey's trial when Armstrong confirmed in cross-examination that she had felt able to refuse having her hair restyled but had remained passive and silent during Mourey's examination and did not speak about it afterwards ("October 1885, Trial of Rebecca Jarrett et al." 2012a). In an interview with Bramwell Booth, confirmation of Armstrong's chastity rather than her general wellbeing or whereabouts brought her mother to tears ("October 1885, Trial of Rebecca Jarrett et al." 2012b).

The ideal and ideology of female sexual innocence had reached extreme heights. Stead, in the *Maiden Tribute*, placed great emphasis upon the utter naivety of young girls procured into prostitution: one was described as having thought a midwife's virginity examination was her seduction. Stead's gloss, expected to be credible to his 'respectable' readership, was that 'if the man had run a needle into the girl's thigh and told her that she was seduced, she would have believed it' (Stead 1885). By focusing upon sexual purity, powerful men could ignore other aspects of women's lives. The fallen woman was outcast because of her lack of chastity, rather than seen within a context of economic and gender oppression. The respectable woman's position as a jewel to her home, the angel of the hearth, could explain her exclusion from professional life without reference to the interests of powerful men. As Lord Neaves explained in his *Jex-Blake* judgment denying women access to medical education, 'Much time must or ought to be given by women to the acquisition of a knowledge of household affairs and family duties, as well as to those ornamental parts of education which tend so much to social refinement and domestic happiness' (p. 582). Stead's resort to pornographic tropes may have been a distinctive feature of the *Maiden Tribute* (Wendelin 2012), but his concealment of the unsexy poverty central to the lives of his 'maidens' and his emphasis upon sexual innocence as a precondition for sympathy were not.

Separate spheres ideology thus worked to naturalise oppressive structures including the double standard of male sexual licence and female chastity. However, it also provided a site of resistance. The Evangelical conception of women's moral role, far from disappearing as the century progressed, informed some feminist challenges to the sexual double standard. Campaigners such as Josephine Butler, leader of the movement against the Contagious Diseases Acts (discussed below) and for the 1885 Act, proved adept at strategically using the mythology of female sexual innocence and passivity to claim moral standing for their campaigns.[10] While it faced increasingly direct challenge later in the century as 'New Women' and the suffrage movement demanded formal equality in the public sphere, appeals to women's special moral role would endure for some time to come.

Sexuality and Insanity

The social regulation which assigned women to a very specific role in the home and the marital bed was supplemented by medical regulation of women who deviated significantly from those norms. Unlike the criminal justice system, which primarily targeted working-class women, the medical profession focused much attention on the middle classes.[11] Indeed, the proliferating private asylums and clinics depended for their financial success upon a more affluent clientele. The feminisation of mental illness, which had begun in the late eighteenth century and continued through the nineteenth, directly equated women's sanity with their performance of normative femininity.[12] Treatment was successful if it returned a

[10] For an overview of Butler's life and activism, see Walkowitz (2004).

[11] And the upper classes, as seen in the treatment of Lady Harriet Mordaunt who was declared insane in 1870 following her confessions of infidelity including with the Prince of Wales (Souhami 1996, chap. 4).

[12] The literature is extensive and largely outside the scope of this book. Its starting points include Foucault's identification of this shift as an internalisation, rather than removal, of restraint, and Showalter's gendering of the new regimes (Foucault 1961; Showalter 1987).

woman to her proper place in the orderly, patriarchal household, a connection made explicit by Florence Nightingale (1860, p. 220):

> It is not only against those esteemed physically insane that commissions of lunacy are taken out. Others have been kept unjustly in confinement by their well-intentioned relations, as unfit to be trusted with liberty. In fact, in almost every family, one sees a keeper, or two or three keepers, and a lunatic.

The psychiatrisation of women, particularly those who were sexually or criminally deviant, rested upon an assumption that the supposed instability of women's reproductive systems made them more vulnerable to insanity (Scull and Favreau 1986, p. 243; Strange 2000). In the words of George Man Burrows, menstruation was 'the moral and physical barometer of the female constitution' with 'the functions of the brain … so intimately connected with the uterine system' that any menstrual disturbance could lead to mental disturbance (Burrows 1828, p. 146; quoted in Scull and Favreau 1986, pp. 243–44). With any move out of traditional female roles seen as a cause or manifestation of insanity, women who sought independence from men were vulnerable to psychiatric intervention. At the same time, the belief in physical causes of insanity led to an interest in physical, and specifically gynaecological, cures.[13] These ranged from Dr Edward Tilt advocating the retardation of menstruation, to W Tyler Smith recommending injections of ice water into the rectum, ice in the vagina, or leeching of the labia and cervix to treat nervous symptoms of menopause (Showalter 1981, pp. 323–24), to the extreme of clitoridectomy.

The interaction of the patriarchal family, respectability, and the coercion of women into sexual and social conformity were at their most evident in the mid-century clitoridectomy scandal. While removal of the clitoris as a cure for mental illness may appear both horrific and ineffectual today, its most influential exponent Dr Isaac Baker Brown was no maverick but enjoyed the respect of his peers. He had been among the

[13] Scull and Favreau highlight in particular 'the newly emerging specialism of neurology … [and] another new group of specialists, gynecologists' (1986, p. 246).

founders of St Mary's Hospital (Scull and Favreau 1986, p. 248), and enjoyed sufficient respect to be elected President of the Medical Society in London in 1865 when he was already performing clitoridectomies (Roy 2004). Nor was he the first doctor to recommend clitoridectomy: for example, Samuel Ashwell had done so in 1848 although in a rather narrower range of cases (Moscucci 1996), and one Dr Fraser wrote to Middlesex County Asylum in 1859 explaining that a patient had undergone a clitoridectomy-type operation due to 'vicious habits of self-indulgence' contracted under 'the evil influence of the worthless maid servant' (quoted in Suzuki 1999, p. 115). Brown's book *On the Curability of Certain Forms of Insanity, Epilepsy, Catalepsy, and Hysteria in Females* was dedicated with permission to the distinguished Dr Brown-Séquard,[14] and drew extensively on the work of Dr Handfield Jones, by whom he was 'pleased to be supported' (Brown 1866, p. 4).[15] He was able to cite by name sixteen doctors 'who have been led to adopt my views and treatment' (p. 13).

The book, apparently designed for the interested potential client as much as medical peers, avoided using words such as 'clitoris' or 'masturbation' as it explained that the disorders susceptible to surgical treatment were those caused by a 'loss of nerve power' due to 'excitement of the pudic nerve' (pp. vi and 7). They were characterised by a series of physical symptoms as well as moral characteristics including being 'indifferent to the social influences of domestic life', 'distaste for marital intercourse', and 'desiring to escape from home' (pp. 15–16). Indeed, there was a moral as well as surgical element to the treatment: 'improvement can only be made permanent, in many cases, by careful watching and moral training' (pp. 17–18). A case presented as paradigmatic involved a reference to past lesbianism: she engaged in masturbation 'having first been taught by a school-fellow' (p. 52). Women's health was equated with lack

[14] Brown-Séquard did important work on sensory pathways in the spinal cord (the area of his research connected to Baker Brown's work) as well as work which led to his being considered the father of endocrinology. He enjoyed many distinctions including election to the FRS and FRCP, and an honorary LLD awarded by Cambridge University. Unfortunately for his reputation, outside medical circles his best-known experiment was when, aged 72, he injected himself with extracts from animal testes and claimed to feel rejuvenated in consequence (Gosden 2004).

[15] Jones was a histologist but also published clinical observations on paralysis, anaesthesia, and neuralgia. In 1888 he became a vice-president of the Royal College of Surgeons (N. Moore 2004).

of autonomous sexual desire; the alternative was unruliness, both sexual and social. Clitoridectomy was therefore an effective and acceptable way of limiting sexuality to accepting penile penetration, meaning 'the objection that, in the event of marriage, [Brown's] operation might interfere with marital happiness' was 'physiologically … untenable' (Brown 1866, p. 70). Cure was defined by appropriate feminine behaviour. While for some patients this was exemplified by passionless submission to marital sexual intercourse, many appear to have been single women old enough that marriage was unlikely. Nonetheless, their newly feminine demeanour was characterised by epithets such as 'modest', 'cheerful', and 'tractable'. Sexuality was thus both a symptom and a cause of a pathologised independence from patriarchal authority.

When Brown became the subject of controversy over his procedures it was not purely because of his dubious physiology[16] or more dubious ethics.[17] Much of his colleagues' outrage was directed to the challenges his conduct posed to patriarchal interests. First, the diagnostic process alone risked compromising patients: daughters might return from consultations 'tainted with filthy inquiries, or branded by filthy suspicions' thanks to the doctor 'bringing a knowledge of evil to minds from which it had been absent' (*Medical Times and Gazette* 1867). Second, the rights of fathers and husbands to control their female relatives' bodies had been breached. A respectable woman's capacity to consent was, given her sexual ignorance, 'like the consent of an infant or lunatic—null and void'. The decision should therefore fall to the male relatives 'on whom she is dependent', particularly as 'the woman's character affects theirs' (*Medical Times and Gazette* 1867). Thus surgeon Mr Haden suggested that the procedure was a type of blackmail, where the husband or father could not complain because that would involve revealing his wife's or daughter's 'disgraceful practices'. The 'victim', to him, was not so much the woman who had 'undergone a dreadful mutilation' as the man who then had to 'write a cheque for 100 or 200 guineas' (Sheehan 1997, p. 331). Finally,

[16] Brown would later describe clitoridectomy as 'neither more nor less than circumcision of the female' (*Medical Times and Gazette* 1867, n. (a)).

[17] He showed a similar attitude to his patients when he began performing ovariotomies: his first three patients died, but he nonetheless performed a fourth procedure, on his own sister, who did survive (Roy 2004).

Brown had breached the silencing of female sexuality through self-promotion. There had been no controversy following reports of his procedure in professional publications (Sheehan 1997, p. 330). The crisis which brought about his downfall began with an article in *The Times* promoting his work (Stothard 1999) and was exacerbated by the publication of his book in bindings the *British Medical Journal* thought better suited 'to a class of works which lie upon drawing room tables' (quoted in Scull and Favreau 1986, p. 253). Even one Dr West, who had himself recommended clitoridectomy to a patient suffering from hysterical symptoms, criticised Baker Brown because 'public attempts to excite the attention of non-medical persons, and especially of women, to the subject of self-abuse in the female sex are likely to injure society' (quoted in Sheehan 1997, p. 330).

On 3 April 1867, a hearing held by the Obstetrical Society of London concluded with Baker Brown's expulsion from the society (Roy 2004). *The Lancet* was not alone in regretting the 'repulsive' duty of examining a subject better never mentioned (Stothard 1999). Baker Brown's reputation and practice were both permanently harmed, and he died less than six years later. The proceedings against him largely ended the use of clitoridectomy in England and Wales but did not end the treatment of women's reproductive biology, mental health, and sexuality as interdependent, unstable, and in need of careful regulation. Thus lesbianism became a moral and psychological issue whose medical management was as coercive as, and more readily compatible with silencing than, criminal prosecution. The expansion and professionalisation of the medical profession, alongside similar processes in the legal system, ensured that the doctor rather than the magistrate or judge was the key arbiter of women's sexual conduct. Yet this process also problematises Foucauldian claims that medicalisation classified homosexuals into existence in the late nineteenth century: not only were lesbians medicalised much earlier but it was done in such a diffuse way that no specific medical identity was created. Instead, women whom we might consider lesbians were subsumed within a larger group whose conditions were essentially a failure to be sufficiently subordinate and sexually desireless. Medicine worked alongside law to silence lesbian possibility by refusing it a distinct name.

The Criminal Justice System

While eighteenth-century criminal justice had depended upon the occasional but spectacular infliction of severe penalties, it moved in the nineteenth century to a more professional and systematic approach which aimed to deter through the likelihood of conviction rather than the severity of punishment (Upchurch 2010, pp. 416–17).[18] Even the spaces in which criminal justice happened were changing: while eighteenth-century magistrates might hear cases in their own homes, purpose-built police courts became common in the following century. In terms of policing and prosecution, Douglas Hay and Francis Snyder (1989, p. 4) have defined the period from 1750 to 1850 as the 'century of transition', a process completed when in 1856 the County and Borough Police Act made police forces compulsory throughout England and Wales. The new police forces not only investigated but, increasingly, prosecuted crimes, reducing the victim to the role of witness. Clive Emsley points out (2018, pp. 186, 202–03) that the changes were gradual, but suggests that prosecution counsel were widespread by the 1840s. All the same the prosecutorial role developed unevenly, with victims still bringing many cases until late in the century (Churchill 2014, p. 141; Turner 2012, pp. 65–65); although typically not in the few female husband cases brought to court.

These changes in prosecution practice prompted corresponding alterations to the defendant's position, beginning with the Prisoners' Counsel Act 1836 which allowed defendants to be represented by counsel at all stages of the trial. The primary vehicle for ensuring truth-telling, which in the first part of the century had been the sworn oath and threat of perjury prosecution (Schneider 2015), became cross-examination. That increasing focus upon witness examination by counsel made the modern adversarial trial a very different proceeding to the much briefer, lawyerless hearings of the eighteenth century (Emsley 2018, p. 205).

The extension of counsel's role was not straightforwardly beneficial to defendants. First, the practical effect of the 1836 Act was limited by the need for an accused to be able to pay for legal representation: many still went

[18] Despite that aim, the police never achieved a monopoly over criminal justice, with informal sanctions remaining important (Churchill 2014, p. 135).

unrepresented. Second, counsel's right to speak stood in contrast to the silencing of defendants who only became competent sworn witnesses at their own trial following the Criminal Evidence Act 1898 (Schneider 2015, chap. 5). The exception was defendants in sexual offences, who gained the right to give evidence under section 20 of the 1885 Act, a provision reflecting the justice system's deep distrust of sexual offences complainants. Third, we saw in Chap. 2 that eighteenth-century courts had used a number of devices to limit the impact of the Bloody Code, including the discretionary exercise of mercy and the sense of the judge as protector of the accused person's interests, both substantially reduced as the nineteenth century progressed. Nonetheless, Mourey's case shows some of the advantages of the professionalised system: she had the benefit of legal representation to put forward technical points of substantive law. While ultimately unsuccessful, those arguments could stand or fall on their own merits rather than her ability to engage the sympathies of the court. As a foreigner, a woman who worked for brothels, and an alleged abortionist, she had a better (albeit slim and disappointed) chance of acquittal through appeals to strict legal justice than discretionary mercy.

Attitudes to the criminal law were also changing among those who made it, particularly Parliament. Compared to the often highly specific offences of the eighteenth century, legislation was wider in scope and increasingly related to the national context (Emsley 2018, p. 13). While efforts at full codification of the criminal law failed, major consolidating and reforming statutes including the Offences Against the Person Act 1861 were passed. As statutory law developed, law reporting grew, and the system and its personnel became more professional, so the relatively informal eighteenth-century approach to finding an offence to charge was perhaps less easy to sustain. H G Cocks suggests that the magistracy, now drawn from a slightly lower social class, also wielded authority with less confident familiarity than its eighteenth-century, ruling-class counterparts (2006, p. 134). The inability to identify offences applicable to the female husbands Chapman and Stoakes, and the consequent disappearance of female husband prosecutions, was symptomatic of these developments, as were the legal arguments in *Mourey* and their reporting in *Justice of the Peace*.

Finally, approaches to punishment were changing significantly. Most important was the shift from public to private punishment, aided by the development of imprisonment as the major sanction available to the courts. Intellectual credibility gained from publications such as Cesare Beccaria's *On Crimes and Punishments* (1769) and Jeremy Bentham's *Panopticon* (1791), and increasing political support, allowed construction of Millbank penitentiary in London between 1812 and 1816 (Emsley 2018, pp. 277–78). Its completion was followed by legislation aimed at producing a more uniform and rational approach nationally.[19] Although progress was uneven, not least because of criticism of prison conditions (Willis 2008, pp. 402, 417–18), imprisonment became the primary sentence for most petty and serious crimes (Emsley 2018, p. 298). Among the cultural consequences was a shift from broadsheets and ballads focused on punishment towards press and literary interest in the surviving public spectacle: the trial itself (Schneider 2015, p. 6). Thus the Armstrong abduction case was a media sensation, making reporters' reticence about Mourey all the more significant.

The Sexual Double Standard

The Armstrong affair was a moment of sensation in a broader and enduring campaign which, for the women's movement, was rooted in opposition to the sexual double standard. In the 1860s, the Contagious Diseases Acts had brought medicine and law together to enforce that double standard.[20] This series of statutes aimed to address high rates of venereal diseases (sexually transmitted infections or STIs) in the armed forces. The specific means chosen was to ensure that uninfected prostitutes were available to military men: women suspected of being engaged in prostitution were subjected to compulsory medical examinations and, if diagnosed with an STI, detention and treatment in a lock hospital (Wendelin 2012, pp. 381–83). Parliament was redefining prostitution as a public health problem, and doctors worked hand in hand with police to enforce

[19] For example, the Gaol Act 1823 and the establishment of a prison inspectorate in 1835.

[20] A series of Acts of the same name were passed in 1864, 1866, and 1869. They were suspended in 1883 and repealed in 1886.

the new laws. They were well aware that the Acts were in fact moralistic and ideologically informed: STIs are not passed only from women to men, and justifications for the decision to police only women's health drew explicitly upon the different value given to women prostitutes and male soldiers. Men's morale was not to be risked by medical inspections, even though far more intrusive measures were being taken against women. The Acts assumed that men had uncontrollable sexual urges to which financially motivated women catered: in the words of the 1870 Royal Commission on the Contagious Diseases Acts:

> There is no comparison to be made between prostitutes and the men who consort with them. With the one the offence is committed as a matter of gain; with the other it is the irregular indulgence of a natural impulse.

The campaigns against these Acts continued until their repeal in 1886. The same campaigners, an uncomfortable combination of feminists and moralists, fought for the 1885 Criminal Amendment Act. Feminist campaigners did not view the Contagious Diseases Acts in isolation but increasingly addressed wider aspects of prostitution and sexual exploitation. The women's movement of the period—diverse in its views and interests, including many at odds with Butler's—was also engaged in wider critiques of marriage and was achieving important changes to married women's property and parental rights, including the Custody of Infants Acts 1839 and 1873, Married Women's Property Acts 1870 and 1882, and Matrimonial Causes Act 1878 (Vicinus 1997, pp. 72–74; Shanley 1989). Butler located the Contagious Diseases Acts within a social framework in which women were either 'set aside, so to speak, to minister to the irregularities of the excusable man' or 'almost forcibly guarded in domestic purity' (Butler 1886). She was alive to issues of class, economic exploitation, and the need to protect the liberty of the person. In particular, working-class girls were legally vulnerable to sexual abuse thanks to the low age of consent, just as they were the main target of state abuse under the Contagious Diseases Acts.

However, the alliance working against the Contagious Diseases Acts and for new age of consent legislation showed varied levels of awareness of the current law's class bias and patriarchal assumptions. Deborah

Gorham describes a coalition encompassing 'Anglican bishops and socialists' as well as feminists and social purity campaigners. The Salvation Army, heavily involved in the 'Maiden Tribute' events, was part of a morally conservative movement opposed to 'vice'. While they had some common ground with the women's movement in terms of the specific law reform sought, their wider attitudes and motivations were often very different. For example, Butler's concerns about young women being 'almost forcibly guarded' ran counter to other reformers' suggestions that sexually active girls should be placed in reformatory institutions (Gorham 1978, pp. 354–65). Those differences would become overt soon after the passing of the 1885 Act, when Butler resigned from the anti-vice National Vigilance Association formed to police its operation (Roberts 1995, p. 104). That Association's constitution defined its purpose as 'to enforce and improve the laws for the repression of criminal vice' (Hunt 1999, p. 161). By contrast, Butler was later ambiguous at best about the 1885 legislation, stating 'I have not a very great faith in law' since however good, it was of little use to 'a half awakened people' (Roberts 1995, p. 101).

Women campaigners had to negotiate a difficult line when speaking publicly about these issues. They needed to show sufficient understanding of the issues to establish their authority, but would be discredited personally and politically if they displayed too much inappropriate knowledge. Stead, as a man outside the mainstream of journalistic practice, was in a very different position. He ignored norms of class and propriety and was eager to take an American-influenced approach characterised as the New Journalism (Goodwyn 2018). He had more in common with the anti-vice than feminist elements of the age of consent campaign, but had approached Butler as early as 1876 with an offer to write something for the cause. She did not accept, and it was only as the Bill looked certain to fail again in 1885 that Stead was approached by the anti-vice campaigner Benjamin Scott to increase the pressure for reform (Wendelin 2012, p. 383). His crusading methods may have been effective in this instance but they also drew considerable criticism for the subject-matter they brought into respectable homes.

Mourey's case therefore occurred at the intersection of feminist, moralist, and paternalist approaches to the law. The courts' concern to preserve men's sexual prerogatives did not mean they had any sympathy for women such as Mourey. She might have been employed by brothels to offer the reassurances their wealthy customers required, but those customers felt no gratitude towards her. Like the prostitutes with whom she worked, Mourey was seen as fallen and immoral. The *Pall Mall Journal*'s pornographic rendering of her encounter with Armstrong, as well as the legal argument about her offence, added unspoken (and unspeakable) hints of lesbian erotics to her actions which could only prejudice her further. The judge's stern insistence upon his own disregard of the accusations that she was an abortionist combined an assertion of impartial justice with a potent reminder of the very allegations he claimed to dismiss: he was doing a distasteful task with all the rationality and neutrality that patriarchal masculine norms required. The lesbian undertones remained a potent but unarticulated aggravating factor.

Louise Mourey and Silencing

Mourey's prosecution was politically viable because it did not directly raise the possibility of a woman gaining her own sexual gratification from sexual activity with another woman. Instead, there was emphasis upon the act having been committed in support of the sexual gratification of men. That was done by positioning Mourey as somebody who worked for brothels: while her midwifery diploma was discussed, her midwifery practice was not. Yet she did have such a practice: not only did she list her services as *accoucheuse* in the Post Office Directory, but Margaret Makepeace has shared the story of her grandmother May Louise Smith, born on 1 May 1885, who was given her middle name for the midwife who delivered her: Louise Mourey (*Post Office Directory: London* 1880, p. 1108; Makepeace 2014).

Mourey's association with prostitution and abortion also served another silencing function by placing her far outside the norms of respectable womanhood which the policy aimed to protect. While the possibility of lesbianism for British, middle-class, properly domestic women was denied, Mourey was none of those things and indeed the court proceedings defined her in contrast to them. That was not the work of the legal personnel alone; it was also the approach of her co-defendants who presented themselves as socially and morally superior. Stead claimed in court that Mourey was 'an old abortionist who had connections with houses of ill fame' ("October 1885, Trial of Rebecca Jarrett et al." 2012a). His strategy was effective, ensuring that the campaigners who had managed the whole affair and, in his case, instigated the examination were sentenced less harshly than this relatively marginal actor.[21]

As a midwife with her own premises bearing a brass plate, Mourey might seem to be part of the respectable, skilled working class. Since that was a class to whom the campaigners particularly wished to appeal, it is unsurprising that they were eager to displace her into the criminal classes by offering information about her alleged practice among brothels and women seeking abortion. Even those wealthy clients whose desires she apparently facilitated were, in Stead's eyes, members of a degenerate aristocracy rather than the respectable middle and upper working classes whose outrage the *Maiden Tribute* sought to provoke.[22] Low social status had also been a theme in the few female husband-type cases brought before the courts in the nineteenth century. While middle-class women were expected not to understand the possible sexual implications of such behaviour, working-class communities seem to have been more knowing and less reticent. Thus John Jones/Ann Hughes, prosecuted in 1862 for causing a disturbance, was discharged by the Manchester magistrates but 'had to be kept in the dock awhile to protect her from being mobbed outside the court' (*Western Daily Press* 1862). Camilla Townsend found that reports of the Geals case in publications for the 'aspiring lower middle class' were most critical of the defendant; working-class journals were 'almost sympathetic' (1993, p. 302).

Midwifery might also have suggested maternal nurturing, but Mourey was presented as deviating from both professional and feminine norms through assertions that she was an abortionist. That would violate not only social but also legal standards, since abortion was a felony under the 1861 Act with no defence even where the mother's life or health were in danger. There may have been truth in the allegation for she had been

[21] Stead, its instigator, received three months' imprisonment, while Jarrett, who was responsible for taking Armstrong, received six months without hard labour.

[22] Butler herself wrote to Stead that 'the rich and aristocratic culprits in this matter should be judged by the people' (quoted in Wendelin 2012, p. 389).

prosecuted in 1873 following the death of her patient Anna Simon whose health had been badly damaged by previous pregnancies and who was reported to have told a neighbour that she would have no more children born alive. If Mourey had supplied Simon with an abortifacient, she had done so in the context of providing ongoing care for Simon and her children. At the inquest, the coroner's jury brought in a verdict of murder against Mourey and she was detained in Newgate Gaol to await criminal trial ("Calendar of Prisoners" 1873, p. 9; *Surrey Comet* 1873a, b, c). However, in the absence of medical evidence of an abortion, the prosecution had formally offered no evidence and the judge had directed a not guilty verdict.

Mourey's foreignness was inescapable in the Old Bailey where, despite having lived in England for some years, the Frenchwoman relied upon an interpreter ("October 1885, Trial of Rebecca Jarrett et al." 2012a). Police Inspector Edward Borner stressed his difficulty in understanding her 'broken English—sometimes she wandered into French', even as he repeated her comprehensive admissions ("October 1885, Trial of Rebecca Jarrett et al." 2012a). Press reports emphasised her nationality both directly and by the repetition of her credentials as a '*diplomée*' rather than 'certified' midwife. Lesbianism had long been constructed as a foreign vice, and Mourey's prosecution played into that discourse even as it downplayed lesbian possibility.[23]

The courtroom depiction of Mourey as a foreign abortionist who provided services to brothels therefore placed her in opposition to virtuous, respectable womanhood. At the same time, the fact that her part in the Armstrong case had been carried out for money played a similar diversionary role to the fraud charges in earlier female husband cases; Harley Street practitioner Dr Heywood Smith, who carried out the same examination for a fee, at Stead's request, and without parental consent, faced no charges ("October 1885, Trial of Rebecca Jarrett et al." 2012b). Any implied association of Mourey with sexual deviancy would pose no threat to the logic of silencing: it would simply displace the faint hints and

[23] Male homosexuality had been similarly treated as a French vice fifteen years earlier in *Boulton and Park*, where the British medical witnesses had to turn for extensive experience of male sodomy to the Frenchman Tardieu, to whose work witness Dr Paul had been alerted by an anonymous letter (Weeks 1981).

troubling undercurrents of lesbian possibility onto those abject and unspeakable elements of society with which respectable women would dread being associated. The myth of female sexual passivity, and its corresponding requirement of female sexual ignorance, were therefore deployed in relation to middle-class, white, British women, while implicitly acknowledging the existence of lesbianism among women outside those norms. The high degree of consensus amongst those making the law that it should operate upon the basis that these myths were true meant they were enshrined in both case law and legislation.

Conclusion: The (Lack of) Impact of *Mourey*

Mourey was in poor health when she went into prison, and soon became seriously ill. Jarrett was taken to the same prison ward for a short time while unwell, and later wrote that fellow prisoners told her, 'do you know who is up here dyeing[.] I said no[.] they said the french woman who had been selling the drugs to stupify poor little children off 13 years of age before they were used by those wretched men' (Jarrett 2018, original spelling). Three months into her sentence, Mourey died in Millbank Prison of kidney disease and 'natural general debility' (death certificate, PRO COL352639/2019); the subsequent inquest found that this was due to her poor state of health and that her care in prison had been good. The legal impact of her case seems not to have survived her.

The ruling had not been legally controversial. Lopes J was in no doubt that section 52 applied to sexual acts between females. Since a girl under the age of thirteen could not give legally valid consent to sexual touching, the section therefore created an age of consent for lesbian sex. Yet, despite the apparent clarity of the law and the publication of the legal ruling in the *Justice of the Peace*, the question of whether such an age of consent did in fact exist tends to be viewed as remaining controversial until the mid-twentieth century. Certainly this was a first-instance decision and the facts of Mourey's case were unusual. However, this interpretation of the law was obvious and relatively uncontroversial to both Lopes and the *Justice of the Peace* commentator who suggested that the point 'deserves to be remembered': in other words, the ruling should be treated as a persuasive precedent.

Prosecutions of women for indecent assault would be extremely rare: the next reported case was almost half a century away. There were good reasons to keep such incidents quiet since they generally posed a direct challenge to myths around female sexuality. A passive and desireless woman would have no means or reason to commit an indecent assault. Mourey's conduct was comprehensible only because she was both assisting others to cater to male sexual desires and, crucially, was far outside the British, middle-class model of virtuous femininity. Factors such as prosecutorial discretion and lack of reporting, rather than legal impossibility, discouraged prosecutions; there was no doctrinal difficulty in interpreting the law to permit a conviction nor controversy over such interpretation. In other words, among those whose professional knowledge and experience entitled them to know 'truths' about female sexuality, there was little hesitation in accepting that such indecent assaults could both occur and be punished.

Chapter 4 will take up the legal and social story after 1885 and explore the next steps in the development of sexual offences, particularly efforts in the 1920s to address the shortcomings of the 1885 Act. However, it is useful to look forward briefly in order to understand the direct consequences of *Mourey*. Rather like the clue of the dog that did not bark in the night,[24] *Mourey*'s significance is found in silence. The degree of legal amnesia is apparent from the Court of Appeal judgment in *Hare* [1934] KB 354. Maggie Hare was convicted in 1933 of indecent assault on a twelve-year-old boy, namely three incidents of sexual intercourse which left him infected with a venereal disease. (That there was no offence of unlawful sexual intercourse with a boy was itself a reflection of the construction of women's role in sex as passive.) The defence argued at trial and appeal that section 62 of the Offences Against the Person Act appeared under the sub-heading 'unnatural offences' and referred only to 'sodomitical offences', so indecent assault upon a boy could only be committed by a man and not by a woman. The argument appeared to have

[24] Sherlock Holmes identified the vital clue in *The Adventure of Silver Blaze* as the silence of a dog which did nothing in the night-time (Doyle 1894).

some academic support, since four years earlier E. Ling-Mallison (1930), apparently unaware of *Mourey*, had asserted that it was 'certain' women could not be convicted under section 62. However, the Court of Appeal had little patience with it and did not even call upon counsel for the Crown. They pointed out that the sub-heading was added after the passing of the Act and 'forms no part of the enactment'. There was no ambiguity in the wording of the section, since the term 'whosoever' admittedly included a woman, and a woman could therefore be guilty of indecent assault upon a male.

Having conceded some sexual agency to women, *Hare* went further, confronting the spectre of lesbianism:

> There is no doubt, in our opinion, that in s. 52 of the Act the word 'Whosoever' includes a woman, and there is no reason for saying that a woman cannot be guilty of an indecent assault on another female.

That point was raised in response to counsel's arguments (themselves probably informed by the high-profile 1929 Colonel Barker prosecution discussed in Chap. 5). The fact that an obiter remark has been accepted by modern commentators as setting out the law while *Mourey* has been overlooked tells us much about our willingness to take Victorian pronouncements on female sexuality at face value. Only in understanding the complicated relationship between public pronouncements and actual beliefs can we develop an accurate assessment of the legal history of sex between women.

References

Acton, William. 1865. *The Functions and Disorders of the Reproductive Organs, in Childhood, Youth, Adult Age, and Advanced Life, Considered in the Physiological, Social, and Moral Relations*. London: J.&A. Churchill.

Armstrong, Nancy. 1987. *Desire and Domestic Fiction*. Oxford: Oxford University Press.

Ashton Weekly Reporter. 1867. Extraordinary Career of a Woman, March 2.

Beccaria, Cesare. 1769. *An Essay on Crimes and Punishments, Translated from the Italian*. London: F. Newbery.

Bell's Weekly Messenger. 1835. Extraordinary Circumstance, February 2.
Bentham, Jeremy. 1791. *Panopticon; or, the Inspection-House*. London: T. Payne.
Bland, Lucy. 1995. *Banishing the Beast: English Feminism and Sexual Morality 1885–1914*. London: Penguin.
Bolton Chronicle. 1862. A Woman Disguised as a Man: Extraordinary Case, September 20.
Brown, Isaac Baker. 1866. *On the Curability of Certain Forms of Insanity, Epilepsy, Catalepsy, and Hysteria in Females*. London: Robert Hardwicke.
Burrows, George Man. 1828. *Commentaries on the Causes, Forms, Symptoms, and Treatment, Moral and Medical, of Insanity*. London: Thomas and George Underwood.
Bury Times. 1867. 'Butter to Butter;' Singular Case of Love-Making between Females, Even to the Brink of Matrimony, March 2.
Butler, Josephine. 1886. The Double Standard of Morality. *The Philanthropist*.
"Calendar of Prisoners in Her Majesty's Gaol of Newgate for the Session Commencing for the Year 1873." 1873. London.
Churchill, David C. 2014. Rethinking the State Monopolisation Thesis: The Historiography of Policing and Criminal Justice in Nineteenth-Century England. *Crime, Histoire & Sociétés* 18 (1): 131–152. https://doi.org/10.4000/chs.1471.
Clark, Anna. 1996. Anne Lister's Construction of Lesbian Identity. *Journal of the History of Sexuality* 7 (1): 23–50.
Cocks, H.G. 2006. Safeguarding Civility: Sodomy, Class and Moral Reform in Early Nineteenth-Century England. *Past and Present* 190: 121–146.
Crosby, Kevin. 2017. Keeping Women off the Jury in 1920s England and Wales. *Legal Studies* 37 (4): 695–717. https://doi.org/10.1111/lest.12169.
Devon and Exeter Daily Gazette. 1886. The Death of Madame Mourey, January 25.
Doyle, Arthur Conan. 1894. *Memoirs of Sherlock Holmes*. London: G. Newnes.
Edwards, Susan S.M. 1981. *Female Sexuality and the Law: A Study of Constructs of Female Sexuality as They Inform Statute and Legal Procedure*. Oxford: Martin Robertson.
Emsley, Clive. 2018. *Crime and Society in England 1750–1900*. 5th ed. London: Routledge.
Essex Herald. 1867. A Female Barman, February 26.
Faraday, Annabel. 1988. Lesbian Outlaws: Past Attempts to Legislate against Lesbians. *Trouble and Strife* 13: 9–16.

February 1867, Trial of Mary Walker (T18670225-341). 2012. Old Bailey Proceedings Online. https://www.oldbaileyonline.org/browse.jsp?id=def1-341-18670225&div=t18670225-341#highlight.

Fletcher, Anthony. 1995. *Gender, Sex and Subordination in England 1500–1800.* Yale University Press.

Foucault, Michel. 1961. *Madness and Civilization: A History of Insanity in the Age of Reason*. London: Routledge.

Goodwyn, Helena. 2018. A 'New' Journalist: The Americanization of W. T. Stead. *Journal of Victorian Culture* 23 (3): 405–420. https://doi.org/10.1093/jvcult/vcy038.

Gorham, Deborah. 1978. The 'Maiden Tribute of Modern Babylon' Re-Examined: Child Prostitution and the Idea of Childhood in Late-Victorian England. *Victorian Studies* 21 (3): 353–379.

Gosden, Roger G. 2004. Séquard, Charles Édouard Brown (1817–1894). In *Oxford Dictionary of National Biography*. Oxford University Press. http://www.oxforddnb.com/view/article/3720.

Hall, Catherine. 1992. *White, Male and Middle-Class: Explorations in Feminism and History*. Cambridge: Polity Press.

Hall, Lesley A. 2001. Hauling Down the Double Standard. *Gender and History* 16 (4): 36–65.

———. 2004. Acton, William John. In *Oxford Dictionary of National Biography*. Oxford University Press. http://www.oxforddnb.com/view/article/39445.

Hay, Douglas, and Francis Snyder. 1989. Using the Criminal Law, 1750–1850: Policing, Private Prosecution, and the State. In *Policing and Prosecution in Britain 1750–1850*, ed. Douglas Hay and Francis Snyder, 3–54. Oxford: Clarendon Press.

Hunt, Alan. 1999. *Governing Morals: A Social History of Moral Regulation.* Cambridge: Cambridge University Press.

Illustrated Times. 1865. Law and Crime, September 23.

Jackson, Lee. 2001. Women—Cross-Dressing. The Victorian Dictionary: Exploring Victorian London. http://www.victorianlondon.org/women/crossdressing.htm.

Jackson, Louise A. 2000. *Child Sexual Abuse in Victorian England.* London: Routledge.

Jackson, Margaret. 1994. *The Real Facts of Life: Feminism and the Politics of Sexuality c 1850–1940*. London: Taylor & Francis.

Jarrett, Rebecca. 2018. Rebecca Jarrett's Narrative (c. 1928). W. T. Stead Resource Site. https://attackingthedevil.co.uk/related/narrative.php.

Kendal Mercury. 1838. A Female Husband, April 21.

Laqueur, Thomas. 1990. *Making Sex: Body and Gender From the Greeks to Freud*. Cambridge, MA: Harvard University Press.

Leeds Times. 1848. Singular Case of Concealment of Sex, October 14.

Liddington, Jill. 1998. *Female Fortune: Land, Gender and Authority: The Ann Lister Diaries and Other Writings*. London: Rivers Oram Press.

Ling-Mallison, Eric. 1930. *Law Relating to Women*. London: Solicitors' Law Stationery Society Ltd.

Makepeace, Margaret. 2014. May Louise and the Marylebone Midwife. *Untold Lives Blog*. https://blogs.bl.uk/untoldlives/2014/05/may-louise-and-the-marylebone-midwife.html.

Marcus, Sharon. 2007. *Between Women: Friendship, Desire, and Marriage in Victorian England*. Princeton, NJ: Princeton University Press.

Mason, Michael. 1994. *The Making of Victorian Sexuality*. Oxford: Oxford University Press.

Matthews, Richard. 1833. *A Digest of the Law Relating to Offences Punishable by Indictment*. London: William Crofts.

Meadowbank, Lord. 1975. Speech of Lord Meadowbank, 25 June 1811. In *Miss Marianne Woods and Miss Jane Pirie against Dame Helen Cumming Gordon*. New York: Arno Press.

Medical Times and Gazette. 1867. Editorial: Clitoridectomy and Medical Ethics, April 13.

Miss Marianne Woods and Miss Jane Pirie against Dame Helen Cumming Gordon. 1975. New York: Arno Press.

Moore, Lisa L. 1997. *Dangerous Intimacies; Toward a Sapphic History of the British Novel*. London: Duke University Press.

Moore, Norman. 2004. Jones, Charles Handfield (1819–1890), Rev. Michael Bevan. In *Oxford Dictionary of National Biography*. Oxford University Press. http://www.oxforddnb.com/view/article/14985.

Morning Chronicle. 1835. Police Intelligence: Hatton Garden, February 2.

Morning Post. 1833. Lavinia Edwards, March 21.

Moscucci, Ornella. 1996. Clitoridectomy, Circumcision, and the Politics of Sexual Pleasure in Mid-Victorian Britain. In *Sexualities in Victorian Britain*, ed. Andrew H. Miller and James Eli Adams, 60–78. Bloomington: Indiana University Press.

Nead, Lynda. 2000. *Victorian Babylon: People, Streets and Images in Nineteenth-Century London*. New Haven: Yale University Press.

Nightingale, Florence. 1860. *Suggestions for Thought to Searchers After Religious Truth Vol 2*. London: Eyre & Spottiswoode.

O'Driscoll, Sally. 2010. A Crisis of Femininity: Re-Making Gender in Popular Discourse. In *Lesbian Dames*, ed. John C. Beynon and Caroline Gonda. New York: Ashgate.

"October 1885, Trial of Rebecca Jarrett, Wiliam Thomas Stead, Sampson Jacques, Louisa Mourez (T18851019-1032)." 2012a. Old Bailey Proceedings Online. https://www.oldbaileyonline.org/browse.jsp?div=t18851019-1032.

"October 1885, Trial of Rebecca Jarrett, William Thomas Stead, Sampson Jacques, William Bramwell Booth, Elizabeth Combe (T18851019-1031)." 2012b. Old Bailey Proceedings Online. https://www.oldbaileyonline.org/browse.jsp?id=t18851019-1031&div=t18851019-1031.

Oppenheim, Janet. 1991. *"Shattered Nerves": Doctors, Patients and Depression in Victorian England*. Oxford: Oxford University Press.

Oram, Alison, and Annmarie Turnbull. 2001. *The Lesbian History Sourcebook: Love and Sex between Women in Britain from 1780 to 1970*. London: Routledge.

Peakman, Julie. 2016. *Amatory Pleasures: Explorations in Eighteenth-Century Sexual Culture*. London: Bloomsbury.

Penny Illustrated Paper. 1867. Mary Anne Walker, November 23.

Plowden, Alison. 1974. *The Case of Eliza Armstrong: A Child of 13 Bought for £5*. London: BBC Publishing.

Post Office Directory: London. 1880. London.

Post Office London Directory. 1880. London: W Kelly and Co.

Rayside, David M. 1992. Homophobia, Class and Party in England. *Canadian Journal of Political Science* 25 (1): 121–149.

Richardson, Angelique. 2003. *Love and Eugenics in the Late Nineteenth Century: Rational Reproduction and the New Woman*. Oxford: Oxford University Press.

Roberts, M.J.D. 1995. Feminism and the State in Later Victorian England. *The Historical Journal* 38 (1): 85–110.

Roy, Judith M. 2004. Brown, Isaac Baker (1811–1873). In *Oxford Dictionary of National Biography*. Oxford University Press. http://www.oxforddnb.com/view/article/50268.

Royal Cornwall Gazette. 1838. A Female Husband, April 20.

Schneider, Wendie Ellen. 2015. *Engines of Truth: Producing Veracity in the Victorian Courtroom*. New Haven: Yale University Press.

Scull, Andrew, and Diane Favreau. 1986. The Clitoridectomy Craze. *Social Research* 53 (2): 243–260.

"September 1865, Trial of Sarah Geals (T18650918-860)." 2012. Old Bailey Proceedings Online. https://www.oldbaileyonline.org/browse.jsp?id=t18650918-860&div=t18650918-860.

Shanley, Mary Lyndon. 1989. *Feminism, Marriage, and the Law in Victorian England.* Princeton, NJ: Princeton University Press.
Sheehan, Elizabeth A. 1997. Victorian Clitoridectomy: Issac Baker Brown and His Harmless Operative Procedure. In *The Gender/Sexuality Reader*, ed. Roger N. Lancaster and Micaela di Leonardo, 325–334. London: Routledge.
Showalter, Elaine. 1981. Victorian Women and Insanity. In *Madhouses, Mad-Doctors, and Madmen: The Social History of Psychiatry in the Victorian Era*, ed. Andrew Scull, 313–331. Philadelphia: University of Pennsylvania Press.
———. 1987. *The Female Malady: Women, Madness and English Culture, 1830–1980.* London: Virago.
Souhami, Diana. 1996. *Mrs Keppel and Her Daughter.* London: HarperCollins.
Stead, W. T. 1885. The Maiden Tribute of Modern Babylon, II. *Pall Mall Gazette*, July 6.
———. 2018. W.T. Stead's Reminiscences of the 'Maiden Tribute' Campaign (Undated). W. T. Stead Resource Site. https://attackingthedevil.co.uk/steadworks/tribute.php.
Steele, R. 1714. *The Ladies Library (Vol. I).* London.
Stothard, Peter. 1999. Women at Our Mercy. *The Times*, March 27.
Strange, Julie-Marie. 2000. Menstrual Fictions: Languages of Medicine and Menstruation, c. 1850–1930. *Women's History Review* 9 (3): 607–628. https://doi.org/10.1080/09612020000200260.
Surrey Comet. 1873a. Peculiar Case of Death, February 22.
———. 1873b. The Mysterious Death of a Lady, March 8.
———. 1873c. The Suspicious Death of a Lady, April 12.
Suzuki, Akihito. 1999. Framing Psychiatric Subjectivity: Doctor, Patient and Record-Keeping at Bethlem in the Nineteenth Century. In *Insanity, Institutions and Society, 1800–1914: A Social History of Madness in Comparative Perspective*, ed. Joseph Melling and Bill Forsythe, 115–137. London: Routledge.
"The Additional Petition of Miss Mary-Ann Woods and Miss Jane Pirie." 1975. In *Miss Marianne Woods and Miss Jane Pirie against Dame Helen Cumming Gordon*. New York: Arno Press.
Townsend, Camilla. 1993. I Am the Woman for Spirit': A Working Woman's Gender Transgression in Victorian London. *Victorian Studies* 36 (3): 293–314.
Turner, Joanne. 2012. Summary Justice for Women: Stafford Borough, 1880–1905. *Crime, Histoire & Sociétés* 16 (2): 55–77. https://doi.org/10.4000/chs.1359.
Upchurch, Charles. 2010. Liberal Exclusions and Sex between Men in the Modern Era: Speculations on a Framework. *Journal of the History of Sexuality* 19 (3): 409–431.

Vicinus, Martha. 1997. Lesbian Perversity and Victorian Marriage: The 1864 Codrington Divorce Trial. *Journal of British Studies* 36 (1): 70–98.
Waites, Matthew. 2002. Inventing a 'Lesbian Age of Consent'? The History of the Minimum Age for Sex between Women in the UK. *Social & Legal Studies* 11 (3): 323–342.
Walkowitz, Judith R. 1992. *City of Dreadful Delight: Narratives of Sexual Danger in Late-Victorian London*. London: Virago.
———. 2004. Butler [Née Grey], Josephine Elizabeth (1828–1906), Social Reformer and Women's Activist. In *Oxford Dictionary of National Biography*, vol. 1. Oxford University Press. https://doi.org/10.1093/ref:odnb/32214.
Weeks, Jeffrey. 1981. *Sex, Politics and Society: The Regulation of Sexuality since 1800*. London: Longman.
Wendelin, Greta. 2012. A Rhetoric of Pornography: Private Style and Public Policy in 'The Maiden Tribute of Modern Babylon. *Rhetoric Society Quarterly* 42 (4): 375–396.
Western Daily Press. 1862. A Woman in Man's Clothing for Six Years, March 29.
Willis, James J. 2008. Punishment and the Cultural Limits to State Power in Late 18th-Century Britain. *Punishment & Society* 10 (4): 401–428. https://doi.org/10.1177/1462474508095318.
Wollstonecraft, Mary. 1792. *A Vindication of the Rights of Woman*. London.
Zedner, Lucia. 1991. *Women, Crime and Custody in Victorian England*. Oxford: Clarendon Press.

4

'Gross Indecency Between Females': The 1921 Parliamentary Debates

The 1921 Debates

In 1921, the men of the Houses of Parliament engaged in what might today be described as a display of fragile masculinity.[1] The First World War had ended less than three years earlier but the social upheavals it had brought accelerated the social changes of previous decades. Independent, career-minded 'New Women' had emerged in the 1880s and the science of sexology in the 1890s; the women's and social purity movements were problematising male sexual behaviour; and women were starting to enter Parliament and the legal profession. Some of Britain's legislators were feeling under threat. Outside the home, their sexual access to young women was being threatened by feminist legal reforms, while the spectre of lesbianism threatened their sexual dominion within. A sense pervaded the parliamentary debates that once women heard of lesbianism, not only would they be likely to try it but, having tried it, they would turn away definitively from their marriages and husbands. The spectre of sex between women, then, was not just a moral danger but a menace to the patriarchal

[1] There was only one woman MP sitting in the House, Lady Nancy Astor, who did not speak in the amendment debates.

C. Derry, *Lesbianism and the Criminal Law*,
https://doi.org/10.1007/978-3-030-35300-1_4

family itself. As judge and Conservative MP Sir Ernest Wild asserted, 'it is a well-known fact that any woman who indulges in this vice will have nothing whatever to do with the other sex' (HC 04/08/1921, col. 1804).

Debating how to meet this threat, fellow Conservative MP Lieutenant Colonel Moore-Brabazon summarised the history of regulation as having involved three options (HC 04/08/1921, cols. 1802–1803):

> The first is the death sentence. That has been tried in old times, and, though drastic, it does do what is required—that is, stamp them out. The second is to look upon them frankly as lunatics, and lock them up for the rest of their lives. That is a very satisfactory way also. It gets rid of them. The third way is to leave them entirely alone, not notice them, not advertise them. That is the method that has been adopted in England for many hundred years.

He was speaking on an amendment to the Criminal Law Amendment Bill 1921, which raised a novel fourth option. If passed, it would have created an offence of 'gross indecency between female persons' criminalising all sexual contact between women. In fact, the amendment did pass the House of Commons but not the House of Lords (HC 04/08/1921, col. 1807; HL 15/08/1921, col. 577).[2] The whole Bill then failed, but not before lesbianism was explicitly discussed—although not named—by the legislature for the first time. As a fresh forum for the exploration of lesbianism's legal status, hitherto only addressed (deliberately obliquely) in the courts, Parliament also provided a venue for a very different *kind* of discussion. Common law courts downplay their lawmaking role, drawing upon notions of precedent, continuity, and deference to the legislature. In parliamentary debate, by contrast, policy underpinnings, strategies, and manoeuvres could be fully spelled out, challenged, and contested, and radical changes could be overtly proposed and considered. Thus the 1921 discussions offer both a unique glimpse of how the United Kingdom's legislators understood the regulation of lesbianism and a different perspective upon wider legal approaches.

---

[2] It passed the Commons with 148 votes in favour to 53 against, meaning that only about a third of MPs voted.

The Criminal Law Amendment Act 1885, which had raised the age of consent for sexual intercourse to sixteen (see Chap. 3), had significant flaws. Section 5 included a defence of reasonable belief that the girl was over 16 and a six-month time limit for commencing prosecutions, which made the law very difficult to use in practice. The age at which girls could legally consent to sexual activity other than intercourse remained thirteen years old. The 1921 Bill would have addressed these shortcomings but was painted by its opponents as an unjustified attack upon young men which 'took away from an accused person a ground of defence' and offered a tool by which unscrupulous young girls might blackmail them (*The Times* 1921b). The gross indecency clause was therefore proposed by Conservative MPs (and barristers) Frederick Macquisten, Howard Gritten, and Sir Ernest Wild as a spoiling amendment, designed not to pass but to be controversial enough that the Bill would run out of parliamentary time before it could become law. Some sense of their perspective on the issues can be gained from a poem penned by Wild about his feminine ideal: not only '[w]omanly, wayward, weak' but '[s]eventeen winters old' (quoted in Davenport-Hines 1990, p. 152).

The controversy, however, was not about the existence or undesirability of lesbianism. As Moore-Brabazon's remarks encapsulate, both sides agreed that sex between women was both real and wrong. Estimates of its prevalence were more contentious: as the Earl of Desart asked, 'How many people does one suppose really are so vile, so unbalanced, so neurotic, so decadent as to do this?' (HL 15/08/1921, col. 1803). It was either a rarity of which '999 woman in a thousand' outside 'sophisticated' city society were unaware (Lord Chancellor, HL 15/08/1921, col. 574) or a growing menace confessed weekly to one leading 'nerve specialist' (Wild, HC 04/08/1921, col. 1803). However, the crux of the disagreement was whether criminal law was the best medium through which to regulate it.

The House of Lords agreed that it was not, even knowing that to reject the amendment was to kill the Bill, since (female) knowledge of sex between women was tantamount to contagion. For the Earl of Malmesbury, the very subject was 'polluting': '[t]he more you advertise vice by prohibiting it the more you will increase it' (HL 15/08/1921, cols. 563, 570). The Earl of Desart, who spoke with the authority of a former Director of Public Prosecutions, posited, 'Suppose there were a prosecution ... It would be made public to thousands of people that there was this offence; that there was such a horror' (HL 15/08/1921, col. 573). The amendment's opponents in the Commons were of the same view: Moore-Brabazon expressed concern for 'the minds of perfectly innocent people'. He endorsed silence not out of any spirit of toleration but to keep that innocence untainted by 'the most revolting thoughts' (HC 04/08/1921, col. 1803).

The price of preserving female innocence was the loss of the wider Bill. The House of Lords rejected the amendment, meaning that further debate would have been required in the House of Commons. Since the government would not make the time for such debate available, the Bill failed. Its opponents' victory was short-lived: the measure was reintroduced as a government Bill the following year and became the Criminal Law Amendment Act 1922, albeit with the defence of reasonable belief retained for young men under 24. In Standing Committee, the Home Secretary seemed to accept that the age-of-consent laws would apply to women perpetrators against young people of either sex, although his remarks were typically ambiguous and allusive (Home Secretary, HC Standing Committees, 12/07/1922, col. 9; Waites 2002, p. 332):

> Take the case of an older man or woman who has got hold of a girl, who has polluted her mind and committed an indecent assault upon her. If that girl is going to be prosecuted, she will never give any information against that man, nor will a boy give any information against that woman. ... I see nothing in this which distinguishes one sex from another.[3]

The issue of gross indecency between women, its immediate purpose served, was not debated again.[4] Why, though, had it been chosen in the first place?

---

[3] The Home Secretary's comments were directed to an amendment making consenting 15-year-olds criminally responsible. The amendment, which he opposed, was rejected.

[4] Macquisten did try to introduce it, and other amendments, in 1922. Again his apparent aim was to delay the Bill. His efforts were unsuccessful as the Speaker ruled the amendment outside the scope of the Bill (Mr Speaker, HC 25/07/1922, col. 365; Waites 2002, p. 331). That was a return to the legislative silencing which had seen the Home Secretary refuse to consider legislation crimi-

Why Was the Issue of Lesbianism Chosen?

The Criminal Law Amendment Bill had widespread support within and outside Parliament. It was promoted by a coalition of over fifty organisations, led by the Association of Moral and Social Hygiene (AMSH) which, despite its name, was a thoroughly feminist body whose aims centred around the decriminalisation of prostitution and elimination of the sexual double standard. The Honorary Secretary of the AMSH, former suffragette Alison Neilans, was thus also a *de facto* leader of the overall campaign for the Bill. Key members of the coalition included the National Union of Societies for Equal Citizenship (NUSEC, formerly the National Union of Women's Suffrage Societies), Women's Freedom League (WFL, founded as a suffragette organisation), and National Council of Women of Great Britain (NCW). There were also decidedly unfeminist supporters, notably the National Vigilance Association (NVA) formed in 1885 to monitor and improve the Criminal Law Amendment Act. Josephine Butler, the feminist at the forefront of the 1885 campaign, had resigned from its original executive to form the organisation which became the AMSH (Attwood 2015, p. 326; Cree 2008; L. A. Hall 2009, p. 190). The NVA's presence in the coalition indicated its breadth, but this did not prevent opponents portraying the Bill as a feminist attack upon male prerogatives: Moore-Brabazon later characterised government support for reform as the Home Secretary's submission to feminist 'henpecking' (Jeffreys 1985, p. 89).[5]

There was considerable support within Parliament for reform. The 1921 Bill originated from three separate Bills introduced in 1920 and referred to a Joint Select Committee. The resulting agreed Bill was introduced into the House of Lords by the Bishop of London. Its opponents therefore had a difficult task, since they faced a broad alliance of diverse interests. Unlikely to win on the merits of their arguments, they resorted to manipulating parliamentary procedure. The government had agreed to

---

nalising sexual conduct between women in 1913 (Wedgwood, HC 04/08/1921, col. 1802; Ferris 1993; Doan 1997, p. 545).

[5] Carol Smart (2000, p. 62) notes that similar perceptions of reform as an attack on men were expressed in the 1922 debates.

give enough time for this Private Member's Bill to pass provided that it remained uncontroversial; there would not be sufficient parliamentary time available for additional debates (*The Times* 1921a). The gross indecency amendment was introduced as material which would render the Bill controversial, ensuring that it ran out of time and would not pass into law.

There were good reasons for its proposers to choose this of all controversial topics for their purpose. Like the Bill itself, the amendment had its roots in the Criminal Law Amendment Act 1885. During the passage of that Act through Parliament, radical independent MP Henry Labouchère had introduced an amendment to criminalise 'gross indecency between males'. The level of support it enjoyed remains unclear: while it was introduced at the last moment when few MPs were in the chamber, the Government not only accepted it but increased the proposed penalty from one to two years' imprisonment.[6] The Labouchère amendment became section 11 of the Act and won notoriety a decade later when used to convict and imprison Oscar Wilde. However, it had been designed to facilitate prosecution of behaviour already criminalised as assault or attempted buggery (Upchurch 2009). As discussed in Chap. 1, no equivalent offences for women existed or had been proposed. The 1921 amendment would therefore have marked a wholly new direction for the law. It was modelled explicitly upon section 11 and referred directly to it:

> Any act of gross indecency between female persons shall be a misdemeanour and punishable in the same manner as any such act committed by male persons under section eleven of the Criminal Law Amendment Act, 1885.

Its proposers may have been inspired by evidence given to the Joint Committee by Cecil Chapman, a pro-feminist stipendiary magistrate who had supported women's suffrage and was a founder member of the British Society for the Study of Sex Psychology (BSSSP), a forum for discussing radical ideas on sexuality and sex reform. Seeking to argue that young girls should have legal protection from abuse by older women (which a higher age of consent to indecent assault would provide), he

[6] For contrasting interpretations, see Weeks (2016, p. 15) and Brady (2016, p. 92).

unfortunately expressed himself in terms which might have suggested he supported a general offence of gross indecency between females (Joint Select Committee 1920, para. 1479; L. A. Hall 2000, p. 102, and see 1995; Doan 1998, p. 203):

> I have had very serious cases in my experience in which women have been in the habit of getting girls to their flats and houses in London, and I remember a case that took place in Bournemouth, where girls were practically being treated as if they were prostitutes. It is an offence which people speak of as if it was almost unknown to the public, but it is very well known to the police, and it is very well known to many people who are students of criminology that women as well as men corrupt girls. There is no question about it that in regard to all these acts there ought to be absolute equality between the sexes as far as is humanly possible. … I know of a Home which was started for the reformation of girls where the police had to interfere because of the girls being corrupted by the woman controller of the Home.

In doing so, he was perhaps repeating a mistake made in 1885: there are some grounds for believing that the Labouchère amendment had been prompted by concerns about sexual exploitation of boys (Funke 2013, p. 144). While Chapman's suggestions were not taken seriously by the Committee (Earl of Malmesbury, HL 15/08/1921, col. 568), they may have indicated subject-matter upon which neither parliamentarians nor feminist campaigners were agreed. They also illustrate how silencing could, perversely, risk over-regulation through its prohibition on naming and defining what was under discussion. As Doan has explained, this vagueness led the Committee to discuss the proposal in terms wider than age-of-consent cases, an approach also adopted by the amendment's proposers (Doan 1997). In Parliament, the reversal was completed by debates about regulating adult relationships to protect the patriarchal family, not protecting girls from abuse.

Prosaically, the regulation of sexual activity between women met the essential requirement of controversy. There was unanimity among parliamentarians that lesbianism was a bad thing, but their views on how to control it were considerably more diverse. Many favoured a continuation of silencing, but some were uneasily aware that this very discussion breached that policy and thereby endangered its effectiveness. Indeed, silencing was already showing early signs of fracture. In 1918 the press had reported, albeit cautiously, on a libel case brought by Maud Allen in response to an allegation of lesbianism—the 'Cult of the Clitoris' case discussed below. Sexology, the scientific study of sex, had also discussed and described homosexuality and the 'female invert', albeit within a privileged field of primarily male medical and scientific knowledge which barely entered into parliamentary consciousness. When Laura Doan examined the 1921 debates to explore how far it had entered legal discourse, she found that MPs and peers showed little knowledge of the sexologists: only Sir Ernest Wild referred to them by name, and he was less concerned with their ideas than the veneer of scientific authority they offered (Doan 1998). Instead, there was an assumption that such sexual knowledge was demarcated by profession, class, and gender: lawyers and doctors would be aware of the issue, women and working-class men would not (Doan 2001, pp. 56–57). In other words, MPs and peers were still drawing upon the discourses of the nineteenth century explored in Chap. 3: as Liberal MP Horatio Bottomley said of the amendment, '[t]he only thing that appealed … was the attempt to maintain the purity of our women' (*The Times* 1921b).

To those who proposed it, the amendment's subject-matter must have seemed inspired. Rather than have to admit its wrecking purpose, they could locate the proposal within the Bill's aims by suggesting that it represented legal equality for women. Had they been prompted by any genuine desire for sex equality, the proposers would have addressed the lack of legal protection for boys from sexual intercourse with women—a shortcoming highlighted to the Select Committee by none other than the AMSH (Joint Select Committee 1920, para. 669). The focus upon gross indecency between women, by contrast, had the advantage of placing feminists and their supporters in a difficult position. To support the amendment might concede ground to opponents' arguments that young women could themselves be sexually dangerous, undermining the moral basis of the Bill. To oppose it could be construed as upholding a sexual double standard. Accepting either alternative therefore opened supporters to charges of hypocrisy—indeed, Lady Astor would be attacked for voting against it (Neilans 1921a)—while neither was guaranteed to see the Bill progress. The possibility that anyone might argue for full decriminalisation of gross indecency does not seem to have been contemplated, and indeed it went publicly unmentioned although we will see that feminist groups discussed it privately.

Some of the leading women campaigners could have been particularly vulnerable to accusations of hypocrisy. The amendment's proposers might not have been aware how close to home they struck, but would have known of these women's now-suspect spinster status. Neilans had recently set up home with Ethel Margaret Turner, with whom she would live for the rest of her life.[7] Dr Mary Gordon, leading the MWF's work on the Act, would later write a book about the two Ladies of Llangollen, Irish aristocrats who eloped to Wales in 1780 and lived there together for fifty years (Gordon 1937); she also commissioned a memorial plaque from her partner, sculptor Violet Labouchère, which features portraits of herself and Labouchère as the Ladies (Pearson 2004, p. 133). Lady Astor's political secretary Hilda Matheson was a lesbian (Doan 2001, p. 220). It is probable that, as Doan concludes (2001, p. 220), feminists were associated in the House of Commons with inversion; but restricted press coverage which paid little attention to sexology, preferring the longer-standing equation of sex between women with insanity, limited wider damage (Oram 2016, p. 172).

The amendment served its primary purpose of ensuring that the Bill failed for lack of time. It had also made lesbianism briefly visible in the legislature as the focus of open parliamentary debate for the first time in English history, if only to confirm that it should be kept silent. Lesbianism continued to be formulated as secret male knowledge which elite men could choose to share or withhold, leaving little space for women's agency. The debates did reveal that lesbianism was gaining a little cultural legibility—enough to render it controversial if not yet an open threat. However, even among most MPs supporting the amendment, that legibility owed little to the emerging science of sexology which would become prominent at the end of the decade (see Chap. 5). Instead, they attempted to

[7] I am indebted to Julia Laite for this information; she discusses Neilans's relationship in an unpublished forthcoming chapter.

draw upon a discourse which had its roots in the First World War: lesbianism as a danger to home and nation.

Lesbianism and Women's Sexuality

Sex and Danger in the First World War

The 1885 Act had been passed near-simultaneously with the suspension and then repeal of the Contagious Diseases Acts, enacted in the 1860s to address sexually transmitted infections (STIs) in the armed forces by facilitating sex with uninfected prostitutes. Women had borne the whole burden of compulsory medical examination and treatment: a very concrete application of the sexual double standard. The Acts' repeal proved a temporary victory. During the First World War, STIs once again became perceived as an urgent threat to the efficacy of the armed forces, and thus to national survival. Regulation 40D, made under the Defence of the Realm Act 1914, allowed compulsory examination of those accused of infecting a member of the armed forces with an STI but would prove so open to abuse that it was repealed within a year (Lammasniemi 2017, pp. 584–86). However, feminist organisations had not been unified in seeing its danger: Alison Neilans remembered unhappily in 1922 that the National Council of Women had initially supported it (Secretary's Memorandum on Further Work of the AM&SH, 1922, WL 3AMS/A/01/04).

Wartime had made all extra-marital sexuality a matter of national concern, but Noel Pemberton Billing created an aura of particular menace around lesbianism and male homosexuality. He was an independent MP and leader of the right-wing Vigilante Society which published its own journal, the *Vigilante*. Both Society and journal opposed a negotiated peace; alleged there was an international conspiracy of Germans, Jews, and Bolsheviks; and claimed that Germany was promoting moral degeneracy in England as a way to fatally undermine the nation and thus win the war. In particular, Billing published an article alleging that a 'black book' belonging to a 'German prince' had been discovered; inside were the names of 47,000 homosexual Englishmen and women known to (and potentially blackmailed by) the German government. Cultivation of their practices, it fulminated, did not only 'hint at the extermination of the race' and a fall of the British empire parallel to Rome's, but also enabled intelligence to be gathered from highly placed people. It hinted in particular at rumours of lesbianism surrounding the former Prime Minister's wife, Margot Asquith (Medd 2002, pp. 22–23). Thus, in the closing months of the First World War, lesbianism was linked with foreign influence, espionage, and threats to the security of wartime Britain. While Billing was at the fringes of British politics, his journal's association of deviant sexuality with foreignness was not novel and had long been an integral element of the way in which lesbianism was silenced.[8]

In February 1918 an announcement appeared for a private performance of Oscar Wilde's play *Salome* (which the Lord Chamberlain had banned from public performance) starring celebrated modern dancer Maud Allan.[9] She was already well-known for her sensual dancing as Salome, while Wilde remained notorious for his 1895 gross indecency conviction. Allan was also suspect as a North American who had been educated in Germany and trained and performed in Continental Europe. The *Vigilante* could not let this go unremarked, publishing an item under the headline 'The Cult of the Clitoris'. The paragraph concluded, '[i]f Scotland Yard were to seize the list of [audience] members I have no doubt they would secure the names of several thousand of the first 47,000' (quoted in Medd 2002, p. 22). Faced with the accusation that she was a lesbian and a traitor, Allan brought a libel action against Billing which was heard at the Old Bailey (see Bland 2013, chap. 1; Medd 2002; Oram and Turnbull 2001; Cohler 2010, chap. 4; Kettle 1977). After a highly publicised trial, in which the judge's primary concern seemed to be Allan's performance in a costume 'worse than nothing', Billing was found not guilty (TNA HO 45/22792).[10] His defence arguments had included that

---

[8] See previous chapters, notably the discussion of *Woods and Pirie v Cumming Gordon* (Chap. 3) and Mourey (Chap. 4).

[9] Until 1968, plays had to be licensed for public performance by the Lord Chamberlain.

[10] Proceedings for criminal libel were more common than civil claims during this period since under the Libel Act 1843, a defendant would only be acquitted upon proving both the truth of the libel and that publication was for the public benefit.

Allen's very knowledge of the word 'clitoris' implicated her as a lesbian. Billing claimed that 'out of twenty-four people who were shown that libel, including many professional men, only one of them, who happened to be a barrister, understood' (quoted in Kettle 1977, p. 68). Similarly, witness Dr Serrell Cooke suggested that only medical men or 'people interested in that kind of thing' would understand what a clitoris was (quoted in Medd 2002, p. 37). Billing would later back-pedal, arguing that the allegation was of general immorality rather than lesbianism. In response, prosecution counsel Sir Travers Humphreys asserted that the meaning of a 'cult of the clitoris' was obvious but expressed his discomfort at mentioning this female organ in front of 'some ladies in Court' (quoted in Medd 2002, p. 32). This was a vivid illustration both of the extent to which silencing policed women's knowledge about their own sexuality, and of its construction as a field of professional medical and legal knowledge. Like the later parliamentary debates, and to the government's concern (Iglikowski 2019), the case also posed challenges to the policy of silencing. Even though the actual nature of the accusation was not reported in the press since the judge had warned the newspapers that it would be 'indecent' (Medd 2002, p. 45), it would have been an open secret to many in Parliament.[11]

The notion of lesbianism as an immediate threat to the British Empire, already hyperbolic when first articulated, was even more so in 1921. With the dangers of the First World War now in the past, a more subtle argument was made: lesbianism was formulated as a symptom of moral and national degeneracy. Its growth would mark 'the beginning of the nation's downfall' (Macquisten, HC 04/08/1921, cols. 1799–1800), and 'must tend to cause our race to decline' (Wild, HC 04/08/1921, col. 1803). After all, '[t]he falling away of feminine morality was to a large extent the cause of the destruction of the early Grecian civilisation, and still more the cause of the downfall of the Roman Empire' (Macquisten, HC 04/08/1921, cols. 1799–1800). Accounts of lesbianism's danger thus fit within a discourse of immorality as symptom and cause of imperial

[11] For further discussion of press reporting, see Doan (2001, pp. 32–33) and Oram (2016, pp. 171–72). Press reports were obscure and unintelligible for many readers, particularly working-class readers (Oram 2007, p. 57; Bland 1998; Cohler 2010, pp. 140–42).

decline for traditionalists, or the new 'science' of eugenics for the modern and progressive.[12] Relationships between women were a long-term menace to nation and empire, and an immediate threat to the sanctity and security of these elite men's own homes. Those perils might yet be averted by keeping such dangerous knowledge from the ears of their wives and daughters.

The conflation of deviant sexuality and national danger had not dissipated by 1921, then, but had certainly lost its urgency. Almost three years after the Armistice was signed, the national mood had shifted towards social reform and reconstruction. I differ here from Deborah Cohler, who argued that these debates demonstrated a sense of lesbianism as a threat 'of grave nationalist, moral, medical, and legal concern' (2010, pp. 143–48). Importantly, her analysis did not account for this being a spoiling amendment rather than a serious proposal. MPs were, though, exaggerating rather than lying. They really did view lesbianism as a threat to the family and the moral and physical health of the nation, even if not as an immediate danger to its survival. As the Earl of Malmesbury explained in vicious terms, 'nervous conditions following on the war' had increased vice generally but 'these unfortunate specimens of humanity exterminate themselves by the usual process' (HL 15/08/1921, col. 570). Moore-Brabazon similarly asserted that such 'examples of ultra-civilisation ... have the merit of exterminating themselves' (HC 04/08/1921, col. 1805). The lesbian was still a potent menace, but her opponents felt able to play a long game.

New Parallels to Male Homosexuality

The parliamentary debates addressed lesbianism as a discrete phenomenon, but some MPs drew parallels with male homosexuality in order to suggest that the amendment would bring sex equality. The drawing of this parallel depended upon movement away from the heights of

[12] Eugenics advocated scientific breeding for the benefit of the race, and childbearing as the duty of every healthy woman. Its followers came from a wide range of political viewpoints and included sexologist Havelock Ellis and a number of socialist and feminist writers (Weeks 2016, p. 91; Richardson 2003).

nineteenth-century separate spheres ideology towards sexological models. Although used to conservative effect in the House of Commons, and by no means easily accepted by the medical profession in general, these models had a powerful appeal to many feminists. Their more negative implications for the regulation of lesbianism would not become apparent until later in the twentieth century.[13]

The AMSH in particular drew upon sexology to envision a very different model of law reform. Publicly, they were constrained in what they could afford to say. When Neilans quickly drafted a statement on the failure of the Bill, she had to walk a careful tightrope between addressing the issues it had raised, not showing inappropriate knowledge, and being careful not to alienate other members of a coalition which had no agreed view on the amendment's subject-matter. In successfully performing her task, Neilans nonetheless managed to express disapproval of the amendment's substantive content as creating 'a new crime for women of an almost unintelligible and unprovable nature, and one which would offer the most certain opportunities for blackmail of a peculiarly revolting kind' (Memorandum, 18 August 1921, WL 3AMS/A/01/04). The restraint she showed here was less necessary in other contexts. Shortly before the House of Lords debated the amendments, Neilans had written to selected peers including the Law Lords, the UK's most senior judges, on behalf of the AMSH and wider coalition suggesting a need for 'more consideration, as to the value or otherwise of this legislation either in the case of men or women'. She quoted that letter and developed the point in an editorial for *The Shield*, the journal of the AMSH (Neilans 1921a, pp. 203–04):

> The truth is that it is being slowly recognised that these laws provide the most fertile source of blackmail against both normal and abnormal men; that the offences are extremely difficult either to prove or disprove, and that modern scientific opinion is opposed to laws which attempt to punish very severely, not only the vicious pervert, but also the invert who is not really responsible for his psychic abnormality, and in whom the normal

[13] For a discussion of the complex relationship between sexology and feminism see Hall (2004).

development of his sexual life is impossible owing to the congenital misdirection of his instinct.

In other words, Neilans was explicitly arguing not only against the criminalisation of gross indecency between women but also in favour of the decriminalisation of gross indecency between men. The language of 'abnormality' and 'congenital misdirection', which today reads as homophobic, was the progressive vocabulary of the time. ('Vicious pervert' referred to men who engaged in sexual activity with boys or without consent.) Neilans had contact with the sex reform movement and was aware of the work of sexologist Henry Havelock Ellis (Neilans 1921a); two years later she wrote to George Ives, an early campaigner for homosexual law reform, that the aim of the AMSH was to repeal laws since attempts to legislate morality did more harm than good (L. A. Hall 2009, pp. 190–91). In effect, she was advocating a legal approach more liberal than the Wolfenden Report's proposals nearly half a century later (see Chap. 6), and which would not be achieved until the Sexual Offences Act 2003 brought full legal equality for same-sex activity between men.

In 1921 such views were more advanced than most legislators were ready to hear. They remained influenced by the Victorian model where male sexuality was utterly different from female. Male homosexuality was therefore considered to have more in common with non-normative male heterosexuality, both being excessive expressions of the active masculine libido, than with women's passive, relatively desireless sexuality. Thus the amendment was characterised by the House of Lords as 'irrelevant matter' (Bishop of Norwich, HL 15/08/1921, col. 565), 'a great change [in] our Criminal Code' (Earl of Malmesbury, HL 15/08/1921, col. 569), and 'a serious alteration in the Criminal Law … not even within the purview' of the Act to be amended (Earl of Desart, HL 15/08/1921, col. 571)—despite that Act having included the Labouchère amendment. Sexology and its parallels between male and female 'inversion' were not understood, let alone accepted, by most parliamentarians.

Sexology was one of many new specialisations to have emerged in the latter part of the nineteenth century, as medicine became more professionalised. While the sexological concept of female inversion would impinge upon legal discourse later in the 1920s, its influence was neither inevitable nor complete. Nor was inversion a unitary concept, as we will see in Chap. 5: there were significant differences between the leading writers, and between British and European sexologists (see Beccalossi 2011). The concept had developed from Carl Westphal's 1869 article on *conträre Sexualempfindung* ('contrary sexual instinct'), which centred on the case study of a woman with normal genitalia but who had desired women since childhood. Further case studies were collected by other European specialists, who increasingly translated Westphal's *conträre Sexualempfindung* as 'sexual inversion' and focused more on male than female cases. In 1886, Richard von Krafft-Ebing published the first edition of his influential *Psychopathia Sexualis*, a catalogue of case studies of 'perversions' including male and female sexual inversion, which appeared in English translation in 1892 (Krafft-Ebing 1886; Krafft-Ebing and Chaddock 1892). He described the female invert as masculine in dress with a scientific bent, an enthusiasm for 'manly' sports, and little interest in feminine toys or employment (Krafft-Ebing and Chaddock 1892, pp. 279–80). Her condition was not only hereditary but a sign of degeneration, the progressive decline of mental as well as physical health through the generations. The idea of sterility as the final stage of this degeneration did appear in the 1921 parliamentary debates, particularly through the notion of 'self-extermination'; Krafft-Ebing would be one of the two sexologists whom Wild mentioned by name. The other was Henry Havelock Ellis, who disagreed with many of his colleague's ideas and, in particular, did not accept theories of degeneration (Bristow 1998, p. 80; Doan 2001, pp. 139–40).

Ellis and John Addington Symonds's own volume *Sexual Inversion* had been published in 1897 in circumstances which illustrate the difficulties faced by this field. Ellis's usual publisher refused the book for fear it would reach a non-specialist audience, if only the compositors who set it for printing (Grosskurth 1981, p. 180). The homosexual Symonds died before the book appeared, and its first edition was mostly bought up and destroyed by his literary executor (Funke 2013, p. 147; Ellis and Symonds 1897). Symonds's name did not appear on the second edition, from which most of his contributions were removed and which was to be sold only to medical and legal professionals: general readers, including MPs, required a certificate from a doctor or lawyer (Doan 2001, p. 133; Ellis

1897). Even so, the *Lancet* had criticised its publication by a non-specialist publishing house ("Editorial" 1896), and breach of the restrictions by radical bookseller George Bedborough led to his conviction for obscenity offences the following year.[14] The *Lancet* and *British Medical Journal*, although supportive of Ellis as a fellow medical professional, were unconvinced by the book itself.

Chiara Beccalossi points out (2011, p. 18) that there was reluctance to adopt the Continental science of sexology in Britain, where women's same-sex desire had been understood through gynaecology rather than psychology. It was considered a 'vice', a term which also appears repeatedly in the legal and parliamentary discourse of the early 1920s, rather than an innate condition. The interaction between women's genitalia and their psyche had been a theme of nineteenth-century medical and legal discourse, not least in courtroom assumptions that women's unstable reproductive biology with its cycles and excretions unfitted them mentally and physically for participation in the public sphere. While understandings of male homosexuality as a medical issue were a largely twentieth-century development, the concern to manage women's sexuality outside the courts had seen this shift made much earlier for sexually 'immoral' women including lesbians. As we saw in Chap. 3, the Victorian understanding of women's reproductive physiology, sexuality, and mental health as intertwined had meant that sexual 'misconduct' could provoke coercive medical interventions including incarceration in asylums and surgical procedures such as the mid-century use of clitoridectomy.

By the 1870s, as the 'New Woman' became a public figure seeking opportunities for education and employment hitherto denied to women, this vulnerability was presented as a reason to thwart her ambitions (Oppenheim 1991, p. 182). What Showalter identified as 'psychiatric Darwinism' (1987, p. 104) came to the fore, led by figures such as Henry Maudsley. They emphasised heredity and physical causes, with lunacy one of the more advanced forms of degeneracy. The field of psychiatry had thus extended far beyond the asylum and overlapped with gynaecology

[14] The primary purpose of the prosecution seems to have been to destroy the Legitimation League, a 'free love' organisation whose meetings provided a platform for anarchists and of which Bedborough was secretary; he pleaded guilty (Weeks 2000, pp. 27–28; Humpherys 2006, pp. 1–2).

and sexology in its interest in female sexuality. A corresponding shift in the focus of medicalisation from the reproductive system to the brain (not mind) was evident in the 1921 debates. Introducing the amendment, Macquisten called lesbianism 'a matter for medical science and for neurologists' (HC 04/08/1921, col. 1799); for Moore-Brabazon it was 'not … crime at all … [but] abnormalities of the brain' (HC 04/08/1921, col. 1802). Unmarried women were not openly described as 'inverts' but were represented as unhealthy, unnatural, and unfulfilled (Jeffreys 1985; Bland 1995, pp. 171–72).

Lesbianism, then, had long been medicalised to an extent that male homosexuality had not. While there was a more distinct shift from understandings of male homosexuality as a moral and legal issue to a medical one, sexology marked a movement from understandings of lesbianism as a (gynaecological) issue of female sexual purity towards its conceptualisation as a condition parallel to male sexual inversion. The 1921 debates show that following the First World War, this new understanding was moving into legal domains whose appeal to medical authority appeared to indicate a new approach to the old policy of silencing. At the same time, they demonstrate the incoherence and incompleteness of understanding among parliamentarians. When the amendment's proposers drew upon sexology to define lesbianism as a growing problem, they simultaneously ignored the implication that it was not a vice but an innate condition which Krafft-Ebing and Ellis had specifically asserted was unsuited for legal management.

Lesbian Sex

What type of sexual activity did parliamentarians think they were debating? If their speeches were the only evidence, we would have little idea since not one of the MPs or peers ventured any kind of explanation and the meaning of 'gross indecency between females' was never articulated. Existing law could offer little illumination: indecency was an ill-defined concept and the scope of its application to sex between women had hardly been clarified by the 1885 *Mourey* case (Chap. 3). However, there is a clue in two letters not intended for publication, which survive in a file held in The National Archives. The Bishop of Norwich wrote to Sir Claud Schuster, Permanent Secretary to the Lord Chancellor's Office, that if the amendment were to be accepted, 'it would be desirable to extend it to the sale of any implements required for the purposes indicated' since the police might thus bring some successful prosecutions. He saw little likelihood of convictions under the main proposed offence (Bishop of Norwich to Sir Claud Schuster, 11 August 1921, TNA LCO 2/469). Schuster replied agreeing that he saw no prospect of convictions, but conveying the Lord Chancellor's view that any further clause regarding 'prohibition of the sale of instruments' would provoke as much debate as the main clause (Sir Claud Schuster to Bishop of Norwich, 13 August 1921, TNA LCO 2/469). This reluctance to extend the debate was informed by awareness of the tactics being used by the Bill's opponents rather than the substance of the Bishop's proposal. Nonetheless, the letters vividly illustrate the legal and cultural illegibility of sex without penetration. While gross indecency between men carried a maximum two-year sentence, compared to the life sentence for buggery, non-penetrative sex between women was not just uncriminalised but near-inconceivable. The Bishop was not raising the eternal question, 'What do lesbians *do*?' but assuming that he knew precisely what they did: simulation by 'instrument' of penis-in-vagina sex. His understanding and imagination allowed for no possibility of sexual activity without a substitute for the phallus.

Was that a general understanding among legislators? We cannot know because the debates offered no indication of what 'gross indecency' might entail. Some MPs claimed to be able to envisage, if not articulate, more than one possibility: it was 'difficult to recite the various forms of malpractices between women' and 'impossible to recite them in the House' (Wild, HC 04/08/1921, col. 1803). Most speakers took refuge in great vagueness, assuming a common but unarticulated understanding gained by 'the ordinary boy' at 'public school from the classics which he reads about what is known as Lesbian vice' (Wedgwood, HC 04/08/1921, cols. 1800–1801). Some shared a discomforting sense that it might not look too different from female friendship, particularly 'the sort of romantic, almost hysterical, friendships that are made between young women at certain periods of their lives' (Earl of Desart, HL 15/08/1921, cols.

572–573).[15] Others achieved the illusion of greater specificity by focusing upon 'cases' who engaged in this unspecified but deviant activity. By speaking in this way and drawing upon medical discourses, these MPs were involved in the construction of women who had sex with women as pathologised individuals. After the more stringent silencing of the nineteenth century, the 'female invert' was beginning to emerge into legal discourse as an anomalous individual. While her masculinity and social non-conformity may have been reminiscent of eighteenth-century female husbands, her conception as an isolated 'case' differed significantly from the situating of those predecessors within marital and wider community relationships.

Social Change

The 1921 debates have received attention from historians primarily in relation to social attitudes rather than legal regulation, not least because they occurred at a time of significant anxieties about sex roles. After the upheavals of the First World War, there were fears that middle-class women were increasingly rejecting marriage and motherhood in favour of new opportunities. There is a broad consensus among historians that the 1921 debates were informed by these anxieties among elite men, although they have differed as to which particular aspect was of primary concern. Sheila Jeffreys and Deborah Cohler argued, from rather different approaches, that it was the threat to nation and race (Jeffreys 1985, pp. 13–15; Cohler 2010, pp. 143–49); Martin Pugh, in failing to account for the amendment's spoiling purpose, overestimated MPs' commitment to criminalisation (2000, p. 79). Laura Doan considered the possibility that it was a pragmatic strategy to counter the (lesbian-led) Women Police Service (Doan 1997). While that particular suggestion is perhaps not convincing, her broader point about the need to take the social context of the Bill seriously is an important one. It was debated just as some of the most powerful patriarchal institutions—including the police,

[15] Euphemisms predominated, with only Macquisten referring directly to 'homosexual immorality' and Wedgwood referencing 'Lesbian vice' (HC 04/08/1921, cols. 1800 and 1801).

Parliament, and the courts—were being invaded by women; those same women were challenging men's behaviour in the private sphere of family and sexuality.

Social Class and Race

When Labour MP Colonel Wedgwood suggested that his fellow party members who lacked a public school background might also lack understanding of lesbianism, he was tapping into contemporary uncertainties about social class. The First World War had unsettled this as profoundly as it did gender. The Representation of the People Act 1918 is now best remembered for giving some women the vote in general elections, but it also opened the franchise to men who had previously been excluded by property qualifications. The end of the First World War had been followed by popular anger as demobilised soldiers faced unemployment. The Liberal/Conservative Coalition Government headed by David Lloyd George was now enacting a programme of social reform including raising the school leaving age, building social housing, and extending national insurance, as well as opening the professions, the franchise, and parliament itself to women.[16]

The issue of class also underpinned the 1921 debates, as it had those of 1885. The daughters of the wealthy enjoyed greater legal, social, and familial protections. Their working-class peers could be vulnerable both in paid employment, which they entered at a much younger age, and on the streets where their presence was liable to be constructed by police officers and those of higher social class as evidence of immorality. Reformers were explicit about poorer girls' need for legal protection (Neilans 1921b).[17] By contrast, opponents framed the age-of-consent issue as one of (presumptively higher-class) young men being entrapped by calculating (presumptively lower-class) young women. After all, their

[16] Key legislation included the Education Act 1918; Housing and Town Planning Act 1919; Unemployment Insurance Act 1920; Sex Disqualification (Removal) Act 1919; Representation of the People Act 1918; and Parliament (Qualification of Women) Act 1918.

[17] Contemporary understandings of female adolescence also fed into the idea of the mid-teens posing greater sexual risk for working-class girls than their middle-class peers (Oldfield 2001, pp. 68–71).

own daughters were relatively well-protected, so their primary concern was for their sons. Their anxieties were perhaps only exacerbated by Wedgwood's reminder that any easy assumptions about the relative class homogeneity of the House of Commons were increasingly untrue.

Less overtly articulated, but equally unsettling, were issues of race. The black population of Britain had grown during the war as many men from British colonies served as soldiers and sailors, including in the merchant navy (Bland 2005, p. 34). Their increasingly visible presence became a focus for working and middle-class reactions when, during eight months in 1919, white crowds rioted in British port cities including London, Liverpool, and Cardiff. Black people were attacked, property was damaged, and five people were killed. This overt antagonism was a significant break with the pre-war situation.[18] The causes of unrest included racism as well as lack of housing and employment for demobilised service personnel, particularly sailors in the merchant navy who had been replaced during the War by black and Asian sailors (Jenkinson 2007). Yet, significant as it was, the perceived economic threat from black men was not the only one which prompted these attacks. Michael Rowe and Lucy Bland have highlighted the role played by fears around sexual activity between black men and white women (Rowe 2000; Bland 2005).

Concerns around miscegenation began to appear in the press and among the authorities only after the disturbances when explanations were sought; while they were clearly a middle-class concern, their significance on the streets was less clear (Rowe 2000, pp. 57–58; Bland 2005, p. 35). Women were held responsible for these troubling sexual relationships: (morally inferior) black men could not be blamed for accepting their advances; nor could white men be blamed for their violent response to such relationships (Rowe 2000, p. 59; Bland 2005, pp. 33, 36). While no explicit link was drawn during the 1921 debates between miscegenation and lesbianism, the 1919 unrest formed an unspoken backdrop to the overt connections drawn between women's sexual purity and the

[18] Jeffrey Green (2003, pp. 47–48) comments upon the lack of a colour line or overt racial antagonism in nineteenth-century Britain in contrast to the United States. While the most visible members of Britain's ethnic minorities at that time were those who formed part of Queen Victoria's court and, at the other social extreme, foreign sailors, black people had lived in every part of Britain in the nineteenth century (Killingray 2003, p. 51).

interests of empire. In a mirroring of the displacement of anxieties about lesbianism onto women of other nationalities and ethnicities, anxieties about other 'races' were displaced onto white, middle-class lesbians.

Feminist Diversity and Resistance

Parliamentarians were right to see the women's movement as a growing threat to the heteropatriarchal family. Some women continued to deploy their maternal role and the mythology of female sexual innocence strategically to claim a moral basis for their activism. However, by the turn of the twentieth century, feminists were able to identify the power of refusing heterosexual relations in radical terms: Lucy Re-Bartlett claimed that '[i]n the hearts of many women today is rising a cry' that 'I will know no man, and bear no child' until men's apathy towards women's suffering was 'broken through—these wrongs be righted' (quoted in Jeffreys 1984, p. 41). Rather than basing rejection of marriage upon women's supposed desirelessness and capacity for self-sacrifice, such arguments posited spinsterhood as a fulfilling alternative to the bondage of matrimony (Hamilton 1909; Jackson 1984, p. 52; Faderman 1981, p. 237). While women's distinctive social role within the family continued to ground some feminists' activism, then, others drew upon a more critical approach often centred upon demands for sex equality.

As critics of conventional sexual morality, many in the women's movement engaged with the work of the sexologists. While the sexological texts themselves could be far from feminist, their ideas were drawn upon and developed in varied directions. Indeed, the AMSH's opposition to the gross indecency amendment is understandable only in that context since its wider position was to favour sex equality in sexual offences. Its report 'The State and Sexual Morality', published the previous year, had argued for the creation of an offence of unlawful sexual intercourse by a woman with a boy and the inclusion of male victims in the offence of incest (AMSH 1920, p. 20).

Such views were not only somewhat unspeakable among the wider public but were far from universally shared by other women's organisations. That is not to say that there was enthusiasm for legal regulation so much as a lack of formulated policy; in 1885, feminist organisations had largely been neutral or unenthusiastic about the unexpected addition of the Labouchère amendment to the 1885 Act (Brady 2016, p. 87; Walkowitz 1992, p. 278; Weeks 2016, p. 18; Smith 1976, p. 170). The AMSH was unusual in the extent of its focus and expertise upon age-of-consent reform, as well as in its abolitionist approach which opposed legal regulation particularly of prostitution (Laite 2008, pp. 207–08). Improving age-of-consent legislation was one of its three priorities alongside opposing solicitation laws and preventing the trafficking of girls and women for prostitution. Its abolitionist stance had left it unable to support amendments to an earlier version of the 1921 Bill, introduced into Parliament in 1917, which included a clause allowing courts to order the detention of girls under eighteen for various forms of sexual misadventure. While the AMSH recognised that 'the liberty of the subject is at stake', it also realised that many of its allies took a different view or did not appreciate the risks.

Some organisations were closely aligned with the AMSH: NUSEC's aims included an equal moral standard and much of its work on the 1921 Bill was done by Chrystal MacMillan who also sat on the AMSH's executive committee. The WFL, of which Neilans was a former member, had shared AMSH concerns about the equal moral standard and opposed Regulation 40D during the First World War (Newsome 1957, pp. 11–12, 19; Normanton 1921, p. 6). Nonetheless, the WFL's main work after the War seems to have been focused on employment and nationality issues (Newsome 1957, pp. 15–17). For others in the women's movement, the Bill was a minor part of their activities and they lacked specialist knowledge. The NCW was primarily concerned at this period with women's representation in local government (Glick 1995). While it held a conference on the 1921 Bill and passed a resolution supporting it, this was not a central focus of its work. The Medical Women's Federation was principally interested in the spread of sexually transmitted infection. Although its report on the Criminal Law Amendment Bill attacked the double standard since 'protection cannot be had by sweeping up diseased girls … and punishing them by detention', it went on to argue that 'the young are especially dangerous. … They are among the most inveterate communicators of disease' ('Précis on Criminal Law Amendment Bill, Sexual

Offences Bill', 1921, WC SA/MWF/D/3; Cheney 2010, p. 117). Its consequent willingness to accept control measures such as licensing of young people's lodgings differed significantly from the AMSH's approach. As Neilans would summarise in a confidential report in 1922, the AMSH was unique not only in its expertise on the topic and in its politics but also in the 'formulated principles' underpinning its work. These allowed it to exert a 'steadying influence' against the risk that its partners 'might, through lack of information and multiplicity of other interests, support and promote proposals which would lead directly to Neo-Regulation' (Secretary's Memorandum on Further Work of the AM&SH, 1922, WL 3AMS/A/01/04).

Women and Lawmaking

Women, like working-class men, were starting to enter previously closed arenas of public life. The Representation of the People Act 1918 had given the vote to certain women. They had to be over thirty, and either meet a property qualification themselves or through their husband, or be entitled to vote as a university graduate. (Certain universities still returned their own MP to Parliament at this period.) Thus only a minority of women were enfranchised. Counter-intuitively, the Parliament (Qualification of Women) Act of the same year was considerably more expansive, allowing women over 21 to stand as MPs. At the time of the 1921 debates, two had been elected: Constance Markiewicz who, as a Sinn Fein member, did not take her seat and Lady Nancy Astor, Conservative MP for Plymouth Sutton. Astor worked with the AMSH to support this Bill. She had pushed for parliamentary time for the Bill as well as sitting on the Select Committee responsible for its drafting (Nancy Astor, Papers: Moral Hygiene VI, UR MS 1416/1/1/549; Doan 2001, p. 35). However, she did not speak in the debates: although 'prepared to do so if necessary', she had apparently agreed with fellow supporters to 'say as little as possible in order to allow the opposition to state its case' (Neilans 1921c). This tactic, which effectively acknowledged that a speech from her would divert attention from the central issues, reveals much about Astor's position as the sole woman in the House of Commons.

Given that she did not speak even in the amendment debate which threatened the entire Bill, it also highlights the extent to which women were silenced about their own sexuality.

Women were also newly entering the courtroom: the Sex Disqualification (Removal) Act 1919 allowed them to join the legal professions and sit as magistrates and jurors. The first women were already training as solicitors and barristers but would not qualify until the following year; thereafter, their numbers would remain low with many of the barristers in particular either never practising or struggling to make a living in the profession. Lay magistrates were much more quickly recruited, and their value in the traditionally feminine fields of family and juvenile courts recognised, but it would be 1945 before a woman was appointed as a stipendiary magistrate (Polden 1999), 1956 before the first woman was permanently appointed recorder (a part-time judge), and 1972 before a woman presided over an Old Bailey trial (Hale 2009). As for jurors, judges retained the power to order all-male juries and frequently did so for sexual offences trials, particularly those involving homosexuality.

In this context, it is unsurprising that the debates proceeded on the basis that the law and its workings were male terrain. Yet there was an underlying awareness among parliamentarians that that was shifting, surely reinforced by Astor's silent presence in the lower house. Those changes both heightened perceptions of female professional and sexual self-sufficiency as acute and growing threats, and exacerbated uncertainties over how best to regulate them. Silencing remained an attractive strategy since women's mere sexual knowledge was constructed as a direct threat to patriarchal authority—but with women entering the very professions afforded the privilege of knowledge, silencing also looked a little more fragile.

Conclusion

Throughout the parliamentary debates on 'gross indecency between females', no female voice was heard. Lesbianism was carefully constructed as an area of male knowledge to be kept from women themselves. Astor broke her silence only at the moment of the Bill's defeat when her anger was so vocal that she was called to order (*The Times* 1921c). Her moment of being overly audible, and its prompt suppression, could serve as a metaphor for the episode as a whole.

The paradoxical combination of hypervisibility and invisibility was not unique to the 1921 debates. At the 1918 'Cult of the Clitoris' trial, prosecutor Sir Travers Humphreys had both referred directly to 'lesbianism' and reverted to calling it 'the nameless vice between women' (Medd 2002, pp. 32–33). Within a few years, Radclyffe Hall would make a public plea for understanding and toleration of the female 'invert' in her novel *The Well of Loneliness.* That in turn triggered a contradictory response: highly publicised press reporting of the book's content, prompting a highly publicised case aimed at silencing the novel. This paradoxically noisy effort at silencing did achieve some long-term success: after being found obscene, *The Well of Loneliness* remained out of print in Britain for decades. It did not disappear immediately or entirely, though, and its immediate influence would be apparent in the prosecution of a marriage whose lesbian elements were firmly silenced even as they were addressed: that of Victor/Valerie Barker in 1929, explored in the following chapter.

References

Association for Moral and Social Hygiene. 1920. *The State and Sexual Morality.* London: George Allen & Unwin.

Attwood, Rachael. 2015. Stopping the Traffic: The National Vigilance Association and the International Fight against the 'White Slave' Trade (1899–*c.* 1909). *Women's History Review* 24 (3): 325–350. https://doi.org/10.1080/09612025.2014.964064.

Beccalossi, Chiara. 2011. Female Same-Sex Desires: Conceptualizing a Disease in Competing Medical Fields in Nineteenth-Century Europe. *Journal of the History of Medicine and Allied Sciences* 67 (1): 7–35.

Bland, Lucy. 1995. *Banishing the Beast: English Feminism and Sexual Morality 1885–1914.* London: Penguin.

———. 1998. Trial by Sexology? Maud Allan, Salome and the 'Cult of the Clitoris' Case. In *Sexology in Culture: Labelling Bodies and Desires*, ed. Lucy Bland and Laura Doan. Cambridge: Polity Press.

———. 2005. White Women and Men of Colour: Miscegenation Fears in Britain after the Great War. *Gender & History* 17 (1): 29–61.
———. 2013. *Modern Women on Trial: Sexual Transgression in the Age of the Flapper*. Manchester: Manchester University Press.
Brady, Sean. 2016. *Masculinity and Male Homosexuality in Britain, 1861–1913*. https://doi.org/10.1007/978-0-230-27236-1.
Bristow, Joseph. 1998. Symond's History, Ellis's Heredity: Sexual Inversion. In *Sexology in Culture: Labelling Bodies and Desires*, ed. Lucy Bland and Laura Doan, 79–99. Cambridge: Polity Press.
Cheney, Deborah. 2010. Dr Mary Louisa Gordon (1861–1941): A Feminist Approach in Prison. *Feminist Legal Studies* 18 (2): 115–136.
Cohler, Deborah. 2010. *Citizen, Invert, Queer: Lesbianism and War in Early Twentieth-Century Britain*. Minneapolis: University of Minnesota Press.
Cree, Viviene E. 2008. Confronting Sex Trafficking: Lessons from History. *International Social Work*. https://doi.org/10.1177/0020872808095249.
Davenport-Hines, Richard. 1990. *Sex, Death and Punishment: Attitudes to Sex and Sexuality in Britain since the Renaissance*. London: Collins.
Doan, Laura. 1997. Gross Indecency between Women: Policing Lesbians or Policing Lesbian Police. *Social & Legal Studies* 6 (4): 533–551.
———. 1998. 'Acts of Female Indecency': Sexology's Intervention in Legislating Lesbianism. In *Sexology in Culture: Labelling Bodies and Desires*, ed. Lucy Bland and Laura Doan, 199–213. Cambridge: Polity Press.
———. 2001. *Fashioning Sapphism: The Origins of a Modern English Lesbian Culture*. New York: Columbia University Press.
"Editorial." 1896. *Lancet*, no. 19, November: 1344.
Ellis, Henry Havelock. 1897. *Studies in the Psychology of Sex Vol. 1: Sexual Inversion*. The University Press.
Ellis, Henry Havelock, and John Addington Symonds. 1897. *Sexual Inversion*. London: Wilson and Macmillan.
Faderman, Lillian. 1981. *Surpassing the Love of Men: Romantic Friendship and Love Between Women from the Renaissance to the Present*. London: The Women's Press.
Ferris, Paul. 1993. *Sex and the British: A Twentieth-Century History*. London: Michael Joseph.
Funke, Jana. 2013. 'We Cannot Be Greek Now': Age Difference, Corruption of Youth and the Making of *Sexual Inversion*. *English Studies* 94 (2): 139–153. https://doi.org/10.1080/0013838X.2012.760255.
Glick, Daphne. 1995. *The National Council of Women of Great Britain: The First One Hundred Years*. London: The Council.

Gordon, Mary. 1937. *Chase of the Wild Goose*. London: Hogarth Press.
Green, Jeffrey. 2003. Reexamining the Early Years of Samuel Coleridge-Taylor, Composer. In *Black Victorians/Black Victoriana*, ed. Gretchen Holbrook Gerzina, 39–50. New Brunswick, NJ: Rutgers University Press.
Grosskurth, Phyllis. 1981. *Havelock Ellis: A Biography*. London: Quartet Books.
Hale, Brenda. 2009. Heilbron, Dame Rose (1914–2005). In *Oxford Dictionary of National Biography*, ed. L. Goldman. Oxford: Oxford University Press. https://doi.org/10.1093/ref:odnb/96231.
Hall, Lesley A. 1995. 'Disinterested Enthusiasm for Sexual Misconduct': The British Society for the Study of Sex Psychology, 1913–47. *Journal of Contemporary History* 30 (4): 665–686.
———. 2000. *Sex, Gender and Social Change in Britain Since 1880*. Basingstoke: Macmillan Press.
Hall, Lesley. 2004. Hauling Down the Double Standard: Feminism, Social Purity and Sexual Science in Late Nineteenth-Century Britain. *Gender & History* 16 (1): 36–56.
Hall, Lesley A. 2009. Suffrage, Sex and Science. In *The Women's Suffrage Movement: New Feminist Perspectives*, ed. Maroula Joannou and June Purvis, 188–200. Manchester: Manchester University Press.
Hamilton, Cicely. 1909. *Marriage as a Trade*. London: Chapman & Hall.
Humpherys, Anne. 2006. The Journals That Did: Writing about Sex in the Late 1890s. *19: Interdisciplinary Studies in the Long Nineteenth Century*, no. 3 (Oct.). https://doi.org/10.16995/ntn.450.
Iglikowski, Vicky. 2019. Maud Allan and 'Unnatural Practices among Women.' *National Archives Blog*. https://blog.nationalarchives.gov.uk/blog/lgbtq-history-maud-allan-unnatural-practices-women/.
Jackson, Margaret. 1984. Sexology and the Social Construction of Male Sexuality. In *The Sexuality Papers: Male Sexuality and the Social Control of Women*, ed. L. Coveney, M. Jackson, S. Jeffreys, L. Kaye, and P. Mahony, 45–66. London: Hutchinson.
Jeffreys, Sheila. 1984. "Free from All Uninvited Touch of Man": Women's Campaigns around Sexuality, 1880–1914. In *The Sexuality Papers: Male Sexuality and the Social Control of Women*, ed. L. Coveney, M. Jackson, S. Jeffreys, L. Kaye, and P. Mahony, 22–44. London: Hutchinson.
———. 1985. *The Spinster and Her Enemies: Feminism and Sexuality 1880–1930*. Melbourne: Spinifex.
Jenkinson, Jacqueline. 2007. Race' Riots, 1919. In *The Oxford Companion to Black British History*, ed. David Dabydeen, John Gilmore, and Cecily Jones. Oxford: Oxford University Press.

Joint Select Committee. 1920. Report by the Joint Select Committee of the House of Lords and the House of Commons on the Criminal Law Amendment Bill [H.L.], the Criminal Law Amendment (No. 2) Bill [H.L.], and the Sexual Offences Bill [H.L.]. London.

Kettle, Michael. 1977. *Salome's Last Veil: The Libel Case of the Century*. London: Granada Publishing.

Killingray, David. 2003. Tracing Peoples of African Origin and Descent in Victorian Kent. In *Black Victorians/Black Victoriana*, ed. Gretchen Holbrook Gerzina, 51–67. New Brunswick, NJ: Rutgers University Press.

Krafft-Ebing, Richard von. 1886. *Psychopathia Sexualis: Eine Klinische-Forensische Studie*. Stuttgart: Enke.

Krafft-Ebing, Richard von, and C.G. Chaddock. 1892. *Psychopathia Sexualis: Translation of the Seventh German Edition*. London: F. A. Davis Co.

Laite, Julia. 2008. The Association for Moral and Social Hygiene: Abolitionism and Prostitution Law in Britain (1915–1959). *Women's History Review* 17 (2): 207–223.

Lammasniemi, Laura. 2017. Regulation 40D: Punishing Promiscuity on the Home Front during the First World War. *Women's History Review* 26 (4): 584–596. https://doi.org/10.1080/09612025.2016.1148506.

Medd, Jodie. 2002. 'The Cult of the Clitoris': Anatomy of a National Scandal. *Modernism/Modernity* 9 (1): 21–49. https://doi.org/10.1353/mod.2002.0015.

Neilans, Alison. 1921a. Editorial. *The Shield*.

———. 1921b. Editorial. *The Shield*, 115–16.

———. 1921c. Editorial. *The Shield*, 155.

Newsome, Stella. 1957. *Women's Freedom League, 1907–1957*. London: Women's Freedom League.

Normanton, Helena. 1921. *The Work for Women M.P.s*. London: Women's Freedom League.

Oldfield, Carolyn. 2001. *Growing up Good? Medical, Social Hygiene and Youth Work Perspectives on Young Women, 1918–1939*. University of Warwick.

Oppenheim, Janet. 1991. *"Shattered Nerves": Doctors, Patients and Depression in Victorian England*. Oxford: Oxford University Press.

Oram, Alison. 2007. *Her Husband Was a Woman! Women's Gender-Crossing in Modern British Popular Culture*. London: Routledge.

———. 2016. 'A Sudden Orgy of Decadence': Writing about Sex between Women in the Interwar Popular Press. In *Sapphic Modernities: Sexuality, Women, and National Culture*, ed. Laura Doan and Jane Garrity, 165–180. London: Palgrave Macmillan.

Oram, Alison, and Annmarie Turnbull. 2001. *The Lesbian History Sourcebook: Love and Sex between Women in Britain from 1780 to 1970*. London: Routledge.

Pearson, Lynne F. 2004. *Discovering Famous Graves*. Princes Risborough.

Polden, Patrick. 1999. The Lady of Tower Bridge: Sybil Campbell, England's First Woman Judge. *Women's History Review* 8 (3): 505–526. https://doi.org/10.1080/09612029900200218.

Pugh, Martin. 2000. *Women and the Women's Movement in Britain*. 2nd ed. London: Macmillan Press Ltd.

Richardson, Angelique. 2003. *Love and Eugenics in the Late Nineteenth Century: Rational Reproduction and the New Woman*. Oxford: Oxford University Press.

Rowe, Michael. 2000. Sex, 'Race' and Riot in Liverpool, 1919. *Immigrants & Minorities* 19 (2): 53–70. https://doi.org/10.1080/02619288.2000.9974991.

Showalter, Elaine. 1987. *The Female Malady: Women, Madness and English Culture, 1830–1980*. London: Virago.

Smart, Carol. 2000. Reconsidering the Recent History of Child Sexual Abuse, 1910–1960. *Journal of Social Policy* 29 (1): 55–71.

Smith, F.B. 1976. Labouchere's Amendment to the Criminal Law Amendment Bill. *Historical Studies* 17: 165–173.

The Times. 1921a. House of Commons, May 13.

———. 1921b. Age of Consent, July 16.

———. 1921c. The Criminal Law Amendment Bill, August 18.

Upchurch, Charles. 2009. *Before Wilde: Sex between Men in Britain's Age of Reform*. Berkeley, CA: University of California Press.

Waites, Matthew. 2002. Inventing a 'Lesbian Age of Consent'? The History of the Minimum Age for Sex between Women in the UK. *Social & Legal Studies* 11 (3): 323–342.

Walkowitz, Judith R. 1992. *City of Dreadful Delight: Narratives of Sexual Danger in Late-Victorian London*. London: Virago.

Weeks, Jeffrey. 2000. *Making Sexual History*. Cambridge: Polity Press.

———. 2016. *Coming Out: Homosexual Politics in Britain from the Nineteenth Century to the Present*. 3rd ed. London: Quartet Books.

5

Victor/Valerie Barker: Sexology and Challenges to Silencing

By the early 1920s, several developing themes in the legal regulation of lesbianism were apparent. Sexual offences legislation was established as a distinct body of law which encompassed certain sexual acts between females, while criminal prosecution had been professionalised as a function of the state. Attention to indecent assault and the age of consent coincided with an absence of reported female husband prosecutions.[1] The House of Lords' clear rejection of the criminalisation of 'gross indecency between females' in 1921 had confirmed silencing as the criminal law's overarching approach (Chap. 4). Meanwhile, sexology's growing status as a specialism was not necessarily inconsistent with the Victorian understanding of women's sexuality as a matter for medical rather than judicial regulation (Chaps. 3 and 4). In those contexts, the 1929 prosecution of a 'female husband' for a non-sexual offence, in a case with strong echoes of both historical trials and the newly described 'congenital invert', seemed to mark an abrupt change of direction. This chapter will explore how and to what extent that was the case.

[1] For earlier female husband prosecutions, see Chaps. 2 and 3.

C. Derry, *Lesbianism and the Criminal Law*,
https://doi.org/10.1007/978-3-030-35300-1_5

The legal basis and cultural background of the Victor/Valerie Barker prosecution were inevitably very different to those of past centuries.[2] The broader context of the case included growing anxiety about 'morbid' relationships between women where friendship might spill over into 'unhealthy' passion. This itself was a manifestation of wider concerns about single women. While the loss of life in the First World War might have created sympathy for women who had apparently lost their chance of marriage as a result, the unsettling effects of women's war work and their post-war gains in legal and economic independence made the unmarried woman an object of social concern.

The Barker case's immediate precursors were women's enfranchisement on equal terms with men under the Representation of the People (Equal Franchise) Act 1928 and the obscenity case against *The Well of Loneliness*. Radclyffe Hall, a novelist of some renown, had drawn upon sexological theories of congenital inversion in this latest work (R. Hall 1928).[3] Its protagonist Stephen Gordon was a masculine lesbian and war hero who acted nobly and self-sacrificingly before ending the novel with a plea for her and her fellow inverts' right to exist.[4] Initial reviews were generally favourable, but the prosecution was prompted by a later, furious—and circulation-boosting—review in the *Daily Express* whose editor James Douglas referred to both 'inversion and perversion' as he claimed that he 'would rather give a healthy boy or a healthy girl a phial of prussic acid than this novel' (Douglas 1928). The Home Secretary, the puritanical Joynson Hix, gave his view that the book should be withdrawn; the publishers agreed to do so but took casts of the type to Paris. When copies printed in France were seized by Customs, legal proceedings were brought

[2] Barker was born Lillias Irma Valerie Barker and changed surname to Arkell Smith on her marriage in 1918. As a woman, Barker was known as Valerie; as a man, Victor Barker although he would later use the names John Hill (*Daily Express* 1934) and James Hunt (Vernon 2000, p. 44). For clarity, 'Barker' is used throughout this chapter. As elsewhere in the book, I use 'he' or 'she' according to whether Barker was presenting as a man or woman; this also reflects the force or even excess with which Barker claimed each identity at different times, as discussed further below.

[3] The foreword was written by Henry Havelock Ellis, while Hall also referred in the text to Richard von Krafft-Ebing and Karl Heinrich Ulrichs and drew upon the work of Edward Carpenter (Doan 2001, chap. 5).

[4] Although *The Well of Loneliness* is generally read as a lesbian novel, that interpretation is not universal: Prosser (2001) argues for a trans reading while Costello (2018) suggests that it is a novel of 'sexual indeterminacy'.

before Bow Street Magistrates' Court (Derry 2018, p. 207). While there was no explicit sexual content in the novel, the courts found it obscene precisely because it argued for toleration rather than condemnation. Although the legal response reflected a clear wish to enforce silence upon the subject, damage had been done: the trial was widely if obliquely reported, and the subject thus carried into the nation's homes (Souhami 1998). Both the *Well of Loneliness* and Barker prosecutions drew more or less overtly upon sexological understandings of 'female inversion'. Indeed, Barker's trial judge was none other than Sir Ernest Wild, the only parliamentarian to refer to sexologists by name in the 1921 debates. However, the Barker case functioned in many ways as a repudiation of sexology by both the legal system and the parties to the relationship, and this brief surge in lesbian visibility was soon followed by a surprisingly successful reimposition of legal silence.

Victor/Valerie Barker

Valerie Barker had been born into an upper-middle-class family in Jersey in August 1895.[5] In April 1918, she married Australian Lieutenant Harold Arkell Smith, but by 1919 she had fallen in love with his countryman Ernest Pearce Crouch. She stayed with Crouch when Arkell Smith returned to Australia, living as his wife although they never legally married. They moved to Paris and then Sussex, and had two children, but Crouch was violent and Barker left him to live as a man. Barker would later tell the press that this was both because men's clothes were more comfortable for work, and because she 'felt that as a woman [she] was helpless' (*The Leader* 1937, p. 7).

Barker was joined by a close friend, Elfrida Haward, who had previously known him as Valerie. He told Haward's parents that he was a man who had impersonated a woman following a war injury, and Haward would later maintain that she herself believed this ("Col. Barker" 1929,

[5] The Barker case papers, including press cuttings, and prison file are in The National Archives (TNA) MEPO 3/439, HO 144/19128, and TNA PCOM 9/272; there is also a fairly extensive secondary literature (e.g. Collis 2001; Jennings 2007, pp. 127–29; Vernon 2000).

p. 2). Although the two posed as fiancés, Haward's parents put pressure on them to marry for the sake of propriety. They did so in a Brighton church on 14 November 1923. What happened next would be a matter of public dispute: Barker insisted that they had a purely platonic friendship ("Col. Barker" 1929, p. 5; *Sunday Dispatch* 1929b), while Haward claimed that their honeymoon (and by implication sex life) 'was a perfectly normal one' (*Sunday Express* 1929, p. 3). In a police interview, she explicitly alleged that sexual intercourse took place during the honeymoon by what she now believed were 'artificial means' (Walter Burmby, Central Officers' Special Report, 1929, PRO MEPO 3/439).

Following the marriage, Barker moved between towns and jobs including acting in Brighton and London, conducting an antique furniture business in Andover, and working as secretary to Colonel Seymour, president of the anti-Semitic National Fascisti Movement (Burmby, MEPO 3/439, pp. 2–3; Pugh 2005, p. 53). Barker claimed to be an ex-soldier who had been awarded the Distinguished Service Order (DSO), and was active in the Movement, teaching boxing and physically fighting communists. He came close to discovery in July 1927 when he and his employer were charged with firearms offences. Having admitted to using a false name, but claimed that there were family reasons for withholding his true identity, Barker strangely attended court with bandages over his eyes claiming temporary blindness as a result of a war wound (J. Partridge to Under Secretary of State, War Office, 20 August 1927, PRO MEPO 3/439; Insp. Briddon, Report, 1927, PRO MEPO 3/439). He was acquitted and although ongoing police inquiries uncovered rumours that he was a woman, these went unproved. Barker and Haward had separated by this time.

Barker's sex was finally discovered in consequence of his next employment. He bought a café in Litchfield Street off Charing Cross Road, London, from Edith Roper Johnson. When the café proved unsuccessful, Barker abandoned it without leaving a forwarding address and went to work as a reception clerk at the Regent Palace Hotel. Johnson brought bankruptcy proceedings in respect of outstanding payments, but the court documents were sent to the empty café and Barker thus failed to attend court as ordered. He was arrested and imprisoned in HMP Brixton for contempt of court. Almost as soon as he arrived there on 28 February

1929, his anatomical sex was discovered by the medical officer. Barker was taken to a room in the prison's Hospital and '[a]s soon as it was apparent that she was a female arrangements were made for her immediate transfer to Holloway Prison' (Minutes to Head Office, 1 March 1929, PRO PCOM 9/272). Very quickly, details of Barker's past life were obtained including her marriage to Haward (R Morton, statement, 1929, PRO PCOM 9/272). Barker was charged with two perjury offences: the first for making a false entry in the marriage register and the second in respect of an affidavit sworn in the name of Victor Barker (Burmby 1929; Information laid 15 March 1929, PRO MEPO 3/439). By the time the case came to court, both Barker and Haward had already given their versions of events to the newspapers (*Sunday Express* 1929; *Sunday Dispatch* 1929a).

When Barker appeared at the Old Bailey there was no trial, as a plea of guilty on the charge relating to the marriage was accepted, but there was a sentencing hearing. The prosecutor, Percival Clarke, had also prosecuted in the firearms case when, he now admitted, he had not suspected Barker's sex. He seems to have placed little emphasis upon the sexual undertones to the case. Rather, for him, its aggravating feature was the use of a church: 'If she wanted to marry another woman she could have done that in a Register Office, but there is no justification, it is suggested, for her abusing the Church for the purpose' (*Evening Standard* 1929).

The judge, Sir Ernest Wild, appeared in Chap. 4 as one of the MPs proposing a 1921 amendment to criminalise 'gross indecency between females'. In the ensuing debate, he had argued that lesbianism, 'a very prevalent practice', 'saps the fundamental institutions of our society' and leads to childlessness, debauchery, neurasthenia and insanity (HC 04/08/1921, cols. 1803–1804). The following year, he had become Recorder of London (the senior judge at the Old Bailey) in which role he now heard Barker's case. Wild chose to take witness evidence from Dr Brisby of Brixton Prison and Elfrida Haward before passing sentence, and while questioning Haward, he raised the legally irrelevant question of whether there had been a sexual relationship (Burmby, 1929, PRO MEPO 3/439; 1929d; see further Collis 2001). Concerned that the press and public should not hear her answers, he adopted a procedure whereby passages of her statement were indicated and she confirmed or denied them. Her somewhat contradictory account was that Barker had told her he was incapable of sexual intercourse following a war injury but had had 'perfectly normal' sexual relations with her during the honeymoon (Burmby 1929, PRO MEPO 4/439 pp. 1–2). On 15 April 1929, Barker was sentenced to nine months' imprisonment. Although Wild was at pains to stress that he was sentencing only for the perjury, he clearly saw the taint of perversion throughout. Thus the publicity around the case was 'part of the punishment of [Barker's] perverted conduct' which had 'profaned the House of God … outraged the decencies of nature, and … broken the laws of man' (*Evening News* 1929).

The Rise of Sexology and the Female Invert

Wild's assertions of perversion owed little to sexology, which had emerged as a discipline in the second half of the nineteenth century. Originally an import from Continental Europe, it developed a specifically British strand by the end of the century with the publication of Henry Havelock Ellis's *Sexual Inversion* (1897).[6] That book introduced the congenital female invert into the British scientific literature. She was not identical with the lesbian but something closer to a composite of lesbian and trans identities: masculine in physiology, character, and appearance as well as exclusively sexually attracted to women. Nonetheless, the invert and the lesbian overlapped significantly in the sexological literature, and perhaps even more significantly in legal discourse.

The latter was influenced by, but never engaged deeply or systematically with, sexology. Instead, it took most notice of those elements which chimed with wider legal and cultural understandings of female sexuality while largely disregarding those which did not. The result was a rather uneven importation of sexological ideas into criminal justice. Notably, the longstanding assumption that someone with female physiology living as a man was unproblematically a woman in disguise was not unsettled

[6] This was not the only British sexological work, or approach (e.g. see Carpenter 1908), but it was the most influential, including in the legal context. When the *Justice of the Peace* commented on the field in 1938, it compared Ellis's work favourably with the 'pseudo-Latin scientific jargon' emanating from Germany (Vernon 2000, p. 45).

by legal interpretations of the sexological literature. Rather, the sense that there was something perverse about female husbands was converted from a suspicion into a certainty, as evident in Barker's treatment. However, the corresponding certainty that these were perverted *women* seems to have remained intact.

We saw in Chap. 4 that *Sexual Inversion* had been labelled obscene after radical bookseller George Bedborough made it available to buyers outside the medical and legal professions. Nonetheless, sexology was read by some laypeople who would identify personally with its description of the 'invert', as well as radical thinkers on sex and sexuality including many in the feminist movement. Indeed, it was more thoughtfully engaged with in those circles than legal ones, despite the latter's apparently privileged access and sexologists' desire to influence the legal climate. Part of Ellis and his original collaborator John Addington Symonds's purpose was to provide scientific support for homosexuality as a congenital condition of medical rather than criminal concern (Somerville 1998, p. 63). Some of the political negotiations involved were self-conscious: the emphasis upon sexual inversion as an innate condition, and the move away from using the ancient Greeks' socially endorsed relationships between men and teenage boys as a cultural precedent, were responses to late nineteenth-century concerns about sexual exploitation and corruption (see Chap. 3; Funke 2013).[7]

Sexology was just one of several discourses around sexuality at this period. In particular, as Britain's imperial identity had strengthened in the nineteenth century, claims for British moral authority were made on a number of fronts extending from religious and cultural 'superiority' to scientific racism. Anxieties about a sufficient supply of fit and healthy men for the armed forces helped focus attention upon the national interest in childbearing and childrearing, expressed in scientific and medical theories around evolutionary biology, race, and eugenics (Cohler 2010, pp. 75–78). These in turn overlapped with, informed, and were informed by sexology: Ellis's sexology, for example, was suffused with his support for eugenics (Somerville 1998, p. 68). Women's maternal role, and thus

[7] This approach can be contrasted with Symonds' appeal to the Hellenic past in *A Problem of Greek Ethics* eleven years earlier (Symonds 1883).

their sexual behaviour, was not a purely private issue but one of vital importance to the future of the nation and race. For eugenicists, suitable women were under an obligation to have children; conversely, the 'excessive' fertility of the unfit was a problem to be addressed. Respectable, heterosexual, white, middle-class mothers were both norm and ideal; those outside, including lesbians, were a risk to the future of the race. This anxiety about sexuality, race, and miscegenation was implicit in much eugenic and evolutionary discourse around reproduction. While the scale of deaths in the First World War and subsequent influenza epidemic would exacerbate those concerns, they were already acute due to a drop in the birth rate at the turn of the century (Cohler 2010, p. 75). In contrast to the United States of America, where the homicidal lesbian was discursively distinct from the black rapist (Duggan 2000, p. 3), the threats posed by racial and sexual otherness were elided, and combined with female criminality, in the writings of Ellis.

Criminality and Female Inversion

Seven years before *Sexual Inversion* appeared, Ellis had published *The Criminal*. Like Cesare Lombroso, the 'father of criminology', Ellis devoted attention to female offenders and made an association between criminality and masculinity. This association was not in itself a novel one, as Ellis illustrated using supposed popular sayings: 'Salute from afar the beardless man and the bearded woman' (1890, p. 63). What was new was its sheen of scientific credibility. Ellis also made a further contribution: his stereotype of the lesbian was remarkably similar to that of his and Lombroso's female criminals (a similarity all the more remarkable since Lombroso's research subjects were working-class criminal and prostitute women, while Ellis's female inverts were primarily middle-class, including his own wife Edith Lees). In essence, both the born female criminal and the born female invert were portrayed as half-male, with all the bad points and none of the charms of conventional femininity. It may not have been entirely accidental that they thereby coincided with popular images of feminists as defective women who lacked proper feminine and maternal instincts.

Lombroso and Ellis exhaustively catalogued the physical characteristics of deviant women. Their interest stemmed from the idea of deviancy as congenital: if this affliction was present from birth, it ought to manifest itself in some identifiable way in the body. Their descriptions reflected as well as reinforced their belief that both lesbians and female criminals were not fully women, but part-male. Such attitudes had a long history; the notion of the lesbian as genitally half-man—in the terms of the age, a hermaphrodite—or as having a penis-like enlarged clitoris had enjoyed currency in the seventeenth and early-eighteenth century (Peakman 2004, pp. 174–78; Chap. 3; Donoghue 1993) and Victorian gynaecologists had continued to associate same-sex activity with clitoral size (Beccalossi 2011, p. 21). However, the deviant woman's masculinity was now systemic. She had a masculine appearance (Lombroso and Ferrero (1895) 1959, p. 99; Ellis 1933, p. 199), with both criminal and inverted women showing 'abundance of hair' or 'hypertrichosis' (Ellis 1890, p. 73, 1933, p. 200), as well as a masculine voice (Ellis 1890, p. 63, 1933, p. 200). She moved in a masculine way: the criminal's 'singular agility and force' and enthusiasm for exercise (Lombroso and Ferrero (1895) 1959, pp. 130–31) were matched by the firm muscles and energetic movements of the inverted woman (Ellis 1897, p. 97). Both were physically and sexually precocious (Ellis 1890, p. 144, 1933, p. 199). That masculinity of body was liable to be enhanced by masculine or male clothing (Lombroso and Ferrero (1895) 1959, p. 187; Ellis 1897, p. 95) and by smoking tobacco (Ellis 1890, p. 120, 1897, p. 97), a significant habit because other authors associated it with menstrual disturbance and sexual delinquency (Talbot 1898, pp. 112–14; and see further Tinkler 2016).

Deviant women's self-sufficiency was unappealing, in both senses of the word, to all but the most effeminate men. Ellis regretted the invert's unattractive lack of shyness and dependence (1897, p. 98). Her repulsion towards men was 'instinctively reciprocated' (Ellis 1897, p. 88). That elision of women's independence with female deviance was not new. In 1876, crime historian Luke Owen Pike had posited similar views, although treating independence as cause and deviancy as effect (1876, p. 527):

> in proportion as [women] have rendered themselves independent of men for their subsistence, they have thrown off the protection against competi-

> tion and temptation which dependence on men implies. It follows that, so far as crime is determined by external circumstances, every step made by woman towards her independence is a step towards that precipice at the bottom of which lies a prison.

Given the alarming autonomy of the female deviant, it was no doubt a great reassurance to Lombroso, Ellis, and their male readers that the born deviant was a rarity (Lombroso and Ferrero (1895) 1959, p. 110; Ellis 1933, p. 190). Just as the female husband trials of the past had carefully glossed over any complicity on the part of the wife, she could now be understood as a pseudo-invert amenable to heterosexual recuperation. Ellis emphasised that the pseudo-invert was susceptible to seduction rather than congenitally inverted: her homosexuality, like her 'sexual impulses', was 'only slightly marked' (1897, p. 87). These women 'of strongly affectionate nature' were not truly independent of men and did not reject them; their attachment to other women was not sexual and they needed only male guidance to be reformed. Conveniently, if a man wanted to reform a woman she was by definition too attractive to be a congenital case, leaving just a small minority of inverts beyond male control.

Allied to this, however, was another message which could be used to undermine women's independence. Pseudo-inverts, with their weakness for the true invert's advances, were most likely to develop into homosexuals in single-sex institutions such as colleges, women's clubs and societies, and settlement houses: all those most associated with the New Woman of the time (Smith-Rosenberg 1986, pp. 266–67). Ellis also quoted Thomas Laycock's argument that inversion was especially common among women working outside the domestic setting, in hotels, shops, and so on (Gibson 1997, p. 120). In other words, the notion of lesbianism as a form of corruption survived intact but was aligned with the social and political concerns of the day.

Given the striking similarities between these definitions of the true lesbian and the criminal woman, it is unsurprising that Ellis himself linked the two genres of female deviancy. Thus, while he was eager to emphasise the high number of male inverts who had artistic talent or high intellect, among women it was prostitutes and criminals who had 'an undue tendency to homosexuality ... and, to a much less extent, among persons of genius and intellect' (1897, p. 102). Indeed, the movement for female emancipation

> has involved an increase in feminine criminality and in feminine insanity, which are being elevated towards the masculine standard. In connection with these we can scarcely be surprised to find an increase in homosexuality which has always been regarded as belonging to an allied, if not the same, group of phenomena. (Ellis 1897, p. 100)

The linking of feminism, inversion, and criminality in women was made even more explicit in a lengthy footnote which stated that 'a considerable proportion of the number of cases in which inversion has led to crimes of violence, or otherwise acquired medico-legal importance, has been among women' (pp. 78–79).

If the invert could serve as a focus for anxieties about women's liberation, she could do the same for anxieties about empire, nation, and race. Thus *Sexual Inversion* devoted a passage to inter-racial lesbian relationships consistent, as Siobhan B Somerville explains, with its focus upon 'somatic differences' (Somerville 1998, p. 63). Discussing relationships between black and white women, Ellis concluded that these were a result of 'the imperative need for a certain sexual opposition' (1897, p. 120). This notion served to construct black lesbians as 'other', explicitly placed in opposition to white lesbians, and again he made a clear association with criminality (1897, pp. 78–79):

> I am told that in American prisons for women Lesbian relationships are specially frequent between white and black women. A Dr. Kiernan informs me that 'of the three murders from perverted sexual jealousy by women in the United States in two decades, one was a negress's; and of four similar attempts to kill, two were [?by] negresses'.[8]

In the 1915 edition of *Sexual Inversion*, Ellis extended his consideration of American cases (Duggan 2000, pp. 174–75), discussing the 'Tiller Sisters' and another murder case which concerned two Russian 'girls'. In

---

[8] Dr Kiernan, Ellis's informant, was '[t]he most prolific and influential U.S. sexologist, James G. Kiernan' who had 'a particular interest in female sexual inverts' (Duggan 2000, pp. 172–73).

three of four cases it was made clear that the violent woman was the 'congenital invert' in the partnership. The careful detailing of racial backgrounds, even to the fastidious description of the Tiller Sisters as quintroons (i.e. with one black great-great-grandparent and fifteen white ones ("Quintroon, N." 2019)), and the identification of the violent partner as a 'congenital invert', tied together lesbianism, masculinity, racial otherness, and violence.

These theories developed in tandem with another nineteenth-century invention, the science of race (Stepan 1982, p. 1). Both fields shared a focus on cataloguing bodily features, and a particular fascination with women's sexual characteristics (Stepan 1982, p. 66). As Judith Raiskin explains (1994, p. 157), nineteenth and twentieth-century scientists used racial hierarchies as a template for the assertion of gender and class hierarchies, Indeed, in the British context, class was particularly important as a focus for eugenic concerns, with anti-Semitism also a significant feature (Richardson 2003, p. 3; Gibson 1997, p. 120; Stepan 1982, p. 126; Pugh 2005, pp. 13–14). Such ideas made relationships between white and black women particularly shocking, mingling as they did sexual degeneracy, undesirable racial mixtures, and the highly visible rejection by white women of their proper (breeding) role in perpetuating the superior English race. Ellis may not have accepted theories of degeneracy, but his work showed a similar fascination with congenital and hereditary features which constructed the female invert as physically, psychologically, racially, and criminally deviant.

Sexology in Legal and Popular Understanding

Sexual Inversion was over thirty years old when Barker appeared before the Central Criminal Court. While the book's availability had been limited, it had come to the attention of a number of people who identified as 'inverts'—not least through the legal proceedings against it. They contacted Ellis and other sexologists (Bland 1995, p. 263); their stories in turn often became 'case studies' for later editions.[9] Ellis was also part of a

[9] Krafft-Ebing in particular significantly expanded later editions of his *Psychopathia Sexualis* in this way, and to some extent changed his own views (Weeks 2001, p. 501).

diverse movement which by the late 1920s included socialists, feminists, psychoanalysts, and a wide range of medical professionals as well as sexologists. Its adherents' views varied significantly on issues including homosexuality and eugenics. Broadly, the British Society for the Study of Sex Psychology (BSSSP) advocated sexual freedom including homosexual rights while the World League for Sexual Reform (WLSR), which was also active in Britain, took a more conservative approach but favoured medicalisation rather than criminalisation. However, there were substantial differences within each organisation (Crozier 2003) as well as considerable crossover between their membership; Ellis himself was a president of the WLSR and allowed his papers to be read at BSSSP meetings.

Nonetheless, this movement for sex reform was a radical rather than mainstream one and small in numbers (L. Hall 2004, p. 37). It engaged a relatively limited group of people drawn mainly from the educated middle classes. Diffusion of its ideas was not only uncertain in extent but also a complex process which Doan characterises as one of knowledge production rather than top-down dissemination (2019, pp. 309–11). General works such as Marie Stopes's best-selling *Married Love* (1918) had introduced some of its ideas on heterosexual relationships to a broader public, but there was no equivalent diffusion of those on less conventional relationships or identities. Wider public awareness, let alone understanding, of lesbianism was much slower to develop. Even the legal profession, which had more access to sexological works, seemed little influenced by them. Although Wild was aware of sexology, his remarks on sentencing Barker hardly reflected it. Similarly, newspapers emphasised Barker's case as a curiosity, even if a potentially disturbing one, and largely ignored the suggestion of sexual transgression (Oram 2016, p. 175) in favour of treating Barker's life as a romantic masquerade (Vernon 2000, pp. 49–50). Popular responses continued to be diverse and not always unfavourable, as encapsulated by an anecdote in the autobiography of Diana Mosley, a fellow fascist activist and wife of British Union of Fascists leader Sir Oswald Mosley. She recalled being considered 'very lucky' to visit Bailiffscourt, Barker's 'hallowed' former home; but once there, discovered that Barker's name was 'taboo' to the new owner, who 'preferred to forget that she had ever existed' (Mosley 1977, p. 61).

Legal narratives, though superficially more direct in confronting the sexual element of this and the *Well of Loneliness* cases, were paradoxically even more conservative in resisting the abandonment of silencing, as is apparent in the banning of *The Well* and the way in which Haward's courtroom testimony was obtained. But what sexological discourse did the courts seek to silence? Barker and Hall may have evoked the congenital invert, but it was not necessarily this figure who preoccupied their peers. Lesley Hall has argued that this period saw a rather different concern around women's relationships: their identification as morbidly hyper-feminine. The emphasis, rooted in popular psychology, was not on the sexual component which might or might not exist in a relationship but upon its irrational and overly emotional nature. For those in the women's movement at least, these morbid relationships could be contrasted with more moderate and sustaining friendships between women (L. Hall 2016, pp. 129–33). Anxiety about feminine, rather than masculine, excess in women's relationships was not incompatible with sexological concepts. First, psychology and sexology were not in opposition; indeed, sexology considered itself to fall at least partly within psychology. Second, this hyper-feminine woman was Ellis's pseudo-invert, pushed by a mixture of inclination and circumstance into a same-sex relationship. That we now pay more attention to the congenital invert and rather neglect her counterpart is a relic of the relative visibility of Barker and *The Well of Loneliness*, the enduring popular fascination with female husbands, and the later cultural association between masculinity and lesbianism.

The specific ways in which sexology influenced wider culture were complex and remain controversial. One the one hand, it has been suggested that sexologists provided a valuable new vocabulary and set of identities which enabled political movements for lesbian, gay and other rights (Weeks 1981, p. 2). On the other, they have been accused of medicalising and pathologising non-normative sexualities (Jackson 1994). Their emphasis upon congenital explanations is antithetical to contemporary feminist or queer understandings of sex, gender, and sexuality, as well as reifying racial and sexual differences. There are also significant anti-feminist elements in their work. Yet their aims were often progressive and some of their more conservative concepts were put forward strategically rather than from conviction; their ideas were influenced, drawn upon, and developed by radical thinkers including leading feminists.[10] Nonetheless, others who identified with their work—particularly the most privileged women including Radclyffe Hall herself and Vita Sackville-West—also shared conservative views on the wider place of women (Doan 2006).

The detail of those debates is largely outside the scope of this book, but it is important to note that the significance of sexology was profoundly different for men and women. Oram has problematised the argument that Ellis and his colleagues imported general suspicion of lesbianism into middle-class women's relationships for the first time, but in the legal context Caroll Smith-Rosenberg's argument to this effect does have value. She points out that while Ellis's discussion of men aimed to defend them from moral and criminal condemnation, there was no equivalent motivation for his discussion of women: 'he initiated those allegations' (Smith-Rosenberg 1986, p. 277). Indeed, Ellis implicitly contrasted the often-exceptional male invert with his potentially criminal, racially suspect female counterpart. This elision of unfeminine and criminal women held obvious dangers for lesbian defendants in the criminal courts; the prosecution of the middle-class Barker was a concrete manifestation of their effects. However, Ellis's appeal to gender norms was both broader and deeper. His equation of femininity with dependency and submission, as when he stated that 'in a very large number of women the sexual impulse remains latent until aroused by a lover's caresses', was part of a normalisation of male dominance and female submission as natural, inevitable, and fundamental to heterosexuality (Ellis 1902; Jackson 1984). It ran counter to feminist challenges to the sexual double standard, just as his equation of feminism with falling mental and moral standards helped distort the feminist challenge to heteropatriarchy from a political to a medical problem (Jeffreys 1985). In doing so, it also undermined many women's moral claims: a refusal of heterosexuality might be no more than a front for or an inducement to less acceptable forms of sexual conduct.

---

[10] See, for example, Alison Neilans' use of sexological ideas discussed in Chap. 4.

When taken up by the wider culture, neither the positive nor the negative elements of sexological thought survived unchanged. They were used in varied and strategic ways by members of the diverse sex reform movement, whose aims ranged from free love to eugenics. Reformers often disagreed profoundly on issues such as the purpose and use of birth control or abortion, the social function and desirability of marriage, or the extent to which the movement should associate itself with homosexual law reform (in fact, it increasingly focused upon heterosexual relationships). Those debates and campaigns, rather than the original texts, were more likely to appear in popular media which themselves misunderstood, distorted, or cherry-picked sexological ideas. They could also be taken up for strategic reasons by broadly unsympathetic readers, as Wild had done in the 1921 parliamentary debates.

Ellis's work did feed a new concern about lesbianism among the middle and upper classes, exacerbated by the *Well of Loneliness* trials. Its influence was apparent in a popular work on criminality by former CID officer Cecil Bishop. Writing on women's 'perversion', which he identified wholly with lesbianism, Bishop also made links between female independence, race, nationality, and sexuality (1931, p. 169):

> The sights to be seen on the Continent have spoiled the minds and ruined the lives of many girl visitors from this country. For instance, I recently learned that two young girls, travelling together to Paris last Easter, were conducted round Montmartre by a designing scoundrel who took them to a place where they saw persons of different colour indecently performing for public show. The girls paid two hundred francs to witness this spectacle.[11]

Although Bishop made no reference to the *Well of Loneliness* or Barker prosecutions, he did focus upon the greater opportunities given to wealthier women who had the financial means to pay for flats or hotel rooms for themselves and their younger lovers. That scenario was also central to Eugenics Society founder's Sybil Neville Rolfe's contrasting (likely fictional) vignettes, similarly premised upon the innocence of respectable women and the dangers of foreign travel. A middle-aged head

[11] The fear of miscegenation which pervaded both this anecdote and Ellis's discussion of female inversion was also to be found in press reports of the period (Oram 2016, p. 176).

teacher's needless concern about her 'sensible' friendship with a widowed postmistress, thanks to a psychological lecture she 'couldn't really understand', was contrasted with the behaviour of a young woman whose friend had 'a lovely car' and spare money, dressed like Radclyffe Hall, and wanted to take her to Italy. An aunt was, unusually, alert to the danger because she was a doctor (Neville-Rolfe 1935, pp. 96–97).

Clearly the publicity around Hall, with her wealth and social status, made the assignment of lesbianism to the working classes alone untenable. Oram has highlighted that the lesbian in the popular press of the 1920s was higher-class and decadent, othered by contrast to the virtues of respectable working and lower-middle-class readers. The middle-brow publications of the 1930s—to which we might add Bishop's book—saw the 'fleeting' appearance of the predatory older woman of the West End nightclubs (Oram 2016, p. 176). This figure could connect lesbianism's growing association with 'a semi-criminal underworld of violence … and sexual depravity' (Oram and Turnbull 2001, p. 158) simultaneously to the lower orders and the affluent, bohemian upper classes—the murky world two British girls allegedly brushed up against in Montmartre. As in earlier centuries, there was a sense that the threat to respectable women was contagion from above *or* below: the logic of silencing, the association with degeneracy theory in some sexological works, and the attention to race and criminality in others helped to displace anxieties back onto their traditional targets.

Unlike the popular press, the court hearing Barker's case could not use her class to portray her as other: she was of similar social rank to the legal professionals. In that context, the new association of middle-class women with lesbianism was significant. The trial's importance should not be overestimated, however: it was in some ways anomalous, coming as it did so soon after the *Well of Loneliness* case and being heard by a judge already familiar with debates around lesbianism. It also came at a period when sexology was facing challenge from other branches of medical science including Freudianism, which emphasised development in infancy and childhood rather than innate characteristics; and endocrinology, which offered hormonal explanations for atypical sexual behaviour. These approaches were already fashionable among parts of the educated public (Rapp 1990) but would only make their way into legal debates after the

Second World War; the general public's understanding lagged even further behind. While Barker's prosecution probably marked a high point of direct sexological impact upon popular understandings of lesbianism, much of the public seems to have been largely untouched by it. For example, the treatment of gender crossing as a matter of comedy was still strong: Barker was 'the cause of great amusement ... one has only to mention her name to raise a laugh' (Surrey Comet, March 1929, quoted in Brody 2004).

Sexology and Silencing

If sexology was co-existing with older discourses in 1929, what did that mean for silencing? The threat posed by the new science was more limited than it might appear. Sexologists themselves did not necessarily oppose a policy of silencing, even if their arguments owed as much to strategy as conviction. Ellis, who presented his work as addressed to an essentially male, higher-class, professional audience, argued that homosexuality should be decriminalised because 'it at once puts a stop to the movement of agitation, and the tendency to the glorification of homosexuality—which is undesirable and even in many respects harmful' (1933, p. 201). Sexual reformers discussed issues such as birth control relatively publicly but gave little space to lesbianism (Cohler 2010, chap. 3). Even *The Well of Loneliness* was published at a significantly higher price than most other novels, and its review copies were more carefully targeted at 'highbrow' journals (Doan 2001, p. 8).

Sir Ernest Wild might have proclaimed his support for an offence of gross indecency between women eight years earlier, but that was in the context of a spoiling amendment designed to prevent a Bill being passed (Chap. 4). When faced with the realities in his courtroom, he was as certain in Barker's case as his parliamentary opponents had been in 1921 that publicity would promote vice. Although he sought evidence as to any sexual relationship, he added, 'let me see it in writing. I do not want anything prurient to be stated in court' (*Evening Standard* 1929).[12]

[12] He was similarly hostile to women sitting on juries for male homosexual offences (Davenport-Hines 1990, p. 297).

Through this device, nothing sexual had to be stated in public: the judge retained his privileged access to Haward's written statement which was rather less coy. This echoed the 'patriarchal distribution of knowledge' which Katherine Costello identifies in *The Well of Loneliness*, where Stephen Gordon's father reads sexological texts and understands their application to his daughter, but chooses not to share that knowledge with her or his wife (Costello 2018, pp. 181–82, fn 17).

Again, though, silencing was not a consequence of either ignorance or toleration. Suspicions about Barker's alleged sexual conduct followed her into prison. While serving her sentence, Barker was allocated sewing work but petitioned to be allowed more mentally or physically strenuous work in a kitchen or library, 'which would keep my brain occupied, in fact anything that will not give me time to think and brood' (Arkell-Smith, Petition from Prisoner, 1929, HO 144/19128). Her petition, which ultimately failed, was opposed by the governor of HMP Holloway on the basis that in the sewing room 'she might work under the direct supervision of an officer, and thus be deprived of opportunities of *seducing another* pr[isoner]' (Governor's Report, 1929, HO 144/19128, emphasis in original). The grounds for this concern were provided in answer to a written question: 'there can be little doubt she is a pervert may seek opportunities of making converts' (Note, 31 May 1929, HO 144/19128). The mixture of courtroom vagueness and outright silence had concealed, not eradicated, suspicion of sexual deviancy.

Since the persistence of silencing ensured that the courts were hardly thronged with lesbian defendants, lesbianism continued to be policed primarily through social, financial, religious, and familial pressures. In the nineteenth century, another form of regulation had also developed: medicalisation. Initially this had, as discussed in previous chapters, focused upon the physical reproductive system as the source of moral and mental disturbance, a logic which had led to the use of clitoridectomy among other surgical 'cures' at mid-century. By the end of the century, regulation was moving into the realms of psychology and psychiatry. Sexology was in conversation with these specialisms, and its emphasis upon 'true' inversion as a congenital condition changed legal perceptions, but not legal treatment, of lesbianism.

Female Husbands and Class

There are clear parallels between Barker's case and those of past female husbands, but also significant differences. The most striking of these is Barker's class. While the female husbands who appeared before the courts in the eighteenth and nineteenth centuries were from the lowest classes, Barker came from a very different social milieu. As a girl she had a bourgeois upbringing; as a man his occupations, claim to military and other titles, and fashionable lifestyle were equally upper-middle-class. In this, as much else, there was noticeable resonance with *The Well of Loneliness*. Despite rejecting the label of 'invert', Barker, like its protagonist Stephen Gordon, claimed to have been 'brought up as a boy' and later drove ambulances in France during the First World War (*Sunday Dispatch* 1929a, p. 5). In the same account, Barker self-described, as Ellis described the congenital invert, as 'highly strung and temperamental' (a characterisation which itself carried classed overtones).

Sexologically influenced writing including Hall's novel was aimed primarily at a middle-class readership. Similarly, the anxieties it fed around girls' boarding schools and independent professional women in London flats were largely specific to upper-middle-class women. The police officer-turned-journalist C.H. Rolph suggested during the *Well of Loneliness* proceedings that knowledge of lesbianism was confined to a sophisticated 'two per cent' whose 'wickedness and profligacy' were a matter of 'horrified enjoyment' for the vast majority of the public (quoted in Doan 2001, chap. 25). That notion of sexual deviance as confined to a small, over-privileged, over-intellectual, and decadent section of society was a new variation on the theme of upper-class corruption. It both explained away and isolated Radclyffe Hall and her supporters, and would persist for some decades as a way of continuing to confine and control this sexual knowledge. Those anxieties could also be literally displaced: during the *Well of Loneliness* proceedings, journalist Evelyn Irons's mother continued to insist that such things could happen in Paris, not England (quoted in Doan 2001, p. xxi). Doan points out that Radclyffe Hall continues to be strongly associated with the French capital despite having spent little time there (2001, pp. xxi–xxii).

If the impact of sexology was limited in middle-class circles, it was even less apparent elsewhere.[13] In the years leading up to the Barker case, a series of newspaper reports had shown a very different culture of working-class cross-dressing. And such reports were fairly numerous: Oram has identified an average five a year in the 1920s, doubling following the 1929 Barker case (2007, p. 3). Only a few of these are discussed here, not least because many reports did not involve criminal proceedings related to the gender-crossing itself, or at all; or did not refer to a specific, putatively sexual relationship, for example with a wife. Even where there are hints that alternative approaches were available, these cases seem to have been more concerned about working-class industriousness and familial control than with criminal or sexological interpretations. For example, in a case of drunkenness brought before a Westminster magistrate in 1904, the defendant Charlie Wilson (identified in court as Catherine Coombes) had been married twice but was now a widower (*Shields Daily News* 1904). Although his age was not given, he had reportedly been wearing male clothes for half a century so was probably over sixty. Once satisfied that the marriages were over and the 'most industrious and well-behaved' defendant would be found work by an unnamed 'gentleman', the magistrate discharged the prisoner stating that 'I know nothing in law to prevent a woman dressing as a man'. It was implicit in the presentation of the case that the defendant's single status, industrious poverty, and oversight by a 'gentleman' rendered the situation unthreatening. There was little motivation, then, to seek a similar charge to the one found against the more feckless, insubordinate, and youthful Barker.

In 1912, Adelaide Dallamore of Acton, London was remanded in custody for 'masquerading as a man'. It was apparent that the case could have been viewed through a sexological lens: the court missionary (a forerunner of the modern probation officer) reported that Dallamore's reason for living as her friend's husband was 'so that no young man should come forward and keep them apart', and a medical report was obtained (*Daily Mail* 1912). There had also been opposition to Dallamore's relationship from her friend's family (Oram 2007, p. 55). However, the court and

[13] For detailed consideration of gender-crossing in popular culture, see Oram (2007).

press took a very different direction. Headlines drew upon older 'female husband' tropes: 'Girl "Husband"' in the *Daily Mail* and 'Woman as Husband' in the *News of the World* (*Daily Mail* 1912; *News of the World* 1912). According to the court missionary, the two young women had run away together after their parents tried to part them; yet even in describing their 'love', the *News of the World* emphasised this was done 'for friendship's sake' by the 'fond' 'pals' (*News of the World* 1912). In other words, while the relationship between the two women was at least part of the case's interest to both the criminal justice system and the press, they seem to have shied away from any public discussion of its more troubling implications. Instead, they reinterpreted it as an exceptional friendship and focused upon the defendant's potential return to obedient femininity. Dallamore had worked for several weeks as a plumber's mate, a suitably subordinate position, and although she later told the press that living as a man offered more freedom, better wages, and more comfortable clothes, she had returned to female dress for the second court hearing and promised that she would 'go home and live as a girl' (*News of the World* 1912). On that basis, she was bound over, with the magistrate telling Dallamore 'she had acted very foolishly' (*Nottingham Daily Express* 1912). (She did not, however, promise to stop seeing her friend; again, the court's silence on that point seems to reflect a wider silencing of the case's erotic overtones.) The medical report was simply dismissed as 'satisfactory' (*Daily Mail* 1912).

The precise charge against Dallamore was not specified but, given the outcome, seems to have been breach of the peace. That was probably also the charge in several cases during the First World War which similarly appear to have included accusations of 'dressing as a man'. Breach of the peace is not a crime but a quasi-offence which, in common law, allows the police to arrest the accused and the court to bind them over for a specific period, requiring them not to behave in a certain way. The person must agree to be bound over by entering into a recognisance, that is, giving the court an undertaking or promise to be of good behaviour. They might also be required to arrange for a sum of money, known as a surety, to be paid into court. A bind-over is not technically a punishment but imprisonment could follow if sureties were not raised, while those sureties were liable to be forfeited if the recognisance was breached (Broadbent

2017; Turner 2012, p. 67). This was only one of several rather vague and flexible powers used to police 'waywardness' in young women, alongside by-laws and powers to detain for 'moral danger' (Cox 2013, p. 37). They served a familiar function: avoiding the need to spell out the sexual element of the conduct by labelling the accused as 'disorderly'.

As we saw in Chap. 4, the war had brought fresh attention to women's extra-marital sexuality as a source of danger. Outside Noel Pemberton Billing MP's overwrought claims of a German 'black book' of British perverts who could be used to bring down the nation, there were more mundane concerns about armed forces morale and the spread of sexually-transmitted infections. In these circumstances, even some feminist organisations had not been opposed to greater regulation of young women's sexuality (see Chap. 4). Prosecutions for cross-dressing appear to have been connected to this new concern about unruly girls, yet the newspaper accounts also show a continuing willingness to treat these events as a pragmatic feature of working-class life rather than a symptom of sexual perversion. This approach mirrors that of earlier centuries towards women who enlisted in the armed forces under male identities.

In January 1918, one such case was reported as an 'escapade'. When eighteen-year-old Charles Capon was called up for military service, the London wire-worker produced a military protection certificate (which would have excused him). However, following further investigation, the youth told the recruiting office that she could not be called up as she was a woman, Ellen Capon. She also told the police officer who took her into custody that she had been 'walking out' with another woman. Capon claimed two motives: 'a bit of daring' and higher wages. Her family was aware of her actions and much of her income went to her parents. She was brought before the court where the magistrate heard that she now intended to work on the land (actually a rather ambivalently gendered proposition, but one likely to involve working under male oversight and direction). He released her, saying he wanted to hear from her father the following week (*Globe* 1918). Capon's father duly attended and told the magistrate that although he had advised her against 'masquerading', this 'most determined girl' was 'a good girl as regards her mother' (*Sunday Times* 1918). She was thus located as the daughter of a patriarchal household and an industrious worker, despite the suggestions of insubordination and a lesbian relationship. The magistrate explicitly returned her to a properly subordinate position when he bound her over on her father's surety to keep the peace.

After the war had ended, Lillian Lewis was prosecuted in Westminster for 'loitering and failing to give a satisfactory account of herself' (*Sheffield Daily Telegraph* 1925). She had been arrested in male dress and with dyed, short hair while walking arm-in-arm with another young woman. Her mother, whom Lewis told police she was in male dress to avoid, had pointed her out. The reason for their estrangement was not given, but Lewis had left her home in Wales a year earlier and worked as a waitress in Weston-Super-Mare before coming to London. This story of female disobedience—Lewis had abandoned the nuclear family and had no obvious occupation at this point—seems to have met with little sympathy. She was remanded in custody (*Western Daily Press* 1925). The press were similarly unenthusiastic about Lewis, and the outcome of the case does not seem to have been reported. That lack of sympathy does not indicate that sexological explanations were being imported wholesale into the courts. On the contrary, sexological ideas had little influence upon the prosecutions of working-class female husbands. Barker's case, like Maud Allen's libel case (Chap. 4) and the *Well of Loneliness* obscenity proceedings, was literally a class apart (see also Oram 2007, pp. 56–58). For some of the popular press reports, Barker could also be placed in the traditional female husband mould; it was higher-class observers such as Radclyffe Hall who expressed straightforward disapproval (Doan 2001, p. 89). For those 'above' popular culture, Barker fell within a different trope: that of upper-class decadence and perversion, which had its own long pedigree. It had been a key factor in support for age of consent reforms in the 1880s, and remained a powerful cultural idea in the 1920s.

Comparison with Earlier Cases

Alongside Barker's social class, the other striking difference from previous prosecutions was the offence charged. The move from financial fraud against the wife to perjury against the state is a reminder of the major changes in married women's legal position over the preceding century:

since a wife's legal identity and property were no longer subsumed into her husband's, a financial fraud charge was no longer appropriate. At the same time, since civil registration of marriage had been introduced in 1837 its increased formality, as well as its secularisation as a matter of state record, offered a new non-sexual alternative. Perjury performed the same function as fraud in keeping the law's focus upon the fact of marriage as a legal (rather than sexual) union. Other charges in relation to Barker's masculine career would have been possible: not only was a second charge of perjury in relation to an affidavit brought but not proceeded with, but an offence relating to Barker's false claim of having a DSO was also contemplated (Burmby 1929, PRO MEPO 3/439). The failure to pursue these alternative charges indicates that the marital relationship was considered the most serious element of the affair, the one most deserving of criminal punishment. While the sexual element was silenced, it nonetheless weighed heavily upon the minds of those bringing the prosecution and hearing the case. Consummation was legally irrelevant to perjury (as it had been to vagrancy or fraud), and the guilty plea meant no evidence needed to be heard at all, but the judge specifically sought further information upon this point.

These barely concealed concerns about sexuality explain why, at the same time as telling a story parallel to that of the congenital invert, Barker felt obliged to vigorously deny charges of perversion and dissociate from sexological concepts. By 1937, Barker was even more emphatic that she had 'never … in the slightest been a sexual pervert'. Despite a heterosexual history of love affairs, marriage, and children, Barker claimed to have 'had very little to do with men and was rather innocent … there had been no sex stuff' (*The Leader* 1937). Like certain eighteenth-century predecessors, Barker seems to have realised that the best hope of safety was to be found in the promise of a return to heteropatriarchal norms. Barker's press accounts claimed economic motivations—supposedly dependent for employment upon a knowledge of horses and farm work, Barker 'simply had to become a man—I had to' ("Col. Barker" 1929). Barker also offered the classic mitigation of a disappointment in heterosexual love, insisting that 'this would never have happened' if she married her one true love, a major twenty years older than her who was taken prisoner in the war (*Sunday Dispatch* 1929a, p. 5). In 1937, she even emphasised her essential femininity: 'I have always been a woman, inwardly yearning for the normal life of a woman … I could wear a girl's clothes with grace'. Implicitly distinguishing herself from unappealing congenital inverts, she portrayed herself as attractive to men and having received multiple marriage proposals (Arkell-Smith 1937). Yet these assertions to the press were contradicted by persistent returns to male life. Barker would appear before the courts under different male names on two later occasions, although not because of relationships with women (Vernon 2000; Collis 2001). A much later press interview, in 1956, gave a more complex account: after living so long as a man, Barker claimed to 'think as one, behave as one,' but to have 'no "tendency" to become a man' (Vernon 2000, pp. 57–58).

Barker fitted into a long history of female husbands performing a masculinity which was not just adequate, but excessive. If Lillias Irma Valerie Arkell-Smith had three given names, Leslie Ivor Victor Gauntlett Bligh Barker would have five. He was not Mr Barker, but a Captain or Colonel or even baronet. He was not just interested in politics, but prominent in the extremist National Fascisti who physically fought Communists. He was not simply an ex-soldier, but the decorated founder of a fellowship of Mons veterans. He not only enjoyed sport, but also taught and excelled at fencing and boxing. He was not merely repudiating his own female past, but overtly misogynist: women were gold-diggers, out for what they could get, and he felt 'loathing and contempt' as he watched them 'preen' ("Col. Barker" 1929).[14]

Just as the female husbands of the eighteenth century had apparently convinced workmates and neighbours, so Barker's acquaintances endorsed his masculinity. According to Haward, 'everything about her suggested that she was really a man' whom waiters admired and women fell in love with, 'extraordinarily handsome', able to 'do a tremendous day's work, and lift weights and dig and plant in a way that would have exhausted any ordinary man' (*Sunday Express* 1929). To a Mons veteran, Barker was 'the finest type of officer and gentleman' ("Col. Barker" 1929). He was not only accepted by the leadership of the National Fascisti, but his membership in turn made him part of a political movement whose appeal to the

[14] It is only fair to mention that he was unimpressed by men, too.

upper-middle and upper classes suited his own role as 'gentleman'.[15] At the same time, it facilitated rather different displays of masculinity: he was 'always ready to join in any of the fracas the young men had with the Communists' (*Sunday Dispatch* 1929b). Ironically, however, Barker would later credit her very femininity for her masculine success with other women: 'being a woman I knew exactly the little attentions which would appeal to them' ("Colonel Barker" 1929).

Finally, the 'wife' remained a secondary figure in the courtroom, visible but silenced, although the growth of print media allowed her some voice elsewhere. The *People* echoed eighteenth-century reports in emphasising the number of 'marriages' in which Barker had been involved: not only the apparently legal marriage to Haward but also common-law relationships with a further two or three women (*People* 1929). Haward was mentioned relatively briefly in Wild's sentencing remarks, and in such confused terms that her position was left more than a little ambiguous. He stated that he 'was impressed' by her evidence but, '[w]ithout expressing any views about the truth or falsehood' of it, he would assume in Barker's favour that Haward entered the marriage knowing Barker's sex (*Evening News* 1929). No direct criticism was made of her conduct: Haward was benefitting from the same steadfast determination to believe in her innocence as had her historical predecessors.

Aftermath: Renewed Silence

If legal history were a linear narrative of progress, this book would now go on to describe lesbianism's growing legal visibility, debates on its regulation, and a gradual move to greater acceptance and equality. If it followed Foucauldian theory, the creation of a medical category would in turn create a regulated identity. However, any sense of linear develop-

[15] This organisation did not attract a huge membership, but was visible and skilled at publicity (Wheelwright 1990, p. 43). It had broken away from the British Fascisti, of which Barker had originally been a member alongside the Earl of Glasgow and Viscountess Downe (Collis 2001, p. 115). The founder of the British Fascisti, Rotha Lintorn-Orman, was herself known as the 'Man-woman' for her habit of wearing men's clothes and enthusiasm for unfeminine skills such as changing tyres (Pugh 2005, pp. 51 and 64).

ment in criminal regulation or social understandings disappears at this point because instead, something improbable happened. After its moment of legal and cultural visibility, sex between women was rendered invisible again, particularly in working-class contexts. This was not a gradual falling-away but an immediate disappearance evident within weeks of Barker's sentencing when William Holton, married father of two, was revealed to be physiologically female upon admission to hospital. He too had performed an excessive masculinity, indulging in heavy drinking and unusually strong tobacco and engaging in hard manual labour. While the story was reported as a parallel to Barker's, Holton was not prosecuted and the older framing of the female husband story was maintained. Thus honest industry was emphasised, along with domestic virtues and the laughable naivety of a wife who apparently still insisted that Holton was the biological father of her younger child (Oram 2007, pp. 68–73). The appropriation of male sexual and social privilege was downplayed, thanks to the desire to reassert silencing rather than risk further publicising the sexological discourses so determinedly aired by the *Well of Loneliness* and resisted in Barker. As Oram comments, the press 'worked hard' in the 1930s to maintain this older approach to the female husband as a remarkable, comical character (2007, p. 75). They and the courts tacitly acknowledged, but simultaneously suppressed, lesbian possibility.

Male professionals in the criminal justice system felt able to write in more knowing ways. In 1930, E. Ling-Mallison offered what was probably a commentary on the Barker case. It is notable that in contrast to older texts, this discussion openly acknowledged the possibility of a sexual element, explaining that 'masquerading' was not an offence in itself 'if induced by sexual motives only'. At the same time, the author was apparently unaware of earlier disorderly conduct prosecutions and drew only upon a comparison with men's prosecutions for incitement to prostitution or conspiracy to commit sodomy (Ling-Mallison 1930, p. 50):

> It would doubtless be the same in the case of a Woman—though there do not seem to be any reported cases, and there could not be a charge of conspiracy, as two women together cannot commit sodomy.

The following year, former CID officer Cecil Bishop showed similar awareness of lesbian sexuality, devoting a chapter of his book *Women and*

Crime (1931, chap. 8) to it. In a complete inversion of Victorian sexual orthodoxy, he argued that 'many women are more highly sexed than men', turning to each other because 'the average man, whose vitality has perhaps been reduced by long hours of uncongenial work, is sometimes physically incapable of meeting their demands' (p. 162). Given such an excess of female sexual agency, '[v]eiled truths may do more harm than lies … until these facts are known there is no certain safety for any woman' (p. 163).[16] Yet his claim does not seem to have resonated with legal or popular culture.

Of course, once spoken aloud, the forbidden knowledge could not be as thoroughly silenced thereafter. Silencing thus became a more fraught process during the remainder of the twentieth century. However, a fairly effective legal silencing was quickly reasserted. *Hare* [1934] KB 354 (and see Chap. 4) confirmed the criminality of non-consensual sex between females in an *obiter* comment. The issue was therefore settled without addressing the material physicalities or specifics of what sex between women might look like. In the same year, Barker returned to court as John Hill, charged with theft (*Daily Express* 1934; *The Times* 1934). The Quarter Sessions bench used his male name in what Jennings suggests was an effort to avoid addressing his gender identity in court (Jennings 2007, p. 128).

In 1937, twenty-year-old Joan Coning was prosecuted for making a false entry in the marriage register after marrying in the role of bridegroom. The coded, psychologised language of 'unhealthy friendship' was used in awkward circumlocutions around the question of sexual activity. According to the prosecutor, 'things that did happen indicate that Miss Coning's mental outlook on certain matters was a little peculiar'. Satisfied that the defendant had been influenced by her older bride, and that the friendship had been permanently ended, the magistrates bound Coning over for three years and placed her under the care and observation of a woman probation officer (Oram 2007, pp. 85–87). Oram emphasises that this was the only pre–Second World War case to use the language of

[16] His approach nonetheless had strong echoes of earlier centuries when he argued that 'self-abuse … leads naturally to the greater perversion', and that '[f]or both purposes special instruments are actually manufactured'; the consequences of their use included loss of 'robust appearance' (Bishop 1931, pp. 163–64).

'unhealthy friendship'. It can be contrasted with Barker's further court appearance for another theft, under the name James Hunt. The magistrate claimed to give no weight to the cross-dressing, and passed a lenient sentence, but nonetheless exhorted Barker to 'not masquerade as a man' (Vernon 2000, p. 44). Even in Coning's case, the scientific and medical language worked as a form of code to obscure and silence, rather than explain, the sexual nature of the relationship between the young women.

The Barker case, then, was a momentary sensation which left few traces in the criminal justice system. No coherent legal narrative or understanding of inversion or lesbianism emerged from it. The biography presented to the court had strong parallels to the sexologically inflected narrative of *The Well of Loneliness*, but those parallels were actively resisted by the parties. The sexologically informed judge rejected inversion in favour of perversion when passing judgment. The press and public either applied traditional working-class tropes to this middle-class defendant or used Barker's class as a reason to distinguish the case from those of working-class female husbands. Given those contradictions and complexities, combined with the determination of the criminal justice system to maintain its policy of silencing, it is perhaps less surprising than it first seemed that this case's subsequent impact was so contained.

Conclusion

Barker's prosecution, coupled with the *Well of Loneliness* trial, marked a high point of lesbian visibility in the criminal courts. Both cases to some extent represent a continuation of the debates of 1921: they show disagreement among the lawyers and legislators not upon the undesirability of lesbianism but upon how it should be regulated.[17] Silencing came under severe challenge but was not abandoned, and indeed shaped both

[17] Doan suggests broader differences of opinion among 'the Establishment' and posits that those involved in suppressing *The Well of Loneliness* were an atypical minority (2001, pp. 20–24). However, they were not so atypical as to be prevented from rising to high office; and it is their virulent, activist response rather than the underlying hostility to lesbianism which was unusual. Most of her counter-examples, while members of gentlemen's clubs, were writers rather than lawyers or legislators.

sets of legal proceedings. The obscenity charges against Hall's publishers were intended to prevent the book's publication and distribution to the public, and no British edition would appear again for over twenty years (R. Hall 1949). Similarly, the method of taking Haward's evidence on her sexual relationship with Barker served only one purpose: to confine the information she gave to the legal professionals present, keeping it from the public and press.

The subsequent success of silencing was also part of a wider response to the sexual reform movement. Co-organiser Dora Russell later wrote that the WSLR's 1929 London congress marked the movement's peak; thereafter, reaction set in (Crozier 2003). Even this 'peak' event, which happened the year after *The Well of Loneliness* was suppressed and had censorship as a central theme, had carefully avoided discussion of homosexuality in favour of presumptively heterosexual issues such as contraception and abortion (Crozier 2003). Seemingly ignored by the courts, and an embarrassment to many sex reformers, lesbianism had little value as a political priority and there was no concerted effort to breach the official silence. The wider consequences of this failure to challenge dominant discourses would become apparent thirty years later, when legal reform became a matter for official discussion by the Wolfenden Committee. As the next chapter explores, the silencing of lesbianism became a mechanism for suppressing not only women's sexual autonomy but also the demands of campaigners for male homosexual law reform.

References

Arkell-Smith, Valerie. 1937. Col Barker—The Man-Woman Who Hoaxed the World. *The Leader*, September 11.

Beccalossi, Chiara. 2011. Female Same-Sex Desires: Conceptualizing a Disease in Competing Medical Fields in Nineteenth-Century Europe. *Journal of the History of Medicine and Allied Sciences* 67 (1): 7–35.

Bishop, Cecil. 1931. *Women and Crime*. London: Chatto and Windus.

Bland, Lucy. 1995. *Banishing the Beast: English Feminism and Sexual Morality 1885–1914*. London: Penguin.

Broadbent, Graeme. 2017. Breach of the Peace. *Westlaw*.

Brody, Simon. 2004. Perfect Gentleman Was a Wily Woman. *Kingston Guardian*. http://www.kingstonguardian.co.uk/news/features/display.var.469340.0.perfect_gentleman_was_a_wily_woman.php.
Carpenter, Edward. 1908. *The Intermediate Sex*. London: George Allen & Unwin.
Cohler, Deborah. 2010. *Citizen, Invert, Queer: Lesbianism and War in Early Twentieth-Century Britain*. Minneapolis: University of Minnesota Press.
"Col. Barker." 1929. I Become a Woman Again. *Sunday Dispatch*, March 10.
Collis, Rose. 2001. *Colonel Barker's Monstrous Regiment: A Tale of Female Husbandry*. London: Virago.
"Colonel Barker." 1929. My Life as 'Man About Town.' *Sunday Dispatch*, March 24.
Costello, Katherine A. 2018. A No-Man's-Land of Sex: Reading Stephen Gordon and 'Her' Critics. *Journal of Lesbian Studies* 22 (2): 165–184. https://doi.org/10.1080/10894160.2017.1342457.
Cox, Pamela. 2013. *Bad Girls in Britain: Gender, Justice and Welfare, 1900–1950*. Basingstoke: Palgrave Macmillan.
Crozier, Ivan. 2003. 'All the World's a Stage': Dora Russell, Norman Haire, and the 1929 London World League for Sexual Reform Congress. *Journal of the History of Sexuality* 12 (1): 16–37.
Daily Express. 1934. 'John Hill' Admits 'He' Is a Woman, September 28.
Daily Mail. 1912. Girl 'Husband', April 4.
Davenport-Hines, Richard. 1990. *Sex, Death and Punishment: Attitudes to Sex and Sexuality in Britain since the Renaissance*. London: Collins.
Derry, Caroline. 2018. DPP v Jonathan Cape and Leopold Hill (1928). In *Women's Legal Landmarks: Celebrating the History of Women and Law in the UK and Ireland*, ed. Erika Rackley and Rosemary Auchmuty. London: Hart Publishing.
Doan, Laura. 2001. *Fashioning Sapphism: The Origins of a Modern English Lesbian Culture*. New York: Columbia University Press.
———. 2006. Women's Place Is the Home: Conservative Sapphic Modernity. In *Sapphic Modernities: Sexuality, Women, and National Culture*, ed. Laura Doan and Jane Garrity, 91–107. London: Palgrave Macmillan.
———. 2019. Troubling Popularisation: On the Gendered Circuits of a 'Scientific' Knowledge of Sex. *Gender & History* 31 (2): 304–318.
Donoghue, Emma. 1993. Imagined More than Women: Lesbians as Hermaphrodites, 1671–1766. *Women's History Review* 2 (2): 199–216.
Douglas, James. 1928. Editorial. *Daily Express*, August 19.
Duggan, Lisa. 2000. *Sapphic Slashers: Sex, Violence and American Modernity*. Durham, NC: Duke University Press.
Ellis, Henry Havelock. 1890. *The Criminal*. The Contemporary Science Series.

———. 1897. *Studies in the Psychology of Sex Vol. 1: Sexual Inversion*. The University Press.

———. 1902. *The Sexual Impulse in Women*. St Louis, MO: Heinemann.

———. 1933. *Psychology of Sex: A Manual for Students*. London: Heinemann.

Ellis, Henry Havelock, and John Addington Symonds. 1897. *Sexual Inversion*. London: Wilson and Macmillan.

Evening News. 1929. Judge on Crime of 'Col. Barker', April 25.

Evening Standard. 1929. 'Col. Barker' Guilty on One Charge, April 24.

Funke, Jana. 2013. 'We Cannot Be Greek Now': Age Difference, Corruption of Youth and the Making of *Sexual Inversion*. *English Studies* 94 (2): 139–153. https://doi.org/10.1080/0013838X.2012.760255.

Gibson, Margaret. 1997. Clitoral Corruption: Bodily Metaphors and American Doctors: Constructions of Female Homosexuality, 1870–1900. In *Science and Homosexualities*, ed. Vernon A. Rosario, 108–132. London: Routledge.

Globe. 1918. Dressed & Worked as a Man: Girl Who also 'Walked Out' with a Girl, January 19.

Hall, Lesley. 2004. Hauling Down the Double Standard: Feminism, Social Purity and Sexual Science in Late Nineteenth-Century Britain. *Gender & History* 16 (1): 36–56.

———. 2016. 'Sentimental Follies' or 'Instruments of Tremendous Uplift'? Reconsidering Women's Same-Sex Relationships in Interwar Britain. *Women's History Review* 25 (1): 124–142. https://doi.org/10.1080/09612025.2015.1047243.

Hall, Radclyffe. 1928. *The Well of Loneliness*. London: Cape.

———. 1949. *The Well of Loneliness*. Paperback. London: The Falcon Press.

Jackson, Margaret. 1984. Sexology and the Social Construction of Male Sexuality. In *The Sexuality Papers: Male Sexuality and the Social Control of Women*, ed. L. Coveney, M. Jackson, S. Jeffreys, L. Kaye, and P. Mahony, 45–66. London: Hutchinson.

———. 1994. *The Real Facts of Life: Feminism and the Politics of Sexuality c 1850–1940*. London: Taylor & Francis.

Jeffreys, Sheila. 1985. *The Spinster and Her Enemies: Feminism and Sexuality 1880–1930*. Melbourne: Spinifex.

Jennings, Rebecca. 2007. *A Lesbian History of Britain: Love and Sex Between Women since 1500*. Oxford: Greenwood World Publishing.

Ling-Mallison, Eric. 1930. *Law Relating to Women*. London: Solicitors' Law Stationery Society Ltd.

Lombroso, Cesare, and Giuglielmo Ferrero. (1895) 1959. *The Female Offender*. London: Peter Owen Ltd.
Mosley, Diana. 1977. *A Life of Contrasts*. London: Hamish Hamilton.
Neville-Rolfe, Sybil. 1935. *Why Marry?* London: Faber & Faber.
News of the World. 1912. Woman as Husband, April 7.
Nottingham Daily Express. 1912. A Female Husband, April 4.
Oram, Alison. 2007. *Her Husband Was a Woman! Women's Gender-Crossing in Modern British Popular Culture*. London: Routledge.
———. 2016. 'A Sudden Orgy of Decadence': Writing about Sex Between Women in the Interwar Popular Press. In *Sapphic Modernities: Sexuality, Women, and National Culture*, ed. Laura Doan and Jane Garrity, 165–180. London: Palgrave Macmillan.
Oram, Alison, and Annmarie Turnbull. 2001. *The Lesbian History Sourcebook: Love and Sex Between Women in Britain from 1780 to 1970*. London: Routledge.
Peakman, Julie. 2004. *Lascivious Bodies: A Sexual History of the Eighteenth Century*. London: Atlantic Books.
People. 1929. 'Colonel Barker's' Red-Haired 'Wife' Vanishes: She Was 'His' Second, March 10.
Pike, Luke Owen. 1876. *A History of Crime in England, Vol. II*. London: Smith, Elder & Co.
Prosser, Jay. 2001. 'Some Primitive Thing Conceived in a Turbulent Age of Transition': The Transsexual Emerging from The Well. In *Palatable Poison: Critical Perspectives on the Well of Loneliness*, ed. Laura Doan and Jay Prosser, 129–144. New York: Columbia University Press.
Pugh, Martin. 2005. *Hurrah for the Blackshirts! Fascists and Fascism in Britain Between the Wars*. London: Pimlico.
"Quintroon, N." 2019. *OED Online*. https://www-oed-com.libezproxy.open.ac.uk/view/Entry/156719.
Rapp, Dean. 1990. The Early Discovery of Freud by the British General Educated Public, 1912–1919. *Social History of Medicine* 3 (2): 217–243.
Raiskin, Judith. 1994. Inverts and Hybrids: Lesbian Rewritings of Sexual and Racial Identities. In *The Lesbian Postmodern*, ed. Laura Doan, 156–172. New York: Columbia University Press.
Richardson, Angelique. 2003. *Love and Eugenics in the Late Nineteenth Century: Rational Reproduction and the New Woman*. Oxford: Oxford University Press.
Sheffield Daily Telegraph. 1925. Girl Dressed as a Man, November 17.
Shields Daily News. 1904. Woman's Wives: Magistrate Says a Woman May Dress as a Man, August 4.

Smith-Rosenberg, Caroll. 1986. *Disorderly Conduct: Visions of Gender in Victorian America*. Oxford: Oxford University Press.

Somerville, Siobhan B. 1998. Scientific Racism and the Invention of the Homosexual Body. In *Sexology in Culture: Labelling Bodies and Desires*, ed. Lucy Bland and Laura Doan, 60–76. Cambridge: Polity Press.

Souhami, Diana. 1998. *The Trials of Radclyffe Hall*. London: Weidenfeld.

Stepan, Nancy. 1982. *The Idea of Race in Science*. London: Macmillan Press.

Stopes, Marie. 1918. *Married Love: A New Contribution to the Solution of Sex Difficulties*. London: A C Fifield.

Sunday Dispatch. 1929a. Colonel Barker, My Story: By the Man-Woman, March 10.

———. 1929b. Man-Woman's Second 'Wife', March 17.

Sunday Express. 1929. Mrs Barker, My Story: By the Man-Woman's Wife, March 10.

Sunday Times. 1918. The 'Girl Boy', January 27.

Symonds, John Addington. 1883. *A Problem in Greek Ethics*. London: Privately Printed.

Talbot, Eugene S. 1898. *Degeneracy: Its Causes, Signs, and Results*. London: Walter Scott Ltd.

The Leader. 1937. No Title, September 11.

The Times. 1934. Woman's Pose as a Man, September 28.

Tinkler, Penny. 2016. Sapphic Smokers and English Modernities. In *Sapphic Modernities: Sexuality, Women, and National Culture*, ed. Laura Doan and Jane Garrity, 75–90. London: Palgrave Macmillan.

Turner, Joanne. 2012. Summary Justice for Women: Stafford Borough, 1880–1905. *Crime, Histoire & Sociétés* 16 (2): 55–77. https://doi.org/10.4000/chs.1359.

Vernon, James. 2000. For Some Queer Reason: The Trials and Tribulations of Colonel Barker's Masquerade in Interwar Britain. *Signs* 26 (1): 37–62.

Weeks, Jeffrey. 1981. *Sex, Politics and Society: The Regulation of Sexuality since 1800*. London: Longman.

———. 2001. Review Symposium: Krafft-Ebing, A Hundred Years On. *Sexualities* 4 (4): 499–503.

Western Daily Press. 1925. Girl Dressed as a Man: Formerly Waitress at Weston-s-Mare, November 17.

Wheelwright, Julie. 1990. 'Colonel' Barker: A Case Study in the Contradictions of Fascism. In *The Politics of Marginality: Race, the Radical Right and Minorities in Twentieth Century Britain*, ed. Tony Kushner and Kenneth Lunn, 40–48. London: Frank Cass.

6

The Wolfenden Report: A Shift in Silencing

The Wolfenden Report

In 1957 the Committee on Homosexual Offences and Prostitution, better known as the Wolfenden Committee, published its Report (Committee on Homosexual Offences and Prostitution (CHOP) 1957). Taken at face value, the Wolfenden Report had little to do with lesbianism. However, this chapter will demonstrate that appearances are deceptive. Not only did the Report conceal a range of witness evidence addressing lesbianism, but it also marked the emergence of a new approach to silencing lesbian possibility. As near-complete silence became increasingly unachievable, lesbians were instead obscured behind the new legal figure of the male homosexual.

The Wolfenden Committee had been appointed in August 1954 by the Home Secretary, Sir David Maxwell Fyfe. Its twelve men and three women members included chairman John Wolfenden, Vice-Chancellor of Reading University (Weeks 2004), as well as church representatives, doctors, lawyers, and academics. Significantly, it was a departmental committee rather than a Royal Commission and so could hear evidence in private. Fyfe was no reformer, having led a campaign against the 'vice',

C. Derry, *Lesbianism and the Criminal Law*,
https://doi.org/10.1007/978-3-030-35300-1_6

and had somewhat reluctantly included homosexuality in the Committee's terms of reference because of a recent increase in prosecutions for homosexual offences (Waters 1999, p. 137). In particular, that year had seen the highly publicised conviction and imprisonment of Lord Montagu of Beaulieu, his cousin Michael Pitt-Rivers, and the diplomatic correspondent of the *Daily Mail*, Peter Wildeblood.[1] (Wildeblood would go on to publish his autobiography and plea for law reform, *Against the Law* (1955), and give evidence to the Wolfenden Committee). There was, as Wolfenden recalled in his memoirs, 'a very odd atmosphere' (Wolfenden 1976, p. 131).

Concerns about the social effect of sensationalised press reporting had drawn varied responses from the establishment, although all aimed at silencing. Winston Churchill favoured press censorship (Lewis 2016, p. 6). By contrast, an editorial in *The Times* suggested partial decriminalisation would keep cases such as Montagu's out of the newspapers (*The Times* 1953). Similar reasoning was used by a Church of England report calling for law reform and a government commission (Church of England Moral Welfare Council 1954; and see Grimley 2009). Fyfe himself had no desire to see the laws criminalising sex between men changed and feared 'embarrassing recommendations' to that effect (David Maxwell Fyfe, 'Sexual Offences', 1954, TNA CAB 129/66). Indeed the Sexual Offences Act 1956, which included the offences of buggery (section 12), gross indecency (section 13), and soliciting or importuning for immoral purposes (section 32), was passed without substantive debate while the Committee was still meeting.[2]

The Wolfenden Report's recommendations on female prostitution accepted its existence as inevitable but aimed to keep it away from public view. Similar aims underpinned Part Two which considered, and recommended the partial decriminalisation of, sexual acts between men. The

[1] The three men were convicted following accusations that during a weekend at Montagu's country estate, they had committed gross indecency with two RAF men, who gave evidence against them in court; Lord Montagu always denied the offences. For a fuller account of the role of sensationalist press reporting in prompting the inclusion of homosexuality, see Bengry (2012).

[2] This was achieved by using the procedure under the Consolidation of Enactments (Procedure) Act, 1949, section 1. Marcus Lipton MP's challenge to the Bill being passed before the Departmental Committee reported was rejected on procedural grounds (HC 06/07/1956, cols. 1750–1751).

Report argued for these recommendations with reference to the figure of 'the homosexual', and in doing so has been identified as the moment when the English law began to shift decisively from regulating acts to regulating a specific identity (e.g. Moran 1996). In 1967, legislation based on the recommendations would introduce the word 'homosexual' into English statute for the first time (Sexual Offences Act 1967, section 1). Yet, crucially, the Wolfenden Report itself had carefully distinguished 'homosexuality' from 'homosexual acts' and only the latter were regulated by the criminal courts, a distinction whose significance was understood by many gay men.[3] From the lesbian perspective, by contrast, the publication of the Report was another moment at which a legal identity was refused. At the very moment of entering legal language, the 'homosexual' was constructed as male. The lesbian was hardly spoken of and then only as his counterpart, invoked in relation to him: a replication of wider gender relations. Lesbianism's treatment as a non-issue both in the Report and in the criminal law means it has received little subsequent attention in relation to either.

Ostensibly, the Report had good reason to be quiet about sexual activity between women since unlike that between men, which was wholly illegal, it was not explicitly criminalised. In reality, though, this silence was actively and deliberately constructed, somewhat in the face of the evidence. Exclusive attention to male behaviour was not an inevitable outcome of the Committee's terms of reference. These were 'to consider … the law and practice relating to homosexual offences and the treatment of *persons* convicted of such offences' (CHOP 1957, p. 7, emphasis added). Wolfenden himself was well aware of this, later pointing out that the lack of legislation 'perhaps explained why so many people thought that the 'homo-' part of 'homosexual' meant man' (Wolfenden 1976, p. 131). In its table of homosexual offences, the Report included indecent assault on a female by a female contrary to section 14 of the Sexual

[3] Indeed the performance of male homosexual identities was common in light entertainment of the period, for example, the polari-speaking 'Julian and Sandy' (Kenneth Williams and Hugh Paddick) in the BBC Radio comedy series *Round the Horne* (1965–1968); or the camp Mr Humphries (John Inman) of BBC TV's *Are You Being Served?* (1972–1985).

Offences Act 1956, which made non-consensual activity criminal and imposed an age of consent (CHOP 1957, p. 59, table (a)). Interestingly, this offence had been excluded from a Home Office memorandum (TN HO 345/7) summarising the existing law.

All the same, the offence was dismissed in a single paragraph of the Report which concluded: 'We have, however, found no case in which a female has been convicted of an act with another female which exhibits the libidinous features that characterise sexual acts between males.' Convictions of females for indecent assault on females, it explained, were 'due *in the main* to the practice of including in the figures relating to any particular offence not only those convicted of the offence itself, but also those convicted of aiding and abetting the commission of the offence' (CHOP 1957, p. 38, emphasis added). Despite the implication that a minority of cases might have involved women as principal offenders, nothing more was said about them. The use of other sexual or non-sexual offences was not considered, a key omission since, as Pamela Cox discusses (2013, p. 37), the courts saw a sexual element to *all* offending by young women. Nor was the detention of young women within the penal system on the grounds of 'moral danger' mentioned, although girls were still being held for 'care and protection' due to sexual misconduct (Walker and McCabe 1973, p. 147). Indeed, in 1960, 64 per cent of girls committed to penal institutions had not been convicted of any criminal offence compared to only 5 per cent of boys (Smart 1995, p. 29). Paul Crane noted that local authority care proceedings for 'moral danger' remained 'a real threat' for young lesbians as late as 1980 (1982, pp. 7, 11).

The contrast between this piecemeal regulation and the blanket criminalisation of sex between men did not mean that witnesses thought the position of women unimportant. In contrast to the brevity of its treatment in the final report, sex between women was a recurring theme in the evidence heard by the Committee. In consequence, the ghost of the lesbian haunts the Wolfenden Report, her rare manifestations a sort of spectral echo of the more substantive discussions with witnesses. She is the shade of a different, more radical approach which haunted the Committee but was firmly exorcised before it could manifest in the Report.

Changing Law: Legislators and Sexual Offences Legislation

From Moralism to Liberalism?

The Wolfenden Report famously drew upon liberal principles, including the harm principle and the distinction between public and private, to assert that 'there must remain a realm of private morality and immorality which is, in brief and crude terms, not the law's business' (CHOP 1957, para. 61). Nonetheless, its approach to the liberal harm principle left room for moralism. John Stuart Mill had stated that '[t]he only purpose for which power can rightfully be exercised over any member of a civilised community against his will, is to prevent harm to others' (1859, p. 13), but also suggested that public offences against decency could constitute harm. The Committee accepted that qualification with enthusiasm, although Mill himself had been more ambiguous (Mill 1859, p. 97). While the Committee asserted that '[i]t is not, in our view, the function of the law to intervene in the private lives of citizens' (CHOP 1957, para. 14), this statement was subject to restrictions. The criminal law could intervene to 'preserve public order and *decency*' and to safeguard others against 'exploitation and *corruption*', and should 'protect the citizen from what is *offensive* or injurious' (CHOP 1957, para. 13, emphasis added).[4]

Although not adopted into sexual offences legislation for another decade, the influence of this approach would be profound. Criminal law reforms were increasingly underpinned by the harm principle, and it is central to legislation in this area today. However, it was compromised from the outset by the space the Report's formulation allowed to moralism, and by its restriction of liberty to a narrowly and heteronormatively defined 'private'. Similarly, the acknowledgement that in applying community moral standards, 'they will not be recognised by all citizens, and ... our estimate of them may be mistaken' (CHOP 1957, para. 15) had

[4] Interestingly, the Church of England report had suggested a potentially narrower state duty 'to protect young people ... to protect society from nuisances and to preserve public decency' (Church of England Moral Welfare Council 1954, p. 19).

little effect then and has not always been honoured in subsequent legal discourse.

The limitations of the Wolfenden Report's liberalism have been overshadowed by the Hart-Devlin debate on the purpose of the criminal law which it prompted (Hart 1962; Devlin 1965). Delivering the 1959 Maccabean Lecture (reprinted in Devlin 1965), judge Patrick Devlin had argued that part of the criminal law's purpose was the enforcement of morality. For Devlin, morality was essential to social cohesion and a matter to be determined by the jury (pp. 90–91). H.L.A. Hart, a legal philosopher, countered that enforcing sexual morality was no part of the law's business, although he did concede that the law could step in to prevent public 'offence'. His rejection of 'an official sexual morality' in favour of 'a number of mutually tolerant moralities' was a signpost to the future direction of the law (1962, pp. 62–63). It was not, though, the approach taken by the Wolfenden Report which, as Matthew Grimley has pointed out (2009, p. 740), formed part of a debate about ideas of the nation as moral community rather than individual rights.

Partial as it may have been, there was clearly a shift in the debate on the role of the criminal law which would find statutory effect with the Sexual Offences Act 1967. However, this shift was achieved at a price. While liberalism might seem to favour equal rights, Wolfenden was proposing something much less revolutionary and indeed the law would not treat sex between men on formally equal terms until the Sexual Offences Act 2003. Rather, while beginning with an apparently liberal proposition, the Report went on to develop a medicalised argument for partial decriminalisation. Its recommendations explicitly aimed to keep male homosexuality out of public view and thus limit its spread, while encouraging medical treatment of existing 'cases'. Not only did this have echoes of the longstanding approach to lesbianism, but the silencing of the female comparator was central to limiting political claims in this way.

Silencing the Lesbian Comparator

Lesbianism featured in a number of the memoranda submitted to the committee by various experts. The Medical Women's Federation (MWF) in particular wrote a lengthy analysis, included in the British Medical Association's Memorandum of Evidence (British Medical Association (BMA) 1955), while a variety of other witnesses included shorter discussions. Among these was the War Office, which indicated that it had included female homosexuality at the request of the Wolfenden Committee (War Office, Memorandum, TNA CHP/47, para. 1). In addition, committee members discussed the issue numerous times and sometimes at length when hearing oral evidence from witnesses in closed meetings.[5]

Above all, the lack of legal parity between male homosexuals and lesbians was raised in experts' submissions and emphasised as a keenly felt unfairness among gay men themselves. An anonymous memorandum from a self-identified homosexual general practitioner (TNA HO 345/8) asked, 'By what principles of Justice does the Law of Britain … permit female homosexuality whilst punishing with imprisonment male homosexuality?' Hugh Klare, Secretary of the Howard League, stated (TNA HO 345/13, qus. 1760–1761) that this 'anomaly' was

> intensely deeply felt by homosexuals themselves. … I believe that every single one of them who came up to us—and some of them were guilty of other offences, they were not just homosexual offenders—brought this point out and obviously felt strongly about it.

His co-author, prison visitor FE Baker added, 'If it is presented to the homosexual that there are moral reasons for ruling out homosexual conduct that completely falls to the ground if it is applied to only one sex and not the other' (qu. 1764).

The inequality was also raised by the Rev. Sherwin Bailey, representing the Church of England Moral Welfare Council. He argued that same-sex acts among both men and women were sinful, but distinguished sins against God from crimes against the community. He went on,

> It seems to us again quite illogical that the Lesbianism which is almost as prevalent as the male homosexual practices should be excluded, especially

[5] See the transcripts of witness evidence, for example TNA HO 345/13, questions 1164, 1342, 1375–1376, 1760–1764, 1960, 2396–2399, 2607, 2630, 2912–2916, 2936, 3024–3025, 3084, 3111–3121, 3223–3224, 3336–3339.

> in view of the pastoral evidence that we have of the most undesirable effects, indeed socially more undesirable one might almost say than acts between men.

Committee member Canon Demant responded, 'I would like to know a lot more about that'; a brief discussion of prevalence followed (qus. 1375–1376).

The Canon was not alone in his curiosity. At various points when such evidence was raised, the Committee tried to pin down the relative prevalence of male and female homosexual behaviour. This was prompted by the assumption that a substantially greater prevalence of male homosexual behaviour could justify different legal treatment. However, the evidence was highly contradictory and incomplete so no support for such a distinction was obtained. In fact, several witnesses were clear that there was no such difference in prevalence: Drs Kelnar and Dicks of the Tavistock Clinic maintained that lesbians were 'equally responsible', could do 'as much harm as the male homosexual', and 'there should be considerable equality in treatment' (qu. 2912). More helpful for the Committee was evidence such as that of Dr J.A. Hobson of the Royal Medico-Psychological Society, who combined estimates of lower prevalence with hearsay impressions that lesbians were 'more under control, [living] more celibate lives' (qu. 3335).

The Committee was much less open to discussion of the unfairness and illogicality of the current law, frequently cutting it short by pointing out that those objections could be met by criminalising gross indecency between women (e.g. qus. 1760, 2396–2399, 3224, 3339). This was something of a warning shot to supporters of decriminalisation that arguments based on formal equality were better avoided. Its strategic nature is evident from the rather different use made of it by solicitor Lord Mischon during the examination of Law Society witnesses. They were speaking to a memorandum based around Jeremy Bentham's rules for criminal legislation; the first of these was that the objectionable practice must produce evils great enough to counterbalance the suffering caused by punishment (Council of the Law Society 1955, TNA HO 345/8). Mischon's questions demonstrated that according to the witnesses' arguments for defining homosexuality as such a harm, lesbianism should also be criminalised.

They pleaded a lack of knowledge of lesbianism in order to avoid expressing a definite view, but Mischon's attack supported the Committee's ultimate conclusions by implying that arguments leading to equal treatment of male and female homosexuals were necessarily flawed (qus. 3111–3121).

None of the complexities of this evidence appeared in the final report. Its dismissal of female homosexuals as apparently less 'libidinous' or prevalent imported a distinction which witnesses had often had difficulty in making or refused to make. That reticence was in tune with other reports of the period: the Royal Commission on Marriage and Divorce reported a year earlier than Wolfenden, rejecting lesbianism as a ground for divorce because sodomy-like physical relations could be neither defined nor proved (Royal Commission on Marriage and Divorce 1956, pp. 30–31). Thus even at a time of very public debate about the legal regulation of sexuality, open discussion of lesbianism was avoided. Instead, Wolfenden drew upon the persisting notion of women as sexually passive, lacking 'libidinous' desire, and to be shielded from sexual knowledge. Yet the Committee, given the evidence it had heard, was conscious that the view of female sexuality asserted here was not accurate.

Limiting Political Claims

There were strong inducements for the Wolfenden Report to offer a desexualised portrayal of lesbianism. If male and female homosexual behaviours were not firmly differentiated, then the law should not be either. However, the Report's recommendations were not intended to radically disrupt the law but to cautiously reform it by advocating non-interference with *private* behaviour. The invisible women of Wolfenden were, implicitly, from the respectable, white middle classes: the same section of society whose homosexual men received limited support from the Report. Lewis notes that Wolfenden seems to have accepted the distinction made by the Home Office, DPP and police between respectable, monogamous homosexuals and those who were corrupting and promiscuous (Lewis 2016, p. 14).[6] Patrick Trevor-Roper, eminent oph-

[6] The former, they claimed, need not fear prosecution. Other witnesses, including the Bar Council, were more sceptical of police practices.

thalmologist and one of three self-identifying homosexual men to give evidence, later recalled a dinner with Wolfenden in which the latter was 'slightly holding his nose in the air' but intimated that the committee preferred to listen to Trevor-Roper than others who were less articulate or balanced (quoted in Lewis 2016, pp. 202–03).[7] The Committee heard from and offered its support to a very narrow range of men, the 'right type of homosexual' (Lewis 2016, p. 203).[8]

The Wolfenden Report emphatically did not advocate equality, yet that was exactly the standard by which witnesses were measuring the law when they criticised its criminalisation of men for behaviour legal among women. Such arguments may seem compelling in a contemporary context where equality arguments have been the basis for legal reforms including equal marriage, an equal age of consent, and the protections of the 2010 Equality Act, but this was a very different era. The Campaign for Homosexuality Equality, which began as a legal reform committee and would prove influential in later decades, was not founded until 1964 (Scott-Presland 2015); the first cautious legal equality measures, the Race Relations Act and Equal Pay Act, would not become law until 1965 and 1970, respectively. In that context, a report advocating legal equality between homosexuals and heterosexuals would have been unlikely to achieve changes to the law. Hostility to even modest reform was such that it would take a further decade for legislation to pass through Parliament, and positive rights were not in prospect.

The Report did draw a parallel between homosexual men and women at one point, but not in a criminal context. Addressing the contention articulated by the Law Society that male homosexual behaviour 'has a damaging effect on family life', the Report accepted this was often true because homosexual behaviour could prevent or break up a man's marriage. While deploring 'this damage to what we regard as the basic unit of society' the Committee went on to note that 'cases are also frequently

[7] Probably a reference to Wildeblood; the third openly gay witness was Carl Winter, Director of the Fitzwilliam Museum.

[8] Leslie Moran (1995, p. 115) also argues that the Committee 'hoped homosexual acts might disappear into a space beyond the law'.

encountered in which a marriage has been broken up by homosexual behaviour by the wife, and no doubt some women, too, derive sufficient satisfaction from homosexual outlets to prevent their marrying'. However, the Report did not focus solely on lesbianism but also made comparisons to adultery and fornication, concluding that 'it is difficult to see why on this ground male homosexual behaviour alone among them should be a criminal offence' (CHOP 1957, p. 22). The inclusion of heterosexual conduct drew attention away from a direct comparison between the position of women and men engaged in same-sex sexual activity, and thus avoided undermining the Report's wider agenda. That was not to endorse or destigmatise homosexuality but to control and limit it, as was apparent in the modifications to the harm principle as well as an emphasis upon the causes and treatment of homosexuality. Jeffrey Weeks has pointed out that the unifying element between this part of the Report and that on prostitution was a shift in the criminal law's role from 'guardian of private morality' to 'protector of public decency' (1981, p. 243). The courts proved willing to take on that role, as seen in the expansion of prosecutions for conspiracy to protect public morals discussed further below. Lord Reid was correct to assert in *Knuller* [1973] AC 435 (HL) that the 1967 Act did not 'indicate that parliament thought or intended to lay down that indulgence in these practices is not corrupting' (p. 437).

The resulting emphasis on private conduct as legally tolerable if out of sight meant that lesbianism was not problematic: constructed as invisible, indeed made so by the Report itself, it would not require criminal prohibition. More specifically, the Report amounted to a confirmation that lesbianism among the 'right sort' of respectable, white, British women was not libidinous or socially problematic. The same might not be true for other, 'psychopathic', promiscuous, or foreign women; as former stipendiary magistrate UP Eddy stated in relation to men, 'We do not take our morals from the Continent' (qu. 4005). Some witnesses also raised another possible source of corruption: women's emancipation (e.g. Sir Laurence Dunne, Memorandum, HO 345/7, para. 19). They were right, insofar as the growth of the women's liberation movement as well as the gay rights movement would make traditional silencing untenable and a new approach had to emerge.

Articulating the Lesbian Comparator

Parliament was not easily convinced that even limited decriminalisation of sex between men was the right course to take. Introducing the Report to the House of Commons over a year after its publication, Home Secretary Richard Austen (Rab) Butler referred to the breadth of views on this issue and articulated his own concerns (HC 26/11/1958, cols. 365–371). In the discussion which followed, MPs were not constrained by a party line since the issue was treated as one of individual conscience, allowing a range of opinions to be expressed. Several supporters of the Wolfenden recommendations explicitly raised the legal position of lesbianism, suggesting an exact parallel which made continued total criminalisation unjustifiable—although they did not go so far as to advocate for homosexual equality. Harford Montgomery Hyde MP was first to raise the comparison, in a speech which would later lead to his deselection from his North Belfast constituency (McDowell 2004):

> [A]dultery and fornication are not offences for which a person can be punished by the criminal law. Nor indeed is prostitution as such. Nor, I may add, is lesbianism or homosexual conduct between females, and here, indeed, is an anomaly. If homosexual conduct between consenting adults in private is to continue to be an offence, is homosexual conduct between consenting female adults in private also to continue not to be an offence? (HC 26/11/1958, col. 392)

Kenneth Younger similarly struggled to see a substantive difference:

> I have never been able to find any fundamental difference except that one is talked about and the other is not. I have never met anyone who, in relation to Lesbianism, does not share the views put forward by the Wolfenden Committee in respect of male homosexuality. (HC 26/11/1958, col. 409)

Sir Hugh Linstead, who had been a member of the Wolfenden Committee, departed from its findings to advocate the formal equality the Report had been so careful to avoid. He stated that male and female homosexuality were equally prevalent and proposed explicitly 'that the same law shall be applied to consenting males as is applied today to consenting females' (HC 26/11/1958, col. 409). However, he also took care to limit rights claims: equal legal treatment would bring with it an equal responsibility 'for behaving themselves in public' (HC 26/11/1958, col. 414).

To opponents, lesbianism was different for reasons which, though difficult to articulate, drew upon traditional constructions of femininity. Frederick Bellenger suggested that decriminalising private homosexual acts would allow 'a malignant cancer' whose spread meant that 'humanity would eventually revert to an animal existence' (HC 26/11/1958, col. 417). Countering him, William Wells challenged him to explain the difference between male and female homosexuality; Bellenger responded that although his service in both world wars meant he knew something of the former, 'I know nothing or practically nothing, except what one may read, about lesbianism' (HC 26/11/1958, col. 418). A fellow opponent of decriminalisation, William Shepherd, asserted that 'Lesbian associations in many cases supply a social purpose, because they tend to be much more lasting or permanent than homosexual associations' (HC 26/11/1958, col. 428).

The proposed reforms were sufficiently controversial within both the Conservative and Labour Parties that there was little enthusiasm for putting forward a government bill. Attempts to raise the issue before Parliament in the early 1960s were unsuccessful. Nonetheless, public and parliamentary opinion was gradually shifting in favour of a change in the law. The equation of male homosexuality with lesbianism helped support that shift, and campaigners were well aware of its possibilities. Tony Geraghty wrote in lesbian magazine *Arena Three* that in the 1965 debates, reference would be made to the growing visibility of the 'legalised homosexual population' (lesbians) to show that 'publicity about it has not demonstrated that it contains the seeds of destruction' and that the differences between lesbians and gay men were not relevant ones (Geraghty 1965, p. 6). The Earl of Arran, bringing a Bill before the House of Lords in May that year, suggested that giving effect to the Wolfenden recommendations would allow male homosexuality to take 'its dreary place side by side with lesbianism or adultery' (HL 12/03/1965, col. 77). Lord James of Rusholme referred to the 'staggering illogicality' of men and women's different legal position (HL 12/03/1965, col. 107). The Lord Chancellor emphasised the equivalency of gay men and lesbians, drawing on the etymology of 'homosexual'—'homos' is Greek for 'same'—as well as the social harm done by divorce (HL 12/03/1965, cols. 169–170). The Bill passed the House of Lords but ran out of parliamentary time. Arran introduced another unsuccessful Bill before sponsoring Abse's successful 1967 Bill through the House of Lords. By this time, the Labour government elected in 1964 had increased its majority in the 1966 general election and Roy Jenkins, a supporter of law reform, had become Home Secretary.

Despite their different uses of the lesbian comparator, both sides of the parliamentary debates shared one common feature with each other and with the Wolfenden Committee's witnesses. They did not discuss lesbianism as an issue of importance in its own right; indeed, some of them were happy to emphasise their ignorance of it. Rather, the lesbian mattered only insofar as she affected the male homosexual. As the Howard League had written in their memorandum to the Committee, women's different legal position 'does nothing to help the social readjustment of male homosexuals' (Howard League for Penal Reform, Memorandum, TNA CHP/45, para. A.I.1). The debates on the 1967 Bill highlight the extent to which lesbian visibility was contingent upon its usefulness to discussions of male homosexuality. In the latter stages of that Bill, the lesbian comparator disappeared again while detailed comparisons with heterosexual acts, and between various permutations of ages, were drawn. It would have been tactically unhelpful to remind a Parliament seeking to justify a higher age of consent for acts between men that for women, it was sixteen. Even an unsuccessful amendment which would have criminalised 'activities tending to promote homosexuality between consenting adults', not limited to male homosexuality, was debated without reference to lesbianism (HC 23/06/1967, cols. 2115–2155).

The conflation of male and female homosexuality, with the male taken as the norm and focus, was largely novel: they had hitherto been treated by legislators as two separate issues. That was apparent, for example, in correspondence between the Lord Chamberlain (the Earl of Clarendon) and the Lord Chancellor William Jowitt in 1951. Faced with the question of whether all representations of lesbianism or male homosexuality should continue to be banned on stage, the Lord Chamberlain had sought Jowitt's advice. The topic had been made urgent, he explained, because he had a play about lesbianism awaiting his decision (Lord Chamberlain to Lord Chancellor, 6 February 1951, TNA LCO 2/4705). To Jowitt, these were separate if connected questions and central to his advice was his 'very high impression' of modern 'girls' who 'would be revolted by an indecent discussion on [lesbianism] even though they know all about [it]'. Tellingly, he acknowledged that straightforward silencing might no longer be a viable option: 'we Victorians are always apt to confuse innocence with ignorance.' His recommendation was that licences should only be withheld from plays who mentioned the subjects in an 'indecent fashion' (Lord Chancellor to Lord Chamberlain, 7 February 1951, TNA LCO 2/4705).

The new conception of lesbianism as part of the same phenomenon as male homosexuality nonetheless treated it as a lesser, quieter version. Following its introduction in discussions of the Wolfenden Report, that approach quickly took root in legal and governmental discourses. Thus in 1978, the UK government argued before the European Court of Human Rights in *Dudgeon v United Kingdom* (A/45) [1981] 9 WLUK 88 that the differences in criminal regulation of male and female homosexuality reflected 'a genuine difference both in the nature and the scale of the social and moral problems' (quoted in Crane 1982, p. 9). The argument was not addressed in the majority judgment, but had been accepted by the European Commission on Human Rights ((1981) 3 EHRR 40, para. 120). A new form of silencing was appearing: the recognition of the lesbian only as a less significant counterpart to the gay man. In the latter part of the twentieth century, her existence would be acknowledged by Parliament and the law but she was rarely allowed her own voice.

From Congenital Inversion to Medicalised Homosexuality

Legal discourses on sexuality, like wider culture, drew upon popularised versions of the medical literature. Earlier sexological models of inversion were already being challenged in the interwar period by Freudian theories of sexual development. Those ideas in turn increasingly informed popular notions of sexuality after the Second World War. Like sexology, psychoanalysis had an uneven cultural impact as it became simplified, reinterpreted, and misunderstood. It also continued sexology's work of formulating lesbianism as flawed and inferior to heterosexuality, albeit now attributed to arrested psychosexual development rather than congenital abnormality. And like sexology, Freudianism developed a peculiarly British strand: Alison Oram (1992) has noted that while the theories of the unconscious, repression, and sublimation were retained, Freud's emphasis upon the primacy of the sexual drive was diluted.

The importance psychoanalysis gave to childhood both emphasised the significance of women's maternal role and posited lesbianism as a developmental failure. That approach was making its way into parts of wider culture—but not legal discourse—by the 1930s. In 1932, Helena Wright advised girls that their task was to develop from the 'more or less sex-unconscious child' into having 'a frank and healthily developed attraction for the opposite sex' (1932, p. 136, repeated in 1956, p. 94). 'Hero-worshipping' same-sex attraction, like the 'childish affair' of masturbation, should be no more than a brief stop along the way (Wright 1956, p. 99; Oldfield 2001, pp. 77–80). The woman who failed to develop into her role as wife and mother was pathologised as not only frigid or perverse but also at risk of mental illness (much as she had risked greensickness in the eighteenth century). And just as the attribution of active desire to eighteenth-century women had been far from uniformly liberatory (see Chap. 3), the modern identification of a universal sexual instinct would throw new suspicion onto lesbians and spinsters (the former generally subsumed within the latter category). Dominant strands of feminism and popular culture emphasised the importance of heterosexual unions to women, accepting the new theories of spinsterhood as necessarily problematic (Jeffreys 1985). Eugenicist Sybil Neville-Rolfe urged that lesbians 'should be looked upon as sick persons' to be sympathised with and treated psychologically if possible, but also recognised as 'a serious social evil' since 'the abnormality is socially and racially very undesirable' (1935, pp. 105–06). Those negative discourses were not universally accepted or adopted, and some feminists did find ways to resist the discrediting of spinsterhood and to create positive spaces and campaigns (Oram 1992).

The psychoanalytically inspired model would start to make its way into legal discourse after the Second World War (Oram 2006). It was brought before the Wolfenden Committee by the MWF submission (BMA 1955, paras. 29–38) which offered a semi-official summary of it as the prevailing model in the medical profession. The MWF account described a number of differences between male and female homosexuality, although any explanation of them through women's reproductive biology was expressly discounted (BMA 1955, para. 32). It offered the 'interesting fact' that during the war there had been 'little homosexuality' among women in the armed forces. (The War Office had made the subtly different claim that very few cases were *reported* (War Office, Memorandum, TNA CHP/47, para. 13)). Situational lesbianism was associated with the criminal classes, occurring in 'prisons, approved schools and remand homes'—but only if there was a 'psychopathic' or 'mentally subnormal' ringleader (BMA 1955, para. 31). Even outside the carceral context, lesbian relationships were apparently prone to 'end in disaster' due to jealousy and possessiveness, while those who were 'incapable of love' and often 'psychopathic' engaged in 'organised vice' (lesbian prostitution). This allegation was all the more extraordinary since the memorandum conceded that '[t]here is … little actual knowledge on this point' (BMA 1955, para. 36). Yet the MWF were not wholly negative about lesbian relationships, instead drawing a distinction between the 'promiscuous Lesbian, sometimes addicted to perverted physical practices' and the (implicitly middle-class) 'women of distinction' for whom a 'faithful love relationship' could be a positive part of their lives (BMA 1955, para. 34).

The memorandum's authors included Albertine Winner, who had been a senior doctor within the Royal Army Medical Corps during the War and served as deputy chief medical officer in the Department of Health from 1947. In a conference paper that year, she had set out her understanding of lesbianism. She emphasised that it did not pose the same social problems as male homosexuality, claiming that in most relationships, 'any real attempt at producing orgasm, is not at all common'. As a result, the child abuse and prostitution she associated with 'the promiscuous male' were absent (Winner 1947, pp. 5–6). The only issues posed by lesbianism were its interference with women's 'proper reproductive function' and the lack of research on the subject by women (pp. 3 and 7).

For those who did find lesbianism to be a problem, there were various new mechanisms for dealing with it: not only could women consult general practitioners and psychiatrists, but Rebecca Jennings highlights the growing numbers of counsellors, psychotherapists, and social workers in post-war Britain (Jennings 2008, pp. 892–98). The relationships between women and professionals varied widely, not least according to the class of the patient and whether they sought NHS or private treatment. Many practitioners did not see lesbianism as necessarily requiring treatment, but others offered 'cures' through treatments including psychotherapy, drug therapy (e.g. use of LSD), behavioural therapy, aversion therapy, and psychosurgery (Jennings 2008, pp. 894–95). While women were unlikely to be coerced into treatment through prosecution for homosexual offences, they were at risk in other encounters with the criminal justice system. Referrals from probation officers and social workers could create a coercive context in terms of both treatment and patient consent. At the end of the 1950s, Luchia Fitzgerald's probation officer referred her to a psychiatrist in the belief that her lesbianism was behind her minor juvenile offending. The psychiatrist suggested brain surgery to which she nearly agreed, although she ultimately refused after speaking about it to a lesbian friend (Jivani 1997, pp. 126–27).

Added to this was the emphasis in the 1950s upon homosexuality as a medical issue, not only in professional and legal discourse but also to some extent in popular culture. Just as Wolfenden recommended medical research and treatment, Oram highlights how newspaper crime stories portrayed lesbianism 'intertwined with discourses of psychiatry' and the lesbian as unbalanced and socially marginal (2007, p. 44). A medicalised approach was not novel (see Chaps. 4 and 5); but the shift from gynaecology to psychiatry was significant. It further aligned the approach to lesbianism with that to male homosexuality. The Wolfenden Report, for example, had recommended that buggery should be reduced to a misdemeanour (a less serious offence) in order to facilitate the seeking of medical advice.[9] The Wolfenden era's psychologically oriented approach to criminal prosecutions owed much to developments in criminology and penology as well as sexology. There was increasing official attention to the reform and treatment of offenders of all kinds, evident for example in the 1939 Home Office Report on the Psychological Treatment of Crime (East and Hubert 1939); the provisions for treatment of offenders in the Criminal Justice Act 1948; and a 1949 appeal for treatment as well as punishment of homosexual offenders (British Medical Association and Magistrates' Association 1949; Waters 1999, p. 142). The Wolfenden Report itself discussed a variety of possible aetiologies of homosexuality without committing to any of them (CHOP 1957, chap. III), as well as acknowledging uncertainties and reservations about the effectiveness of treatment. It did not dismiss the usefulness of such attempts, but did delegate responsibility to the medical profession by recommending further research (CHOP 1957, paras. 214–17). This rather uneven and strategic appeal to medical expertise was a recurring theme in legislation of the 1950s and 1960s: it would also be apparent, for example, in the Abortion Act 1967's reconstruction of abortion as a medical rather than moral issue, but one kept under legislative control.

The effects of this shift from morality to medicine were evident in the criminal courts from the 1940s onwards, not so much in medical reports as in the comments of 'police, probation officers and lawyers' (Oram 2007, p. 140). Yet it is important to remember that the lesbian was also marginalised in the psychiatric literature. Her status was that of little-studied 'other' to the healthy married woman or the troublesome male homosexual. Winner (1947) observed that there was a paucity of psychiatric literature on lesbianism, since most research on 'homosexuality' in fact referred only to men. W Lindsay Neustatter would attribute this to a lack of lesbians consulting psychiatrists, a medical under-representation which was connected to legal silencing (Neustatter 1955, pp. 99–100; quoted in Jennings 2008, p. 887). With no pressure from the criminal justice system to seek treatment, fewer lesbians did so. Popular science

[9] Failure to disclose a felony (a serious offence) to the police was itself a crime, misprision of felony, albeit there had been no prosecutions of doctors ("Report of the Departmental Committee on Homosexual Offences and Prostitution" 1957, p. 640).

books such as Eustace Chesser's *Odd Man Out* and Pelican paperbacks by D.J. West and Anthony Storr nonetheless considered lesbianism (Chesser 1959; West 1955; Storr 1964; and see Jennings 2008). Using Freudian theories of delayed psychosexual development, they explained it in terms of arrested development, penis envy, and a consequent hostility to men founded in feelings of inferiority.[10] The message for their largely middle-class readers was clear: relationships with other women were immature, inferior, and needed to be supplanted by married heterosexuality. Lesbianism thus appeared as a failure or lack rather than a positive identity. Nonetheless, did this mark a substantial fracture in the policy of legal silencing?

Cracks in the Wall of Silence?

Wartime Regulation

The silencing reasserted following the *Well of Loneliness* and Colonel Barker prosecutions at the end of the 1920s (Chap. 5) had endured through the 1940s. During the Second World War, many women served in branches of the armed forces including the Women's Auxiliary Air Force (WAAF); the Women's Royal Naval Service; and the Auxiliary Territorial Service (ATS), the women's branch of the Army. These all-female institutions were subject to military discipline which prohibited same-sex sexual conduct, meaning that the issue of lesbianism had to be considered. At the same time, strenuous efforts were made not to recognise lesbianism in practise. Those efforts were helped by the pseudo-Freudian explanation of such conduct as evidence of immaturity rather than perversion. Interpreted as a passing phase rather than an inclination, it was considered most likely to spread through gossip and bad influences, meaning that silencing continued to be the best tactic to address it. The overall approach in the women's services was to say nothing where

[10] In his evidence to the Wolfenden Committee, Chesser expressly opposed the criminalisation of female and male homosexuality (qu. 3224).

possible: while sex education talks were given, mention of lesbianism was actively prohibited (Vickers 2009, p. 434).

As the War Office explained in its written submission to the Wolfenden Committee, a memorandum had been prepared for the ATS by 'a woman medical adviser' (Letitia Fairfield, Senior Woman Medical Officer and also a qualified barrister) but was issued only on request, 'for fear of creating a problem by drawing attention to it'.[11] The number of cases was allegedly 'exceedingly small' and dealt with by posting the women concerned apart; only 'promiscuous Lesbians' had to be discharged from the service (War Office, TNA CHP/47, para. 13). Albertine Winner later emphasised that there was no 'ignorance of the possibilities' of lesbianism among senior personnel but rather 'a very sensible approach' which recognised gossip as more dangerous to other women than 'unfortunate Lesbians'. Such gossip could be contained because knowledge of lesbianism was still considered to be largely confined to medical professionals: as Fairfield later wrote, they had to explain 'rudimentary matter' since 'a great many women have not the remotest idea what we are talking about' (Dr. Letitia Fairfield, Papers: Homosexuality, LMA PH/GEN/3/19). The limited availability of the memorandum was credited with ensuring that out of a quarter of a million ATS women, only about half a dozen had to be discharged, with most cases due to 'a promiscuous psychopath' (Winner 1947, p. 6). Emma Vickers has identified a similar approach in the Women's Auxiliary Air Force, where a 1941 case described as involving 'misfits' in a 'highly temperamental and peculiar state of mind' was resolved by reposting the women (Vickers 2009, p. 431).

In a familiar discursive manoeuvre, inappropriate behaviour was associated with the lower classes: much behaviour the middle-class authorities might otherwise interpret as lesbian was ascribed to working-class norms. Women accustomed to sharing beds with their sisters might do so with friends; displays of physical affection could be 'normal customs of factory life'; while sexual practices were the preserve of a 'self conscious intelligentsia' (Fairfield, quoted in Vickers 2009, p. 434). Squadron Leader A.P. Doran, looking back from the vantage point of the 1970s,

[11] While the War Office stated it was produced in 1941, Vickers dates it to 1943 and identifies its author (2009, p. 432).

suggested that this approach was driven by wartime expediency (Vickers 2009, p. 432), but in fact it continued into the following decades. That was explicitly confirmed in the War Office's evidence to the Wolfenden Committee. It had extended, not retreated from, its wartime position: not only did cases remain 'extremely rare' but it was now possible to deal with them by discharging those involved as 'services no longer required', ostensibly an administrative rather than disciplinary discharge. Most incidents continued to be seen as involving possible misconstruction of 'ignorant but perfectly harmless behaviour' (War Office, TNA CHP/47, para. 14).

Meanwhile, the tensions between legal silencing and social speech remained unresolved in the civilian courts. In a 1942 decision which both acknowledged lesbianism and worked to legally silence it, Asquith J. held that an allegation of lesbianism amounted to an imputation of unchastity. In other words, it fell within one of the exceptions to the general rule that a slander claim required proof of pecuniary loss in order to succeed. He repeated pre-war themes of lesbianism as elite male knowledge: 'I should be much surprised if, under whatever name, the parliamentary draftsmen of the 1890's were ignorant of [lesbianism's] existence. To assume this to be the case one must assume that they had little or no knowledge of the literature of the ancient world: an assumption which I make bold to repel' (*Kerr v Kennedy* [1942] 1 KB 409 at p. 412).

The Post-war Lesbian Marriage-Breaker

After the Second World War, silencing remained central to the policing of lesbian sexuality. Laura Doan describes how Radclyffe Hall's partner Una Troubridge wrote to the Home Office in 1948 asking them to reconsider the ban on *The Well of Loneliness*. Not only was her request refused but the case files were 'severely purged' and closed until 2048 (Doan 2001, p. ix). The BBC apparently had a '[h]igh-level shush-shush policy' on lesbianism (Benno 1964). Even the complex cultural figure of the female husband, whose sexuality was simultaneously hinted at and denied, was moving out of public view: Oram has identified a significant decrease in reporting of women's gender-crossing following the War.

From a high of around ten reports a year in the decade following the Colonel Barker case, the number fell to just one or two a year between 1940 and 1960 (Oram 2007, p. 3). There were, though, other cultural changes which set such legal silencing increasingly in tension with the wider culture. It is difficult to assess how much was known by the general public: while cases such as the *Well of Loneliness* trial had been widely reported, Wolfenden claimed that when his Committee was formed, '[m]ost ordinary people had never heard of homosexuality' between men or women (Wolfenden 1976, p. 132).[12] Campaigner Allan Horsfall recollected that gay men could be 'well into late adolescence' before they decoded press reports of 'gross indecency' to realise that their sexual activity was criminal (Bedell 2007). What can be perceived, however, is that knowledge was *increasing* as a result of cultural changes. We have seen that popular science publications were disseminating knowledge of lesbianism more widely, at least for educated middle-class readers, although their loosely Freudian approach condemned lesbians as failed heterosexuals.

Lesbianism was also beginning to be raised overtly in court. In 1947, a female husband case initially reported in traditional, mostly humorous terms took an unusual turn. Ellen/Alan Young was prosecuted for making false declarations in relation to her 1946 marriage to Irene Palmer. The issue of lesbian sexuality was raised during the plea in mitigation: defence counsel referred to a sexual experience with an older woman in Holloway Prison which 'brought [Young] into contact with a form of perversion.' Even so, the defence also called upon the older trope of thwarted heterosexual love, here for a soldier lost in Singapore. It had limited success in court, where she was sentenced to nine months' imprisonment, but won a measure of sympathetic treatment from the *News of the World* (Oram 2007, pp. 134–37). Significantly, the issue of lesbian sexuality had not been raised by the prosecution.

External pressure upon legal silencing continued to mount. The lesbian had gained a new image as a 'wife-stealer' in the popular press before the War (Oram 2016, pp. 172–74). In the post-war period, while the

[12] My informal discussions with several people who grew up in the 1940s and 1950s suggest that there was truth in that claim.

press moved on to more pathologised representations (Oram 2007, pp. 140–42), there were efforts to invoke the marriage-breaking lesbian in the civil courts and the Wolfenden Report (CHOP 1957, p. 22). This was both a reflection of post-war concerns about family breakdown (Waters 2013; Smart 1981, pp. 46–47) and a continuation of earlier tropes. The predatory lesbian threatening marriages had something in common with pre-war stereotypes of the congenital invert or degenerate pervert, preying upon women who were not innately lesbian and would otherwise accept heterosexuality. Eagerness to reassert women's domestic and maternal roles after the disruptions of wartime, coupled with ongoing concern about the birthrate, once more saw the single woman problematised and pathologised (Thane 1999; Smith 1951; Hutton 1960). This legal anxiety about lesbianism as a threat to marriage made itself felt when lesbian magazine *Arena Three* was founded: it initially required married women to provide their husband's written consent in order to subscribe, following advice on the legal implications of allowing such subscriptions (Jennings 2007, p. 157).

Yet the marriage-breaker proved surprisingly elusive once actual evidence was sought, as the Wolfenden Committee found when hearing witnesses. The Chief Metropolitan Magistrate, Sir Laurence Dunn, argued that lesbians abounded in certain clubs and pubs; but he defined the social problem posed by lesbianism as its 'pernicious' role in breaking up marriages. However, he had only known of 'one or two cases' himself (qus. 3024–3025). The Law Society's witnesses were questioned on their experience of a wife's lesbianism breaking up a marriage. Two had no personal experience of it at all; two had been involved in only a single case each (qu. 3112). Their memorandum had dismissed lesbianism in a sentence, concluding that 'there is no public demand for any [criminal] legislation and no problem of any significant proportions' (Law Society 1955, p. 4). The witnesses from the Tavistock Clinic argued that lesbianism was prevalent but could point to only one current case where they were seeing 'the very depressed and depressive husband' (qu. 2916). In the House of Lords a decade later, the Lord Chancellor took refuge in vague appeals to 'anyone with a divorce practice' knowing of such cases (Lord Gardiner, HL 12/03/1965, col. 169).

The wife-stealing lesbian's legal presence was even more circumscribed. It was felt primarily in the divorce courts, which proved ambiguous about her appearance. In 1949, a husband was granted a decree nisi on the ground of desertion but the judge emphasised that the wife would never have left him had she not fallen under the 'ghastly and baleful influence' of an 'evil' and 'curious' woman who dressed like a man. The news report described an attempt to separate the women as a 'rescue' which failed when the other woman threatened suicide. The relationship was thus recast as a morbid friendship in the pre-War mould, a matter of personality rather than sexuality, although the echoes of congenital and pseudo-inversion were also apparent. The judge deemed the husband 'entitled to the utmost sympathy' (*Nottingham Evening Post* 1949).

The possibility of a sexual relationship was denied even in the face of apparently strong evidence in *Spicer v Spicer (Ryan intervening)* [1954] 3 All ER 208. The husband petitioned for divorce on the grounds of cruelty, alleging that his wife had formed a lesbian relationship with another woman. The wife formally conceded that her friendship was 'of such a kind as to give her husband grave cause for anxiety as to the precise nature of that association' but denied lesbianism. Karminski J. accepted that her subsequent refusal to give up the association despite her husband's 'entreaties' and 'best endeavours' amounted to cruelty. He was effectively endorsing an agreement reached by the parties, but when left to make the decision themselves, courts were reluctant to find that a same-sex friendship could amount to cruelty. In another case the same year the petitioning husband, a vicar, described how his wife and her female friend (who sometimes wore 'mannish' clothes) walked hand in hand, kissed on the lips, addressed each other as darling, sometimes shared a bed, and holidayed together. Davies J found that the friendship was 'a very odd business' but 'perfectly innocent' and the husband could not reasonably believe it 'improper' (*Daily Mirror* 1954; Oram 2007, pp. 141–42). Even where a couple had agreed before marrying that the wife's woman friend would sleep with her after the marriage, the court which considered a maintenance order following divorce emphasised 'there was never any suggestion' of a 'physical or emotional' lesbian relationship (Oram 2007, p. 142). While the courts may have been reluctant to endorse husbands' suspicions of lesbianism, a wife who sought to divorce her husband on similar grounds met outright hostility from the Court of Appeal in *Buchler v Buchler* [1947] P 25. Petitioning on the ground of constructive desertion as a result of a similarly suspect relationship between her husband and his pig-man (later bailiff), the wife was condemned in the Court of Appeal for her 'dereliction of duty' in leaving the marital home and her attitude characterised as, if not snobbish, something close to it. In other words, the divorce courts' priority in these cases was to police wifely obedience to patriarchal authority.

The Post-war Unnatural Friendship

The criminal courts, though, were developing in a different direction more aligned with press representations. They did not deal with the lesbian 'marriage-breaker' since she committed no crime. Instead, a female husband case heard the same year as *Spicer v Spicer* suggests they seized upon the 'unnatural friendship' model. Vincent/Violet Jones and Joan Lee married in Catford, with Jones presenting as the bridegroom. Both spouses pleaded guilty to making a false statement for the purpose of obtaining a marriage certificate and were fined £25 each. Jones was trans, attending court in male clothing and explaining that he felt he was really male and had attempted to obtain medical treatment (*Lancashire Evening Post* 1954). This was accepted by his solicitor and largely respected by the press; a medical report confirmed Jones's 'delusion' (Oram 2007, pp. 146–48). Yet the magistrates' court treated this as a clearly lesbian case, convicting and punishing the wife as well as her husband and castigating both defendants for their 'unnatural passions' (Oram 2006). It is ironic, if all too consistent with the long history of criminal regulation, that when a court did overtly recognise a 'lesbian' relationship it did so for a relationship that was not actually lesbian.

That magistrates' court's approach was perhaps anomalous. In the 1948 murder prosecution of Margaret/Bill Allen, legal, prison, and medical personnel worked together to deny the possibility of lesbianism. Allen was tried for murdering elderly, eccentric acquaintance Nancy Chadwick with a hammer. Allen confessed the killing but denied the motive was robbery, saying, 'I was in one of my funny moods' (*Manchester Evening*

News 1948). The evidence of her close friend Annie Cook pointed to Allen being lesbian or trans. Cook claimed in her witness statement to have refused a sexual relationship, apparently with great pragmatism (Annie Cook, 'Statement', 1948, TNA MEPO 3/3024 17):

> [Allen] said to me, "We have been going out long enough now together. Can't we start having connections". I told her, "No. I am parted from my husband and I don't want to bother". That was all that was said. As far as I known [*sic*] I don't know what she was going to have connections with from her point of view.

The friendship continued and when they were out together, Allen asked to be called Bill and used men's lavatories.

Although Allen's defence was insanity, it was effectively thwarted by the prison Medical Officer who gave evidence that she was not insane. He placed her deviancy within discourses around women's unruly reproductive biology rather than pathological sexuality, concluding that any symptoms Allen experienced were a feature of the menopause rather than mental illness. According to his report, Allen told him that she wore trousers and a jumper as a bus conductress and thereafter found them 'convenient'. She denied any homosexual tendencies and 'frankly admit[ted] occasional normal sexual intercourse' (EWA Cormack, 'Report of Medical Officer, HM Prison Manchester', 1948, TNA ASSI 86/20). The jury rejected a plea of insanity after fifteen minutes' deliberation, and the judge passed a death sentence (DCI Stevens, Central Officer's Special Report, 1948, TNA MEPO 3/3024 18A). The Home Secretary refused clemency (J.A. Newsam to Commissioner of Police of the Metropolis, 3 January 1949, TNA MEPO 3/3024 21A). Allen was executed in January 1959, the first woman to be hanged since before the Second World War. National press reports focused on the 'woman with mannish ways' without overt reference to lesbianism (Herald Reporter 1948; Oram 2007, p. 143). It was lesbian magazine *Arena Three* which identified the failure to extend mercy offered to other killers 'where circumstances were less extenuating' as due to Allen's apparent lesbianism (Gulston 1966).

Four years later, the issue of lesbianism was harder to avoid when Bertha Scorse was tried for murdering her lover. They had met in a sanatorium while being treated for tuberculosis. When the other woman ended the relationship, Bertha stabbed her. Again, the defence was insanity; this time, a prison medical officer did discuss 'perverted emotion'. However, his conclusion was that it may have led to Scorse's 'lack of self-control' but not insanity. Dr Roy Neville Craig, instructed by the defence, diagnosed her as a legally insane psychopath with a 'gross perversion' but her position, stricken with tuberculosis and lying on a stretcher while the sentence was pronounced, attracted more press attention than her 'perverted passion' (Oram 2007, pp. 144–45). To the *Daily Mail*, she was a 'Cornish girl' who had murdered 'her friend' (*Daily Mail* 1952a, b). The *Daily Mirror* reported that the 'stretcher girl' had an 'abnormal friendship' but mostly focused upon defence counsel's interpretation of it as the desperate affection of a dying woman rather than the 'matter of horror' it would be between 'normally healthy persons' (*Daily Mirror* 1952a, b). The judge apparently concurred, suggesting that the jury would 'be glad' to find her not guilty by reason of insanity if the evidence allowed (*Daily Express* 1952). In fact, the jury rejected the insanity defence and Scorse was sentenced to death. Her almost immediate reprieve helped ensure that the case made little impact upon wider legal cultures. There was no allusion to it in the Wolfenden Report or the witness evidence heard by the Committee.

Rights Claims and an Emerging Movement

The possibility of decriminalisation raised by the Wolfenden Report had quickly prompted a backlash among legislators and the criminal justice system. While the recommendations on prostitution were enacted in the Street Offences Act 1959, those on homosexuality took a decade to become law. Prominent among the parliamentary opponents of reform was the man who had commissioned the Report, David Maxwell Fyfe, now sitting in the House of Lords as Lord Kilmuir. When the Sexual Offences Act 1967 did come into force, the police responded not with a more tolerant attitude but with an increase in prosecutions for homosexual offences, which rose by 55 per cent between 1966 and 1974 (Cocks 2016, p. 279). This backlash served to emphasise both the extent of hostility towards same-sex relations and the complex and uneven relationship between statutory law reforms and criminal justice system practice.

Thus, for example, the common-law offence of conspiracy to corrupt public morals enjoyed an apparent renaissance immediately after the Report's publication. Notorious among the dozens of prosecutions between 1965 and 1970, which encompassed prostitution and pornography as well as homosexuality, was that of *International Times* for publishing contact advertisements by gay men (*Knuller* [1973] AC 435 (HL)).[13] The use of this offence against publications and bookshops represented an attempt to silence the newly legal possibility of gay sex. Its prominence also made the legal position of lesbians more precarious. While sexual acts between women may not have been explicitly criminal, that was not a prerequisite for the commission of the common law offence. Thus its repressive silencing effect was able to extend to lesbian as well as gay activism: for example, *Arena Three* was initially available only to 'private subscribers' for fear of prosecution (Langley 1965). Nonetheless, the use of public proceedings was not only counterproductive but brought criticism on legal and civil rights grounds, and for that reason the offence was placed on a statutory footing by sections 1 and 5(3) of the Criminal Law Act 1977.

Lesbians were facing a new form of legal silencing in which increasingly overt hostility was articulated through condemnations of 'homosexuality' which implicitly encompassed women while ignoring the specificities of their experiences. At the same time, cultural developments were taking a slightly different direction. Women's sexuality was recognised, but firmly limited to a monogamous heterosexual context (Smart 1981, p. 48), making the lesbian both less impossible and more obviously threatening. She began to be visible in popular publications written for a heterosexual audience, notably through 1950s 'pulp' novels on lesbian themes. Their lurid covers and blurbs did little to challenge the pathologisation of lesbianism as a pornographic, 'twilight world of strange desires'

[13] For discussion of this case and whether conspiracy to corrupt public morals had existed historically as a single offence, see Cocks (2016).

(D.M.C. 1964) but did increase its visibility. In the late 1960s, depictions of lesbians began to appear more frequently in mainstream popular culture: among the best known was the film *The Killing of Sister George* (1968). Lesbians themselves actively sought visibility and social change. They challenged psychiatry and its categorisation of lesbianism as a mental illness at the same time as using scientific research to challenge public attitudes (Jennings 2008). They also formed organisations to support and campaign for lesbians, as well as social spaces such as the famous Gateways club (Jennings 2008, p. 898). The first lesbian social group, the Minorities Research Group formed in 1964, produced the monthly magazine *Arena Three*. 1969 saw the first National Women's Liberation Movement Conference, although it was not initially welcoming to lesbians, and 1970 the first meetings of the Gay Liberation Movement, attended by lesbians as well as gay men. In 1974, an end to discrimination against lesbians was added to the Women's Liberation Movement list of demands (Jennings 2007, pp. 169–75). Maureen Colquhoun came out as lesbian in 1976, becoming the first openly homosexual Member of Parliament (Jennings 2007, pp. 184–85). It was apparent that lesbians were no longer willing to be silenced and that, albeit unevenly and slowly, the law had to evolve in their wake.

Conclusion

The Wolfenden Report has been understood as a key moment in the history of male homosexuality. Not only did it start the slow process of decriminalising male homosexual acts; it also brought into legal being 'the homosexual'. For lesbians, its impact has been neglected but was both significant and quite different. At the very moment that the Report introduced homosexual identity into legal discourse, it both gendered it as male and made a parallel move to silence lesbianism. That has been little remarked upon because it appeared to be a natural result of the existing criminal law. However, consideration of the Committee's terms of reference and the evidence it sought and heard demonstrates that the silence was far from inevitable: it was a strategic move in the effort to achieve partial decriminalisation of male homosexual acts. The Report offered a template for reform which did not challenge existing beliefs about the wrongfulness of homosexuality or the undesirability of its public visibility. Instead, it presented a novel tactic for achieving the repression of male homosexuality: its silencing in the public domain through limited toleration in the private. Lesbianism, already similarly silenced, need not be discussed. More than that, it should not, since such discussion would raise challenging questions about an alternative ground for law reform: equality. Thus the Report dismissed lesbianism through comparison to male homosexuality. Lesbians were less active, less sexual, less assertive, and so less needful of legal consideration.

The Report was not the last word on the issue. Subsequent parliamentary debates and wider social changes developed a new context for the criminal regulation of lesbianism, in which total silencing was no longer possible. By the time the Sexual Offences Act 1967 became law, new possibilities for networking and campaigning were being created; second-wave feminism and the gay rights movement were developing; and lesbians would soon be demanding that their voices be heard. Yet while Wolfenden's immediate tactic was unsustainable, the same was not true of its underlying approach: the treatment of lesbianism as a subset of male homosexuality. Subjected to the social, economic and political constraints of womanhood as well as medical and societal censure for her sexuality, the lesbian was not offered liberation by this legal acknowledgement. Instead, she was consigned to a new obscurity within the shadow of the male, albeit the homosexual man rather than the paterfamilias. As the next chapter explores, this shift in approach brought an associated transformation in the criminal law's regulation of lesbianism: cases would increasingly be prosecuted as sexual offences.

References

Bedell, Geraldine. 2007. Coming Out of the Dark Ages. *Guardian*, June 24.

Bengry, Justin. 2012. Queer Profits: Homosexual Scandal and the Origins of Legal Reform in Britain. In *Queer 1950s: Rethinking Sexuality in the Postwar Years*, ed. Heike Bauer and Matt Cook, 167–182. Basingstoke: Palgrave Macmillan.

Benno, Hilary. 1964. Scouting for … The Public Image. *Arena Three*, January.
British Medical Association. 1955. *Homosexuality and Prostitution*. London.
British Medical Association, and Magistrates' Association. 1949. The Criminal Law and Sexual Offenders: A Report from the Joint Committee on Psychiatry and the Law. London.
Chesser, Eustace. 1959. *Odd Man Out: Homosexuality in Men and Women*. London: Victor Gollancz.
Church of England Moral Welfare Council. 1954. The Problem of Homosexuality. London.
Cocks, Harry. 2016. Conspiracy to Corrupt Public Morals and the 'Unlawful' Status of Homosexuality in Britain after 1967. *Social History* 41 (3): 267–284. https://doi.org/10.1080/03071022.2016.1180899.
Committee on Homosexual Offences and Prostitution. 1957. *Report of the Committee on Homosexual Offences and Prostitution*. London: Her Majesty's Stationery Office.
Cox, Pamela. 2013. *Bad Girls in Britain: Gender, Justice and Welfare, 1900–1950*. Basingstoke: Palgrave Macmillan.
Crane, Paul. 1982. *Gays and the Law*. London: Pluto Press.
D.M.C. 1964. More Thoughts on the 'Public Image.' *Arena Three*, September.
Daily Express. 1952. Stretcher Girl Is Sentenced to Death, February 22.
Daily Mail. 1952a. Cornish Girl May Appeal, February 25.
———. 1952b. Reprieved Girl Writes Home, February 27.
Daily Mirror. 1952a. You Are Trying Dying Girl, Jury Told, February 21.
———. 1952b. Stretcher Girl Guilty of Murder, February 22.
———. 1954. Her Nagging Made the Vicar a Secret Drinker—of Tea, June 1.
Devlin, Patrick. 1965. *The Enforcement of Morals*. Oxford: Oxford University Press.
Doan, Laura. 2001. *Fashioning Sapphism: The Origins of a Modern English Lesbian Culture*. New York: Columbia University Press.
East, Norwood, and W.H. de B. Hubert. 1939. *Report on the Psychological Treatment of Crime*. London.
Geraghty, Tony. 1965. The 'Blackmailers' Charter'. *Arena Three*, April.
Grimley, Matthew. 2009. Law, Morality and Secularisation: The Church of England and the Wolfenden Report, 1954–1967. *Journal of Ecclesiastical History* 60 (4): 725–741.
Gulston, Laura. 1966. The Damning of Margaret Allen. *Arena Three*, February.
Hart, H.L.A. 1962. *Law, Liberty and Morality*. Oxford: Oxford University Press.
Herald Reporter. 1948. The Woman Who Was Too Sure. *Daily Herald*, December 9.

Hutton, Laura. 1960. *The Single Woman: Her Adjustment to Life and Love*. London: Barrie & Rockliff.
Jeffreys, Sheila. 1985. *The Spinster and Her Enemies: Feminism and Sexuality 1880–1930*. Melbourne: Spinifex.
Jennings, Rebecca. 2007. *A Lesbian History of Britain: Love and Sex Between Women since 1500*. Oxford: Greenwood World Publishing.
———. 2008. 'The Most Uninhibited Party They'd Ever Been to': The Postwar Encounter Between Psychiatry and the British Lesbian, 1945–1971. *Journal of British Studies* 47 (4): 883–904.
Jivani, Alkarim. 1997. *It's Not Unusual: A History of Lesbian and Gay Britain in the Twentieth Century*. London: Michael O'Mara Books.
Lancashire Evening Post. 1954. Woman 'Bridegroom' Was Dressed as a Man—Court Told, December 13.
Langley, Esme. 1965. November Mailbag: Editor's Comment. *Arena Three*, November.
Law Society. 1955. *Memorandum of the Council of the Law Society*. London.
Lewis, Brian. 2016. *Wolfenden's Witnesses: Homosexuality in Postwar Britain*. Basingstoke: Palgrave Macmillan.
Manchester Evening News. 1948. Woman: I Put Body on Road, December 8.
McDowell, R.B. 2004. Hyde, Harford Montgomery [H. Montgomery Hyde] (1907–1989). In *Oxford Dictionary of National Biography*. Oxford: Oxford University Press. https://doi.org/10.1093/ref:odnb/40874.
Mill, John Stuart. 1859. *On Liberty*. London: Parker.
Moran, Leslie. 1995. The Homosexualization of English Law. In *Legal Inversions: Lesbians, Gay Men and the Politics of Law*, ed. Didi Herman and Carl F. Stychin, 3–28. Philadelphia: Temple University Press.
———. 1996. *The Homosexual(Ity) of Law*. London: Routledge.
Neustatter, W. Lindsay. 1955. Homosexuality in Women. In *They Stand Apart: A Critical Survey of the Problems of Homosexuality*, ed. J. Tudor Rees and V. Harvey. London: Heinemann.
Neville-Rolfe, Sybil. 1935. *Why Marry?* London: Faber & Faber.
Nottingham Evening Post. 1949. Woman Dressed as a Man: 'Ghastly and Baneful Influence' Says Judge, April 29.
Oldfield, Carolyn. 2001. *Growing Up Good? Medical, Social Hygiene and Youth Work Perspectives on Young Women, 1918–1939*. University of Warwick.
Oram, Alison. 1992. Repressed and Thwarted, or Bearer of the New World? The Spinster in Inter-War Feminist Discourses. *Women's History Review* 1 (3): 413–433. https://doi.org/10.1080/09612029200200010.

———. 2006. Cross-Dressing and Transgender. In *The Modern History of Sexuality*, ed. H.G. Cocks and Matt Houlbrook, 256–285. London: Palgrave Macmillan.

———. 2007. *Her Husband Was a Woman! Women's Gender-Crossing in Modern British Popular Culture*. London: Routledge.

———. 2016. 'A Sudden Orgy of Decadence': Writing about Sex Between Women in the Interwar Popular Press. In *Sapphic Modernities: Sexuality, Women, and National Culture*, ed. Laura Doan and Jane Garrity, 165–180. London: Palgrave Macmillan.

"Report of the Departmental Committee on Homosexual Offences and Prostitution." 1957. *British Medical Journal*, no. 14 (Sep.): 639–640.

Royal Commission on Marriage and Divorce. 1956. *Report of the Royal Commission on Marriage and Divorce*. London.

Scott-Presland, Peter. 2015. *Amiable Warriors: A History of the Campaign for Homosexual Equality and Its Times*. London: Paradise Press.

Smart, Carol. 1981. Law and the Control of Women's Sexuality: The Case of the 1950s. In *Controlling Women*, ed. Bridget Hutter and Gillian Williams, 40–60. London: Croom Helm.

———. 1995. *Law, Crime and Sexuality: Essays in Feminism*. London: SAGE Publications.

Smith, Marie Blanche. 1951. *The Single Woman of Today: Her Problems and Adjustment*. London: Watts & Co.

Storr, Anthony. 1964. *Sexual Deviation*. Harmondsworth: Pelican.

Thane, Pat. 1999. Population Politics in Post-war British Culture. In *Moments of Modernity: Reconstructing Britain, 1945–1964*, ed. Becky Conekin, Frank Mort, and Chris Waters, 114–133. London: Rivers Oram Press.

The Times. 1953. A Social Problem, November 1.

Vickers, Emma. 2009. Infantile Desires and Perverted Practices: Disciplining Lesbianism in the WAAF and the ATS during the Second World War. *Journal of Lesbian Studies* 13 (4): 431–441. https://doi.org/10.1080/10894160903048163.

Walker, Nigel, and Sarah McCabe. 1973. *Crime and Insanity in England, Volume 2*. Edinburgh: Edinburgh University Press.

Waters, Chris. 1999. Disorders of the Mind, Disorders of the Body Social: Peter Wildeblood and the Making of the Modern Homosexual. In *Moments of Modernity: Reconstructing Britain, 1945–1964*, ed. Becky Conekin, Frank Mort, and Chris Waters, 134–151. London: Rivers Oram Press.

———. 2013. The Homosexual as a Social Being in Britain, 1945–1968. In *British Queer History: New Approaches and Perspectives*, ed. Brian Lewis, 188–218. Manchester: Manchester University Press.

Weeks, Jeffrey. 1981. *Sex, Politics and Society: The Regulation of Sexuality since 1800*. London: Longman.

———. 2004. Wolfenden, John Frederick [Jack], Baron Wolfenden. In *Oxford Dictionary of National Biography*, ed. Lawrence Goldman. Oxford: Oxford University Press. https://doi.org/10.1093/ref:odnb/31852.

West, D.J. 1955. *Homosexuality*. Harmondsworth: Pelican.

Wildeblood, Peter. 1955. *Against the Law: The Classic Account of a Homosexual in 1950s Britain*. London: Weidenfeld.

Winner, Albertine. 1947. Homosexuality in Women. *Medical Press*, No. 3 (Sep.): 219.

Wolfenden, John. 1976. *Turning Points*. London: Bodley Head.

Wright, Helena. 1932. *What Is Sex? An Outline for Young People*. London: Williams and Norgate.

———. 1956. *Sex: An Outline for Young People*. 3rd ed. London: Williams and Norgate.

7

Allen: Sexual Offences Prosecutions in the Late Twentieth Century

R v Allen

Sexual offences enacted in the Victorian era continued to frame the criminal law in the latter part of the twentieth century. Since 1861 there had been a statutory offence of indecent assault against a female, and since 1880 there had been an age below which a girl could not give legally valid consent. However, as Chap. 3 explored, the caselaw establishing that the offence could be committed by a woman was subject to a strange anomaly: it did not actually involve sexual activity between women. *Mourey* (1885) 49 JP 745 concerned an examination by a midwife, while the indecent assault in *Hare* [1934] 1 KB 354 was committed by a woman upon a boy. Neither challenged the view that, in the words of the 1957 Wolfenden Report, indecent assaults between females lacked 'the libidinous features that characterise sexual acts between males' (Committee on Homosexual Offences and Prostitution 1957, p. 38). Instead, they fed into the perception of relationships between women as potentially pathological, but essentially non-sexual, friendships. For the courts, penis-in-vagina sex was the only 'real' sex, and sexual activity without a penis was not really sex at all.

C. Derry, *Lesbianism and the Criminal Law*,
https://doi.org/10.1007/978-3-030-35300-1_7

Nevertheless, in the decades after the 1957 Wolfenden Report, the ways in which the law silenced lesbian possibility evolved significantly. A blanket denial that (respectable, higher-class, white, British) women could engage in sex together was increasingly untenable. Instead, the existence of lesbians was acknowledged but they were treated as a lesser version of gay men: less visible, less troublesome, less sexual. Those who did appear before the courts were othered not so much by being outside respectable social classes as by being recast as perverted, in ways which paralleled longstanding legal myths around male homosexuality. Sex between women thus gained limited visibility within the criminal law, including between middle-class, white women.[1] It is notable that the ethnicity and nationality of the defendants discussed in this chapter was generally not apparent from law reports, and as far as can be judged from the press reports they were white and British. Race was therefore mostly unmentioned, with whiteness taken as an unspoken norm.

The first case to appear in the law reports (though not the first prosecution) was *Allen* [1996] 2 Cr App R (S) 36. That case offers a starting point for exploring the criminal law's response to these cultural changes.

The defendant, Donna Allen, was a twenty-year-old woman of good character who pleaded guilty in May 1995 to one sample count of indecent assault on a female and one of gross indecency with a child,[2] alongside an assault occasioning actual bodily harm and two assaults with intent to resist arrest. The charges of indecent assault and gross indecency related to her sexual relationship, when she was aged seventeen or eighteen, with a girl, R, aged about thirteen. It had lasted for about a year and ended in June 1994. R was described by the Court of Appeal as a willing participant in the relationship and sexual activities. The actual bodily harm charge related to an occasion upon which the defendant assaulted R, 'happily, not very badly' (p. 37). At Leicester Crown Court, HHJ Benson passed a sentence of two years' detention for the indecent assault (with one year concurrent for gross indecency and four months concurrent

[1] While some of the defendants discussed here were working-class, that was by no means true of all of them. In particular, the chapter later considers the prosecution of teachers: defendants in a normatively middle-class profession.

[2] Although the *Criminal Appeal Reports* headnote states there were two counts and the *Criminal Law Review* casenote repeats this, the judgment specifies one.

for the assault on the girl), plus a consecutive six months' detention for the two assaults on police officers. Allen's total sentence was therefore two and a half years' detention; the two years' detention for the sexual offences was the main focus of her appeal.[3] The Court of Appeal held that it was too severe given the appellant's age, her plea of guilty, and the lack of force or coercion to overbear the will of the girl. The sentence for indecent assault was reduced to fifteen months' detention and that for gross indecency with a child to eight months.

The judgment and sentence involved an unspoken (and perhaps unconscious) negotiation of two conflicting approaches. On one side, the apparently 'lesser' nature of lesbianism supported a less punitive view, apparent in the consideration given to Allen's youth and compliance with the judicial process and in the lack of weight given to the common assault. On the other side, and as discussed later in this chapter, lesbianism was increasingly associated with negative characterisations of gay sexuality including 'corruption'. Those contributed to the imposition of a substantial sentence in circumstances where a heterosexual man would probably have received a non-custodial disposal.

Allen was convicted under section 14 of the Sexual Offences Act 1956, which had essentially re-enacted section 52 of the Offences Against the Person Act 1861. It defined the offence of indecent assault upon a woman, and established the age of consent as sixteen:

1. It is an offence ... for a person to make an indecent assault on a woman.
2. A girl under the age of sixteen cannot in law give any consent which would prevent an act being an assault for the purposes of this section.[4]

Indecent assault was any touching with an 'indecent' (usually sexual) purpose to which the complainant did not consent. The perpetrator was referred to as 'a person': hence the Act was gender-neutral as to the offender, rather than explicitly including women.

[3] Because she was under twenty-one, Allen was sentenced to detention in a young offenders' institution rather than to imprisonment in an adult prison.

[4] A parallel clause, section 15, governed indecent assault upon a male.

The possibility of women being prosecuted for indecent assault upon a female may have been largely theoretical when silencing was at its height in the nineteenth century. Louise A Jackson found that of her sample of 1590 people prosecuted for sexual offences in Yorkshire, Middlesex, and London between 1830 and 1910, only 14 were woman: an average of one conviction every six years. Of those, only one had committed the offence for her own sexual satisfaction rather than in conjunction with a man; she had indecently assaulted a boy (Jackson 2000, pp. 108–12). In more recent decades, that has no longer been the case. Home Office research found that in 1973, six women had been convicted of indecent assault on a female (Walmesley and White 1979). Writing in 1982, Paul Crane found that there were 'on average fewer than ten' convictions of women for indecent assault on girls each year (1982, pp. 9–10). Statistics for 1994 (Tatchell n.d.) showed that twenty-seven women and girls were prosecuted for indecent assault on a female, of whom three received custodial sentences; a further twelve, all under eighteen, were cautioned. In 2003, seventeen women were convicted of the same offence (Bartlett 2005).

One particularly notable feature of the statistics is the very young age of some of the girls cautioned or prosecuted for committing this offence. It is also clear that although the prosecution of women and girls for indecent assault has remained relatively rare, it has increased significantly.[5] The more recent statistics do not indicate the presence or absence of factual consent, or whether the girls and women were principals or accessories. However, we know from *Allen* that at least some involved women principals and complainants who had given factual consent. Crane gave another example: a 1978 case reported in the *Daily Mirror* concerned a friendship between a fifteen-year-old and her teacher which later developed into a sexual relationship. The court, accepting that the girl was a 'willing partner' and that the defendant had tried to cool the relationship, imposed a two-year probation order (Crane 1982, p. 10).

The growing importance of the offence was not confined to the courtroom. Matthew Waites (2002, p. 337) identifies the 1990s as the decade in which a 'lesbian age of consent' emerged in political and cultural

[5] To provide a little context for these figures, in 1994 total recorded indecent assaults upon a woman exceeded 17,000 while by 2003, they exceeded 25,000 (Home Office 2006).

discourse as well as legal practice. This was driven by debates on the age of consent for sexual acts between males, which also produced new rationales for the age of consent for sex between females (Waites 2003, p. 642, 2002, pp. 336–37). However, attention to the latter was limited in both legal and social contexts. It was also not the only form of criminal regulation: Jennifer/Jimmy Saunders's conviction in 1991 marked the reappearance of female husband-type cases (referred to here as gender fraud cases, given the absence of marriage).[6] Kelly Trueman's prosecution, arising from offences committed just before the 2003 Sexual Offences Act came into force, combined age of consent and gender fraud elements. This chapter seeks to understand not only the particular ways in which lesbianism was regulated by the criminal courts in these cases, but also how that regulation was visible. In order to do that, both consideration of the social context and comparison of *Allen* with the prosecutions of Saunders and Trueman are enlightening.

A New Social Context

In his 1976 memoir, John Wolfenden looked back at his work chairing the Committee on Homosexual Offences and Prostitution and writing its Report. He concluded the chapter by mentioning recent interviews with young people who viewed it as 'old-fashioned', and expressed his amusement that what was 'outrageous' in 1957 seemed 'Victorian' two decades later (Wolfenden 1976, p. 146). His wry humour was rooted in a cultural reality: social understandings of same-sex relations had undergone a significant evolution. The Wolfenden Report's cautious evasion of equality arguments had long since been rejected by activists who refused to see their sexuality as a disability or source of inferiority. Lesbian visibility and self-organisation were increasing enormously, but would be met with significant challenges and backlash, as the following examples illustrate.[7]

[6] This terminology is further considered, and subsequent similar cases examined, in Chap. 8.
[7] Histories of this period include Weeks (1981, 2016), Jivani (1997), and Jennings (2007).

The Minorities Research Group was the first British group to openly represent lesbians, and had the explicit aim of collaborating in medical and scientific research. It achieved this within a few years of its founding in 1964, doing much to ensure the inclusion of women in research projects and extending the population of research subjects beyond those who had sought medical treatment. Until it closed in 1971, the organisation was also part of a critical engagement with the medical literature in which lesbians saw themselves as more than passive objects of study (Jennings 2008, pp. 899–903). However, by the time the American Psychiatric Association removed homosexuality from its list of disorders in 1973,[8] sexuality had been clearly established as falling within the remit of the 'psych' professions. That association was reinforced by the arguments of liberal law reformers: just as the Wolfenden Report had supported the understanding of homosexuality as a medical issue (Rubin 1989), medical evidence remained central to debates around the age of consent in the 1990s (Waites 2003, p. 645). Indeed, Wolfenden's concern to minimise the threats posed by theories of latent homosexuality and the Kinsey Scale had hardened into claims about the fixity of sexual identity as medical 'fact' (Waites 2003, pp. 644–48).

Counter-narratives from the subjects of this regulation were proliferating. The Sexual Offences Act 1967 had decriminalised sexual activity between men only in narrow circumstances, but did allow a new openness in discussing both male and, to a lesser extent, female homosexuality. Unfortunately, lesbians often found themselves forgotten in the spaces between a feminism focused on heterosexual women's issues and a gay liberation movement dominated by men's interests. Nonetheless, lesbian activism was diverse with aims ranging from modest legal reforms to the revolutionary overthrow of patriarchy. While the former may seem to have been achieved, the picture is of course more complex. Liberal campaigns for law reform did not produce an even progression towards equality. Rather, there was another significant backlash against lesbian and gay rights in the 1980s. The AIDS crisis, which ought to have brought

[8] The change would later be reflected in DSM-III (American Psychiatric Association 1980). The influence of this manual extends internationally: it is widely used in the United Kingdom, for example, where in addition to its clinical use, it is regularly cited before the courts on issues of mental illness.

sympathy and horror at the tragedies it wrought, was instead used as evidence of the 'polluting' nature of homosexuality. That pollution was now not only moral but physical: the Chief Constable of Greater Manchester described people with AIDS as 'swirling around in a human cesspool of their own making' and, despite criticism, was privately supported by Prime Minister Margaret Thatcher (*Telegraph* 2012). By the twisted logic of such attacks, lesbianism should have been lauded since HIV transmission was less likely through sexual activities between women than through acts involving penile penetration. That did not happen, of course: the undifferentiated grouping of lesbians and gay men is an ideological one, based upon their deviation from a heterosexual norm. (It is also distinct from alliances between lesbians and gay men, which do have the scope for recognising common interests without assuming homogeneity.) Subsumed within the 'lesbian and gay' category, lesbians shared the political consequences even as their own needs were ignored.[9] The British Social Attitudes survey showed a fall in tolerance of gay sexuality in the 1980s, reversing only at the end of the decade (S. Jackson and Scott 2004, pp. 244–45).

Hostility could be manifested through appeals to law, as when a lesbian couple kissing goodbye at Leeds Central station in 1980 were detained by transport police for an alleged breach of the peace before being released without charge (Crane 1982, p. 19). Its most visible legal manifestation was section 28 of the Local Government Act 1988, considered below, whose terminology of 'pretended family relationships' was a deliberate counterpoint to lesbian campaigns around child custody (and based upon an ideology of the ideal nuclear family which was increasingly being abandoned by heterosexual partners and parents (Plummer 1992, p. 20)). It had been met with a highly visible lesbian response: the most famous actions in the anti-section 28 campaign were both carried out by lesbians. On 1 February 1988, a small group of lesbians abseiled into the House of Lords from the public gallery; another group invaded the BBC *Six O'Clock News* on 23 May (Carter 1992, p. 221). However, lesbians were

[9] Beth E. Schneider (1992) identified six areas in which AIDS affected lesbians' lives: through their friendships and work with gay men; through HIV infection; through debates around lesbian sexual practices; in concerns around sperm donation; through work—greater homophobia in paid employment, plus unpaid caregiving responsibilities; and politically.

effectively seen but not heard, as mainstream organisations opposed section 28 through arguments founded on the fixity of sexual identity (Waites 2003, p. 651; Auchmuty 2015, p. 6).

Lesbian activism also addressed the criminal law in the early 1990s. The magazine *Lesbian London*, published between December 1991 and June 1994, featured the conviction of Jennifer Saunders on its very first front page (Lavelle 2014, p. 92). In 1994, the Lesbian Avengers group carried out their first protest before a statue of Queen Victoria in reference to the legal myth with which this book opened (Jennings 2007, p. xi). Yet such express articulation of connections between lesbianism and the criminal law proved fleeting. There was little general enthusiasm for Cherry Smyth's call for banners proclaiming 'Lesbians Solicit and Fuck Too' or 'Grossly Indecent Lesbians' (Smyth 1991), slogans themselves shaped by the representation of lesbianism as a lesser variation ('too') of gay male sexuality.

Within higher-profile, mixed campaigns for an equal age of consent for sex between men, women's legal position was silenced to such an extent that it was assumed there was *no* age of consent for lesbians. As Allen maintained in her police interview, 'There isn't no law for lesbians anyway' (*Allen*, p. 37). Lesbians shimmered in and out of view throughout the debates, alternatively invoked and ignored even by the same speakers. Thus before an equal age of consent to male homosexual acts was achieved, Stonewall dismissed lesbian age of consent issues on the basis that '[f]or lesbians the criminal law is roughly the same as for heterosexuals' (Stonewall n.d.-a). 'Roughly' acknowledged different treatment even as it was simultaneously swept under the carpet in order to further the aim of formal legal equality for gay men. It dismissed the onerous sentences imposed upon lesbians convicted of relationships with girls under the age of consent, or the sentencing approaches in *Saunders*, as effectively none of its concern. Once formal equality had been achieved in the Sexual Offences Act 2003, Stonewall's website went further: as late as December 2006, it still claimed that prior to the 2003 Act, 'there was no age of consent relating to lesbians' (Stonewall n.d.-b). Social and legal understandings of lesbianism, then, combined to leave it unspoken even when it was not unspeakable.

A New Legal Context

Like outright silencing, the criminal justice system's positioning of lesbianism as a less troublesome version of gay male sexuality did not equate to toleration. Once lesbians did enter the criminal justice system, they were perceived as specially deviant due to their sexuality and failure to conform to gender norms. Bertha Scorse, whose murder conviction was considered in Chap. 6, had been dying of tuberculosis when her death sentence was commuted to life imprisonment in 1952. However, the removal of a lung saved her life and in 1972, journalist Jill Tweedie drew attention to her subsequent treatment: Scorse remained in prison far beyond the period even someone subject to a life sentence might have expected, and had served 'the longest sentence of any woman now in gaol' (Tweedie 1972). Tweedie described her as a verbally aggressive woman who had been released several times on licence but recalled after behaviour which was non-violent but construed as threatening. She explained how Scorse was subject to unusual levels of scrutiny, was considered too unstable for release but denied treatment, and suffered from the unconscious bias of others towards her lesbianism. That hostility to lesbian defendants accused of offences related to sexual or violent conduct persisted throughout the century.[10]

Other forms of legal regulation remained significant, perhaps most obviously in family law. When women left heterosexual marriages in order to live as lesbians, they found in the 1970s and 1980s that their new freedom was met with a punitive response by the family courts, particularly in child custody cases. Divorce law also denied lesbian sexuality as a serious alternative to heterosexuality, through a refusal to imagine meaningful sexual activity which did not involve a penis. The 1956 Royal Commission on Marriage and Divorce concluded that lesbianism could not be a ground for divorce because of the difficulties of 'a workable definition' and 'proof' of 'a physical relationship analogous to sodomy' (Royal

[10] By contrast, the courts were not consistently hostile when dealing with non-sexual offences. For example, in 2000 a police officer who had lied about a car accident in order to conceal her lesbian relationship was found not guilty by a jury of perverting the course of justice. The judge, Paul Downes, then criticised the homophobic attitudes of her colleagues as 'alarming' (Flanagan and McGowan 2000).

Commission on Marriage and Divorce 1956, pp. 30–31). Instead, it endorsed the existing practice of considering such a relationship under the cruelty ground (see Chap. 5). That also had the unspoken benefit of keeping the courts' focus upon male expectations of their wives rather than women's own agency.

The notion of lesbianism as cruelty to a husband was consistent with the family courts' wider approach to it as something destructive of the patriarchal family. In this, they were arguably correct—but their response was to use their disciplinary powers to protect that institution. Thus the family courts which, in the 1940s and 1950s, had gone out of their way not to see lesbianism now directly confronted and were confronted by it in child custody cases. The best interests of the child were decided by reference to the welfare principle, defined by the House of Lords in *J v C* [1970] AC 668 as including an assumption that parents' rights had a special significance endowed 'by nature' (p. 175). The supposed *un*natural status of lesbianism was fundamental to subsequent court decisions. These distinguished between 'good' (discreet, feminine) lesbians and 'bad' lesbians whose behaviour raised similar issues to those we will see preoccupying the criminal courts: lesbianism as a source of corruption and embarrassment.

In *Re P (A Minor) (Custody)* [1983] 4 FLR 401, the Court of Appeal was narrowly persuaded that the child could remain in the lesbian mother's custody rather than local authority care. Importantly, this mother was 'discreet' and thus posed little risk of 'corruption'; but the court was troubled by the likelihood of 'embarrassing conduct and comment, particularly among the child's friends' (Arnold P, p. 404). A 1991 case awarded care and control to a lesbian mother but confirmed that 'militant lesbians trying to convert others' would not have kept custody. Even discreet 'lesbians in private' raised two issues: 'the effect upon the sexual identity of the child', that is, corruption, and 'the effect of stigmatisation', that is, embarrassment (*B v B (Minors) (Custody, Care and Control)* [1991] 1 FLR 402, Callum J, 410). Another case the same year problematised lesbianism even as the court paid lip service to 'vast change … in the attitudes of our society': it was apparently 'axiomatic' that a heterosexual couple provided 'the ideal environment' for a child (*C v C (a minor) (custody: appeal)* [1991] 1 FLR 223, Glidewell LJ, 228). While the civil and criminal courts did not offer identical discourses around sexuality, their interplay is apparent here. The family courts' requirement of discretion effectively replicated the criminal law's confinement of lawful male same-sex acts to the private. The theme of lesbianism as a source of corruption and embarrassment to others would be taken up by the criminal courts in the 1990s, as discussed further below. The division of lesbians into private, respectable women and public, corrupting, embarrassing and thus punishable women replicated criminal responses to relationships between women.

The family courts' approach did evolve, thanks to determined activism drawing upon a growing body of evidence (Harne and Rights of Women 1997). Substantial change came at the turn of the century after not only societal attitudes, but also social structures had changed (L. Smith 2006). Cases before the courts increasingly involved families which had never fit the heteropatriarchal norm, while Parliament had enacted civil partnership legislation giving legal status to same-sex couples. In *Re G (Children)* [2006] UKHL 43, Lady Hale offered a new and broader definition of 'natural parent' encompassing genetic, gestational, and psychological parents. However, as Beresford (2008) points out, she still withheld the term 'mother' from the female ex-partner of the genetic and gestational mother.

In 2013, Parliament enacted apparent equality for lesbian families through the recognition of same-sex marriage. More radical feminist critiques have pointed out that this is equality to, or assimilation into, a heterosexual norm within a patriarchal institution (Auchmuty 2004; Barker 2012). Further, full formal equality has been withheld since same-sex marriages have no element of consummation, and adultery with a person of the same sex continues not to be a ground of divorce. In other words, Parliament has followed the courts' lead in shying away from recognising lesbian sexuality (or indeed, endorsing buggery). The positive consequence, that the state does not prescribe how (or even if) sexuality should be manifested in marriage, is undermined by its continuing to do so for marriage between men and women. Heterosex thus retains its privileged position in legal discourse, with penis-in-vagina sex carefully distinguished from and promoted above all other forms of sexual activity.

Even so, this was the culmination of a significant change in parliamentary attitudes: the original entry of lesbianism into legislation had been motivated by considerable hostility.[11] Section 28 of the Local Government Act 1988, introduced in an amendment and enthusiastically adopted by the Conservative government, is understood as marking the first occasion upon which lesbians were explicitly included within a statute. However, the L-word was not articulated: instead, the umbrella term 'homosexuality' was used, leaving lesbians both newly visible and newly occluded. It was also contested from conservative as well as lesbian perspectives: earlier official characterisations of lesbianism as not requiring regulation because it did not pose the apparent social problems of male homosexuality (Chap. 6) had been reiterated in the House of Lords debate (Hansard, HL 18/12/86, 310). The operation of the legislation was itself a complex dance of speech and silencing. It prohibited 'promotion of homosexuality as a pretended family relationship' by local authorities, a limitation apparently intended to encompass schools.[12] The direct aim of the section was therefore a silencing one, but not straightforwardly so. It did not forbid any mention of homosexuality but prohibited its *promotion*, leaving space for hostile or condemnatory expression. Its proponents also claimed, as opponents of decriminalisation had done before the Wolfenden Committee (Chap. 6), that the well-behaved and discreet had nothing to fear from the law (Smith 1992, p. 202). Thus the section did not so much aim to prevent discussion as to control the terms upon which homosexuality could be discussed. Further, its impact was substantially extra-legal. Liability was civil rather than criminal, and dependent upon the interpretation of undefined and ambiguous terms (Thomas and Costigan 1990, pp. 10–14). That made the absence of litigation a mixed blessing since uncertainty about the section's scope induced more caution about what might be done or said. While no court cases were brought under the section, several were threatened (Thomas and Costigan 1990, pp. 30–31) and it had a repressive effect and significant symbolic force.

That silencing impulse had also been felt by the Policy Advisory Committee on Sexual Offences, whose final report in 1981 failed to mention sexual activity between women at all (Policy Advisory Committee

[11] A snapshot of the evolution in House of Commons and House of Lords attitudes to same-sex relationships can be seen in the 'gay age of consent' debates (Waites 2003).

[12] In fact, it was not clear whether the legislation did so and no cases were brought to test its scope. The content of sex education was legally a matter for a school's governors, not the local authority.

on Sexual Offences 1981). Putting forward his own proposals for law reform, Tony Honoré adopted the characterisation of lesbians as less libidinous as well as fewer in numbers, attracting less hostility, less socially visible, and less economically damaging than gay men (1978, pp. 100–10).[13] While there were obvious benefits for women in being spared the attentions of the criminal justice system, there were also disadvantages to the terms on which this happened. The new approach to silencing ignored the legal and extra-legal means by which women's sexuality was extensively policed, gave no attention to women's needs or interests, and considered lesbianism only in relation to men's sexuality. As Chap. 6 explored, it also served to justify unequal legal treatment of male same-sex acts which in turn justified wider discrimination against lesbians as well as gay men. Further, it encouraged the criminal courts to consider women defendants who showed libidinous behaviour as multiply deviant. In addition to their double deviancy as criminals and women (Lloyd 1995), they had deviated both from heterosexuality and from the courts' gendered expectations of the female homosexual. The threat they posed was felt all the more keenly when combined with cultural and social changes. These factors combined to provoke a harshly punitive response in the 1991 sentencing of Jimmy/Jennifer Saunders, where Crabtree J claimed that 'these days of openness about lesbianism' required a deterrent sentence.

Court Attitudes

Jennifer/Jimmy Saunders

Jimmy Saunders had had sexual relationships with two young women.[14] It was common ground that the first complainant, R, met Saunders at a

[13] The argument in relation to economic damage is itself interesting: it suggested that men who choose a gay lifestyle and do not marry thereby deny a woman economic support (p. 103).

[14] The case received extensive press coverage (e.g. *Sun* 1991a, b; M. Sharpe 1991a, b; *Guardian* 1992). There is a full transcript of the trial (A.M. Smith 2000). See also the discussions in Smith (1995, 1998) and Sharpe (2018).

family party.[15] They entered into a relationship which lasted five months with daily meetings. R was fifteen at the start of the relationship but the charges of indecent assault were based upon lack of factual consent rather than R's age (Smith 1998, p. 180). The defendant, identified in court as Jennifer Saunders, was sixteen or seventeen.

By R's account, after two months the couple had vaginal sexual intercourse for the first time, with the light off. It hurt so much that R pushed Saunders away and asked if he had a banana. His response was that he had had a sharp tube put in his penis for medical reasons and R had embarrassed him by raising the issue. Despite that horrible first experience, R went on to have sex with Saunders in this way multiple times a week for the remainder of their relationship, always in the dark. R was never allowed to touch Saunders's genitals, and he remained clothed; on several occasions, he used a condom. He claimed that his chest was covered because of a boil and/or that the breasts were the result of cancer. He also told R that they would marry and have a family one day; spent time with R's family; and briefly shared a flat with R's uncle. R's friend H allegedly had sex with Saunders on one occasion. She described it as so painful that she asked Saunders to stop, but he didn't. R's uncle described hearing the sexual activity and H's pleas, but did not intervene. However, after he became suspicious at a number of callers asking for 'Jennifer', and then found tampons in Saunders's wardrobe, he did raise his discovery of her sex with other family members. R's parents questioned Saunders all night without eliciting any admissions before involving the police.

Saunders's account at trial was that while she and R initially met when Saunders was in male clothing, she quickly told R that she was in fact female. R was initially reluctant to believe this, and pursued Saunders for a relationship, inaccurately telling others that 'Jimmy' was already her boyfriend. When R did accept the truth, she did not want her family and friends to know that her boyfriend was in fact a woman. Saunders agreed to present herself as male to R's family, but claimed in court that there

[15] The law at this time granted anonymity only to rape complainants. As the charge against Saunders was indecent assault, the names of the complainants were reported in full. However, in line with current law and practice, only initials are used to identify them here. Similarly, I have randomly allocated initials to identify complainants in other cases where this was not done in reports.

had been no sexual contact between them and she ended the relationship because she was tired of the deceit and had a boyfriend.

In September 1991, a jury at Doncaster Crown Court took an hour and a quarter to find Saunders guilty of two counts of indecent assault (Smith 2000, p. 263). She had already pleaded guilty to offences of burglary, handling stolen goods, theft of a vehicle, and assault. She was initially sentenced to six years' imprisonment for the indecent assaults, with the trial judge asserting that a deterrent sentence was required and that the complainants would have preferred to be raped: a comment which, combined with the severity of the sentence, led to protests (*Pink Paper* 1991). Saunders gave a further account in a brief press interview, claiming that she and R had been in a lesbian relationship and it was at R's request that she pretended to be male to R's family. Saunders's sentence was reduced on appeal to two years' probation, given both her youth and the Court of Appeal's doubts as to the effectiveness of a deterrent sentence (*Guardian* 1992).[16]

Saunders's case was interpreted as one of sex between women although her identity was presented in complex and contradictory ways. According to the trial judge, the defendant was not a lesbian and had been living as a man; she presented herself in court as a woman with a boyfriend; campaigner Megan Radclyffe was confident Saunders was a lesbian, having contacted her in prison; and Saunders herself told the press she had had a girlfriend in prison (*Capital Gay* 1991a, 1992). Following her conviction, during the sentencing hearing, a senior probation officer from the hostel in which she had resided told the court that Saunders dressed as a man on occasion and was aggressive. However, when dressed as 'a very attractive young woman', her personality was different (Smith 2000, pp. 271–72).

Perversion and Corruption

Saunders's original sentence of six years' imprisonment was partly justified by the judge's characterisation of her as 'a menace to young girls' who

[16] The Court of Appeal also referred to, but gave no details of, a social inquiry report (Smith 2000: Court of Appeal judgment).

enjoyed deception (Smith 2000, p. 277). The Court of Appeal reduced her sentence to one of probation, in contrast to Allen's notably harsher fifteen months' detention. The discrepancy between their punishments is not easily explained, but the notion of corruption seems to have underpinned it. There are other possible reasons including time already spent in custody, Saunders's personal mitigation including an 'exceptional background and disturbed childhood' (*Capital Gay* 1992), the campaign supporting her, and the ages of the complainants. However, Allen was of good character (i.e. had no previous convictions), while Saunders was not and had pleaded guilty to a range of non-sexual offences in the same proceedings; the complainant in *Allen* had given factual consent; and the *Allen* judgment was four years later than that in *Saunders*. It is noteworthy that during this period lesbians were making significant advances in other areas of law, particularly child custody cases.

The courts' fear of lesbian corruption, expressed more or less overtly in both cases, was ultimately more serious in Allen's since her sexually activity was with a girl who consented knowingly to a same-sex relationship. The Court of Appeal referred to Allen's 'malign influence', a significant term since it was not generally applied to men who introduced girls to sexual activity. The malignity, then, must have come not just from the sexuality but from the lack of *hetero*sexuality: it was specific to the lesbian, not older, more sexually experienced persons in general. After all, heterosexual activity is viewed as a natural development, so that the law has been concerned that a girl is not unduly rushed into it rather than that she does not do it at all.

The complainants in the Saunders case presented themselves as sexually naïve but heterosexual, and publicly and vigorously rejected lesbianism. They thus allayed any fears that they had been 'corrupted' into a lesbian lifestyle, and promised a return to heterosexuality. The sexual activity was also more closely modelled on heterosexual norms. While the growing legal attention to indecent assault between women theoretically allowed for a more expansive understanding of lesbian sex, the courts continued to perpetuate a hierarchy of sexual activity. Penis-in-vagina sex was 'real' and legitimate; penis-in-anything-else was sexual but deviant and often criminal. Non-penile penetration was a facsimile of 'real' sex, but non-penetrative activity was hardly comprehensible as sexual at all.

That was made explicit in the *Allen* judgment, which presented the sexual activity between Allen and the complainant as a linear progression in both time and severity:

> [It] proceeded to 'kissing and cuddling' and then to repeated acts of sexual familiarity. The appellant then, on many occasions, indecently assaulted her by digitally penetrating her vagina and also using her tongue in order to do the same. She then proceeded to get the child, digitally, to penetrate herself and fondle her own vagina. (p. 37)

'Sexual familiarity' appears in this context to be used to refer to non-penetrative sexual activity other than 'kissing and cuddling', although on its face, it ought to refer to both these and penetrative activities as well. There was no attempt to enumerate the specific acts it included, as there was for the penetrative acts. That vagueness suggests a failure of judicial comprehension of or interest in sexual activity which does not include penetration. The word 'familiarity' evokes a kind of cosiness which places such non-penetrative activity alongside 'kissing and cuddling' as something not really fully sexual. The impression is strengthened by the exclusion of 'sexual familiarity' from the list of acts by which the complainant was indecently assaulted. The only activities considered significant during this process were the various methods of vaginal penetration. It is almost inconceivable that no other forms of sexual activity took place simultaneously with these, but nothing else was given legal significance. The emphasis upon penetration was at the court's (and probably prosecution's) election, rather than dictated by the legal framework of the offences.

The greatest perversity in *Allen* was apparently found in the failure to mimic penis-in-vagina sex. In the hierarchy of activity imposed by the court, the ultimate stage was the girl's active role in touching and penetrating her own vagina. That act of taking on the 'active', 'male' sexual role for herself was more corrupting, more serious than the passive acceptance of penetration by another woman. Not only was her seducer of the wrong sex, but she had been incited to act outside norms of acceptable female sexuality, passing from the expected female role of penetrated to the privileged male role of penetrator. Indeed, as both penetrator and penetrated, she had engaged in a self-sufficient form of sexual activity which not only denied female passivity but left no space for penile involvement at all.

A decade later, sixteen-year old Jake Trueman befriended G, a twelve-year-old girl, and became her boyfriend (*News of the World* 2004; *Ripley and Heanor News* 2004; *Derby Evening Telegraph* 2004a, b). After he told the girl's family that he had been thrown out by his father, G's mother allowed him to stay at their home. Trueman and G kissed and he gave her love-bites on her neck and stomach. He also asked G to allow oral sex to be performed upon her, but G refused; there was no attempt at penetrative sex. When Trueman's father heard about the relationship, he informed a neighbour that 'Jake' was his twenty-two-year-old daughter, Kelly. The neighbour told the complainant's family, who confronted Trueman. She made no admissions, but immediately moved out of the house; she later told police that she was a lesbian and had done this as a joke. She was convicted at trial of eight counts of indecent assault. Press reports gave elaborate detail of how she had achieved the deception including bandaging her chest, wearing baggy clothes, and speckling shaving foam on her face in the mornings to give the impression she had shaved. Details of her defence were not reported, although she apparently claimed she was pushed into sexual contact to maintain her friendship with the girl, and denied getting any sexual gratification. The court was told that Trueman had previously had a relationship with a woman and now had a boyfriend. On 8 March 2004, after Stoke on Trent Crown Court heard that she had a history of anorexia and mental illness and was 'grossly immature', feeling happier in the company of children, she was sentenced to two years' imprisonment.

Trueman's case overlapped with the passing of the Sexual Offences Act 2003 which apparently ushered in a new era of non-discrimination in sexual offences law. It formed part of a new legal climate which had an effect upon this case and its reporting. The press headlines did not emphasise the strangeness of the facts but focused solely upon the defendant's sexuality and the complainant's youth. The implied association between lesbianism and paedophilia in the *Daily Mail*'s 'Lesbian convicted of girl's assault' was made explicit in the local press: *Derby Evening Telegraph* headlines labelled Trueman a 'lesbian pervert' and 'lesbian predator'. No such linkage is made between 'straight' and 'paedophile'; nor did Trueman's apparent bisexuality make any difference to these reports.

Such overt linking of a sexual interest in children with homosexuality might be increasingly disavowed by the judiciary, but it has lingered on nonetheless. Its application to lesbianism assumes a parallel between female and male homosexuality which may seem obvious now but was not drawn routinely in the legal context before the Wolfenden Report (see Chap. 6). In turn, that parallel drew lesbianism into the dangerous myth associating male homosexuality with paedophilia, as evident in these cases. Indeed, the *Equal Treatment Bench Book* of 2000 felt it necessary to include a 'key point' that '[b]eing lesbian or gay has nothing whatsoever to do with paedophile desire' (Judicial Studies Board 2000, p. 219), while the 2018 edition still refers to it as 'a common and extremely offensive stereotype' (Judicial College 2018, pp. 10–13). Yet the shift was not total even at the turn of the twenty-first century: the sentencing remarks in these cases also identified particular harms rooted in conventional gender norms.

Questioning as Harm

The interpretation of gender fraud cases as involving corruption was an uneasy one since the complainants had apparently believed themselves to be in heterosexual relationships. That point was smoothed over by presenting the process of being forced to question one's sexual identity as a primary form of harm. In *Saunders*, the trial judge expressed particular anxiety on this point, telling the defendant 'you have called into question their whole sexual identity and I suspect both these girls would rather have been actually raped by some young man' since they might forget that more easily than 'the obvious disgust they now feel' (Smith 2000, p. 277). Both the seriousness of rape itself and associated risks including pregnancy and serious sexually transmitted infections were glossed over in these remarks and viewed as less serious than exposure to sexual 'deviancy'. It is unclear from his remark whether he assumed that the girls would suffer from questioning something he believed to be already fixed, and therefore disgusted at acting against something innate in themselves;

or from questioning something open to change so that they were disgusted at the real possibility of their being or becoming lesbian. The courts have not moved away from that approach although they no longer express it so overtly. In *R (on the application of 'Monica') v Director of Public Prosecutions* [2018] EWHC 3469 (QB), the High Court spoke of 'the centrality of an individual's sexuality to his or her identity'. On its face that might seem unobjectionable, but they were specifically contrasting this 'centrality' with the relative legal unimportance of the (political activist) applicant's deeply held social and political convictions. A notion of sexuality as binary, fixed, and fundamental was implicitly invoked.

By contrast to the assumption that women complainants' identities were thrown into question, men's have been treated as essentially stable. The Wolfenden Committee had struggled with the troubling idea of latent homosexuality, which threatened the presumption that all but an identifiable minority of men are heterosexual. This disturbing possibility seems to have been diluted into an assumption that youth was a time of vulnerability to corruption; if a man passed through that delicate period uncorrupted, he would be securely heterosexual. If he did not, he might be recuperated later but that was by no means certain. The reassuring notion of sexual fixity gained fresh life in the 1990s age of consent debates, and the worrying implications of Freudian notions of essential bisexuality or the seven-point Kinsey Scale were quietly ignored in legal discourse outside the context of child protection. It was the very stability presumed to attach to male heterosexual identities which informed the sentencing comments in *Duarte Xavier* (unreported, 9 November 2018). Xavier was convicted of six counts of causing a person to engage in sexual activity without consent, contrary to section 4 of the 2003 Act. A gay man, he had posed on dating and contact apps as a woman seeking sexual encounters involving role play. The complainants were thus induced to be blindfolded or otherwise unable to see Xavier while they anally penetrated him, believing themselves to be vaginally penetrating a woman, or he fellated them. Sentencing Xavier to fifteen years' imprisonment, the judge said '[a] heterosexual man who is tricked into penetrating another man must find that a horrible experience' (Murphy 2018). There was no suggestion that the complainants' sexual identity would thereby be called into question. On the contrary, the judge further emphasised the firmly heterosexual identity of the complainants when he addressed the officer in the case immediately after sentencing Xavier. 'It's very rare for a heterosexual male to be the victim of a sexual offence,' he claimed, continuing, 'I hope the fact that these victims were heterosexual males didn't cause them to be put rather lower on the list of priorities' (*BBC News* 2018). That might seem a surprising comment to make when police failings in relation to crimes against women and gay men are well known, and particularly so when directed to the police force responsible for the systemically inadequate investigations into serial rapist John Worboys (Bowcott 2018) and Stephen Port who killed four gay men (Davies 2019).

Lesbianism as Embarrassment

In both the Trueman and Saunders cases, there was a strong assumption by the courts that lesbian relationships were a source of embarrassment. They further identified such social embarrassment as a particularly serious form of damage to a young woman. This attitude has a long legal history: the assumption that a woman's reputation is essential to her value to men was made explicit in *Kerr v Kennedy* [1942] 1 KB 409. That civil case held that an accusation of lesbianism was an imputation of unchastity under the Slander of Women Act 1891 since it was 'calculated both to bring her into social disfavour and, as the phrase runs, to damage her prospects in the marriage market and thereby her finances'. Related arguments around stigma and embarrassment had later been deployed in child custody cases; even after such claims that non-lesbians suffered by association had been discredited in the family courts, they continued to hold sway in the criminal justice system.

In Saunders's case, such themes of social embarrassment coalesced in Crabtree's sentencing remarks. In response to criticism of his suggestion that the complainants would have preferred to be raped, he issued an explanation that in a rape case he could have made an anonymity order—an order not then available for an indecent assault trial (*Capital Gay* 1991b). His original remarks do not bear out this gloss on them, but it does highlight the insistence upon embarrassment as a major harm. Crabtree had asserted during the sentencing hearing that '[f]or a long time, vicious and unthinking people are likely to jeer at these unhappy girls as a result of the misery [Saunders had] caused them really by [her] evil behaviour' (Smith 2000, p. 277). Addressing her apparent lack of remorse, he told her that 'however many unkind girls might laugh at these girls in public you are not going to be one of them for a long time' (Smith 2000, p. 278). This emphasis upon negative public comment about the girls was a reversion to the idea of sexual assault as damaging primarily to a woman's reputation. In Crabtree's formulation, the greatest injury they suffered was not any physical or mental distress occasioned by the acts themselves but the damage to their value in the eyes of the public. Media reports similarly emphasised the naivety and humiliation of Kelly Trueman's victim, a 'gullible youngster' who was 'taken in' by 'puppy love' (*News of the World* 2004). The theme was made explicit through comments by the victim's mother about her being taunted and questioned by other children at school (*Derby Evening Telegraph* 2004b).

While the embarrassment was real and unpleasant for the complainants, it was not an intrinsic feature of the offences. It occurred because the complainants were made to feel embarrassed after the event, notably by their peers and the press. Thus the courts were both colluding in the creation of embarrassment and punishing the defendants for it above other harms their (alleged) conduct had caused. From Quarter Sessions to Crown Courts, from Henry Fielding's pamphlets to today's newspapers, throughout the centuries the expected (even required) response of audiences to lesbian relationships has been derision and contempt; that of the protagonists, embarrassment and shame.

Sentencing Comparisons

The combination of harms identified in *Allen, Saunders*, and *Trueman*—corruption, challenge to sexual identity, and embarrassment—was specific to cases involving sexual contact between girls or women. If the harms were distinctive, was the sentencing approach equally so? Comparisons of sentencing are notoriously difficult, given that each case is decided not only upon its own facts but also in light of the personal mitigation of the offender as well as, in some cases, perceptions of the need for deterrent sentencing at a particular time. These cases were also decided within a statutory framework which created different maximum penalties depending upon the sex of the complainant and the presence or absence of penile penetration. Courts did not have the benefit of the comprehensive sentencing guidelines now available, although guideline cases offered some assistance. Despite all these caveats, a brief comparison of Allen's sentencing with that of other offenders at this period is suggestive.

Allen had engaged in factually consensual activities with a girl of thirteen, about five years her junior. Their friendship had developed into a sexual relationship where the sexual acts included digital penetration. While she was sentenced to fifteen months' detention, similar offences committed by heterosexual men against girls were met with greater leniency. The courts sentencing Allen could have drawn an analogy to the offence of unlawful sexual intercourse with a girl under sixteen (USI), contrary to section 6 of the Sexual Offences Act 1956. It carried a maximum two-year sentence, while that for indecent assault on a female was now ten years (section 3, Sexual Offences Act 1985). The analogy was routinely drawn for men convicted of indecent assault which could have been charged as USI (e.g. *Quayle* (1993) 14 Cr App R (S) 726; *Hinton* (1995) 16 Cr App R (S) 523; *Brough* [1997] 2 Cr App R (S) 202; *Reeves* [2001] EWCA Crim 1053). The guideline sentencing case for USI, *Taylor* (1977) 64 Cr App R 182, stated that where a youth aged sixteen, seventeen, or eighteen had a 'virtuous friendship' with a girl under sixteen which ended in sexual intercourse, the appropriate response was not a punitive sentence but 'a warning to the youth to mend his ways' (i.e. a caution or conditional discharge). Allen's case would appear to fit that pattern, but the point does not seem to have been considered (*R v Allen* [1996] Crim LR 208). The reformulation of the relationship as an 'association' through 'malign influence' where sexual activity occurred 'within' rather than after months enabled the court to close its mind to the *Taylor* parallels.

Even in cases where 'virtuous friendship' was absent, a fine could be appropriate and prison sentences were generally lower. *Taylor* advised a custodial sentence near the two year maximum only for cases where a person in a position of authority deliberately set out to seduce a girl under sixteen for his own sexual gratification. There was no suggestion that such aggravating features were present in *Allen*. As a result, Allen's fifteen-month sentence was significantly higher than a heterosexual man would have received. For example, in *Attorney General's Reference No. 80 of 2000 (Anthony Keegan)* [2001] EWCA Crim 198 the defendant had also had a relationship with a thirteen-year-old girl. He was significantly older than Allen at the time (twenty-nine years old) and had had sexual intercourse with, and later briefly ran away with, the girl. When the prosecution appealed against a sentence of one hundred hours' community service, the Court of Appeal indicated that a sentence of twelve months' imprisonment would have been appropriate. Thus the presence of aggravating factors including the greater age gap, the attempt to run away, and the risk of pregnancy did not lead to a similar or higher sentence.

If Allen was disadvantaged by comparison to heterosexual men—on grounds which amounted to a rejection of all but penetrative heterosex as 'natural'—then on the logic of the court's approach, the appropriate comparator would arguably be a man committing the same offence against a boy. Such a comparison is difficult, not least because of the lack of reported cases with similar facts. For example, those reported in *Current Sentencing Practice* (Thomas 2004, pt. B4) did not include any where friendship developed into a consensual relationship. Even when the sexual activity occurred over a period of time, it appeared either to lack consent or to be on a different basis, for example, one of financial or other inducements from a much older man. Many of the cases involved breach of trust.[17] Insofar as any comparison can be made, it appears that Allen's sentencing was no less severe than in cases of indecent assault by men upon boys (e.g. *Smith* (1987) 9 Cr App R (S) 228; *Roe* (1988) 10 Cr App R (S) 435; *Lee* [1998] 2 Cr App R (S) 272).

Our final option for a comparator is that of a woman who engages in sexual activity with a boy of a similar age. It should by now come as no surprise to find that the approach of the court differed yet again, and that any attempt at comparison uncovers serious discrepancies. *Sant* (1989) Cr App R (S) 441 concerned a woman of twenty-eight who had a sexual

[17] This is not to suggest that all prosecutions of homosexual men for age of consent offences, still less all such offences, involved breach of trust, absence of consent, or inducements. Rather, it suggests that the latter were more likely to reach the Court of Appeal and/or to be selected for reporting.

relationship, at her instigation, with a boy of ten which lasted about three weeks. A sentence of nine months' imprisonment was upheld by the Court of Appeal. The rather less harsh sentence is again explicable by the particular approach to sexuality taken by the courts. It is deemed natural for men to want to take an active sexual role, so some persuasion into that by an older woman was perceived as essentially not corrupting. Rather, the boy was doing earlier what he would soon have done in any event. His active role was preserved, and patriarchal power structures unchallenged. Indeed, the courts seemed determined to view heterosexual women accused of these offences through a highly ideological lens, particularly where they could be allocated to another role which the lesbian defendant could rarely claim: that of the good mother.[18] Thus in *Angela C* [2006] EWCA Crim 1781, the forty-three-year-old's sentence for sexual intercourse with a fourteen-year-old boy to whom she was in loco parentis on the night in question and to whom she had supplied alcohol was reduced from twenty-six months' imprisonment to nine. For the Court of Appeal, the most important mitigating factor was 'the position of her children for whom she is the sole carer' (para. 25). It referred to *Susan S* [2003] EWCA Crim 2300 whose sentence for sexual intercourse with a thirteen-year-old boy at her school was reduced to five months because of personal mitigation 'relating to the position of her children' (para. 22). For the heterosexual woman, then, the role of mother was particularly effective in countering the suggestion she was a corrupter; the result was significantly lower sentences than those received by childless lesbian defendants.

The Sexual Offences Act 2003

Liberal Principles

In July 2000, the government published a consultation paper on sexual offences, *Setting the Boundaries*. The command paper *Protecting the Public*

[18] While many lesbians are of course mothers, they would have had difficulty being regarded by the criminal courts as *good* mothers. (For a stark illustration of the division and its effect upon punishment, see the magistrates' interviews in Carlen (1993)). Similarly, the willingness to imprison mothers for non-sexual offences is a matter of national and international concern (Gerry and Harris 2015).

followed in 2002, and the following year the Sexual Offences Act 2003 passed into law. It aimed to be a comprehensive reform and consolidation of sexual offences law, founded on liberal principles including formal equality and gender neutrality, although in practice those principles were unevenly applied (Lacey 2001). Their practical impact for lesbian defendants has been far from uniformly positive, as Chap. 8 will explore. Particularly pertinent at this point is the extent to which the Act both promoted lesbian invisibility and reinforced existing hierarchies of sexual activity.

Liberalism has been an important thread in sexual offences law since the 1957 Wolfenden Report was published (see Chap. 6). The 2003 Act shifted its liberal emphasis from the public/private divide towards formal equality, although the former division and a strong moral element persisted.[19] The government looked to liberal reformers in shaping the 2003 Act; Davina Cooper has pointed out that hierarchical structures and use of formal equality discourse made such organisations' approaches more congruent with the practices and ideologies of the state than those of radical feminists (Cooper 1993, p. 196). In particular, Stonewall was the most influential lesbian and gay group, much as it had been in earlier age of consent campaigns. Stonewall's main concern with the new legislation was the legal position of gay men; relatively little attention was paid by them to lesbians.[20] The assumption that formal equality equated to non-discrimination resulted in an emphasis upon male homosexual offences as the sole area of discrimination in the pre-2003 Act law. Further, equality was implicitly measured against a heteronormative model. As Peter Bartlett commented in the context of earlier legislation, a focus upon equality has a silencing effect, removing any space for discussion of the distinctiveness of experiences or of 'any alternative substantive vision' (Bartlett 1998).

One of the Act's key principles is gender neutrality. This was an attempt to eliminate the inequalities of the old law, which differentiated between male and female perpetrators and victims. With the exception of rape,

[19] The consultation paper asserted that 'the law should be based on a public morality that protects the individual from danger, harm, fear or distress' (Sexual Offences Review 2000, sect. 6.2.4).

[20] For example, the group's summary of the 2003 Act made no references to lesbians (Stonewall 2003).

which requires penile penetration, the main offences in the Act apply regardless of the sex or gender of the complainant and accused. Gender neutrality has faced feminist criticism for its failure to acknowledge either the highly gendered ways in which both law and society continue to operate or the persistence of inequality between men and women, perhaps more blatantly in the area of sexual offences than elsewhere.[21] Within the specific context of the 2003 Act, gender neutrality was only partially achieved and where it was enacted, has failed to provide substantive equality. However, Nicola Lacey (2001) pointed out that even the attempt meant that feminist questions about the relationship between gendered social norms and sexual violence 'tend to drop out of the picture'. That was particularly true for lesbian and bisexual women: silenced by the law before 2003, they were not given specific consideration during the passage of the Bill. Instead, attention was focused more or less exclusively upon the position of heterosexuals and gay men. As the Gay and Lesbian Association of Doctors and Dentists pointedly commented in their response to *Setting the Boundaries*, '[i]t would be helpful in any further proposals to mention offences involving lesbians' (Gay and Lesbian Association of Doctors and Dentists 2001, p. 2). The needs and specificities of women who have sexual relationships with other women have been disregarded, with no recognition that they face different social, legal, and political challenges to heterosexual women or gay men.

One departure from gender neutrality, and one superimposition of gender neutrality onto a formerly gendered offence, each reveals much about why this new principle did not mean an end to discrimination. First, the offence of rape remains gendered: only penetration with a penis can satisfy the actus reus, limiting potential perpetrators to men and some trans women. That decision was not informed by feminist critiques of gender-neutral laws but seems to have been the consequence of a highly ideological approach to male sexual agency. Seems, because the White Paper struggled to articulate a principled basis for why rape could not be committed by a woman. In a single paragraph, it referred to public understanding of rape; sexed anatomical differences; and apparent uncer-

[21] Such feminist critiques substantially pre-dated the Bill (e.g. Mackinnon 1987, pp. 35–38; Naffine 1994, pp. 24–29).

tainty as to whether a woman could compel a man to penetrate her without consent (Home Office 2002, p. 22). This limitation upon gender neutrality for the most serious sexual offence had a pervasive effect upon the structure of offences as a whole. Once the special status of the penis was accepted, there was no reason to depart from a conservative hierarchy of offences. Consequently, the Act replicates a fairly crude taxonomy in which the most serious crime is penile penetration of a bodily orifice without consent; next comes penetration with something other than a penis; while non-consensual activity without penetration remains significantly less serious.

This hierarchy is founded upon the conceptualisation of men's sexuality as active, women's as passive. That myth lingers on even where an effort has been made to remove one of its most egregious legal expressions. The Punishment of Incest Act 1908 notoriously spoke of men 'having' and women 'permitting' sexual intercourse. The 2003 provisions use gender-neutral language to achieve a very similar result. 'Sex with an adult relative' is criminalised in two separate offences: 'penetration' (section 64) and 'consenting to penetration' (section 65). While technically gender-neutral since they include non-penile penetration, the offences specifically draw upon an active/passive model which could have been avoided by a single offence of 'engaging in' such activity. They also reinforce the assumption that only penetrative activity counts as 'sex'.

A different but related mechanism was at work in the enactment of section 71, a new, gender-neutral offence of sexual activity in a public lavatory. This was clearly intended to replace previous offences used specifically against male same-sex activity. Public sex is adequately criminalised elsewhere,[22] so a superficially 'equal' statement was a powerful declaration of uneasiness about gay equality. The process revealed much about the limitations of gender neutrality and formal equality. It also demonstrated the continuing invisibility of lesbians within the 'lesbian and gay' formulation, as during discussions sexual activity between men and women was generally labelled 'heterosexual', that between men 'homosexual', but that between women 'sex between women'. For exam-

[22] For example, a woman was convicted of outraging public decency for 'romping half-naked' with another woman in a park (*Daily Mirror* 2016).

ple, Baroness Noakes argued for a public toilet offence on the basis that 'the same principles apply to heterosexual sex or to sex between women' (HL 13/02/2003, col. 778). She was echoing *Setting the Boundaries*' statement that the law 'permits a wide range of heterosexual (and implicitly same-sex female) behaviour' (para. 6.2.2), which erased lesbians a few sentences later: '[s]exual activity in public that offends, irrespective of whether the people engaging in the activity are *heterosexual or homosexual*, will remain criminal' (Sexual Offences Review 2000, para. 10, emphasis added). Thus 'homosexual' was recast as gender-specific and the L-word silenced. More subtly, this language echoed wider and older cultural beliefs around lesbianism as a transient state which should and would cede to heterosexuality (Love 2007, p. 22).

Gender neutrality, like formal equality more broadly, has not solved the issues facing lesbians under the criminal law. Rather, it allows discrimination to persist in more subtle ways which can be more difficult to fight. As Nicola Lacey warned in relation to gay men, the Act's apparent non-discrimination would not remove the need for critical analysis and reform. Rather, it left 'more subtle, yet potentially equally discriminatory, images of and assumptions about sexuality' continuing to pervade the criminal justice system (Lacey 2001).

Key Offences Under the Act

The criminal law on sex between women was, despite its absence from the preceding discussions, significantly changed by the Sexual Offences Act 2003. Consent was given a new statutory definition, which will be explored in Chap. 8. Indecent assault was divided into two new offences: assault by penetration and sexual assault. Both of these apply only to factually non-consensual assaults and are gender-neutral as to both perpetrator and victim. Section 3 defines sexual assault as where A intentionally touches another person sexually; that other person does not consent; and A does not reasonably believe that they consent. The offence is triable either-way with a maximum sentence of ten years' imprisonment. However, if the assault involves intentional penetration of the vagina or anus with a body part or object, then the more serious offence of assault by penetration is committed contrary to section 2. This offence carries a maximum sentence of life imprisonment, the same as for rape, and applies not only to cases involving use of a dildo but also to, for example, penetration using fingers. It therefore covers a huge range of situations and degrees of physical risk and harm, and offers the courts enormous potential discretion in sentencing.

The age of consent is now enforced through specific offences, several of which are particularly relevant here. Section 9, 'sexual activity with a child', criminalises any sexual activity by a person over eighteen with a person under sixteen. If the sexual activity involves penetration of the child's anus or vagina with an object, or penile penetration of the mouth, anus or vagina, it is indictable-only and has a maximum sentence of fourteen years' imprisonment (section 9(2)). An offence is committed under section 16 if the younger person is under eighteen while the defendant is over eighteen and in a position of trust in relation to them; the maximum sentence is five years' imprisonment.

A person under eighteen who engages in sexual activity with a person under sixteen commits a discrete offence of sexual activity between minors, contrary to section 13. The maximum sentence is five years' imprisonment, lower than for sexual activity between adults and minors. However, the breadth of criminalisation of consensual conduct between peers—and the consequent wide discretion given to parents, police, and prosecutors in deciding whether to prosecute—is a matter of concern. Relationships of which families or criminal justice personnel disapprove are potentially more likely to result in a caution or prosecution, and in a society where homophobia remains common that poses obvious dangers for young lesbians. The scope given to courts and prosecutors by the Act means that the exercise of discretion is a matter of vital importance. We need to turn to policy and practice, particularly the guidance for prosecutors and sentencers, in order to understand the Act's impact upon defendants accused of same-sex activity with girls or women.

Prosecution and Sentencing Guidelines

Prosecution and sentencing guidance were soon produced for the new Act. Unfortunately, the guidelines for prosecutors (Crown Prosecution

Service 2004) did little to engage with the potential for prejudice. For the offence of sexual activity with a child, they offered a determinedly gender-neutral list of factors to consider. The absence of any specific guidance upon same-sex relationships left ample room for the prejudices of prosecutors and other parties to affect such decisions. In particular, although the list of factors itself referred to 'exploitation, coercion, threat, deception, grooming or manipulation', the summary immediately following reduced this to 'aggravating features, such as coercion or corruption'. Given corruption's long history as a code-word for same-sex activity, such guidance was potentially dangerous.

The most recent guidance does use the less loaded 'exploitative or coercive', but 'corruption' is then reintroduced as an aggravating feature (Crown Prosecution Service 2017). Where an offence was committed by a child against a child under thirteen, the guidance allows the views of the victim's family to be taken into account 'where appropriate'; the views of many families will be fundamentally affected by the same-sex nature of the offence, again allowing prejudice to influence prosecutorial decisions. The impact of these policies is not easy to assess. Statistics now do not routinely distinguish between offences by and against males and females, since there is no distinction in the offences themselves, while proceedings against defendants under eighteen are conducted in the youth courts and are not public.

Sentencing practice poses similar issues for women convicted of same-sex assaults. While the maximum penalty for sexual assault remains ten years' imprisonment, assault by penetration carries a maximum life sentence. Assaults involving penetration would therefore be likely to attract higher sentences, but how were courts to respond to the enormous variety of possible acts and instruments? Guidelines were not issued immediately although the Court of Appeal offered guidance in *Attorney General's Reference (No 104 of 2004)* [2005] 1 Cr App R (S) 177. Assault by penetration was to be treated as more closely equivalent to rape than to sexual assault but the starting point of four years' imprisonment was lower because there was not the 'risk of pregnancy or infection inherent in rape' (p. 670). The sentences for young offenders, should, however, be 'significantly shorter' (p. 671). As a result, the outcome in cases similar to *Saunders* could be closer to her original sentence than the reduced penalty handed down on appeal. In other words, the parallel with rape had resurfaced; but on a different and less inappropriate basis than that put forward by Crabtree.

Two years later, the first Definitive Guideline was published (Sentencing Guidelines Council 2007). Some pre-2003 sentencing principles were imported, perhaps not always consistently with the new ethos: for example, consensual sexual activity immediately before the offence was committed could reduce culpability (Sentencing Guidelines Council 2007, p. 21). In non-consensual offences, the 'primary indicator' of the degree of harm was the nature of the sexual behaviour (Sentencing Guidelines Council 2007, p. 19).[23] For Saunders, the penetration was with an object rather than a body part so the starting point would have been three years' custody; since R was initially fifteen, a starting point of five years was possible. Thus a sentence under the 2007 Guideline would have been closer to the original six-year term than the probation order with which the Court of Appeal replaced it. As for Allen, since there was factual consent, she would have been guilty of offences of sexual activity with a child under sixteen. Because they included penetration with the fingers and tongue, the starting point would have been four years' custody, substantially higher than the actual sentence at first instance or appeal. Although the apparent gender neutrality of the new sentencing approach should have benefitted lesbian defendants by removing their lesbianism as an unspoken aggravating factor, in fact the mechanistic focus upon types and degrees of penetration suggested the imposition of higher sentences while the failure to explicitly reiterate the importance of non-discrimination left space for its covert reappearance.

In 2014 a new Definitive Guideline came into effect, bringing a revised approach. For assault by penetration, the focus has moved from specific types of acts to the degree of harm caused to the victim. Problematically, the greater flexibility of the factors also increases the subjectivity of the approach, and with it the possibility of prejudice. That risk might be

[23] For assault by penetration, the starting point was four years' imprisonment; for sexual assault involving contact between the offender's naked genitalia and a naked part of the victim's body, two to three years; and for contact with the victim's naked genitalia using something other than genitalia, twenty-six weeks to eighteen months. Where genital contact was not involved, the starting point was a community order.

heightened by, for example, the inclusion of 'additional humiliation' as a factor increasing the level of harm (Sentencing Council 2013, p. 14). Therefore after 2014, Saunders might have faced a starting point of six years' custody if the court treated the harm as including penetration using a dangerous object, additional humiliation, or a sustained incident. If they did not, the starting point would drop to two years (Sentencing Council 2013, p. 15). Again, the sentence could be closer to (and potentially even higher than) her original custodial sentence rather than the probation order which was substituted on appeal. For sexual activity with a child, the emphasis upon the type of activity remains so Allen might have faced a higher starting point because there was vaginal penetration (Sentencing Council 2013, p. 46). If her culpability was deemed to be relatively low then the starting point would be one year's custody. However, if the court again rewrote the facts from 'virtuous friendship' to something like grooming, that could give a starting point of five years' custody (Sentencing Council 2013, p. 47). The current sentencing guidelines continue to suggest substantially higher sentences for lesbian defendants and leave space for courts to sentence according to stereotypes.

It is not easy to assess the consequences of these policies on young defendants, given the lack of reporting or detailed published statistics. If the newspaper reports are to be believed, then almost every prosecution of an adult woman for sexual activity with a girl involves a teacher/pupil relationship.[24] There are factors which might make such prosecutions more common, including the higher age of eighteen where a defendant was in a 'position of trust' and the greater likelihood of prosecutors deciding that court proceedings are justified in such cases. However, it seems improbable that the preponderance is as great as the newspaper stories indicate. Rather, the reason for this emphasis is probably found in the headline to one such story: 'The Corrupter' (Byrne 2007). Drawing upon the discourses of corruption discussed earlier, as well as fears stirred up by the section 28 debates, these reports continue to associate lesbianism with the 'malign influence' invoked by *Allen*.

[24] There are numerous examples (e.g. Chapman 2009; *Daily Mirror* 2010, 2011, 2013; Aspinall 2018; *BBC News* 2014; *Daily Star* 2013; Twomey 2016); another case emphasised the defendant was a social worker/youth worker, although the relationship did not occur in the course of her work (Willey 1999). Exceptions include *Leicester Mercury* (2000), Hawken (2014), and Sharman (2018) whose subtitle refers to a 'dangerous predator'.

Conclusion

The period from the late 1960s to the late 1990s included significant conservative backlash and the tragedy of the AIDS crisis, but ultimately brought social and legal liberalisation around male homosexuality. It also marked growing, but partial and selective, legal visibility for lesbianism. Treated as a shadow of the gay man, the lesbian was sometimes fully obscured and always less clearly visible. Her legal position remained ambiguous and was distorted in popular understanding, as evident in the enduring myth that there was no lesbian age of consent. Despite its long legal history, the 'lesbian age of consent' has grown in both symbolic and practical importance only relatively recently. Although prosecutions remain unusual—they are a tiny proportion of total prosecutions for these offences—their court and media appearances are nonetheless significant. They represent part of the progression from complete silencing of lesbianism to its limited appearance as a lesser form of male homosexuality. That is apparent, for example, in the prominence of corruption as an aggravating factor.

While the Sexual Offences Act 2003 introduced important new principles, it was not entirely the radical departure from the old law that it claimed. A theme apparent throughout its passage was the lack of attention to lesbians in their own right.[25] Instead, a new form of silencing was evident: lesbians were subsumed within the 'homosexual' or 'lesbian and gay' category, which quickly slipped into consideration of gay men alone. The sentencing guidelines for the Sexual Offences Act 2003 suggest that the Act has advanced that association. Its benefits for gay men in reducing their potential criminalisation and in requiring a formally equal approach to sentencing are manifest, but the gains for lesbians are to say the least more ambiguous. In particular, the covert discrimination which was a defining feature of cases such as *Allen* is not explicitly challenged under the new regime. Lesbians may continue to be sentenced more

[25] This was not an isolated incident in contemporary parliamentary debate. Discussing the debates on repeal of section 28 and equalisation of the age of consent, Stychin comments that while young gay men were desexualised and young heterosexuals of either sex hypersexualised, '[y]oung lesbians, for the most part, seem not to exist at all' (2003, p. 36).

harshly as the courts take into account factors such as the 'embarrassment' caused.

This has been mirrored by wider cultural processes. In the social sphere as well, men have too often become the norm for 'lesbian and gay', 'homosexual', or 'queer'. Most recently, LGBT and its variants have emerged as the dominant term, favoured for their apparent ability to acknowledge a range of identities both separately and collectively, yet the same pattern tends to repeat itself. Sometimes the term is used as if it is a universal adjective, so that a single individual is described—impossibly—as 'LGBT'. At other times, there is slippage into the old habit of giving greatest attention to gay men unless specific effort is made to offer a diverse selection of examples. The term has therefore fallen into the same trap as 'queer', where component members are frequently treated as an undifferentiated, presumptively male mass. This is not a matter of terminology alone but one which has practical consequences in and beyond the law. When a diverse range of interests and perspectives are subsumed under a single label, those of the most privileged are likely to dominate public discourse. Within the 'queer' umbrella, that means white, middle-class gay men. A recent example of this is offered by Sarah Beresford (2014) in her exploration of 2013 debates around lowering the age of consent. She found that the debates focused upon the criminalisation of boys and young men, at the expense of girls' interests and lived experiences. An apparently inclusive debate which affected all identities was 'inherently privileging of patriarchy' (Beresford 2014, p. 762). That privileging of patriarchy remains manifest in the courtroom, most obviously in the gender fraud cases considered in the following chapter.

References

American Psychiatric Association. 1980. *Diagnostic and Statistical Manual of Mental Disorders*. 3rd ed. Washington, DC: American Psychiatric Association.

Aspinall, Adam. 2018. Lesbian Head Escapes Sex Offender List. *Daily Mirror*, October 9.

Auchmuty, Rosemary. 2004. Same-Sex Marriage Revived: Feminist Critique and Legal Strategy. *Feminism & Psychology* 14 (1): 101–126. https://doi.org/10.1177/0959-353504040307.

———. 2015. Feminist Approaches to Sexuality and Law Scholarship. *Legal Information Management* 15: 4–7. https://doi.org/10.1017/S1472669615000055.

Barker, Nicola. 2012. *Not the Marrying Kind: A Feminist Critique of Same-Sex Marriage*. Basingstoke: Palgrave Macmillan.

Bartlett, Annie. 2005. "Sex Offenders: Madness, myth and modern monsters". Lecture, Dana Centre, London, June 29.

Bartlett, Peter. 1998. Silence and Sodomy: The Creation of Homosexual Identity in Law. *Modern Law Review* 61 (1): 102–114.

BBC News. 2014. Teacher Emily Fox Jailed for Having Sex with Pupil, September 5.

———. 2018. Tinder User Jailed for Tricking Blindfolded Men into Sex, November 9.

Beresford, Sarah. 2008. Get Over Your (Legal) 'Self': A Brief History of Lesbians, Motherhood and the Law. *Journal of Social Welfare and Family Law* 30 (2): 95–106. https://doi.org/10.1080/09649060802469785.

———. 2014. The Age of Consent and the Ending of Queer Theory. *Laws* 3 (4): 759–779. https://doi.org/10.3390/laws3040759.

Bowcott, Owen. 2018. John Worboys' Victims Win Human Rights Case against Police. *The Guardian*, February 21.

Byrne, Paul. 2007. The Corrupter. *Daily Mirror*, October 19.

Capital Gay. 1991a. Judge Hits Back Over Criticism: Demo Sparks Outburst, November 15.

———. 1991b. Judge Crabtree, November 22.

———. 1992. Judge Frees Jailed Lesbian, June 19.

Carlen, Pat. 1993. *Women's Imprisonment: A Study in Social Control*. London: Routledge.

Carter, Vicki. 1992. Abseil Makes the Heart Grow Fonder: Lesbian and Gay Campaigning Tactics and Section 28. In *Modern Homosexualities: Fragments of Lesbian and Gay Experience*, ed. Ken Plummer, 217–226. London: Routledge.

Chapman, John. 2009. Jailed Lesbian Teacher to See Lover, 15, When Freed. *Daily Express*, September 22.

Committee on Homosexual Offences and Prostitution. 1957. *Report of the Committee on Homosexual Offences and Prostitution*. London: Her Majesty's Stationery Office.

Cooper, Davina. 1993. An Engaged State: Sexuality, Governance and the Potential for Change. In *Activating Theory: Lesbian, Gay, Bisexual Politics*, ed.

Joseph Bristow and Angelia R. Wilson, 190–218. London: Lawrence & Wishart.

Crane, Paul. 1982. *Gays and the Law*. London: Pluto Press.

Crown Prosecution Service. 2004. Legal Guidance: Sexual Offences Act 2003. http://www.cps.gov.uk/legal/section7/sexoffencesact2003.html#50.

———. 2017. Rape and Sexual Offences—Chapter 2: Sexual Offences Act 2003—Principal Offences, and Sexual Offences Act 1956—Most Commonly Charged Offences | The Crown Prosecution Service. Code for Crown Prosecutors. https://www.cps.gov.uk/legal-guidance/rape-and-sexual-offences-chapter-2-sexual-offences-act-2003-principal-offences-and.

Daily Mirror. 2010. Tutor on Sex List, November 11.

———. 2011. Pupil Affair Tutor Jailed, May 14.

———. 2013. Lesbian Fling Teacher Jailed, November 23.

———. 2016. Park Lesbian's Drink Therapy, August 20.

Daily Star. 2013. Teacher Is Caged, November 23.

Davies, Caroline. 2019. Police Escape Misconduct Charges over Case of Serial Killer Stephen Port. *The Guardian*, July 5.

Derby Evening Telegraph. 2004a. Lesbian Pervert Guilty of Abusing Girl, February 10.

———. 2004b. Victim of Lesbian Predator 'Taunted' at School, March 9.

Flanagan, Padraic, and Bob McGowan. 2000. My Gay Hell in the Police. *Express*, October 20.

Gay and Lesbian Association of Doctors and Dentists. 2001. *Consultation on Setting the Boundaries: Reforming the Law on Sex Offences*. London.

Gerry, Felicity, and Lyndon Harris. 2015. *Women in Prison: Is the Justice System Fit for Purpose?* London: Halsbury's Law Exchange.

Guardian. 1992. Sex Case Girl Released on Appeal, June 13.

Harne, Lynne, and Rights of Women. 1997. *Valued Families: The Lesbian Mothers' Legal Handbook*. London: The Women's Press.

Hawken, Abe. 2014. Sex Attack at Navy Base by Lesbian Sailor. *Daily Mirror*, October 10.

Home Office. 2002. *Protecting the Public—Strengthening Protection Against Sex Offenders and Reforming the Law on Sexual Offences*. London: HMSO.

———. 2006. Sexual Assault on a Female'—Long-Term National Recorded Crime Trend. http://www.crimestatistics.org.uk/output/Page28.asp.

Honoré, Tony. 1978. *Sex Law*. London: Duckworth.

Jackson, Louise A. 2000. *Child Sexual Abuse in Victorian England*. London: Routledge.

Jackson, Stevi, and Sue Scott. 2004. Sexual Antinomies in Late Modernity. *Sexualities* 7 (2): 233–248.

Jennings, Rebecca. 2007. *A Lesbian History of Britain: Love and Sex Between Women since 1500*. Oxford: Greenwood World Publishing.

———. 2008. 'The Most Uninhibited Party They'd Ever Been to': The Postwar Encounter Between Psychiatry and the British Lesbian, 1945–1971. *Journal of British Studies* 47 (4): 883–904.

Jivani, Alkarim. 1997. *It's Not Unusual: A History of Lesbian and Gay Britain in the Twentieth Century*. London: M. O'Mara Books.

Judicial College. 2018. *Equal Treatment Bench Book*. February. London: Judicial College.

Judicial Studies Board. 2000. *Equal Treatment Bench Book*. London: Judicial Studies Board.

Lacey, Nicola. 2001. Beset by Boundaries. *Criminal Law Review*: 3–11.

Lavelle, Ashley. 2014. 'Wham Bam Tap Scratch Screech': The Brief—But Proud—History of *Lesbian London*, 1991–1994. *Journal of Lesbian Studies* 18 (1): 88–100. https://doi.org/10.1080/10894160.2013.774679.

Leicester Mercury. 2000. Woman Is Jailed for Molesting Schoolgirl, May 19.

Lloyd, Ann. 1995. *Doubly Deviant, Doubly Damned: Society's Treatment of Violent Women*. London: Penguin.

Love, Heather. 2007. *Feeling Backward: Loss and the Politics of Queer History*. Cambridge, MA: Harvard University Press.

Mackinnon, Catharine. 1987. *Feminism Unmodified*. Harvard University Press.

Murphy, Neil. 2018. Gay Tinder User Jailed for Tricking Blindfolded Men into Sex by Dressing as Woman. *Mirror*, November 9.

Naffine, Ngaire. 1994. Possession: Erotic Love in the Law of Rape. *Modern Law Review* 56: 10–37.

News of the World. 2004. Lesbian, 22 Posed as Boy of 16 to Seduce Girl of 12, February 29.

Pink Paper. 1991. Off with His Wig, October 26.

Plummer, Ken. 1992. Speaking Its Name: Inventing a Lesbian and Gay Studies. In *Modern Homosexualities: Fragments of Lesbian and Gay Experience*, ed. Ken Plummer, 3–28. London: Routledge.

Policy Advisory Committee on Sexual Offences. 1981. *Report on the Age of Consent in Relation to Sexual Offences*. London.

Ripley and Heanor News. 2004. Woman Posed as Teenage Boy to Assault Child, February 12.

Royal Commission on Marriage and Divorce. 1956. *Report of the Royal Commission on Marriage and Divorce*. London.

Rubin, Gayle. 1989. Thinking Sex: Notes for a Radical Theory of the Politics of Sexuality. In *Pleasure and Danger: Exploring Female Sexuality*, ed. Carole S. Vance, 267–319. London: Pandora.

Schneider, Beth E. 1992. Lesbian Politics and AIDS Work. In *Modern Asian Studies*, ed. Ken Plummer, 160–174. London: Routledge.

Sentencing Council. 2013. *Sexual Offences Definitive Guideline*. London: Sentencing Council.

Sentencing Guidelines Council. 2007. *Sexual Offences Act 2003 Definitive Guideline*. London: Sentencing Guidelines Secretariat.

Sexual Offences Review. 2000. *Setting the Boundaries: Reforming the Law on Sex Offences, Vol. 1*. London.

Sharman, Jon. 2018. Woman Jailed for String of Sex Attacks on Young Girls. *Independent*, September 27.

Sharpe, Alex. 2018. *Sexual Intimacy and Gender Identity "Fraud": Reframing the Legal & Ethical Debate*. London: Routledge.

Sharpe, Martyn. 1991a. Blonde Dressed as Boy Seduced 2 Girls. *Sun*, September 19.

———. 1991b. I've Got a 36D Chest, How Can I Be a Boy? *Sun*, September 20.

Smith, Anna Marie. 1992. Resisting the Erasure of Lesbian Sexuality: A Challenge for Queer Activism. In *Modern Homosexualities: Fragments of Lesbian and Gay Experience*, ed. Ken Plummer, 200–213. London: Routledge.

———. 1995. The Regulation of Lesbian Sexuality Through Erasure: The Case of Jennifer Saunders. In *Dyke Erotics*, ed. Karla Jay, 164–179. New York: New York University Press.

———. 1998. The Hegemonic Regulation of Butch Performance: Regina v Saunders. In *Butch/Femme: Inside Lesbian Gender*, ed. Sally R. Munt, 177–190. London: Cassell.

———, ed. 2000. *Regina v Saunders: A Collection of the Official Documents Relating to the 1991 Crown Court Trial and the 1992 Court of Appeal Hearing*. Cornell University.

Smith, Leanne. 2006. Principle or Pragmatism? Lesbian Parenting, Shared Residence and Parental Responsibility after Re G (Residence: Same Sex Partner). *Child and Family Law Quarterly* 18 (1): 125.

Smyth, Cherry. 1991. Get Out! Get Angry? *City Limits*, February 14.

Stonewall. 2003. Sexual Offences. http://www.stonewall.org.uk/information_bank/criminal_law/69.asp#History.

———. n.d.-a Age of Consent. Accessed December 13, 2006. http://www.stonewall.org.uk/information_bank/criminal_law/66.asp.

———. n.d.-b Love. Accessed October 30, 2002. www.stonewall.org.uk.

Stychin, Carl F. 2003. *Governing Sexuality: The Changing Politics of Citizenship and Law Reform*. Oxford: Hart Publishing.

Sun. 1991a. This Is a Woman Who 'Pretended She Was a Man Then Seduced Two Young Girls', September 19.

———. 1991b. 6 Years for Blonde Who Posed as a Boy to Bed Girls, September 21.

Tatchell, Peter. n.d. Consent at Sixteen: Protection or Persecution? Accessed September 23, 2004. www.petertatchell.net/age20%25of%2520consent/consent%2520at%252016.htm.

Telegraph. 2012. Margaret Thatcher Saved Career of Police Chief Who Made Aids Remarks, January 4.

Thomas, David, ed. 2004. *Current Sentencing Practice*. London: Sweet and Maxwell.

Thomas, Philip, and Ruth Costigan. 1990. *Promoting Homosexuality: Section 28 of the Local Government Act 1988*. Cardiff: Cardiff Law School.

Tweedie, Jill. 1972. Who Goes Home? *Guardian*, September 11.

Twomey, John. 2016. Lesbian PE Teacher Jailed for Grooming Schoolgirls for Sex. *Daily Express*, January 30.

Waites, Matthew. 2002. Inventing a 'Lesbian Age of Consent'? The History of the Minimum Age for Sex Between Women in the UK. *Social & Legal Studies* 11 (3): 323–342.

———. 2003. Equality at Last? Homosexuality, Heterosexuality and the Age of Consent in the United Kingdom. *Sociology* 37 (4): 637–655.

Walmesley, Roy, and Karen White. 1979. *Home Office Research Unit Study No. 54: Sexual Offences, Consent and Sentencing*. London: HMSO.

Weeks, Jeffrey. 1981. *Sex, Politics and Society: The Regulation of Sexuality since 1800*. London: Longman.

———. 2016. *Coming Out: Homosexual Politics in Britain from the Nineteenth Century to the Present*. 3rd ed. London: Quartet Books.

Willey, Garry. 1999. Youth Worker Is Jailed for Sex Assaults—Woman Sacked After Lesbian Affair with Under-Age Girl. *Evening Chronicle*, December 18.

Wolfenden, John. 1976. *Turning Points*. London: Bodley Head.

8

McNally: After the Sexual Offences Act 2003

The Sexual Offences Act 2003 promised a new approach based upon liberal principles of non-discrimination. Their imperfect realisation, and concerns about subsequent official guidance, were considered in Chap. 7. Judicial interpretation of the Act has raised further questions, particularly around the meaning of consent. Section 74 provides a statutory definition which was intended to transform it from passive agreement, coded as feminine submission to masculine demands (e.g. *Olugboja* [1982] QB 320), into a positive exercise of agency assessed without resort to gendered assumptions. However, that is not what has happened. *McNally (Justine)* [2013] EWCA Crim 1051, in which the Court of Appeal set out its approach to consent in gender fraud cases, demonstrates that lesbians and trans men continue to face discrimination and disadvantage. The questions raised by these cases are complex and challenging, and the chapter concludes by suggesting future approaches rather than definite solutions.

C. Derry, *Lesbianism and the Criminal Law*,
https://doi.org/10.1007/978-3-030-35300-1_8

R v McNally

Teenager Scott Hill met M, a girl a year younger than him, through an online game. They became close, talking on the phone as well as online, agreeing to an exclusive relationship, having phone sex, and discussing marriage and children. After three and a half years, and shortly after M's sixteenth birthday, Scott travelled from Scotland to London to meet her in person for the first time. M's mother did not want Scott staying in the family home and arranged for him to stay with a family friend. Nonetheless, the two teenagers engaged in sexual activity for which M bought condoms, and further visits followed.

The facts alleged by the prosecution were that unknown to M, Scott Hill was actually Justine McNally. During the first visit, McNally remained clothed throughout their sexual activity and, after performing oral sex on M, refused M's offer to reciprocate. (It was also claimed that McNally penetrated M's vagina with a dildo which M believed to be a penis, but McNally denied this and the charge relating to it was ordered to remain on file.) During a second visit, McNally again performed oral sex on M as well as using fingers to penetrate her vagina. The reports are unclear as to whether sexual activity occurred during the third visit, but that visit certainly took a very different turn. The family friend hosting McNally had seen women's clothing and a dildo in McNally's bag. When challenged by M's mother, McNally admitted to being a girl. M was described as 'devastated', although she apparently suggested that things might have been different if she had known from the start (*McNally*, para. 10). McNally returned to Scotland but further contact between her and M prompted M's mother to complain to McNally's school. When McNally confirmed to the headteacher that sexual acts had taken place, the police were contacted and prosecution followed.[1]

The prosecution case was that the complainant had believed McNally to be a boy and consented to sex on that basis. On 4 December 2012, McNally pleaded guilty to six charges of sexual assault by penetration, all relating to digital penetration of M. The case was adjourned for reports

[1] The trial and appeal were widely reported in the press (e.g. O'Shea and Phillips 2013; Dixon 2013; Shaw 2013a, b; Greenwood 2013; *Daily Mail* 2013).

and on 21 March 2013, McNally was sentenced to three years' detention in a young offenders' institution. The judge, somewhat oddly, identified breach of trust as the main aggravating factor. A breach of trust occurs where a defendant occupies a position of authority or responsibility over the complainant, for example, as a teacher or doctor (Sentencing Council 2019), which clearly did not apply in McNally's case.

Having pleaded guilty, McNally did not put forward an alternative version of events in the Crown Court but she had already given a prepared statement to police and would later offer accounts to her lawyers, to a probation officer and a psychologist preparing pre-sentence reports, and when giving evidence before the Court of Appeal. In the statement to police, she suggested that M had known her real identity for several years and knew or suspected she was a girl. She repeated this in her initial instructions to her solicitors, stating that she had admitted her gender when challenged by M and two friends (*McNally*, para. 28). However, in a conference with counsel, she said that she had not in fact told M she was a girl (para. 32). Pre-sentence reports noted both that McNally assumed M 'knew her true gender' and that she was 'worried and scared her gender would be apparent' to M (paras. 42–44). McNally's evidence before the Court of Appeal also seems to have been rather confused: despite asserting that she believed M knew she was female, McNally admitted she didn't want to tell M the truth for fear that M would end the relationship.

McNally appealed against both conviction and sentence. The appeal against conviction revolved around the circumstances in which she pleaded guilty: if she had been wrongly advised by counsel, and was not in fact guilty in law, then her pleas could be vacated by the court and the convictions overturned. The offence of sexual assault by penetration (section 2) is committed where the accused intentionally sexually penetrates the vagina, anus, or mouth of the complainant with something other than a penis; the complainant does not consent; and the accused does not have a reasonable belief that the complainant consents. Here, the issue was whether the complainant's apparent consent was legally invalidated by McNally's deception as to her sex. Even if it was, however, McNally would not be guilty if she had had a reasonable belief that M was consenting. Her appeal centred on the argument that she had not been properly advised on these points and would not have pleaded guilty had they been explained.

The Court of Appeal concluded that McNally had in fact been properly advised by counsel, and that the deception as to her sex was sufficient to vitiate (legally invalidate) M's consent. It did, however, recognise that there had not been an abuse of trust and reduced McNally's sentence to nine months' detention suspended for two years, with a two-year supervision order. The legal ruling on consent will be considered in detail later in this chapter. However, it is first worth exploring the context of this case.

Modern Female Husbands?

The parallels with female husband cases from previous centuries are strong, and sometimes surprising. McNally was a working-class outsider to her partner's home area. Her discovery and prosecution were the result of actions by family members, not the complainant herself. There was uncertainty as to whether the complainant knew that her partner was female before the moment of public discovery, but the courts were predisposed to accept that she did not. The reasons for McNally's male presentation were also left uncertain: there was mention of her talking about a sex change to M's mother, but elsewhere she asserted a lesbian identity, while her pre-sentence report spoke of confusion around both sexuality and gender.

Another similarity between this and earlier cases was its portrayal in the media as a unique and extraordinary event, despite its being one of a small series of such prosecutions. Although McNally was convicted of an offence created by the Sexual Offences Act 2003, the legislation had not marked a point of rupture or revival: there had been several similar prosecutions in the previous decades under the old law. Both of these were discussed in Chap. 7 and will be considered further here: Jennifer/Jimmy Saunders was convicted of indecent assaults on two women in 1991, while Kelly/Jake Trueman was prosecuted in 2004 for indecent assault committed before the 2003 Act came into force. Thereafter, McNally was one of several people prosecuted under the new Act's provisions on the basis that consent was vitiated by deception, namely that they were women falsely representing themselves as male. This chapter will use the term 'gender fraud' as convenient shorthand to refer to those cases, even though it is not entirely accurate (not least because any fraud was as to biological sex, but 'sex fraud' would be confusing). Alex Sharpe (2018) has identified four further prosecutions in England: *Gemma Barker* (unreported, 5 March 2012, Guildford Crown Court), *Gayle Newland* [2016] All ER (D) 85 *Kyran Lee (Mason)* (unreported, 16 December 2015, Lincoln Crown Court), and *Jennifer Staines* (unreported, 24 March 2016, Bristol Crown Court). Before exploring the common themes in these cases, it is useful to briefly consider the facts of each.

The Cases

Gemma Barker

When fifteen- and sixteen-year-old friends J and K became friendly with eighteen-year-old Gemma Barker, two years above them at school, she decided to create the 'ideal boy' each girl had told her they wanted to meet.[2] In late 2009, she set up Facebook profiles in various male names including Aaron Lampard, Connor McCormack, and Luke Jones; each had a different email address and mobile phone number, and they went on to have online relationships with J and K which developed into offline sexual relationships. J dated Luke, who claimed to have bone cancer, but she ended the relationship when he pushed her to engage in sexual activity and groped her. She then fell in love with Connor, a very shy young man who offered sympathy after she broke up with 'cocky' Luke. Connor always wore a baseball cap which obscured his face. Meanwhile, K started going out with Aaron whose backstory included the deaths of his mother and two brothers. As well as these three personae, Barker created other characters including Connor's twin brother and several friends who sent online messages to J. Barker also met the parents of one complainant both as a boyfriend and as a woman.

[2] The case was reported in a range of media (e.g. *BBC News* 2012a, b; Rach 2015; Sabey et al. 2012). J subsequently waived her anonymity to give several interviews about her experience (Blake 2012a; Stretch 2012).

The girls became suspicious that Aaron and Connor might be the same person, so when Connor fell asleep in J's company she removed his hat. She recognised him as Aaron, but not as Barker. J would later describe how, when she discovered that Connor and Aaron were the same person, her own fears and her concern for K led to suicidal thoughts. After three weeks, she went to the police. Aaron initially claimed falsely to have been in hospital at the time of the discovery, then put Gemma Barker forward as an alibi. Barker later fractured her own jaw, claiming to police as Connor that Luke had done this and forced him to pose as Aaron. It was only after Aaron's arrest, when police took some of his clothing from him in the cells area, that they discovered he was physically female and identified him as Barker.

Barker pleaded guilty to two specimen counts of sexual assault relating to kissing, cuddling, and non-penetrative 'sexual touching', and one fraud: an attempt to claim criminal injuries compensation for the broken jaw (*BBC News* 2012b). In March 2012, she was sentenced to thirty months' imprisonment after HHJ Peter Moss described her as either 'bad and dangerous to know or mad and dangerous to know' with 'a very mean and manipulative streak' to her 'cunning, deceptive and cruel' offending. The two or three-year age difference between her and the complainants was identified as a serious aggravating factor: Moss described them as 'much younger than her'. Although according to psychological reports she had an autistic spectrum condition, ADHD, and a history of self-harm, the judge expressed concern that the report writers were being manipulated by a 'deceptive and deceitful' Barker (*BBC News* 2012a).

Gayle Newland/Kye Fortune

Gayle Newland was charged with five counts of sexual assault committed in the first half of 2013.[3] She was tried and convicted in 2015; appealed successfully; but was convicted again in a second trial in 2017. The facts

[3] In her longer article about the case, Sophie Wilkinson (2017) says that the correct spelling is 'Gail', with the alternative spelling originating in a court report typo. I have retained the more common spelling, consistent with the wide range of press reports (e.g. Hattenstone 2017; Pidd 2017; Humphries 2015a, b, c, d; Swerling 2017).

were therefore heavily contested, although it was not disputed that Newland and the complainant C were close friends and that C also had a sexual relationship with Newland's alter ego Kye Fortune (Hattenstone 2017; Wilkinson 2017; Pidd 2017; Humphries 2015a, b, c, d; Swerling 2017).

C's account was that after she got to know Kye online, he put her in contact with Newland and the two women became friends. Meanwhile, C's relationship with Kye progressed to physical meetings in hotels and her home, during which he insisted that C wear a blindfold at all times, even while watching television or going for a drive. He explained that he had been injured in a car accident following which a brain tumour was discovered, and was self-conscious over surgery scars and lost muscle tone due to ongoing medical treatment. Kye wore a swimming costume and bandages, supposedly for his circulation and to keep a heart monitor in place, and handcuffed C during sex so that she couldn't touch him. She agreed to his conditions because she was 'desperate to be loved' (Traynor 2015). His higher-pitched voice was explained by his mixed Asian and Filipino heritage, though C denied that it was outside a male range. When C tried to end the relationship, Kye threatened suicide and they met once more. In that final encounter Kye asked C to lick his penis, but something didn't feel right so she ripped off the blindfold. She saw that Kye was Gayle wearing a hat to hide her long hair and a 'prosthetic penis'. C denied having suspected that Kye and Newland were the same person, despite having seen Kye leave her flat in Newland's car and knowing they shared a birthday and had dogs with the same name.

According to Newland, she first met C at a nightclub's LGBT night and told C that she used a male persona online. Only then did C choose to contact Kye's profile. Newland's use of the Kye persona was role-play; both were struggling with their sexuality and this allowed C to have a 'boyfriend' in public. Newland described C as taking the initiative sexually, including in the purchase of a dildo, and never wearing a blindfold. In June 2013, C had abruptly ended the relationship after Newland told her that she intended to come out to her parents. They argued and C pushed Newland down the stairs and left. After an exchange of messages and C's refusal to speak on the phone, Newland attempted suicide; meanwhile, C had contacted the police.

Both parties' lawyers pointed to implausibilities in the other's account. Defence counsel emphasised that C's version involved her spending more than one hundred hours in Kye's company and having sexual intercourse at least ten times. Prosecution counsel pointed to messages Newland sent to C appearing to admit she had deceived her; called another witness similarly deceived online by Newland; and asked why C would make a false allegation whose consequences were 'excruciating embarrassment', scrutiny and judgment (Humphries 2015d). After a summing up by the trial judge which later formed the basis of her appeal, Newland was convicted and sentenced to eight years' imprisonment. Following retrial, she was sentenced to six years' imprisonment in 2017.

Kyran Lee/Joey Crislow

Joey G-Star Crislow and H, a single mother, met on Facebook (*Telegraph* 2015a, b; L. Smith 2015; Mann 2015; *Guardian* 2015; *BBC News* 2015). Their relationship progressed to text messages and telephone calls; Crislow also sent H gifts including toys for her children and jewellery. He described himself as a tanned, muscular single father. They later met in person and in autumn 2012, three weeks after that first face-to-face meeting, they had penetrative sex. The defendant claimed this only happened because H said the relationship could not continue unless it became sexual (L. Smith 2015). According to the prosecution, Crislow remained fully clothed and wore a 'bodysuit', and the lights were off. H had consented to penile penetration, but was unaware that Crislow used a 'sex toy'. When H discovered through a friend that Crislow was working in a restaurant as Fiona Manson, it emerged that Crislow was Kyran Lee, a trans man receiving treatment for gender dysphoria but still presenting as a woman at work. Lee pleaded guilty to assault by penetration and in 2015, was sentenced to two years' imprisonment suspended for two years.

Jason Spiller/Jennifer Staines

Over a period of five years, Jason Spiller had sexual relationships with three complainants whom he met on social media; one lasted over a year.

He would be identified in court as Jennifer Staines (Churchill 2016; *Telegraph* 2016; Osborne 2016; *BBC News* 2016; Crossley 2016). The first complainant, O, was twelve or thirteen years old at the time of their relationship and Staines was seventeen; they chatted using webcams before Staines travelled from Preston to Bristol on several occasions to stay with her. O refused to have 'sex' with Staines, but they kissed and O sent photographs of herself naked. The relationship ended because of Staines's controlling behaviour.

When Staines was twenty-one and P was seventeen, they engaged in sexual activity during which Staines remained clothed with a bandaged chest, supposedly due to stab scars. P was not permitted to touch him; he told her that being touched was painful as he had been circumcised. Staines used condoms and on one occasion P visited her doctor because she was afraid she might be pregnant. However, sex apparently did not 'feel right'.

Aged twenty-two, Staines had a relationship with another Bristol woman, Q, who was seventeen. During sexual activity she believed he was using his penis; in fact, it was an 'imitation'. When Q's family discovered that her boyfriend was female, Q refused to accept this and continued to talk about having children with him. Q's mother contacted the police and Staines was prosecuted in relation to all three relationships, pleading guilty to four counts of sexual assault and two of assault by penetration as well as charges relating to the photographs of O. Although defence counsel described Staines as having gender dysphoria, he also said that at the time of sentencing, Staines was in a lesbian relationship. It is therefore unclear how Staines identified. Judge Barry Cotter QC declared himself unable to determine whether the offences were committed 'for love, love and sex, or just sex' (*Telegraph* 2016) and sentenced Staines to three years and three months' imprisonment in March 2016. Dismissing an appeal against this sentence, the Court of Appeal said it was at the lower end of the scale (*Lancashire Post* 2016).

Overlapping Identities

All the defendants except Kyran Lee presented themselves as women at trial. However, uncertainties around sexual and gender identity were common to most.[4] McNally had mentioned wanting a 'sex change', albeit in the fraught circumstances of the 'discovery'; her pre-sentence report described confusions around sexuality and gender identity 'which were resolving' (*McNally*, para. 47). After McNally's release, a new girlfriend spoke to the *Daily Record* about their relationship referring to McNally as 'she' throughout; McNally was described as 'lesbian' (Jenkins 2013).

Newland's identity was represented as complex and confused. She presented as a woman throughout both trials, and in most areas of her daily life. In her second trial, she told the court of her isolation when she realised she was attracted to girls: 'You'd use the word lesbian for name-calling' (Wilkinson 2017). Mitigating, her barrister told the court that she had long-term difficulties with both sexuality and sex, for which she had sought professional support (Pidd 2017). Jennifer Saunders, discussed in Chap. 7, had presented herself at different times as heterosexual, lesbian, and possibly trans (*Capital Gay* 1991, 1992). Staines's counsel referred to both a diagnosis of gender dysphoria and a current lesbian relationship. Barker's barrister suggested the adoption of male identities was a reaction to the complainants' desires rather than her own: she became the boy her friends wanted (Sherriff 2012a). Trueman also claimed to have been motivated by the expectations of her (much younger) friends. She described herself as lesbian to police but told the court her most recent relationship was with a man.

Lee was unusual in being clearly trans. His 'transsexuality' was highlighted in court, and distinguished by the sentencing judge from 'a ruse to practise lesbian behaviour' (HHJ Michael Heath, quoted in 2015a). Nonetheless, the judge referred to Lee as 'he' and 'she' interchangeably. The complainant was no less confused, and referred to 'him' even as she talked about discovering he 'was a female' (*Telegraph* 2015b).

The legal issues raised by overlapping, uncertain and unstable identities are considered later in this chapter. However, if we are to respond appropriately to the parties in these cases—defendants and complainants—then our responses must accommodate these uncertainties. We

---

[4] It is therefore difficult to share the confidence of authors who state, for example, that McNally and Newland 'are transgender men, or at least considered themselves to be' (Brooks and Thompson 2019, p. 4).

cannot focus separately upon the interests of lesbians, trans people, or indeed normatively heterosexual young women, as no such neat separation is possible in practice—and all these groups are disadvantaged in a criminal justice system which has developed primarily around the interests of privileged, straight, white men.

Prosthetic Penises

For all their echoes of the eighteenth-century cases, there are some crucial differences in the contemporary prosecutions. One of the most telling is that while the female husband trials of the eighteenth century left the 'instruments' at their centre largely unnamed and undescribed, that is increasingly untrue for recent cases. Reports of *Saunders* largely echoed the older pattern: close mimicry of patriarchal, heterosexual relationships was emphasised along with the inadequacy of the imitation, but the actual dildo (should it have ever existed) never seems to have been found.[5] If there was no dildo involved in the offences, why would one have been invented? Saunders herself later gave the most probable explanation: the assumption that sex was only possible if a 'penis' was involved (*Capital Gay* 1992). That inability to imagine sexual activity without a (substitute) penis may have been a contributory factor in some convictions. To a jury unfamiliar with the idea of sexual activity which does not involve the penis, a version of events relying upon just such activity may well seem inherently less credible than one which does involve at least a facsimile.

The discourse of the phallus being a natural and essential feature of 'real' sex has been reinforced in recent reports. While the prosecution keep the actual item elusive, the term 'prosthetic' now predominates. The dildo was both strangely absent and hyper-visible in Newland's trial (the 'fake penis trial' to the *Liverpool Echo*: Stewart 2015; Graves 2015). Empty packaging for an 'ultra cyberskin penis' was shown in court, and identified by the complainant, but the prosecution did not produce an actual dildo (Pidd 2015a). That was left to defence counsel, described in

[5] Diane Hamer (1992, pp. 49–50) argued that Saunders marked a 'discursive shift', with the dildo discussed but no evidence of it produced in court. In fact, as was seen in Chap. 2, its absence was also a feature of historical prosecutions.

the *Guardian* as 'brandishing' an example of the 'lurid pink' item (Pidd 2015b). No exhibits were produced in Kyran Lee's case since he had pleaded guilty, but defence counsel spoke of a 'prosthetic', glossed as a 'fake penis' in the *Guardian*'s headline (*Guardian* 2015). Although the *Telegraph* called it a sex toy, they reminded readers about the Newland case and its 'prosthetic penis' (*Telegraph* 2015a, b). Similarly, the *Sun*'s report on Staines kept the dildo out of sight, invoking it only by mentioning that she used condoms, but ended with a brief mention of the McNally case including her use of a 'sex toy' (West 2016). The *Telegraph* put the 'prosthetic penis' in its headline; for the *Independent* Staines's device was a 'rubber penis' but it too concluded with a recap of *Newland* referring to a 'prosthetic penis' (*Telegraph* 2016; Osborne 2016).

The term 'prosthetic' implies a lack of the authentic thing: it is a replacement for something missing. For the courts, it is an inferior facsimile: as Dutton J. said when sentencing Newland, the complainant was deceived into believing she had experienced heterosexual intercourse 'and nothing *less*' (Stewart 2015, emphasis added); prosecuting counsel in *Saunders* told the court that H 'lost her virginity to a piece of plastic' (M. Sharpe 1991). Nonetheless, they do not confront the implication that if the dildo replaces something that the person should have, then the courts are asserting the very trans identity which in practice, they disregard. Instead, 'prosthetic' is used to emphasise their understanding of the defendants as women who have attempted to usurp male roles, even going so far as to adopt an artificial 'penis'.[6] None of that would be conveyed by the word 'dildo'. The real mischief, for the criminal justice system, is the appropriation of male sexual privileges and pleasures, not the deceit pervading the relationship as a whole. This context helps us to understand why part of Kyran Lee's mitigation was that he was attempting to save a relationship rather than 'gain pleasure': it reassured the court that his purpose was not to usurp (genitally) male sexual agency. The judge responded that had Lee's motive been sexual gratification, he would have received an immediate custodial sentence (*Guardian* 2015).

[6] For discussion of the complex cultural implications of the dildo, including masculinist interpretations of it as a prosthetic indicating lesbians' penis envy, see Hamming (2001, pp. 329–32).

Pervert or Paedophile?

The evolution in legal and media discourses around gender fraud convictions from a language of congenital perversion towards one of predation and paedophilia, considered in Chap. 7, has continued. Relatively narrow age gaps are used to hint at something darker. The judge who sentenced Barker described her victims, two or three years her junior, as 'much younger than her'. The press followed his lead, contrasting the 'woman' defendant with the 'girl' complainants (*BBC News* 2012b; Stretch 2012). There was only a one-year age difference between McNally and M, but defence counsel referred to 'grooming' (Shaw 2013b) while the *Telegraph* contrasted the 'woman' posing as a 'boy' with her 'girl' victim (Dixon 2013); the use of age to set the tone of the headline is notable. *Staines* was reported in the *Sun* under the headline '"Boy" was paedo girl wearing fake willy; perv jailed'. The report concluded with an unsympathetic look back at *McNally* being 'caged' after having sex with a 'schoolgirl' using 'a sex toy attached to her waist' (West 2016). The *Telegraph* also framed *Staines* in terms of paedophilia, its lede stating that she abused 'young teenage girls' although two of the complainants were seventeen while Staines was twenty-one and twenty-two (*Telegraph* 2016).

Newland's unusual allegations and adult complainant initially saw a return to the older media focus upon the strangeness of the facts and use of a 'fake penis' (Humphries 2015c). However, after Newland's conviction at retrial, the *Times* called her a 'lesbian sex abuser'; although she remained 'fake penis woman' in the *Mirror*, its report also described her seeking 'bizarre satisfaction' (Swerling 2017; Hurst 2017). In his sentencing remarks, the judge used the loaded term 'grooming' (HHJ Dutton 2015, p. 3). Reporting of *Lee* was more muted, acknowledging that the case involved adults one of whom was trans, but none of the newspapers except the *Metro* consistently treated Lee as a trans man even when reporting the case under his male name. Instead they used terms such as 'conned' and 'tricked' to headline a more complex story (Mann 2015; *Telegraph* 2015a, b).

The resort to tropes of paedophilia, perversion, and unnaturalness is disturbing not only in itself but also in its application of longstanding, harmful myths about gay male sexuality to lesbian and trans people. It is a reminder that we should not be complacent about progress: the work in challenging those stereotypes has neither wholly eliminated them from their original context nor prevented their emergence here. It also highlights the dangers inherent in silencing, even in its more partial form. Legal silencing meant there was little obvious need to consider the specific position of lesbians when discussing the criminal justice system; as a result, lesbian (and to a large extent, trans men) defendants have been swept up in both sides' characterisations of gay male sexuality. Breaching that silence was contrary to the interests of campaigners for liberal law reform: defendants criminalised for non-consensual offences, whether their partner was below the age of consent or claimed that there was no legally valid consent, could only trouble appeals to equal rights. Yet addressing these cases is important both to protect potential complainants and defendants, many of whom are vulnerable, and to prevent dangerous stereotypes taking further hold in our culture.

Heterosexuality and Abuse

To fully understand the depth of prejudice underlying the association of lesbianism with perversion, one must contrast it with the assumptions about heterosexual relationships implicit in the cases. By accepting the complainants' accounts as credible, judges and juries are also finding plausible a striking level of controlling, humiliating, and even abusive behaviour. Further, that behaviour is not always seen as a significant aggravating factor by the courts. McNally's case perhaps involves the fewest such elements but even so, the facts accepted by the court included that the sexual activity was heavily one-sided and the defendant remained largely clothed while her partner was undressed. That was apparently key to concealing her sex, but both the complainant and judges accepted it as credible behaviour from a male partner.

Such imbalances were more pronounced, but still unremarked, in the prosecution version of events in other cases. Barker refused to allow J to touch him on the one occasion they engaged in consensual sexual activity, and had already sexually touched her without consent in another persona. Trueman's prosecution largely passed over as unproblematic the (illegal) relationship between a twelve-year-old girl and a sixteen-year-old boy, which had seemingly been accepted by the girl's family too. Newland was alleged to have imposed incredibly restrictive conditions upon C including the wearing of a blindfold and handcuffs; pressured her to give up a job she loved; and threatened suicide to secure a final sexual encounter. Staines's behaviour towards O was so controlling that she ended the relationship, while P was not allowed to touch Staines during sex.

The tacit acceptance of such behaviour was most striking in *Saunders*. According to the prosecution, Saunders had to stop penetrative sex during the first sexual encounter with long-term girlfriend R after it became too painful for the complainant. Although scope for subsequent improvement was limited since the problems were caused by the 'fake penis', Saunders and R allegedly went on to have frequent sexual relations for several months. Throughout that time, R was not allowed to touch Saunders who remained mostly dressed. Meanwhile, H described a single sexual encounter during which penetration was so painful that she asked Saunders to stop. He not only continued but laughed and told her shut up. That behaviour would clearly have amounted to rape had Saunders had male genitalia (*Kaitamaki* [1985] AC 147) but was apparently met with indifference. R's uncle described hearing H shouting at Saunders to stop, but said that he did not interfere because it was nothing to do with him; while the trial judge suggested that H would have preferred to be raped rather than noting that she effectively had been. The cases therefore throw a disturbing light upon the kind of heterosexual relationships which are credible to a jury, apparently unremarkable to a judge and, implicitly, preferable to a lesbian relationship. Despite the significant progress made by feminists in gaining legal recognition of rape within relationships, the courts seem unable to incorporate those analyses into their approach to gender fraud cases.

This normalisation of abuse also casts a different light upon Alex Sharpe's argument, drawing upon Eve Kosofsky Sedgwick, that the complainants may have had the 'privilege of unknowing'. For Sharpe, their ignorance was itself a form of knowledge, an active rather than passive state in which they had learned not to know and which allowed them not to recognise difference even when it was in plain view. This is not to suggest that their belief in their partner's maleness was not genuine, but rather that it was an effect of wilful blindness (A. Sharpe 2018, pp. 11–12, 25–26, 116–18). Thus far, the argument is not unpersuasive; but the suggestion that this is a form of cisgender *privilege* does not take account of the rather more complex context. Women's ignorance has been deliberately produced and cultivated, through mechanisms such as silencing, for men's benefit and not their own. Silencing did not seek to keep women ignorant in order to allow them to avoid confronting their own desires, but in order to prevent them from recognising and exploring them. That is perhaps why the most persuasive example of privileged unknowing available to Sharpe (2018, pp. 116–17) was the male protagonist of the film *The Crying Game* rather than a woman.

According to the complainants' accounts in some of these cases, knowledge was also foreclosed by the defendants. They discouraged questioning through emotional blackmail, claiming distress at discussing traumatic illness and injuries. There is also a gendered context to the acceptance of such untruths: women are told that a substantial element of their own worth comes from relationships with men, yet many will experience significant abuse in those intimate relationships. That context was drawn upon by the complainant in *Newland* when she described herself as 'so stupid and needy' in her eagerness to believe Kye offered love she had not received from family or previous partners (*Crosby Herald* 2015b). Young women's susceptibility to deception may be better understood not as cisgender privilege but as a feature of women's oppression: the expectation that they will endure and excuse abusive male behaviour.

The sexual and emotional abuse alleged in these cases is not a side issue, and placing it at the centre of discussion of the 'gender fraud' prosecutions may offer a better way to analyse the issues, allowing recognition of defendants' subjectivities without dismissing the harms done to complainants. For example, a focus upon power, agency, and consent would allow a different perspective on Lee's case which could take account of the pressure placed upon him to engage in 'penile' penetration of the complainant. Attention to the dynamics of the relationship, then, could fundamentally shift legal interpretations of these cases and remove the criminal justice system's self-appointed role as arbiter of gender boundaries, explored in the next section.

Fraud and Consent

Parliament and the criminal courts have been tolerant of male 'seduction techniques' even when they cross the line into outright deception, with the result that fraud very rarely vitiates consent to sexual activity. By contrast, there seems to have been little questioning of the assumption that fraud as to gender did render complainants' consent legally void. The legal complexities, which are considered in more detail below, have largely been swept aside in these cases by 'common sense'. For all the apparent attention to gender neutrality and equality in contemporary sexual offences law, it still fails to seriously question men's right to aggressively pursue sexual access to women's bodies. The gender fraud defendants are, from this perspective, doubly fraudulent. Perceived as women fraudulently claiming masculine privileges, they are deceiving the complainants not only about the nature of sexual activity but also about their own entitlement to engage in sexual pursuit.

In sharp contrast to the courts' approach, a lesbian-centred analysis requires us to shift the legal focus away from men's perspectives and sexual prerogatives. It demands that we take seriously not only the defendant's but also the complainant's interests. It accordingly diverges from the trans-centred analysis offered by Sharpe which focuses upon the defendant's interests, although both share substantial areas of common concern. The lesbian perspective will be explored through three questions. First, why are these complainants' accounts credible to police, prosecutors, and courts when so many others are not? Second, why are gender frauds criminalised when almost no others are? Third, can the courts' focus upon consent to the immediate, physical sexual act give a wide enough view?

Why Are These Allegations Credible to the Criminal Justice System?

When complainants in sexual offences cases are routinely disbelieved, how did the unusual accounts of these young women come to be accepted as credible by the police, Crown Prosecution Service and, in the few cases which went to trial, juries? This is not to assert that they should not have been: some were admitted by the accused, and where accounts are contested we cannot be certain of the truth. It is easy to be sceptical of the extraordinary evidence of multiple identities, extended relationships conducted in the dark, and so on; but media reports are inevitably selective, evidence can come across very differently in the courtroom to the printed (or electronic) page, and many of the defendants pleaded guilty.[7] Even an assumption that every allegation was true, though, would not explain the contrast between the apparent inevitability of conviction in gender fraud cases and the difficulties in prosecuting other sexual offences against women.[8]

Factors which may have made prosecuting authorities and courts more inclined to believe complainants in these circumstances include attitudes towards female sexuality in general, and towards the desirability of lesbianism (or heterosex with a trans partner) in particular. The model of consent as passive agreement to masculine demands has survived culturally despite the Sexual Offences Act's efforts to replace it legally. These complainants' accounts conformed to that model's norms of femininity including a lack of sexual assertion. On the other side were defendants who breached all those expectations and were perceived as having falsely claimed masculine sexual privileges, making them less credible from the outset. The alleged conduct also engaged the assumption that normative heterosex is always superior to lesbian sex or sex with a trans man, providing a cultural context which gave the complainants' accounts greater perceived credibility from the outset.

We have seen in previous chapters that the courts have invested great effort into denying women's sexual agency. They have proved eager to believe that feminine women are sexually passive, susceptible to masculine desire but lacking proactive desires of their own. They might be taken in by the advances of a masculine, and thus presumptively sexually aggressive, lesbian but left to themselves they would not instigate sexual activity. Those attitudes might sound hopelessly archaic, yet these cases suggest

[7] For the general susceptibility of victims to repeat victimisation in deception involving romance, even where the fraud should be obvious, see Gillespie (2017, p. 221).

[8] In 2017/2018, only 6 per cent of sexual offences cases reported to police resulted in a charge or summons (Office for National Statistics 2018, p. 20).

that they have not disappeared but persist less explicitly, perhaps even less consciously, in the minds of at least some judges, jurors, and prosecutors. That should perhaps not surprise us very much, since conformity to the same female norms is an important factor in building the credibility of a woman complainant in other kinds of sexual offences case.

The complainant's evidence in *Newland* also drew upon racialised stereotypes of Asian men as more feminine than white men: Kye's alleged mixed ancestry was used to explain features such as the pitch of his voice. This was a rare example of such stereotyping appearing overtly in recent gender fraud cases, but previous chapters have explored how the identification of sexual and gender deviance, and specifically lesbianism, with foreignness or minority ethnicity has been a persistent undertone to the law's approach for centuries. Rather than offering a blanket denial of the possibility of same-sex activity between women, the law displaced that possibility onto women who were racially or ethnically other, as well as those outside the respectable middle classes. The shift from outright silencing to the construction of lesbians as lesser gay men has seen a move away from such displacement: *Newland* is now unusual in explicitly raising ethnicity at all. Nonetheless, gender fraud defendants are predominantly working class to an extent untrue of those convicted of age-of-consent offences (Chap. 7), though their backgrounds tend not to be explicitly discussed. Saunders, who was involved in criminal activity and had lived in a youth shelter, was most clearly located towards the bottom of the class hierarchy (Smith 1998, p. 184). Newland was an exception, with her private school education referred to in press reports; it may not be entirely coincidental that she was one of the minority of defendants to plead not guilty, a decision which typically takes into account likely prospects of acquittal as well as factual guilt or innocence.

Significantly, several of the accused were also located outside the stable nuclear family in a way untrue of, or at least not emphasised for, the complainants. This was conveyed relatively subtly in *McNally*, where the complainant's mother was actively involved in pursuing the prosecution while McNally's own family did not appear. More obvious were Saunders, with a 'complicated social background' (Smith 2000, p. 275); Trueman, whose estranged father reported her activities to a neighbour; and Lee, whose claimed familial role as a single father proved imaginary. The complainants' families in *Saunders*, *Trueman*, and *Staines* were actively engaged in bringing the cases before the police.

If feminine young women's claims to be innocent of and about same-sex desire have cultural credibility, the converse is also true. Masculine women's claims that complainants were genuinely attracted to them lack that ready cultural legibility, as do trans men's. In consequence, if a complainant can establish herself as gender-conforming then much of the work of building her credibility and undermining the defendant's has already been done. It is here in the criminal justice system's responses that we most clearly find the 'privilege of unknowing', rather than that privilege attaching to the complainants themselves. The courts have the privilege of defining whether difference is legally visible. In doing so, they are responsive to the wider cultural context, but the power of law is such that they are by no means entirely dependent upon it.

Why Are Gender Deceptions Criminalised?

As in the female husband prosecutions of the past, fraud remains a vital component of contemporary cases, even if the offence charged is sexual rather than financial. It continues to do its work in shifting the focus from the mutual elements of the relationship to the defendant's 'deceit', enabling the presumption of the complainant's innocence to be maintained. But why is deception as to gender sufficient to vitiate consent when other profound and sustained frauds are not? To attempt an answer, it is first necessary to consider the criminal law on fraudulent sexual consent in general.

While there was no statutory definition of consent to sexual activity before 2003, the common law allowed fraud to vitiate consent only in certain, narrow circumstances: fraud as to either identity or the nature and quality of the act. Counter-intuitively perhaps, it is the second ground which applied to the 'gender fraud' cases since identity fraud was confined to impersonation of an actual husband or, latterly, boyfriend. The nature and quality of the act was also narrowly defined. In *Flattery* [1877] 2 QBD 410 and *Williams* [1923] 1 KB 340, fraud vitiated consent where a complainant believed she was consenting to something other than sexual intercourse (in both cases, the defendant claimed to be carrying out medical treatment). Once consent was given to penile penetration, it would not be vitiated by deception as to surrounding circumstances, however fundamental, since according to Morland J in *Linekar* [1995] QB 250, the basis of *Williams* and *Flattery* was that 'non-consent to sexual intercourse rather than the fraud … makes the offence rape.' The common law's approach, then, was centred firmly upon the importance of the penis. It was that logic which led the judge in *Saunders* to direct the jury that unlike '[a]ll sorts of lies' a male defendant might lawfully tell, they could decide that Saunders's was a 'fundamental deception' (Smith 2000, pp. 240–41). This legal context constructed lesbian sexuality as always aberrant, and less desirable than heterosex, at the same time as literally protecting women's sexual ignorance. Only unawareness of whether the act was sexual intercourse sufficed: the courts would punish particularly egregious exploitation of the naivety silencing produced, but did not safeguard women's sexual agency.

The Sexual Offences Act 2003 brought important changes in the law's approach to consent, now defined in section 74 as 'agreement by choice' which requires 'freedom and capacity to make that choice'. Fraudulent consent is explicitly addressed in section 76, which provides that if either of two specified circumstances apply then as a matter of law there is no consent and no reasonable belief in consent. Those circumstances mirror but are not identical with the common law: either deliberate deception as to the nature or purpose of the act, or where the complainant is deliberately induced to believe the defendant is another person known personally to her. For the first circumstance, 'purpose' replaced 'quality' in order to codify *Tabassum* [2000] 2 Cr App R 328 which had held that consent to touch women's breasts obtained by pretending to be a medical researcher was vitiated by fraud as to the quality of the act (i.e. it was sexual rather than non-sexual). The second circumstance has been extended beyond husbands and boyfriends but continues to exclude most identity frauds, including those with which we are concerned.

Section 76 has been kept within very narrow bounds in practice. In only one appeal has use of the section 76 presumption been upheld: *Devonald* [2008] EWCA Crim 527, where a man pretended to be a woman online in order to induce the young male complainant to masturbate in front of a webcam. The court ruled that there was deception as to the purpose of the act since the defendant intended to humiliate the complainant rather than achieve sexual gratification. Heteronormative assumptions about the fixity of sexuality subtly underpinned the court's certainty as to his singularity of purpose, as evident in the failure to follow *Devonald* on the broadly similar facts of *B* [2013] EWCA Crim 823. The defendant had used online deceptions to coerce his girlfriend into performing sexual acts in front of a webcam. The Court of Appeal concluded that at least part of B's purpose may have been sexual gratification and thus section 76 was not engaged. Instead, the deception might mean there was no consent under the general definition in section 74.[9] In both *Assange v Swedish Judicial Authority* [2011] EWHC 2849 and *R (on the application of F) v DPP* [2013] ECA Crim 823, express conditions had been agreed in relation to the sexual act (to wear a condom and to withdraw before ejaculation, respectively); their breach was held to remove the complainant's freedom and capacity to agree by choice. *Jheeta* [2007] EWCA Crim 1699 involved an elaborate and prolonged deception which led the complainant to believe police were ordering her to engage in sexual relations with the defendant. It was not so much the deception per se as the coercive threat of police prosecution which led the Court of Appeal to uphold the conviction.

Only two post-2003 Act gender fraud cases have reached the Court of Appeal. *Newland* [2016] All ER (D) 85 was appealed on the basis that the judge's summing up of the facts was unfair and unbalanced, not the law on consent. *McNally* [2013] EWCA Crim 1051 did address the law on deceptive consent. Lord Leveson stated there was not deception as to 'nature and purpose' under section 76 as, 'in a physical sense, the acts of assault by penetration of the vagina are the same whether perpetrated by a male or a female' (para. 26). He then followed *Assange* and *F v DPP* to hold that deception might nonetheless remove the complainant's freedom or capacity to agree by choice. The judgment drew a distinction between the physical act of vaginal penetration (performed alongside oral sex) and its sexual nature; the latter 'is, on any common sense view, different where the complainant is deliberately deceived by a defendant into

[9] The defendant was convicted on that basis following a retrial (Byrne 2012).

believing that the latter is a male' (para. 26). This distinction is not obvious: such an act would seem to be sexual by its nature, rather than because of its circumstances or the defendant's purpose (section 78), so no legal distinction exists between the physical and sexual act. Its consequence was that the complainant's freedom to choose to have sex with a boy was held to have been removed by the deception. Therefore she did not 'agree by choice', so there was no legally valid consent to the sexual activity. In the earlier cases, though, there had been explicit conditions set by the complainants which McNally's defence argued related to features of the act itself. They were thus distinct from deception as to attributes such as age, marital status or HIV status. The Court of Appeal rejected that view: since the 'act' is legally limited to the fact of penetration, features such as condom use are extraneous to it.

In reaching the conclusion that penetration by a male was a condition of consent here, the Court of Appeal drew upon the notion of deliberate deception. Sharpe discusses the law's approach as centring upon 'active deception' but deliberate deception seems to be a potentially wider concept encompassing anything not purely 'implied'. Although *McNally* uses the term 'active deception' at one point,[10] it does not adopt it as the *ratio decidendi*. Rather, it concludes that approaching the evidence '["]in a broad commonsense way" identifies the route through the dilemma' (para. 25). Deception as to gender would remove freedom to choose 'on any common sense view' (para. 26.). 'Common sense' is a highly problematic concept, too often a cloak for lack of knowledge, unexamined biases, or heteropatriarchal ideologies.[11] It allows no room for alternative views or opinions (Beresford 2008). Its appeal to normative assumptions is immediately apparent in *McNally*: deception about an accused's wealth is 'obviously' not criminal, while deception as to sex unarguably is. But why is it 'obvious' that a deception as to wealth does not remove consent? Unless the case involved casual sex, then a high level of deceit would probably be involved including misrepresentations of the person's intentions, living situation, friendship circle, employment or economic activ-

[10] At para. 21, apparently as a gloss on *Assange*. Bunting also sees this as an open question (Bunting 2013).

[11] In relation to 'common sense' in these cases, see Doig (2013) and Laird (2014). More generally, see Finch and Munro (2006) and Rosenfeld (2014).

ity, and so on. The accused might also be putting forward an assumed character (honest and confident rather than deceitful and insecure or ruthlessly self-serving). In effect, they would have represented themselves as a completely different person: a deception arguably as profound as a deception as to gender. The 'common sense' distinction here has more to do with normative views of permissible seduction techniques than any principled approach.

Is a Focus on the Sexual Act Adequate?

Let us assume for the moment that in all the gender fraud cases, the complainants' versions of events were entirely accurate. What harms do they reveal? The courts have focused upon sex between women as 'less' than heterosex (e.g. Stewart 2015) and in particular upon some complainants' apparent revulsion at having sex with a woman or a trans man. This approach serves two purposes: first, it limits recognition of harms to those sustained during specific sexual acts, allowing the wider context to be ignored. Second, it enables the courts to disavow their own homophobia by locating it in the complainants' responses. While some responses may have been rooted in homophobia and transphobia, that does not exclude the presence of other harms. One must also bear in mind both that the complainants' accounts have been heavily mediated through the filters of the legal process and selective news reporting; and that they were trying to present their experiences in ways comprehensible to their parents, the police and the courts—and themselves. Teenage confusion, particularly around desires and emotions, can be intense even for those who are apparently heterosexual and gender-conforming. Complainants therefore need to be listened to when they describe the full extent of the harms experienced.

It is apparent that these were not limited to the circumstances of one (or even multiple) sexual interactions; nor were they necessarily primarily about the defendant's sex or gender. Rather, a central harm was the profound deception which underpinned the entire relationship, and which created the context in which consent was given. In *Barker*, the report to police was triggered by the discovery that two boyfriends were the same *man*. Barker had used her friends' intimate confidences to craft her alter egos as each complainant's 'perfect boy' (Sherriff 2012b), while her own confidences were invented. The complainant in *Lee* described the damage done when he 'manipulated', 'deceived' and 'lied' to her (*Telegraph* 2015b). Newland apparently used her dual identities to increase pressure on the complainant: when C argued with one, the other would suggest that she was at fault (*Crosby Herald* 2015a). The emotional manipulation of C was said to have extended to persuading her to leave a job, and to threatening suicide if she ended the relationship (Stewart 2015).

In other words, harm in these offences results from the social and emotional deceptions as well as the sexual ones. They are experienced by their victims as more than purely sexual violations. Just as we would not centre our critique of eighteenth-century female husband cases upon the valuation of pawned clothes, it is unhelpful to take the contemporary law's approach at face value by focusing upon the information to be exchanged in a purely sexual encounter. Complainants were accepting a whole persona and life history which was fraudulent. Discovery of the deception did not just affect their understanding of the physical sexual acts; it profoundly breached their trust in the essential character of the relationship which underpinned their consent. Some of the complainants described experiencing something akin to a bereavement. According to C, when she found out that Kye Fortune was Gayle Newland, 'Kye died that day' (*Crosby Herald* 2015a). J described a similar response to the discovery that Luke Jones was Gemma Barker: 'I was like he had just died' (Blake 2012b).

These bear striking similarities to the harms done to victims of undercover police officers who engaged in relationships under assumed activist identities. Those men misrepresented their beliefs and character as well as all the details of their lives including, in some situations, existing spouses and children (McCartney and Wortley 2018). As the Court of Appeal accepted in relation to those covert policing cases, such sustained deceptions invade 'a most intimate aspect' of the privacy protected by Article 8 of the European Convention on Human Rights (*AJA v Commissioner of Police for the Metropolis* [2013] EWCA Civ 1342 at para. 22). Nonetheless, the Crown Prosecution Service (CPS) and courts have ruled out any prosecutions. The courts have persisted in refusing to recognise any criminal harm outside the immediate sexual act, holding that the consent given to undercover officers was legally valid (*R (on the application of 'Monica') v Director of Public Prosecutions* [2018] EWHC 3508 (Admin)). That is despite their not only sharing the harmful features found in the gender fraud cases but also having the exceptional aggravating factor of state complicity.

If we recognise that harms in gender fraud cases emanate from the relationship as a whole rather than a single moment of sexual contact, they can be acknowledged without resort to homophobic or transphobic assumptions. That spares us from having to make potentially dangerous arguments into which critics have been drawn when considering single acts. For example, Sharpe has argued (2018, pp. 86–89) that the 'harms' were irrational emotional responses too nebulous to outweigh defendants' rights to privacy. That characterisation has echoes of gendered legal norms which treat the emotional as both feminine and unimportant, and expect women to show physical injury in order for sexual crimes against them to be taken seriously.[12] As well as leaving open the question of how to distinguish these from the harms in other sexual offences cases, it also underplays the alleged injury in some cases including suicidal feelings and a PTSD diagnosis (Humphries 2017); psychological illness is well-established as a criminal injury (*Ireland; Burstow* [1998] AC 147; *Dhaliwal* [2016] 2 Cr App R 24).

Is the difference between gender fraud and other cases that, as Sharpe has argued (2018, p. 61), the intimacy was desire-led with no coercion? Complainants' evidence frequently suggested that too often, the intimacy was not truly desire-led on their parts. The courts largely glossed over this point, but it ought to be a central factor in critical readings of the law's approach to these cases—and again, it is one more easily examined from the perspective of the wider relationship. Crucially, this approach does not depend upon prosecutors or courts assessing the validity of a defendant's trans identity. By contrast, accepting the law's focus upon individual acts encourages such assessments and they have been implicitly accepted at least to some extent by critics as well. For example, the suggestion that harms to complainants should be weighed against defen-

[12] This is effectively the route taken by Rubenfeld when he argues for a force requirement and asserts that 'deceptive sex, however bad it may be, isn't *that* bad' (2013, p. 1416; emphasis in original).

dants' privacy rights requires evaluation of the identity for which privacy is claimed. Where a defendant claims to be trans, the CPS or courts are left to determine if privacy rights were in fact engaged by deciding whether the defendant's gender presentation was 'genuine'.[13] Where they claim a different or confused identity, the criminal justice system will be left to decide if privacy rights should attach to it. Inviting the court to adjudicate upon whether an individual defendant was 'really' trans, or to decide how far it will recognise gender fluidity, or to define the line between butch and trans presentations, would both presume and reinforce that the courts have power to define the limits of acceptable feminine or masculine behaviour: a power most lesbians, feminists, and trans people would prefer they not have.

How might we better understand the harms involved in relationship deceptions? Chloe Kennedy's suggestion that they might be conceptualised as identity nonrecognition offers scope to recognise the subjectivities of both parties and to take account of the difference between a relationship and a single encounter. This approach to identity is very different to the courts' assumption, explored in Chap. 7, that questioning an otherwise static sexual identity is a powerful form of harm. Rather, Kennedy (2019) frames long-term relationships as central to identity formation through a dialogic process. This is a much more promising way of considering the issues than the current legal resort to 'common sense'. Its ability to encompass issues affecting both accused and complainant would allow a more nuanced approach to lesbian and trans defendants. However, as Kennedy acknowledges, it still requires decisions to be made about what kinds of identity nonrecognition should engage the law.

The shift of legal attention to the wider circumstances in which consent was apparently given does seem crucial. If this could be achieved, then a different view of consent in these cases should follow. That might not always mean different outcomes: an extensive fake history, constructed and maintained over time, may well be considered incompatible with genuine consent. However, prosecutors and courts would have to proceed more carefully in order to reach that conclusion and would not

[13] For further discussion of the dangers of allowing the law to use and define rigid divisions of sexuality and gender, see Gross (2009, pp. 217–24).

be able to limit the principle to gender fraud cases. Such a change of approach might arguably be consistent with the existing statutory regime: the courts' choice to focus narrowly upon the sexual act and disregard its context was not inevitable under the 2003 Act's definition of consent. However, there are two key problems with urging a different use of the current law: first, would the courts be willing to do this? Second, would we want them to?

The caselaw to date shows that while deceptions do not need to directly concern 'features of the act' in order to vitiate consent, they cannot extend far beyond them either. The Court of Appeal in '*Monica*' emphasised that the deceptions in *McNally*, *Assange* and *F v DPP* were 'closely connected with' the nature and purpose of the act (paras. 74–76). Crucially, that approach draws its logic from a deeply gendered model of sexual activity as something engaged in by an active male seducer and passive, seduced female.[14] Its rigid gender demarcations underpin *Monica*'s gloss on McNally, that there 'was all the difference in the world between sexual activity with a boy and similar activity with a girl' (para. 81). As a result, the courts accept that men's seduction 'game' may involve exaggerations, omissions, or outright lies, with legal scrutiny considered an unjustified constraint upon men unless they clearly cross a line into outright coercion. Conversely, gender fraud defendants are seen as wrongfully claiming the masculine role and its prerogatives, and their presumption attracts harsh judicial responses: they have not only broken the rules, but should not have played the game at all. None of that suggests that we can trust common law developments to protect women's or trans men's sexual agency.

Given those issues, should we even ask the courts to take on the role of interpreting consent differently in order to recognise relationship deceptions? Sharpe is rightly wary of giving them carte blanche to imply conditions into apparent consent: feminist and trans critics of sexual offences law should not encourage courts to impose whatever implied terms they deem appropriate. Such a move would further empower the criminal justice system to enforce normative, highly gendered expectations of sexual-

[14] The same model more or less explicitly underlies Hyman Gross's arguments on deceptive consent (2007).

ity, as they currently do when assuming that gender fraud is fundamental in a way that other frauds are not.

Instead, might the wrong done when apparent consent is obtained through systematic deception be better addressed through a specific offence? The Law Commission and Sexual Offences Review had both favoured retention of the offence of procuring a woman to have sexual intercourse by false presentences (section 3, Sexual Offences Act 1956), extended to cover non-penile penetration (Law Commission 2000, para. 5.45; Sexual Offences Review 2000, paras. 2.18.4–2.18.5). For unknown reasons, it was not retained in the 2003 Act (Laird 2014, pp. 499–500), perhaps because it was apparently little used by the time of its repeal. Sjolin (2015) notes the lack of figures to confirm this. There is broad agreement, although with varying degrees of enthusiasm, that an offence of obtaining consent by deception would be preferable to the current approach.[15] A carefully defined offence on these lines would help ensure that criminal liability and sentencing are kept within appropriate bounds. In the gender fraud context, it would limit rather than extend criminalisation. However, it would preserve some of the dangers of the current law and would not accurately label the wrongs done in cases where deception is the basis of, and sustained during, a continuing relationship. Instead, an offence specifically framed to address deceptive relationships could be even more carefully confined, and might also help to address the growing issue of online relationship fraud (Gillespie 2017). It would allow both definition and sentencing to be considered afresh, so that they could better accommodate the concerns of lesbian, trans, and feminist critics. Sentencing guidelines could focus upon the culpability and harm involved in the deception rather than the physical acts alone, since such harms are not primarily measurable through the physical nature of the sexual activity.

This approach would raise its own challenges. For example, how do we define a suitably narrow actus reus while not undermining the section 74 test for consent? And what would we require as mens rea? Specific and robust CPS guidance would also be required—indeed, is required for existing sexual offences in the meantime—and its formulation must

[15] Laird (2014) supports such an offence; Bunting and Sharpe are unenthusiastic but consider it preferable to expanding existing offences (Bunting 2013; A. Sharpe 2018, p. 62).

involve consultation in order to ensure that the complexities of these cases are properly considered. The current guidance added in response to *McNally* (Crown Prosecution Service 2017) is, by those standards, seriously flawed. The issues begin with its heading, 'Transgender suspects', whose application to many of the defendants discussed here would not be obvious. Faced with a suspect who states that she is a lesbian, as McNally did, a prosecutor might not consult this section nor gain much assistance if they did. The substantive content invites the prosecutor to determine the genuineness of an accused's trans identity. This approach risks reliance on normative understandings of gender, and ignores sexuality altogether. Indeed, it may implicitly *encourage* prosecution in cases where the defendant is not manifestly trans, disadvantaging lesbian and non-binary suspects. Its lack of attention to most of the crucial context shows the urgency not just of reform, but of the engagement of a range of feminist, lesbian, and trans perspectives in that reform process.

Even with better guidance, the exercise of prosecutorial discretion and the apparently greater willingness of juries to convict in these cases would remain of concern. Experiences to date suggest that prosecution and conviction are more likely when the accused is a member of a disadvantaged group. One factor is the cultural connection drawn between lesbianism and perversion, discussed above. Another, almost paradoxically, is the courts' lack of understanding of the difficulties young women face in being open about same-sex attraction. After all, women can marry each other and there have even been lesbians on *Coronation Street*: surely equality has been achieved? That narrative of legal and social generosity obscures the realities which prevent young lesbians from being open about their sexuality. They face bullying and an environment of heterosexism at school; vulnerability to homophobia at home; heightened risks of hate crime and homelessness; and consequently, higher rates of depression and self-harm. Lesbian sex remains outside the imagination of legislators who recently, in trying to reach a definition of adultery encompassing same-sex relationships, could do so 'in every instance bar that of a lesbian relationship' (Lord Ali, quoted in Beresford 2016, p. 476). And the lesbian storylines on *Coronation Street* have ended in violent deaths rather than happy marriages (Moss 2019).

Conclusion

Given the difficulties involved in engaging with the criminal justice system, it is tempting to say that gender fraud cases should not be prosecuted at all. However, decriminalisation or non-criminalisation is only superficially an easier alternative. Even if we accept its cost to women's sexual and bodily autonomy, it would almost certainly not work to protect potential defendants. The criminal justice system has long proved creative in criminalising behaviours of which it does not approve: consider the eighteenth-century cases explored in Chap. 2, where financial fraud charges were founded on material benefits no more substantial than the board and lodging provided to McNally by M's family friend; or Colonel Barker in Chap. 5 and Violet/Vincent Jones and Joan Lee in Chap. 6, convicted of perjury rather than a sexual offence. Consider also the age-of-consent cases: Staines's prosecution for sexual activity with a child would probably not have occurred were it not for the gender deception, since the family seem to have condoned the relationship until they became aware that Staines was biologically female. Decriminalisation of gender fraud would offer little protection to some of the most vulnerable potential defendants, young people whose slightly younger partners' age would provide a basis for conviction even if it was not the primary trigger for prosecution.

Limiting the hard-won sexual agency of complainants, who are overwhelmingly women, is therefore a high price to pay in order to achieve very uncertain benefits. Women's bodily integrity is legally fragile. While formally codified by the 2003 Act, it is undermined in practice by the criminal justice system's practices, biases and mythologies. We should not encourage further legal retreat from the recognition of women's right to make free and informed choices about sexual activity. A specific sexual offence might better control the extent of criminalisation and achieve fairer labelling and penalties when prosecutions are brought. Such proposals may seem modest and tentative, but in the context of sexual offences, there are particular concerns about the ways in which feminist reforms can be co-opted or subverted by both legislature and courts. 'Victims' rights' have too often been an excuse for reducing defendants' protections, even though having the correct person convicted is surely very much in victims' interests.

We should be concerned that complainants' sexual autonomy is recognised and legally protected so much more easily where the defendants are women or trans men than otherwise. The apparent legal and cultural unintelligibility of lesbianism and transgender as anything but undesirable or unfortunate, the persistent tropes of female sexual innocence and passivity, and highly normative assumptions about acceptable heterosexual relations all inform current approaches to gender fraud prosecutions. Given the complicated combination of influences on the law in this area, it is unsurprising that there are no easy solutions. Any statutory reforms will be only one step in a longer process.

References

BBC News. 2012a. Staines Woman Dressed as a Boy to Assault Girls, March 5.

———. 2012b. Staines Woman Dressed as Boy Jailed for Sexual Assaults, March 5.

———. 2015. Fake Penis Assault Woman Given Suspended Term, December 16.

———. 2016. Woman Who Posed as Man Jailed for Sexual Assaults, March 23.

Beresford, Sarah. 2008. Get Over Your (Legal) 'Self': A Brief History of Lesbians, Motherhood and the Law. *Journal of Social Welfare and Family Law* 30 (2): 95–106. https://doi.org/10.1080/09649060802469785.

———. 2016. We're All Same (Sex) Now?: Lesbian (Same) Sex; Consummation; Adultery and Marriage. *Journal of GLBT Family Studies* 12 (5): 468–490. https://doi.org/10.1080/1550428X.2015.1104273.

Blake, Matt. 2012a. 'I Felt Repulsed and Dirty and Wanted to Kill Myself': Schoolgirl Victims of Teenage Girl Who Dressed as Boy to Date Them Speak of Their Anguish as She Is Jailed. *Daily Mail*, March 6.

———. 2012b. 'They Were Completely Different People, Even When We Kissed': Teen Duped into Dating Two Boys without Realising They Were Both the SAME GIRL. *Daily Mail*, March 7.

Brooks, Victoria, and Jack Clayton Thompson. 2019. Dude Looks Like a Lady: Gender Deception, Consent and Ethics. *The Journal of Criminal Law* (Mar.): 1–14. https://doi.org/10.1177/0022018319834373.

Bunting, Dan. 2013. When Is Consent Not Consent? *UK Criminal Law Blog*. http://ukcriminallawblog.com/when-is-consent-not-consent/.

Byrne, Paul. 2012. Facebook Faker Jailed. *Mirror*, March 27.

Capital Gay. 1991. Judge Hits Back over Criticism: Demo Sparks Outburst, November 15.

———. 1992. Judge Frees Jailed Lesbian, June 19.

Churchill, Laura. 2016. Woman Posed as Man to Have Sex with Teenage Girls. *Bristol Post*, March 24.

Crosby Herald. 2015a. Woman's Life 'Ruined' after Finding Boyfriend She Had Sex with Was a Woman Wearing a Prosthetic Penis, September 8.

———. 2015b. Woman Tells Court How the Boyfriend She Always Craved Turned out to Be a Female Wearing a Fake Penis, September 8.

Crossley, Lucy. 2016. Woman, 23, Who Used a Rubber Penis to Have Sex with Teenage Girls—And Was so Convincing One Victim STILL Doesn't Accept She Was Duped—Is Jailed. *Daily Mail*, March 23.

Crown Prosecution Service. 2017. Rape and Sexual Offences—Chapter 3: Consent. *Code for Crown Prosecutors*. https://www.cps.gov.uk/legal-guidance/rape-and-sexual-offences-chapter-3-consent.

Daily Mail. 2013. Sex Attacker Who Posed as Boy Freed, June 12.

Dixon, Hayley. 2013. Woman Posed as Boy for Sex with Girl. *Daily Telegraph*, March 22.

Doig, Gavin A. 2013. Deception as to Gender Vitiates Consent. *The Journal of Criminal Law* 77 (6): 464–468. https://doi.org/10.1350/1740-5580-77.6.464.

Finch, Emily, and Vanessa E. Munro. 2006. Breaking Boundaries? Sexual Consent in the Jury Room. *Legal Studies* 26: 303.

Gillespie, Alisdair A. 2017. The Electronic Spanish Prisoner: Romance Frauds on the Internet. *Journal of Criminal Law* 81 (3): 217–231.

Graves, Steve. 2015. Gayle Newland Fake Penis Trial. *Liverpool Echo*, November 24.

Greenwood, Chris. 2013. Schoolgirl Jailed for Posing as Man to Seduce Girl, 16. *Daily Mail*, March 22.

Gross, Hyman. 2007. Rape, Moralism, and Human Rights. *Criminal Law Review*, 220–227.

Gross, Aeyal. 2009. Gender Outlaws before the Law: The Courts of the Borderland. *Harvard Journal of Law & Gender* 32 (1): 165–231.

Guardian. 2015. Woman Who Used Fake Penis to Have Sex with a Woman Avoids Jail, December 15.

Hamer, Diane. 1992. The Invention of the Dildo. *Australian Gay and Lesbian Law Journal* 2: 41.
Hamming, Jeanne E. 2001. Dildonics, Dykes and the Detachable Masculine. *European Journal of Women's Studies* 8 (3): 329–341.
Hattenstone, Simon. 2017. 'I Was Pretending to Be a Boy for a Variety of Reasons': The Strange Case of Gayle Newland. *Guardian*, July 15.
HHJ Dutton. 2015. *Sentencing Remarks.* Chester: Judiciary of England and Wales.
Humphries, Jonathan. 2015a. Victim 'knew All along' That Her Boyfriend Was a Female Friend Who Wore a Fake Penis, Court Hears. *Crosby Herald*, September 9.
———. 2015b. Gayle Newland Fake Penis Sex Assault Accused Breaks down in Court. *Crosby Herald*, September 10.
———. 2015c. Gayle Newland Fake Penis Sex Assault Trial: Claims Are 'incredible, Implausible and Impossible' Say Lawyers. *Crosby Herald*, September 11.
———. 2015d. False Penis Assault Trial Draws to a Close as Jury Hear Closing Speeches. *Crosby Herald*, September 14.
———. 2017. No Winners as Fake Penis Attacker Gayle Newland's Cries Tear through Courtroom. *Liverpool Echo*, June 29.
Hurst, Pat. 2017. Fake Penis Woman Who Tricked Female Friend into Sex with Blindfold and Prosthetic Strap-on Sentenced Today. *Daily Mirror*, July 20.
Jenkins, Kelly. 2013. My Lesbian Lover Is Not Bad. She's Just a Bit Mixed Up. *Daily Record*, March 25.
Kennedy, Chloe. 2019. Sex, Identity and Recognition: Re-Thinking 'Rape by Deception.' *Inherently Human.* https://inherentlyhuman.wordpress.com/2019/02/07/sex-identity-and-recognition-re-thinking-rape-by-deception/.
Laird, Karl. 2014. Rapist or Rogue? Deception, Consent and the Sexual Offences Act 2003. *Criminal Law Review*, 492.
Lancashire Post. 2016. Preston Woman's Sentence for Posing as a Man 'Not Excessive' Say Judges, October 12.
Law Commission. 2000. Consent in Sex Offences. London.
Mann, Tanveer. 2015. Trans Man Spared Jail after Using Fake Penis to Trick Woman into Having Sex. *Metro*, December 15.
McCartney, Carole, and Natalie Wortley. 2018. Under the Covers: Covert Policing and Intimate Relationships. *Criminal Law Review* 2: 137–156.
Moss, Molly. 2019. Why Does Coronation Street Keep Exploding Its Lesbians? *Guardian*, March 22.

O'Shea, Gary, and Rhodri Phillips. 2013. Girl, 17, Posed as a Boy to Bed Girl, 16. *Sun*, March 22.
Office for National Statistics. 2018. *Sexual Offending: Victimisation and the Path through the Criminal Justice System*. London.
Osborne, Samuel. 2016. Woman Posed as Man to Have Sex with Teenage Girls. *Independent*, March 23.
Pidd, Helen. 2015a. Woman Who Claims She Was Tricked into Sex with Friend Was Lesbian, Court Told. *Guardian*, September 9.
———. 2015b. Woman Convicted for Impersonating Man to Dupe Friend into Having Sex. *Guardian2*, September 15.
———. 2017. Woman Who Posed as Man to Dupe Friend into Sex Is Jailed After Retrial. *Guardian*, July 20.
Rach, Jessica Anais. 2015. Gemma Barker: The Girl Who Disguised Herself as Three Guys to Seduce Her Female Friends. *Closer*. https://closeronline.co.uk/real-life/news/gemma-barker-girl-pretended-three-guys/.
Rosenfeld, Sophia. 2014. *Common Sense: A Political History*. Cambridge, MA: Harvard University Press.
Rubenfeld, Jed. 2013. The Riddle of Rape-by-Deception and the Myth of Sexual Autonomy. *Yale Law Journal* 122 (6): 1372–1443.
Sabey, Ryan, Emily Nash, and Andy Crick. 2012. Boy-Girl Groper Gemma Barker Ruined My Life. *Sun*, March 7.
Sentencing Council. 2019. General Guideline: Overarching Principles. https://www.sentencingcouncil.org.uk/overarching-guides/crown-court/item/general-guideline-overarching-principles/.
Sexual Offences Review. 2000. Setting the Boundaries: Reforming the Law on Sex Offences, Vol. 1. London.
Sharpe, Alex. 2018. *Sexual Intimacy and Gender Identity "Fraud": Reframing the Legal & Ethical Debate*. London: Routledge.
Sharpe, Martyn. 1991. Blonde Dressed as Boy Seduced 2 Girls. *Sun*, September 19.
Shaw, Adrian. 2013a. Female Posed as a Boy to Bed Girl. *Mirror*, March 22.
———. 2013b. Justine Poses as Boy to Have Sex with Girl, 16; Three Years for Twisted Deception. *Daily Record*, March 22.
Sherriff, Lucy. 2012a. Gemma Barker, Girl Who Dressed as Boy, Created Identities 'To Grope Friends.' *Huffington Post*, January 18.
———. 2012b. Gemma Barker, Girl Who Dressed as Boy to Seduce Underage Friends, Jailed. *Huffington Post*, March 5.
Sjolin, Catarina. 2015. Ten Years on—Consent under the Sexual Offences Act 2003. *Journal of Criminal Law* 79: 20–35.

Smith, Anna Marie. 1998. The Hegemonic Regulation of Butch Performance: Regina v Saunders. In *Butch/Femme: Inside Lesbian Gender*, ed. Sally R. Munt, 177–190. London: Cassell.

———, ed. 2000. *Regina v Saunders: A Collection of the Official Documents Relating to the 1991 Crown Court Trial and the 1992 Court of Appeal Hearing.* Cornell University.

Smith, Louie. 2015. Woman Pretended to Be a Man by Wearing Body Suit and Sex Toy to Trick Single Mum into Sex. *Mirror*, October 28.

Stewart, Gary. 2015. Gayle Newland Fake Penis Trial: The Judge's Sentencing Remarks in His Own Words. *Liverpool Echo*, November 12.

Stretch, Euan. 2012. My Boyfriend Was Really a Girl: Teenage Victim of Sex Con Woman Tells of Her Horror. *Mirror*, March 6.

Swerling, Gabriella. 2017. Jail for Lesbian Sex Abuser Who Posed as a Man. *The Times*, July 21.

Telegraph. 2015a. Woman Posed as a Single Father to Con Facebook Friend into Sex, October 28.

———. 2015b. Woman Tricked into Having Sex with Transsexual Tells How She Was Manipulated, December 15.

———. 2016. Woman Abused Three Young Girls by Pretending to Be Man with Prosthetic Penis, March 23.

Traynor, Luke. 2015. Woman 'Tricked into Having Sex with Girl She Thought Was a Man' Even Wore a Mask While They Watched TV. *Daily Mirror*, September 9.

West, Alex. 2016. 'Boy' Was Paedo Girl Wearing a Fake Willy: PERV JAILED. *Sun*, March 24.

Wilkinson, Sophie. 2017. Consent, Dildos and Deception: Reexamining the Trial of Gayle Newland. *Vice*, December.

9

Conclusion

The overarching theme of this book has been the silencing of lesbian possibility: its deliberate concealment from 'respectable' women by lawyers and legislators. We followed the arc of its development from its eighteenth-century emergence, through its Victorian heights, to the complexities of the twentieth century and controversies of the present. Importantly, silencing was never absolute or universal and its progression through this broad historical arc has not been smooth or uniform. Nonetheless, there have been common themes; yet the commonalities shift and evolve. In Traub's evocative image, they 'shimmer unsteadily and unevenly' (2015, p. 93). To consider the similarities between contemporary and historical prosecutions is not to assume that these simply reflect some essential feature of lesbian identity. On the contrary, they are worthy of note precisely because so much of their surrounding context has changed.

Silencing was made plausible by ideologies of gender intimately connected to those of class, nationality, and race. The 'respectable' woman was and is classed, although her precise social standing could vary according to the historical period and context. She could be middle class; she might also be a member of the gentry, particularly at the beginning of our arc, and from the later nineteenth century might also be part of the

C. Derry, *Lesbianism and the Criminal Law*,
https://doi.org/10.1007/978-3-030-35300-1_9

upper-working class. Social status was discernible not only from representations of virtuous womanhood but also from who was positioned as outside it: the maidservant or criminal who might corrupt the respectable woman from below, the decadent aristocrat or urban sophisticate who might do so from above. While the former were more likely to appear before the courts as a result of lesbian relationships, the latter also had their moments of legal visibility, as seen in Chap. 5.

Imperialism, racism, and xenophobia make it no surprise that the respectable woman was British—and usually English. However, her nationality was not a side-effect of these discourses but closely implicated in them. What is more notable, and merits further research, is the relative absence of women of colour from the criminal courtroom; all the more striking given their overrepresentation there for other offences. One foreign woman, Louise Mourey, was prosecuted for indecent assault on a girl but was not presented as lesbian. As far as we can tell from the reports of other cases, the defendants were white. While that may not be correct, it would be surprising for the earlier cases in particular if a defendant's minority ethnicity was not made apparent. However, that lack of physical presence did not mean that women of colour were ignored by the courts. Rather, they were visible but silent: referred to as possible sources of corruption in a racist discourse which assigned abnormal physiology, lack of morality or self-restraint, and forbidden knowledge to those who were not white and British. Such discourses were a central part of the imperial project which justified colonialism on the basis of white women's supposed moral superiority and the need to 'civilise' the peoples of colonised lands.

Belonging to a socially and ethnically privileged group has been necessary but not sufficient to ensure a woman's respectability. That status has also depended upon her behaviour, itself heavily policed by heteropatriarchal familial and societal structures. Deviation from norms of respectable femininity was liable to see her cast out or condemned as 'fallen'. While the fallen woman may have been confined to history, her contemporary sister faces both social and legal slut-shaming, as most obviously experienced by women who dare to accuse men of sexual misconduct. However, the boundaries of these norms have always been poorly defined, forcing women to self-police more thoroughly to avoid narrowly drawn but elusive boundaries.

One vital boundary marker has been 'innocence': a lack of sexual knowledge or active desire which helped to ensure that sexual activity was confined to marriage (itself necessarily heterosexual until 2013). An innocent woman would demonstrate neither inappropriate knowledge nor sexual initiative. Those requirements ensured that lesbianism was inaccessible, since understanding of one's own body and desires was withheld. A closely related and central feature of respectability, female sexual passivity, was constructed through medicalised discourses whose models of women's sexuality in general and of same-sex attraction in particular underwent significant transformations as the centuries progressed. While Galenic and Aristotelian models had offered some space to female desire, women's cooler humours made this a passive longing in which they craved men's superior heat: there was no space for lesbian desire. The two-sex model, emergent by the eighteenth century, did not even require that degree of sexual agency. Some (though by no means all) Victorian doctors viewed women as naturally desireless; for most others, women's sexuality was a shadow of, and response to, men's. While women's sexuality was increasingly acknowledged in the twentieth century, it continued to be assumed lesser than men's: thus the Wolfenden Report and subsequent parliamentary debates established lesbianism's characterisation as a less libidinous version of gay male sexuality.

The idea of the wrong sort of sexual activity as a cause of lesbianism, and the right (heterosexual) sort as its cure, has proved persistent. Eighteenth-century greensickness was curable only by heterosexual intercourse. Nineteenth-century moral insanity could be treated by preventing autonomous sexual activity, a logic which reached its extreme in the use of clitoridectomy. In the twentieth century, lesbianism was cast as a failure to develop appropriate heterosexual attachments. In other words, lesbianism was medicalised long before the appearance of sexology or the Wolfenden Report, with heterosexual marriage both treatment and proof of cure. Meanwhile, understandings of male sexual pursuit as natural and beneficial continue to be reflected in the legal protection of men's 'seduction' prerogatives: these underpin the current approach to fraudulently obtained consent.

Also enduring is lesbianism's equation with corruption, evident in the eighteenth-century concerns around maidservants and nineteenth and twentieth-century concerns about single-sex environments. It has recently gained fresh force through age of consent prosecutions where 'malign influence' and 'grooming' are invoked by the courts. The media focus upon cases involving teacher-pupil relationships, and headlines linking 'lesbian' with perversion, reinforce an association which was not generally made in the past. While early sexology had treated male and female sexual inversion as somewhat parallel, the criminal justice system had not followed suit. Indeed, their equivalence was expressly disavowed when lesbianism's supposed differences from gay sexuality were used to justify the continuing criminalisation of male homosexual acts. Those disavowals, paradoxically, helped open the door to the current associations by tying lesbian and gay male identities together as legal comparators. The shift to equality discourses has depended upon *under*playing differences in order to support equal legal treatment. That positioning of lesbianism as a sub-species of gay male sexuality has meant a lack of attention to lesbian specificities in the criminal courts, in favour of the projection onto lesbians of negative myths about gay male sexuality.

Alongside perversion, the association of lesbian sexuality with fraud continues. It has been the preferred type of offence for prosecuting lesbian relationships since the late seventeenth century, and it too has gained new impetus in recent decades. Elaborate deceptions are not the most common forms of lesbian relationship today, and fairly certainly were not in previous centuries either. Their persistence in the criminal courts and relatively high cultural profile are instead consequences of the function such cases have served and the low risk to silencing ideologies they present. First, their central message is that most women will only choose a relationship with another woman (or a trans man) if they are deceived into doing so. Emphasis upon complainants' naivety or even gullibility underlines that point. Second, these cases have been presented as a close—and inadequate—mimicry of the most traditional and patriarchal of heterosexual relationships. The narratives of sexual activity (or its absence) between the couple and the discovery of the deception highlight this inadequacy.

The criminal courts have shown particular interest in—and coyness about—the use of dildos. Their representation as instruments of fraud (i.e. fake penises), and explicit labelling as 'prosthetic penises' in contemporary reports, construct them as an attempt to directly compensate for the lack of a 'real' penis. Their invocation thus underpins a wider legal insistence upon the primacy of penile penetration, with a corresponding devaluation of lesbian sexuality. In particular, approaches to consent have largely operated on the premise that what matters is whether penile penetration was both expected and provided, as is still evident in many of the gender fraud cases. Thus the relationships are portrayed as not just inferior, but downright ridiculous or vicious versions of the 'real' heterosexual thing. They are bizarre, surprising, strange; what they are not is serious. The emotions involved are reduced to the callousness of the deceiver and the public shame of the deceived: there is relatively little discussion of the feelings of attachment, betrayal, and so on, which must surely have been involved in any such close, intimate relationship.

That may also be part of the explanation for why so little sustained attention has been offered previously to lesbians and the criminal law. The cases discussed here pose problems for purely celebratory or recuperative accounts, since many of their subjects had apparently behaved badly within and outside their relationships. Academic historians have moved away from such approaches to produce more nuanced histories, but discussion of lesbian criminalisation is still at odds with the dominant political agenda. Recent campaigns for LGBT rights have used equality claims to seek law reforms such as equal marriage based upon the positioning of lesbians and gay men as model citizens. The campaign for pardons for men convicted of gross indecency gained much of its mainstream political momentum from a focus on Alan Turing, presented as a martyr who had saved the nation through his exceptional work in the Second World War. That is an exceptionally high bar to set, and one none of the defendants in this book would meet. We need to find ways to talk about past and present injustices which encompass even those who are not good citizens. As Heather Love has urged in relation to queer history, such a refusal to 'write off … the least presentable' is a form of resistance to 'gay normalization' (Love 2007, p. 30).

Despite their continuities, there are important differences between the cases too, and the most crucial of these relate to the growing visibility of lesbianism. One is a simple shift of emphasis occasioned by the type of offences charged. Since these are now not financial but sexual, and since sexual matters are raised openly and explicitly both in the courtroom and in the general media, recent reports have more explicit detail of the sexual activity involved. Nonetheless, it remains shrouded in euphemism and allusion, presented as comprehensible only through (unfavourable) comparison to heterosex. Another difference is the overt identification of relationships as same-sex in contemporary trials and reports. The eighteenth-century press either described the facts without ascribing motivation, or ascribed a financial (rather than emotional or sexual) motive. That approach reflected a more favourable context within which to silence lesbian possibility. Today, official silence is no longer viable in that form since both the growth of fields of 'expertise' and the openness of lesbians themselves have ensured that lesbianism cannot be satisfactorily rendered as 'secret'. However, its associations with the bizarre and the emotionally shallow, with deceit and inadequacy, and with predation and paedophilia, work to portray it as an unattractive option; and there are only a limited range of alternative representations of lesbians in the news media and criminal justice system.

If this is where we are now, what directions might future research take? This book does not say all that could be said about lesbianism and the criminal law. Indeed, that is its point: to demonstrate that this is a rich and important field of study which cannot be dismissed with the statement that there was never a specific offence. We must move out of the shadow of the Queen Victoria myth and take seriously the ways in which lesbianism has been regulated by the criminal justice system. Rather than attempting to distinguish it from the regulation of trans men, or leaving it obscured by the criminalisation of male homosexuality, we must explore its complex interactions with both and their importance for understanding the past and present legal treatment of lesbianism—but also for properly comprehending how trans and gay men were regulated, and how legal regulation is never more than a part of the story.

There are many perspectives on, and theoretical approaches to, these cases which would repay further attention. One is their materiality: while the dildo has carried great ideological weight in reasserting the phallic nature of 'real' sex, it is also a physical object (albeit often a surprisingly elusive one). Other material elements have persisted in the female husband/gender fraud cases, notably the attention of courts and media to clothes. Occasionally they had direct legal significance: in the eighteenth century, Mary Parlour's pawned clothing formed the subject-matter of a fraud charge. More commonly, the male and female clothes of male-presenting accused have been described, disputed, judged, and, in the case of Samuel Bundy/Sarah Paul, destroyed. The homes in which these offences occurred were rarely described in the eighteenth century, yet much more attention was given to Louise Mourey's house with its brass plaque and to the locations of Jennifer Saunders's possessions in her bathroom and wardrobe. What is the significance of those changes?

Temporality is also important: temporal reframing of the facts has been consistently present in the criminal cases but inconsistent in form. Eighteenth-century prosecutions made the whole of a relationship relevant since the wedding provided the legal basis for the fraud (it was the moment a husband became the legal owner of his wife's possessions) but the benefits were obtained during the course of the marriage. Yet reports underplayed the length of those marriages: when Mary Price discovered Charles Hamilton's sex 'soon' after their 1746 wedding, that represented a period of several months. By contrast, the use of sexual offences means that contemporary cases focus not upon the flow of a relationship but upon specific moments of sexual contact within it. The harms of the deception are therefore occluded by an emphasis not upon sustained deceit—comparable to that in undercover policing cases which the criminal justice system has strongly resisted criminalising—but upon the non-equivalency and implied inferiority of lesbian to heterosexual sex acts.

The geographies of criminal regulation offer multiple possibilities for further exploration. The regional differences within England, and the elusive evidence for Wales, have been touched upon here but could reward further research. For example, the local political situation in Glastonbury threw light upon the decisions made in Mary/Charles Hamilton's prosecution (and see Derry 2008). These were also influenced by media interest, partly due to the town's proximity to fashionable Bath, whose newspapers in turn ensured the case became known to historians.

As for national geographies, the scope for comparative work is considerable and has particular contemporary importance given debates around legacies of colonialism and the criminalisation of same-sex sexualities in a number of Commonwealth countries.

Returning to England, where should the law go from here? This book does not presume to offer definitive answers to that question. However, it may make some contribution to a more historically informed discussion in which assumptions of tolerance for lesbianism are finally put aside. By mapping out the distinctive criminal legal history of lesbianism, and the persistence of its effects and assumptions, it demonstrates that lesbians cannot simply be subsumed within the rubrics 'lesbian and gay' or 'LGBT' as a less libidinous, less troublesome, and less interesting subgroup of gay men. Nor can we be ignored within the category 'women' as somehow having escaped the attentions of a patriarchal criminal justice system.

Understandings of the regulation of sexuality will fail women who have sex or relationships with women unless the specificities of our history, our present experiences, and our future needs are taken into account. Without them, we will have only a partial and distorted account of the regulation of sexuality as a whole. Whether we are considering eighteenth-century understandings of fraud, the path to the Sexual Offences Act 1967, or the development of sexual assault law, our accounts will be incomplete if they do not consider the silencing of lesbianism. This book could thus be one step in building the groundwork for a shift from the legal history of lesbian sexuality to, borrowing Lanser's concept (2014), the lesbian sexuality of legal history.

This project remains urgent, within and beyond the criminal justice system. As I write this conclusion, there are protests against LGBT-inclusive lessons in Birmingham schools (Iqbal 2019). The Home Office continues, in the pursuit of its racist 'hostile environment' policy, to refuse sexuality-based claims through resort to stereotypes such as the insistence that previously married women cannot be lesbian (Powell 2019). Assumptions about the continuing liberalisation of social attitudes and official reactions no longer hold true. The British Social Attitudes survey had consistently found increasing tolerance of same-sex sexuality since the 1980s; but in 2019, it recorded a decrease in the percentage of people who think sexual relations between two adults of the same sex 'not wrong at all' (NatCen Social Research 2019, chap. 5). As a corollary, reported homophobic hate crimes are increasing dramatically (PA Media 2019).

To end on a more optimistic note, these are times for vigilance rather than despair. Lesbian invisibility persists unless challenged, even in surprising places, but challenge can be effective. The law responds to societal changes, even if it does so at its own pace. Those changes are themselves complex, and not uniformly positive, but historical research and activist campaigns both have the power to inform them. In 2018 a plaque was erected to Ann Lister, whose encoded diary entries detailed her sexual relationships with other women in early nineteenth-century Yorkshire. However, the rainbow-edged plaque on Holy Trinity Church, York described her only as 'gender-nonconforming', the word 'lesbian' conspicuous by its absence (Churches Conservation Trust 2018; *BBC News* 2018). Lister's contemporary moment of visibility was simultaneously a concealment of lesbian possibility. In 2019 though, a reworded plaque was erected (*BBC News* 2019). A few months later, a drama serial based upon Lister's life was shown on BBC One (Wainwright and Harding 2019) and ended with the 'marriage' commemorated by that plaque. Granting a version of the most traditional of happy endings to a lesbian couple is simultaneously a valorisation and a disruption of patriarchal expectations—and a subversive departure from the 'bury your gays' trope of misery and death. Neither cultural nor legal narratives are unchanging or unchangeable.

References

BBC News. 2018. Anne Lister: Plaque to 'First Modern Lesbian' Sparks Anger, August 3.

———. 2019. Anne Lister: Reworded York Plaque for 'First Lesbian', February 28.

Churches Conservation Trust. 2018. UK's First 'Rainbow Plaque' Unveiled at Holy Trinity Goodramgate in York. https://www.visitchurches.org.uk/what-we-do/news/uk-s-first-rainbow-plaque-to-be-unveiled-at-holy-trinity-goodramgate-in-york.html.

Derry, Caroline. 2008. Sexuality and Locality in the Trial of Mary Hamilton, 'Female Husband'. *King's Law Journal* 19 (3): 595–616. https://doi.org/10.1080/09615768.2008.11427709.

Iqbal, Nosheen. 2019. Birmingham School Row: 'This Is Made Out to Be Just Muslims v Gays. It's Not.' *Observer*, September 21.

Lanser, Susan S. 2014. *The Sexuality of History: Modernity and the Sapphic, 1565–1830*. Chicago: University of Chicago Press.

Love, Heather. 2007. *Feeling Backward: Loss and the Politics of Queer History*. Cambridge, MA: Harvard University Press.

NatCen Social Research. 2019. *British Social Attitudes 36*. London.

PA Media. 2019. Homophobic Hate Crime Reports Soar But Charges Fall. *Guardian*, September 11.

Powell, Alex. 2019. Interviews with Asylum Seekers Reveal Why the Home Office Rejects So Many LGBT Claims. *The Conversation*. http://theconversation.com/interviews-with-asylum-seekers-reveal-why-the-home-office-rejects-so-many-lgbt-claims-122905.

Traub, Valerie. 2015. The Present Future of Lesbian Historiography. In *Thinking Sex with the Early Moderns*, 82–100. Philadelphia: University of Pennsylvania Press.

Wainwright, Sally, and Sarah Harding. 2019. *Gentleman Jack*. UK: BBC

Name Index[1]

[1] Note: Page numbers followed by 'n' refer to notes.

C. Derry, *Lesbianism and the Criminal Law*,
https://doi.org/10.1007/978-3-030-35300-1

Subject Index[1]

[1] Note: Page numbers followed by 'n' refer to notes.

C. Derry, *Lesbianism and the Criminal Law*,
https://doi.org/10.1007/978-3-030-35300-1

The manufacturer's authorised representative in the EU is Springer Nature Customer Service Centre GmbH, Europaplatz 3, 69115 Heidelberg, Germany. If you have any concerns regarding our products, please contact ProductSafety@springernature.com

Printed and bound by CPI Group (UK) Ltd, Croydon, CR0 4YY
30/09/2026
02225442-0014